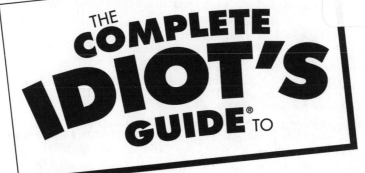

THE **COMPLETE** **IDIOT'S** **GUIDE**® TO

Ghosts and Hauntings

Second Edition

by Tom Ogden

ALPHA

A member of Penguin Group (USA) Inc.

For Mom, Dad, Jeanne, Wayne, and all my other family spirits.

ALPHA BOOKS

Published by the Penguin Group

Penguin Group (USA) Inc., 375 Hudson Street, New York, New York 10014, USA

Penguin Group (Canada), 90 Eglinton Avenue East, Suite 700, Toronto, Ontario M4P 2Y3, Canada (a division of Pearson Penguin Canada Inc.)

Penguin Books Ltd., 80 Strand, London WC2R 0RL, England

Penguin Ireland, 25 St. Stephen's Green, Dublin 2, Ireland (a division of Penguin Books Ltd.)

Penguin Group (Australia), 250 Camberwell Road, Camberwell, Victoria 3124, Australia (a division of Pearson Australia Group Pty. Ltd.)

Penguin Books India Pvt. Ltd., 11 Community Centre, Panchsheel Park, New Delhi—110 017, India

Penguin Group (NZ), 67 Apollo Drive, Rosedale, North Shore, Auckland 1311, New Zealand (a division of Pearson New Zealand Ltd.)

Penguin Books (South Africa) (Pty.) Ltd., 24 Sturdee Avenue, Rosebank, Johannesburg 2196, South Africa

Penguin Books Ltd., Registered Offices: 80 Strand, London WC2R 0RL, England

Copyright © 2004 by Tom Ogden

International Standard Book Number: 978-1-59257-250-2
Library of Congress Catalog Card Number: 2004106743

10 09 08   8 7 6 5 4 3 2

Interpretation of the printing code: The rightmost number of the first series of numbers is the year of the book's printing; the rightmost number of the second series of numbers is the number of the book's printing. For example, a printing code of 04-1 shows that the first printing occurred in 2004.

Printed in the United States of America

Note: This publication contains the opinions and ideas of its author. It is intended to provide helpful and informative material on the subject matter covered. It is sold with the understanding that the author and publisher are not engaged in rendering professional services in the book. If the reader requires personal assistance or advice, a competent professional should be consulted.

The author and publisher specifically disclaim any responsibility for any liability, loss, or risk, personal or otherwise, which is incurred as a consequence, directly or indirectly, of the use and application of any of the contents of this book.

Most Alpha books are available at special quantity discounts for bulk purchases for sales promotions, premiums, fund-raising, or educational use. Special books, or book excerpts, can also be created to fit specific needs.

For details, write: Special Markets, Alpha Books, 375 Hudson Street, New York, NY 10014.

Publisher: *Marie Butler-Knight*
Product Manager: *Phil Kitchel*
Senior Managing Editor: *Jennifer Chisholm*
Senior Acquisitions Editor: *Randy Ladenheim-Gil*
Development Editor: *Lynn Northrup*
Production Editor: *Megan Douglass*

Copy Editor: *Ross Patty*
Illustrator: *Jody Schaeffer*
Cover/Book Designer: *Trina Wurst*
Indexer: *Tonya Heard*
Layout/Proofreading: *Angela Calvert, Donna Martin*

Contents at a Glance

Contents

Foreword

ZELDA RUBINSTEIN

"They're here!"

When I was asked to create the role of Tangina Barrons, the medium who's able to contact and exorcise the evil spirits in the movie *Poltergeist*, I became very excited. It was a dream role for an actress: She's a colorful character who seems just this side of crazy, but she's completely committed to what she knows is true.

And what Tangina knew was this: Ghosts and poltergeists *can* and *do* exist, and, if they want to, they can *find* you!

Up until the time I was cast as "ghostbuster," I'd given very little thought as to whether poltergeists, much less ghosts or other spirit entities, actually exist.

I had heard the stories—they were in all the tabloids—that poltergeist phenomena and other odd events had occurred on the sets of other high-profile supernatural thrillers such as *The Exorcist* and *The Amityville Horror*.

But I guess we were the lucky ones: Nothing of that sort took place during the shooting of the three *Poltergeist* movies. Fortunately, all those animated skeletons and spirited spooks you saw in our films were special effects for the screen.

The book you hold in your hands isn't exactly spooky, but some of the stories do get pretty scary! It's a fun and sometimes frightening read.

Tom Ogden's spent a lifetime studying magic and the supernatural, so you're really in for a treat. He's collected some of the most famous ghost stories of all times. You'll see how ghosts have haunted people throughout history and how we of the living have tried to communicate with those on the Other Side. (Having portrayed a medium myself in several films and TV shows, I felt right at home with the chapters on séances!) And, this book tells you how to become a ghost hunter yourself. That is, if you dare!

Do I believe in ghosts? I'm not sure. But I'll tell you what: *They* believe in *you*.

Happy hauntings,

Zelda Rubinstein

Zelda Rubinstein is probably best known for her portrayal of the medium in *Poltergeist*, *Poltergeist II: The Other Side*, and *Poltergeist III*, as well as her recurring role as Ginny Weedon on the television series *Picket Fences*. Her other film credits include

Lover's Knot, Little Witches, Timemaster, Teen Witch, Guilty as Charged, Anguish, and *16 Candles.* She has also guest starred on such television shows as *Caroline in the City, Martin, Sable, Whiz Kids, Poltergeist: The Legacy,* and many others.

Introduction

When my friends heard I was writing the second edition to my book about ghosts and hauntings, they all asked me what else could I tell the readers? Hadn't I covered it all the first time around?

Hardly!

Since *The Complete Idiot's Guide to Ghosts and Hauntings* was published in 1999, hundreds of people have told me about their firsthand encounters with ghosts. You'll find many of these tales in this expanded and updated second edition. Many are told here for the first time anywhere!

And many of the stories have been expanded. I've had readers contact me, saying, "Well, yes, that tale's true—as far as you went, but did you *also* know that …" So now you'll hear "the rest of the story."

In the past few years I've been able to visit many more haunted places personally. I've been able to investigate recent claims of spirit activity. And I've been able to include new and previously unpublished photographs of several of the sites in this edition.

After all this time, people still ask me: Do I believe that ghosts exist?

Well, yes, I believe it's *possible* that they do. But then, I've been a professional magician for more than 30 years. And in Magic 101 we're taught to believe that *anything* is possible. (In fact, that's what we magicians do for a living: We make the impossible possible.)

Have I ever seen a ghost?

Well, no, not that I know of. But have I ever experienced a chill as I walked beside a cemetery at night? Sure. Have I ever felt someone—or some invisible presence—standing in the room with me, even though I knew I was all alone? Or heard strange, unexplained noises in the dark? Well, yes, and yes again. What were these experiences? Were they ghosts? Or was it just my medication kicking in?

The answer I give my friends is very simple: I don't have to *see* something to know it exists. Who hasn't been fascinated with what—if anything—lies beyond this life of ours? And is it ever possible to return, in any form, to the world of the living? The answers are the stuff of which ghost stories are made.

Throughout the centuries, too many people have reported too many things for us to ignore them or to say with certainty that ghosts don't exist. People have seen, heard, or felt *something*. What could their experiences have been? Spirits? Ghosts? And if not, what? It's my sincere hope that as you read these pages you'll keep those questions in your mind, but also find a few answers along the way.

How to Use This Book

The Complete Idiot's Guide to Ghosts and Hauntings, Second Edition, is divided into five parts, each of which examines some segment of the world of ghosts.

Part 1, "The Great Beyond," takes us back to when humankind first started to question the mysteries of life and the afterlife. We'll trace Western beliefs in ghosts through the eyes of the Egyptians, the ancient Greeks and Romans, and the early Christian church. Then we'll take a walk on the wild side to visit some poltergeists.

Part 2, "Don't Call Us, We'll Call You," traces the rise and fall of the Spiritualism movement in America and abroad. We'll meet some of the stars of Spiritualism and follow along into the séance room to see what goes on when the lights go down. Then, if you want to fool your friends, you'll find some fun ways to transform your own home into a (pseudo) haunted house.

Part 3, "Who Ya Gonna Call?" may be where you want to turn first if you think you've seen a ghost. This section of the book introduces some famous psychic societies, paranormal investigators, and skeptics. We'll look at their methods and learn for ourselves how to become ghost hunters and ghostbusters!

Part 4, "Make Yourself at Home: The Hauntings," is my favorite part of the book because it's filled with scary stories from the literally thousands of legends, case histories, and reports of ghost sightings. You'll find the chapters broken down by the types of places that spirits haunt: houses, cemeteries, castles, theaters—you name it!

Part 5, "Apparitions and the Arts," looks at some of the ways in which ghosts and spirit phenomena have been reflected in popular culture. First, you'll discover the magic connection—how illusionists have used their secret art to seemingly create spirits and phantoms. Then I'll review some of the more popular books, plays, and movies that have featured ghost characters and stories.

On top of all that, I've added three appendixes. For the serious student, I think it's important information and worth a read.

Appendix A, "Continuing the Ghost Hunt," is a collection of the names and addresses of some of the major psychical societies and paranormal investigators. You'll also find the website listings for a few of the top ghost tours worldwide.

Appendix B, "Boo-Boo-Boo, Books!" is a list of recommended reading about ghosts, spirits, and hauntings. Bear in mind that, at any given time, there are hundreds of books in print about ghosts. These are a few that have stood the test of time, are readily available, or that highlight a particular area of interest.

Appendix C, "Seeing Is Believing: Haunted Places You Can Visit!" gives the addresses, phone numbers, or directions to many of the major haunted sites mentioned in this book that are open for tourism, are public properties, or that welcome your business patronage.

Spooky Extras

Throughout this book, I've added four types of boxes that give you extra information:

Phantastic Tips

Here are some special hints and advice to help you contact the spirit world, see a ghost, or learn more about spookdom.

Boo!

You don't want to wind up being a ghost yourself, do you? Here's what to avoid when you're out there in the dark looking for spooks.

Phantom Phrases

Don't worry: All of the spirit-related words are explained in the book. But in "Phantom Phrases" I also draw special attention to jargon or unfamiliar words—as well as some common words with really unusual meanings—used by ghost hunters, ghostbusters, and people involved in the paranormal.

Ghostly Pursuits

These colorful side stories give you background information or provide a different point of view for our tales of ghostly terror.

You'll also find a feature new to this edition, called First-Person Phantoms. Most ghost stories seem to have taken place in the long-distant past, are now urban legends, or happened to someone's second cousin on their mother's side. *These* tales are first person encounters with the Beyond, as told to me by the people who experienced them!

Acknowledgments

There are many people I have to thank for putting me in touch with the spirit world. My special thanks go out to Max Maven, Michael Kurland, Eugene Burger, Gordon Bean, Vincent O'Neill, David Shine, Lilly Walters, and the late Marcello Trucci for their advice and research assistance.

Thank you to all those who supplied photographs or made my quest for them so much easier: Patrice Keane and the American Society for Psychical Research (ASPR); Gill Crawford and The Strathmore Estates (Scotland); Betty Jean Morris and Peggy Ebright of the Pasadena Playhouse; Pamela Young for the excellent spirit photo of Invisible Irma; the Magic Castle; Mark Willoughby of Collectors Book Store in Hollywood (CA); Mel Pierce Camera; Norman Deery; *Country Life* magazine; Vanni Pulé; Greg Bordner and Abbott's Magic Manufacturing Company of Colon (MI); Dave Ngan and Van Tran at Davco Printing; and Richard Kaufman. Thank you, Greg Farber, for explaining how to create spirit photographs of your own.

A special thanks goes out to my patient and supportive team of editors for this revision: Randy Ladenheim-Gil, Lynn Northrup, Megan Douglass, and Ross Patty.

And, finally, thanks to all of you who shared with me the stories of your own ghost encounters. I hope you're happy, people: Those stories are the reason I'm too darn scared to turn out the lights at night.

Trademarks

OUIJA®

Reality and Proof Disclaimer

Part 1

The Great Beyond

"Tell us some ghost stories! Please?" I know that's what you want, so don't worry: There are plenty of spooky tales coming up. But, first, we should put the whole realm of ghostdom in context against the world in which these legends have evolved. In this part, we'll take a peek into the distant past to find out what ancient civilizations thought about survival after death and what they believed happens to us after we, well, bite the dust. And, if our spirits do come back, in what form do they return?

Then we'll look at some of the first recorded ghost stories in Western culture and how the early Christian Church reinterpreted them into doctrine. That's not to ignore the old wives' tales, superstitions, urban legends, and friendly folklore that have grown up about phantoms. Those pesky pranksters, the poltergeists, are here, too.

So don't be frightened—turn the page!

Chapter 1

Let's Enter the Spirit World

In This Chapter

- ◆ Ghosts or apparitions?
- ◆ Survival after death
- ◆ The destination of the soul
- ◆ Festivals of the dead

There are ghosts among us! At least, that's what people have claimed since the earliest of times. Ghost stories filled folklore long before the written word. Members of animistic societies saw the spirits of their ancestors. To foretell the future, ancient seers called up spirits (at least what passed for spirits) of the dead. By the first century A.D., historians were beginning to write down popular ghost tales and legends.

Two thousand years later, our quandary continues. There've been too many reports of spectres and spooky ghostly phenomena to be ignored: Something must be out there! But—and here's the big but—what is it that everyone's seeing and hearing and experiencing?

Are they really ghosts? Are *any* of them ghosts? Hopefully, by the end of this book, you'll have some answers—and probably even a few more questions of your own.

So first, we have to make sure we're all speaking the same language. Do we all mean the same thing when we say "ghost"? Don't be so sure! Let's take a look at some of the simple yet sometimes misunderstood vocabulary that's specific to the study of ghostly phenomena.

Is It a Ghost or an Apparition?

Most people use the word *ghost* to mean any phantom object when what they really mean is the spirit of a deceased human being. In this book, I'll concentrate on the latter.

What's the difference, you ask? Much of the reported phenomena over the centuries has involved objects that are not or were never human. For example, people have reported seeing spectral animals and phantom trains. They weren't human, and they certainly didn't have a soul or spirit (as they're usually defined) that could return from the dead.

Phantom Phrases

A **ghost,** as most people use the word, is the visual appearance of a deceased human being's spirit, life force, essence, or soul. A more general term, an **apparition** is the visual appearance of any spirit phenomenon. Laypeople use the words interchangeably. Paranormal investigators prefer to use the word apparition; to them, a ghost is only one kind of apparition.

So to avoid any confusion, paranormal researchers prefer to use the more general word *apparition* to mean the visual appearance of a disembodied entity. This encompasses all types of phantoms, human or otherwise. For example, the appearance of an angel by your bedside would be an apparition, but you'd never call it a ghost.

Now I realize that these are distinctions not normally made by people on the street. But to avoid confusion as to what claims are actually being made, investigators feel it's best to stick to the word "apparition" unless you specifically mean a ghost.

Think of this way: All ghosts are apparitions, but not all apparitions are ghosts.

To add to the confusion, here are just a few more synonyms for an apparition, all used colloquially to mean "ghost":

- Essence
- Manifestation
- Nightshade
- Phantasm
- Phantom
- Presence
- Shade
- Shadow
- Soul
- Spectre or specter
- Spirit
- Spook
- Vision
- Wraith

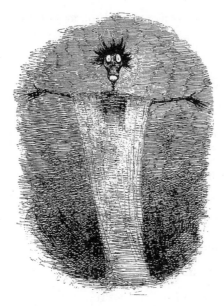

An apparition.

(Nineteenth-century engraving by George Cruikshank)

And poltergeists are another thing altogether. We'll take a special look at them in Chapter 5.

There are all sorts of ghosts, and they keep all sorts of schedules:

- Some have been sighted only once. For example, there's a documented case of the luminous ghost of a boy appearing in Corby Castle in Cumberland, England, on a single night—September 8, 1824.

- They appear at a certain date or time of night. You'll read in Chapter 20 about a female ghost at Simpson College in Indianola, Iowa, who appears at midnight every Friday the 13th.

- Some mark the anniversary of an event. A phantom hitchhiker most often appears on the anniversary of his or her death (see Chapter 4).

Phantom Phrases

The person who sees an apparition is called the **percipient**. The apparition, especially one that wills itself into visibility, is the **agent** of a paranormal sighting.

- Many—the focus of this book—tend to take up residence at a particular place and are seen there with some frequency. They haunt a specific location.

In paranormal parlance, the person who sees the apparition is called the *percipient*. The apparition that's seen is called the *agent*. (The term "agent" is especially used when referring to an apparition that deliberately makes itself visible, that wants to be seen, particularly if it's there to deliver some sort of message.)

I Can't Be Bothered

You have to ask yourself: If someone's crossed over to ghosthood, why bother to come back? There must be something that keeps the spirit here or draws it back to *this* side of veil.

Well, sometimes death occurred so suddenly that the ghost doesn't know it's dead. The spirit's just hanging around, clueless that it doesn't belong there.

Here are just a few more reasons ghost experts have hypothesized that spirits return:

- To give a warning, or to help, comfort, or advise mortals.
- To confess their guilt or sins.
- To obtain a proper burial so that they and their remains may "rest in peace."
- To return to a place they loved, loathed, or were otherwise attached to during life.
- To guard, protect, or simply watch over the premises or, less frequently, a person.
- To provide for their heirs (especially if there was a large inheritance) by telling where treasure was hidden.
- To seek revenge, right a wrong, or obtain justice (especially if the deceased had been murdered).

Ghostly Pursuits

A traditional ritual of indigenous tribal members of the Wayuu Indians of northern Colombia and Venezuela involves the exhumation of a deceased relative's remains after about 10 years, stripping any remaining flesh, cleaning the bones, and then burying them. The remains themselves are usually handled by only one woman, who has neither eaten nor slept two days before the rite in order to prevent being hurt by the soul she has stirred. The ceremony, which is begun before dawn because the dead don't like sunlight, is thought to reintroduce the spirit to ancestors and to prevent it from returning to wander the earth without end.

First-Person Phantoms

Destrehan Plantation, located just outside New Orleans, is the oldest documented plantation home in the lower Mississippi Valley, having been founded in 1787. Someone who once lived there seems to have a hard time moving away. During a walk through the historical house in 1971, my friend Kim Roach spied a small key wedged between the floorboards and the wall in the corner of one of the rooms. Thinking that the key had been accidentally dropped and lost, she picked it up and put it into her pocket so she could turn it in at the front desk. As soon as she took her hand out of her pocket, however, she felt a cold and clammy, but invisible, hand grab hers. It would not let go. With the ghost hand still clutching hers, Kim took out the key and studied it. She got the message and put the key back where she found it. As soon as the key was in place, the spectral hand released its grip and was gone.

Do You Believe?

In an October 1999 Gallup Poll, one out of three people surveyed said that they believe in ghosts—three times as many as in the 1970s.

But do ghosts really exist? *Can* they exist? For those who say, absolutely not, no way, to both questions, consider these things everyone once knew to be absolutely, uncontrovertibly true:

- The world is flat.
- The sun and stars revolve around the earth.
- The moon is made of green cheese.

Yet all three have since been proven false. (Well, we haven't explored the entire moon yet, but the chances of finding any Gruyère or Brie aren't very promising.)

A good researcher carries a healthy dose of skepticism, but not cynicism. Perhaps all that's required is to be open to the possibility.

It's been said that those who believe in ghosts don't need hard evidence to prove it. Conversely, no amount of evidence would ever be enough to convince those who don't believe that ghosts exist.

But it's not a black-and-white issue. It's hard to separate the believers from the nonbelievers. Much of it's tied up with whether you believe that there's life, or any type of survival, after death.

For example, there are those who:

- Don't believe in survival after death. Therefore, the deceased couldn't possibly return as ghosts.

- Believe in survival after death, but they don't think the deceased can return to the world of the living in the form of ghosts.

- Believe in survival after death, and in the possibility that the deceased can return as ghosts.

And it's not even that simple. Many people who may or may not believe in life or survival after death believe in other spirits, such as angels and demons, that can make themselves look like humans, even though they're not the ghosts of human beings.

Then there are apparitions of the living (people who are currently alive but not physically present). In other words, while a person is still alive in one place, his or her "ghost double" appears somewhere else. But more about that in Chapter 3.

And, of course, there are those literal folks who don't believe in anything: life after death, ghosts, heavenly spirits, or demons. They may see or experience something paranormal, but they insist there must be a logical, natural explanation for it.

It's a Bird, It's a Plane, But Is It Supernatural?

Most researchers and theorists of spirit sightings tend to shun the word *supernatural*. I'm not sure why. It's a perfectly good word with a very clear meaning: "existing or occurring through some agency beyond the known forces of nature." The word comes from the Latin *super*, meaning "above," and *nasci*, meaning "to be born." In other words, the phenomenon was created; we just don't know how. It's beyond anything we know or understand.

Phantom Phrases

Something that's **supernatural** cannot be explained by any known means or force of nature. It's above or beyond natural explanation. The word generally carries the suggestion that some divine, demonic, or Higher Power is involved in making the event occur. To avoid this mystical connotation, researchers prefer to use the term paranormal, which also means something beyond the range of everyday human experiences or scientific explanation.

Yet the study of ghosts is a quirky and questionable subject to begin with. And for investigators who want to be taken seriously, perhaps the word "supernatural" carries too many divine, occult, or even satanic connotations. So they prefer to use a related word: *paranormal*.

Many people who are interested in ghosts have a general interest in all psychic phenomena. The related field of parapsychology looks for evidence of phenomena caused by the mind but which can't be explained. In layperson's terms, it's the study of ESP (extrasensory perception). We'll take a closer look at some of the ESP connections in Chapter 12.

After Life, What Next?

Since the beginning of recorded time, and no doubt eons before that, people have wondered what happens to us when we die. Don't you? Unless you subscribe without argument to a particular philosophy or religion, any and all answers to that eternal question are theoretical at best. Why? Because no human being has ever died and returned to this mortal world with the memory to tell us, conclusively, what was on the other side—unless you know something I don't.

But there's been lots of conjecture as to what does happen when we bite the dust.

Is That All There Is?

Almost every recorded culture in history has believed in some form of life after death. As you might expect, beliefs in what happens to the soul, or life force, after death vary greatly from one society to another. Among the many theories, some say:

- The spirit continues a similar existence, but in another realm.

- The spirit is judged and assigned to "heaven" or "hell," based on one's deeds during life.

- The spirit undergoes a series of rebirths or reincarnations, trying to improve toward a higher spiritual plane.

- The spirit waits for an eventual rebirth or resurrection.

Almost every society has had a class of people who could communicate with spirits of the deceased. A *medium* is someone who can communicate with spirits on behalf of another living being. The word suggests that the "medium" acts at a midway point, halfway between the worlds of the living and the dead. In tribal societies the medium is the *shaman*, who is considered a sort of wizard and who acts as a healer and an intermediary for messages between the worlds of the living, the dead, and the gods.

In classical times, oracles and priests related messages and warnings from the deceased to the living. *Necromancers* were seers and prophets who used magical spells and ritual to contact the dead or call up their spirits to obtain information about the future. In some faiths, priests can accept alms and penance from the living to lighten the punishment of the deceased. In spiritualism, a faith we'll examine in some detail in Part 2, a medium acted as a go-between to the worlds of the living and the dead, especially in contacting the spirits of the dearly departed at séances.

Boo! _____

Not all shamans are good guys! Tahquitz Canyon outside Palm Springs, California, is said to be haunted by the ghost of the ancient Cahuilla shaman after whom the canyon is named. According to tradition, the shaman Tahquitz was originally good but turned to the dark side, at first being playfully wicked, then downright evil. He was exiled to the canyon, where he later died. Tribal members say, his spirit still has the power to devour a person's soul, and meteors and earthquakes are often attributed to him. Tahquitz also sometimes appears in downtown Palm Springs.

A shaman, or witch doctor, from Zimbabwe in Africa.

(Photo by author)

Which Way Do We Go?

So if the soul survives death, where does the spirit go? Belief in the location of the spirit realm varied tremendously from one society to the next:

- Ancient Greeks wrote of an underworld found literally in the bowels of the earth. Caves, crevices, and cracks in the earth's surface acted as doorways to Hades.

- Animistic societies believe that spirits of their deceased ancestors exist side-by-side with them, but unseen.

- Occultists and cabalists described ethereal concentric layers or plateaus around the earth, each inhabited by different types of spirits.

- Most Christians think of heaven, the afterworld reserved for the good, as being skyward; hell, the realm of eternal damnation, is thought of as being downward, though not necessarily literally underground.

- Some cultures put the deceased on "hold," assigning them to an invisible nether world or dimension while they wait for judgment or rebirth.

How the spirits got to the Other World was another problem. In Egypt during the time of the Pharaohs, the walls of the tombs and the sarcophagi were decorated with hieroglyphs (collectively known today as the *Book of the Dead*), which instructed the dead on how to proceed to be judged, then be reborn into Eternity. It was the job of the wizard-priests, through ritual prayers and mummification of the corpse, to ease this passage.

Even so, the ancient Egyptians believed that the soul had a spirit double, which in turn had *two* parts, the *ba* and the *ka*. The *ba* held the characteristics, traits, and personality of the human; the *ka* was the life force.

Although the actual soul of a person moved on after death, the *ba* and *ka* remained in the burial chamber. Both were able to leave the grave, however, and walk in the cemetery at night. In fact, if the corpse was broken apart or corrupted, the *ba* could not return to the vault—hence the importance of mummification. Likewise, if the priests failed to make adequate offerings to the deceased, its *ka* had to travel among the living to find food and drink.

Personally, I wouldn't want to run into either a *ba* or *ka* in a darkened pyramid.

The myth that the soul had to travel over a river to judgment actually began in Egypt at the time of the Pharaohs. Classical Greece expanded the belief, teaching that the soul had to cross the River Styx into Hades on a small boat piloted by the ferryman Charon. The legend was adopted and adapted into the Roman mythology.

One of the big "selling points" of early Christianity was St. Augustine's declaration that there wasn't any River Styx or Charon that you had to pass to reach the Kingdom of God. In the next chapter, we'll learn the path that most modern Western civilizations (well, at least those since the tenth century or so) believe the soul takes after death.

A tomb in the Valley of the Kings, in Luxor, Egypt, decorated with hieroglyphs from the Book of the Dead.

(Photo by author)

Celebrate the Soul

Festivals to honor and ward off the dead date back thousands of years. Ancient Greeks held the Anthesteria in late February or early March. You invited the spirits of your ancestors into your home to eat, but afterward you politely asked to them leave for a full year. The hope was that by throwing them a party once a year, the ghosts would remain contented and nonmalicious.

The ancient Romans believed in all sorts of different types of spirits of the dead. Lares were good spirits, welcomed into people's homes and towns, where they acted sort of like guardian angels. Many families had their own individual lares (usually a deceased relative); but there were also lares for the public at large.

On the other side of the coin, larvae were evil spirits, who tried to scare or even harm others. Among them were the lumures, ghosts of people who died without any surviving family. So, too, were the ghosts of those who died prematurely, violently, or by murder or drowning. These malevolent spirits were thrown a three-day party every year in early May. If they went away happy, maybe they'd just stay away.

Today, many cultures hold an annual Day of the Dead to honor the deceased. Usually, the festivals involve parties and feasts. The Chinese, who are known throughout the world for honoring their ancestors, hold three special rituals to honor the souls of all humankind. Hindu *sraddhas*, rites to honor the ancestors, last for 10 days. The Hungary Ghost Festival is two weeks of feasts and parties; even the spirits of those who died without descendants are specially remembered.

Día de los Muertos, the Day of the Dead festival, is celebrated in Mexico on November 2. (Traditionally, the day is set aside to recall adults who have passed on. Children are remembered the day before on *Día de los Angelitos*, or Day of the Angels.) Preparations and parties often begin on Halloween. The Mexican Day of the Dead is a time for family reunions and feasts. Decorations include graphic and macabre depictions of skeletons, especially skulls. (Can you believe it? Until the twentieth century, actual skulls were sometimes dug up for the big event!) Often, families hold picnics on the gravesites of their relatives who have passed to the Great Beyond. The prayers, meals, and merrymaking are all intended to calm the dead and allow them to rest comfortably for another year.

Halloween, or All Hallows Eve, is the best-known festival of the dead. It started as a pagan ritual in Celtic lands, observed on the night of October 31 to mark the end of the autumn harvest and the onset of winter. Meanwhile, down at the Vatican, Pope Boniface IV introduced All Saint's Day in the seventh century to replace the Roman Feralia, a springtime pagan event intended to give peace to the dead. Later, Boniface moved the date of All Saint's Day from February 21 to November 1, and over the years the Celtic, pagan, and Christian festivals somehow merged into one big celebration: Halloween.

Today, it's primarily celebrated, at least in the United States, as a night of costumed trick-or-treating and revelry.

Ghostly Pursuits

What do Halloween costumes and bags of candy have to do with Celts and Christians? The candy connection probably comes from the celebration of a plentiful harvest. The costumes, however, come from folklore about demons and the dead. Many believed that the barrier between the worlds of the living and the dead, as well as the scared and the satanic, was thinnest on All Hallows Eve. On that night, ghosts could cross over, and devils were free to walk the earth. Thus, the tradition of dressing up in scary costumes goes back to the swaggering, if uneasy, practice of imitating the demonic spirits that traveled the earth on Halloween.

Now it's time to take a look at some of the earliest recorded ghost stories, starting back in ancient Greece. Then we'll see how those tales of terror were first embraced, then modified by the early Catholic Church and later Protestant reformers, then eighteenth- and nineteenth-century mystics.

The Least You Need to Know

- Since the beginning of recorded time, humans have contemplated the possibility of life after death.

- All ghosts are apparitions, but not all apparitions are ghosts.

- Paranormal research is the investigation of experiences beyond the range of normal human or scientific explanation.

- Belief systems on ghosts and the afterlife vary enormously from one civilization to the next.

- Most cultures have celebrated some form of a festival or rites honoring the dead, especially the spirits of family ancestors.

Chapter 2

In the Beginning: The First Famous Phantoms

In This Chapter

- ◆ Necromancy and the Witch of Endor
- ◆ The first ghost stories
- ◆ Ghost beliefs of ancient Greece, the Roman Empire, and the early Christian Church
- ◆ Ideas on apparitions change in the sixteenth through eighteenth centuries
- ◆ Laying the groundwork for the arrival of spiritualism

Ready for about 2,000 years of ghost history? Almost all civilizations have believed that there's some form of existence after death. Many have taught that the soul, or essence, of the departed "lives" in some ethereal plane where the spirits aren't bound by the earthly concept of time. Thus, they thought their ancestors, in a sense, floated beyond or "above" time and should, therefore, be able to see the past, the present, *and* the future. (And if you want to find out what's going to happen tomorrow, who better to ask than those who really know?)

Fortunately, there were specialists who could help people contact the spirits: wizards, sorcerers, and enchantresses. They conversed with the dead using a specific type of divination or fortune-telling known as necromancy.

Phantom Phrases

Necromancy is a form of divination, or foretelling of the future, by calling up and consulting with the spirits of the dead. The word necromancy is derived from the Greek word *nekromantia,* which in turn came from the two roots *nekros* ("a dead person") and *manteia* ("divination").

Voices from the Grave

Today the word *necromancy* is used interchangeably with "magic," although it usually carries an occult connotation. Originally, however, the term simply referred to the art of being able to call on the spirits of the dead so that they could foretell the future.

Summoning a spirit involved great preparations and pains on the part of the fortune-teller, often including fasting, arcane rituals, and the recitation of secret incantations.

Which Witch Was Which?

The most famous recorded case of necromancy is that of Saul consulting the Witch of Endor, told in the book of I Samuel: 28:7–16 in the Old Testament of the Holy Bible.

The Law of Moses strictly forbade the use of necromancy and witchcraft: "There shall not be found among you … any one who practices divination, a soothsayer, or an augur, or a sorcerer, or a charmer, or a medium, or a wizard, or a necromancer. For whoever does these things is an abomination to the Lord." (Deuteronomy 18:10–13) Saul himself had outlawed sorcery among the Israelites. Nevertheless, the beleaguered king felt the need to seek out just such a necromancer.

Why? David (of Goliath fame) had collected an army against Saul. The king needed advice, and fast. He decided to call up the ghost of Samuel, his predecessor, to get guidance. Saul asked around and found out that there was a necromancer living in the town of Endor who might be able to perform the forbidden deed.

Saul disguised himself so that he wouldn't be recognized and visited the so-called "Witch of Endor." She conjured up Samuel, but the deceased ruler was so infuriated at being "disquieted" that he refused to help or counsel Saul.

Current thinking is that the Witch of Endor was probably not a witch or sorceress in the modern sense of the word, but closer to our conception of the *oracle* in ancient Greece.

King Saul consults with the Witch of Endor, who conjures the spirit of Samuel.

(Joseph Glanvil, Saducismus Triumphatus, *1681 ed.)*

The Oracle of Apollo at Delphi was the most famous of numerous seers (almost all of whom were female) situated at temples throughout ancient Greece. To consult with the gods, an oracle would first enter a trance. (Today, scientists suggest that the oracles at Delphi probably entered their "trances" after breathing in hydrocarbon gases, especially ethylene, which may have seeped from geological fissures under the temple and at a nearby sacred spring.) The oracle would then deliver her answer, often in cryptic phrases that required the person receiving the message to decipher or interpret its true meaning.

On occasion, oracles would contact spirits in the underworld. But it was accepted that not all ghosts could foretell the future. In fact, it was only after the end of the classical Greek period and the collapse of many oracular sites that more and more ghosts seemed to develop the ability to predict future events.

Phantom Phrases

The **oracle** of classical Greece received messages from the gods (and sometimes from the deceased) concerning the future. Usually female, the prophetess-priestess would be set up in a temple dedicated to a particular god.

The temple of the Oracle of Apollo at Delphi.

(Photo by author)

Early Apparitions

It's difficult to tell, thousands of years after they were written, whether the earliest records of ghosts were literary inventions or whether apparitions had, indeed, been observed.

Ghost stories dating from ancient Greek and Roman periods were often based on legends rather than first-hand experience. *Marchen* stories, as they were called, were generally assumed to be fictional. *Sagen* legends, on the other hand, were thought to be fact with literary embellishments.

Phantastic Tips

The belief that a living being and its phantom double can exist simultaneously (as in the case of Hercules being in both Hades and on Mount Olympus at the same time) is reflected in the modern concept of the astral body or spirit double. If you're fascinated by the legends and lore from ancient Greece and Rome, check out *The Complete Idiot's Guide to Classical Mythology, Second Edition* (Alpha Books, 2004).

The epic poems the *Iliad* and the *Odyssey*, both traditionally attributed to the eighth-century Greek epic poet Homer, ghosts are benign, passive spirits. They didn't bother the living, and the living didn't particularly worry about them. Once the proper burial and rituals were performed for the deceased, the dead pretty much were left to fend for themselves.

After death, the spirit of the deceased departed for Hades, a nether region below the earth's surface ruled by the god Hades. At one point in the *Odyssey*, the hero Odysseus travels to Hades to get advice from the spirit of the long-dead prophet Tiresias.

After Tiresias made his revelations, Odysseus also spoke with the ghosts of his mother, Achilles, Agamemnon, the wife/mother of Oedipus, and more. Ulysses also met Hercules, but he presumed it to be a phantom double (*eidolon*), since the actual Hercules had been accepted onto Mount Olympus to live with the gods.

The spirits in Hades were restless and constantly screaming, but otherwise, they were harmless. They also had no substance: When Ulysses attempted to hug his mother, for example, his arms passed right through her.

There was a great change in beliefs about ghosts and their nature by the time of the Greek philosopher Socrates (469?–399 B.C.E.). Ghosts were still thought to be generally helpful and consoling, but they could just as easily turn into threatening, noisy, and restless beings that might hurt or kill those who upset them—particularly if they wandered too close. For centuries, seers had called up spirits to do their bidding; now, ghosts sometimes made demands of the living! The ghosts of those who had died prematurely or violently were thought to be especially dangerous.

It was common knowledge that the spirit of a deceased person sometimes hovered near its grave, especially in the case of a suicide or a violent or premature death. Writing in his *Phaedo*, the Greek philosopher Plato (427–347 B.C.E.) warned against "prowling about tombs and sepulchers, near which, as they tell us, are seen certain ghostly apparitions of souls which have not departed pure."

The First Ghost Story

Perhaps the first extant report of a haunted house comes from a letter written by Roman author, statesman, and orator Pliny the Younger (C.E. 62?–c.113). He wrote his patron, Lucias Sura, about a villa in Athens that no one would rent because it had a resident ghost:

> At the dead of night, horrid noises were heard in the villa: the clanking of chains, which grew louder and louder. Suddenly, the hideous phantom of an old man appeared, who seemed the very picture of abject filth and misery. His beard was long and matted, his white hair disheveled. His thick legs were loaded down by heavy irons that he dragged wearily along with a painful moaning; his wrists were shackled by long, cruel links. Every so often he raised his arms and shook his shackles in a kind of impotent fury. Once, a few mocking skeptics who were bold enough to stay all night in the villa were almost scared senseless at the sight of the apparition. Worse, disease and even death came to those who ventured inside those cursed walls after dusk.

The notorious reputation of the villa didn't stop another Athenian philosopher, Athenodorus, from leasing it. Short on money, he found the inexpensive rent too attractive to turn down.

According to Pliny, Athenodorus met the ghost his first night at the villa. The philosopher heard the faint rattle of chains, and the spectre appeared. The ghost silently motioned for Athenodorus to follow him. When he refused, the spectre loudly clanked his chains until the philosopher agreed to come along. The phantom floated into the garden, where he pointed to a spot on the ground, then vanished.

The next day, Athenodorus told his story to the local authorities, who dug up the garden. At the very spot indicated by the ghost, a human skeleton, bound in chains, was uncovered. The bones were properly buried, the house was ceremoniously purified, and the ghost, apparently finished with his earthly business, never returned.

Why Bother to Come Back?

The appearance of ghosts demanding proper burial rites is a recurrent theme in classic Greek and Roman literature. Here are just three more examples:

- ◆ During the war at Troy, the spectre of Patroclus appeared to his comrade Achilles, asking to be properly cremated. (The ghost also delivered the bad news that Achilles, too, would be killed in battle at Troy.)

- ◆ Elpenor, one of Ulysses' crewmembers, fell to his death on Circe's island. His spirit appeared on the ship after it had sailed, asking his leader go back to suitably bury him.

- ◆ The ghost of the Roman emperor Caligula, who had been assassinated and quickly cremated, haunted the Lamian Gardens where his ashes were entombed until rites befitting an emperor were held. (He, or some other ghost, also haunted the theater where Caligula was murdered up until the structure was destroyed by fire.)

There were many other reasons why ghosts returned to the world of the living. One was to show gratitude. Roman statesman and author Cicero (106–43 B.C.E.), told of Simonides, who buried the body of a stranger. The man's ghost later appeared to Simonides, advising him not to board a ship on which he intended to sail. Fortunately, Simonides followed the spectre's warning: The ship was lost at sea.

Spirits came back to offer assistance or to give advice, especially to loved ones. For example, according to the fifth-century B.C.E. Greek historian Herodotus, a Corinthian tyrant named Periander was visited by his deceased wife to help him find a precious object that he had lost.

Ghosts also returned to console the bereaved. After Aeneas's wife was burned during the sacking of Troy, her ghost returned to comfort her husband.

Still others who had met violent ends returned as ghosts to help the living find their murderers. Roman poet Ovid (43 B.C.E.–C.E. 18) wrote about the spectre of Remus returning to name his assailant. In *De divinatione*, Cicero describes an innkeeper who murders one of two men staying at his tavern. The victim's ghost returns to help his companion find the corpse and to request a proper burial.

Some ghosts didn't wait for intermediaries to do their bidding. There are dozens of legends of spirits returning to harm their murderers or assailants. Although ghosts were usually thought of as insubstantial, in some cases they were able to physically assault their offenders. Many of these wronged spirits had also been deprived of proper burials.

Ghosts could be disruptive creatures. In his *Life of Cimon*, the Greek biographer Plutarch (C.E. 46?–120?) writes that the baths at Chaeronea were haunted, reportedly by the ghost of Damon, a violent man who was murdered there. The spectral occurrences, including moans and other noises (though apparently no sighting of an actual ghost), became so disturbing that nearby residents sealed up the baths.

In the second century C.E., the Greek author Pausanias described the ghostly night-time sounds of men in combat near the grave mounds on the field where the battle of Marathon had taken place more than 600 years earlier. As you'll discover in Chapter 17, haunted armies form an entire genre of ghost phenomenon.

Throw Them to the Lions

By the third century, Christianity was making strong footholds in ancient Greece and Rome. To make conversion attractive to pagans, the early Christian Church had to adopt (or adapt) many of the prevalent popular religious beliefs, especially those concerning ghosts and the afterlife.

Early Christian writers (such as Justin Martyr) acknowledged life after death. But they also claimed that because ghosts exist in spirit form only, after death, all people would be social equals. (This concept must have been mighty attractive to the masses.)

The big decision the Christian Church had to make, though, was difficult: Just where did the soul go after a person died?

Purgatory: Neither Heaven Nor Hell

Even the great Christian theorist Saint Augustine (d. 430) didn't want to commit as to exactly where the soul went immediately after death. But by the thirteenth century, as the Middle Ages were drawing to a close, the concept of *purgatory* had been firmly established by the Catholic Church.

Phantom Phrases

An ethereal realm somewhere "between" heaven and hell, **purgatory,** in Roman Catholic theology, is an ethereal state or place in which the souls of people who have died in grace must suffer while being cleansed of or while atoning for their venial (or pardonable) sins before being admitted into heaven.

The word "purgatory" might have had its first "official" use in an ecclesiastical letter written to Pope Innocent IV in 1254. Purgatory was discussed at the Council of Lyons in 1274 and again at the Council of Florence (1438–1443). At the Council of Trent (1545–1563) the Catholic Church confirmed its belief in a spirit-inhabited purgatory. The Councils declared that communication to and from the dead was a reality. The Church also established that performing good deeds or services on behalf of the dead could lessen the number of years a spirit would have to spend in purgatory. So, too, could the purchase of indulgences, notes of official forgiveness from the Church.

Apparitional sightings continued throughout the Dark and Middle Ages. Many times the ghosts appeared in dreams. According to most descriptions from the time, ghosts were typically pale and wore sad expressions. They usually showed the marks (such as burns and scars) from the suffering they were enduring in purgatory. Occasionally, a ghost appeared in a nonhuman form, such as a ball of light or a dove.

The Christian dead returned for any number of reasons—often, to make a confession, to beg the pardon of those sinned against, and to atone for their wrongs. But almost all ghosts of the era warned the living of the need to obey the sacraments and laws of the Church.

When Good Ghosts Go Bad

Catholic writers such as N. Taillepied (d. 1589), a Capuchin monk and a Doctor of Theology, suggested that, in addition to the ghosts of the dead, satanic spirits also existed, and they could take the form of loved ones. He listed several ways to tell if you were dealing with a demon in ghost form, as opposed to a good or neutral spirit. According to Taillepied, an evil phantom was more likely to:

◆ Hurt you or damage your belongings.

◆ Flatter or tempt you.

◆ Appear as a lion, bear, black dog, toad, snake, or cat. (Good ghosts manifest themselves as doves, lambs, handsome men with halos, or people dressed all in white.)

◆ Have loud, harsh voices, speak heresy, and are conceited. (Good spirits, it was noted, have soothing, musical voices.)

Phantastic Tips

By the beginning of the sixteenth century, Christian writings were describing how unseen spirits would often announce their presence by knocking or tapping on a table or other solid object. Sorcerers of the period also often asked spirits to knock to make themselves known. So who are we to disagree? If you hear a tapping noise but no one's around, look out: You might have a ghost on your hands. In Chapter 6, we'll see how this form of rapping communication was adopted by the early spiritualists.

Fortunately, Taillepied offered several suggestions for what to do if you saw an evil ghost. As a practical matter, he explained that swordplay would be useless, of course. Instead, you should pray, say the Lord's name, make the sign of the cross on your forehead, and avoid speaking any blasphemy (which the demon could use as an excuse to take you away). Then, just to be safe, you should spend the rest of your life obeying and taking part in the sacraments of the Church. That oughta do it.

Ghostly Reforms

In the sixteenth century, Protestant writers and thinkers of the Reformation began to question the nature—even the existence—of ghosts. Many Protestant leaders taught that ghostly apparitions were illusionary and caused by angels or, more likely, demons; likewise, they disavowed the existence of purgatory as a spirit-filled domain.

One of the best-known early Protestant books on ghosts was *De Spectris* (1570) by the Swiss reformer Louis Lavatar. In 1572 it was published in English as *Of ghostes and spirites walking by nyght, and of strange noyses, crackes, and sundry forewarnynges.* Now there's a title!

Lavatar thought that most Catholic ghost sightings could be explained away as trickery, human error, or natural causes. Also, he dismissed all reports from women because they were, for the most part, "given to fear more than men" and think that they see and hear things that aren't really there. He did concede that "drunken men see strange things" that they mistakenly report as being ghosts.

Despite the Protestants' official position, most sixteenth-century followers *did* believe in ghosts. There were just too many sightings, and the concept of apparitions was just too culturally ingrained for people to completely deny their existence.

The Age of Alchemy

During this period, the practice of necromancy didn't disappear, it just went underground.

In their search for eternal truths and unlimited knowledge, a series of metaphysical thinkers in the sixteenth through eighteenth centuries embraced the Kabbalah, a collection of esoteric Jewish writings. The mystics felt that the keys to unlock all of life's (and the afterlife's) secrets could be found in the books' obscure texts. The practice of necromancy among such occultists was almost commonplace. Often the secret rituals took place at night in the local cemeteries.

Spain was considered the capital of necromancy during the Middle Ages. The nefarious craft was actually taught in Toledo, Seville, and Salamanca, deep in caves outside the cities. When rumors started to circulate that witches were seen eating human flesh as part of these rituals, Queen Isabella, a fervent Catholic, sealed up the caverns.

> ### Ghostly Pursuits
>
> Although the Kabbalah has its roots in ancient Hebrew mysticism, cabalistic teachings and principles are still popular today. In fact, its teachings have many celebrity adherents. To learn more about the Kabbalah, check out the New Age section of any major bookstore; you'll find plenty of books on the subject.

The English wizard John Dee (1527–1608) and his partner, medium Edward Kelly (1555–1595), performing necromancy in a churchyard around 1582.

(Engraving from Mathieu Giraldo's Histaire curieuse et pittoresue des sorciers, *Paris, 1846)*

Ghost Stories of the Seventeenth Century

Following the Restoration in seventeenth-century England, several important collections of ghost stories were assembled, including one by Joseph Glanvil (1636–1680), an Anglican minister and chaplain to Charles II. His stories were published the year after his death under the title *Saducismus Triumphatus; or a full and plain evidence concerning Witches and Apparitions*. Glanvil had a hands-on approach to the paranormal; in 1661, he investigated the site haunted by the famous poltergeist, the Drummer of Tedworth (see Chapter 5).

Glanvil believed that there were two "aspects," or parts, of the soul. At death, what he called the "astral body"—the higher aspect—returned to its heavenly home. The "aerial body"—the lower aspect—sometimes remained as a spirit here on Earth.

Compare Joseph Glanvil's concept of a soul with two "aspects" to the ancient Egyptian belief in the *ka* and the *ba* (see Chapter 1). Sometimes the more things change, the more they stay the same.

 Boo!

Be precise when talking about ghosts. Often the same word can mean two different things, depending on who's doing the talking. For example, Glanvil thought the astral body was only half of a soul or spirit—the part that, after death, ascended to a higher plane. In an out-of-body experience (which we'll examine in our next chapter), the astral body is a whole spirit; it simply leaves a still-living body to take a short vacation.

The ghosts in stories of the Restoration period also tended to share certain attributes:

- They didn't materialize suddenly, float, or pass through solid objects, such as walls. They would open and shut doors, sometimes being polite enough to knock first.

- They appeared "normal" in voice and behavior.

- Two thirds of the ghosts could be recognized by the people they were haunting.

- They resembled the corpse at the time of death. Thus, the ghost of a murder victim might show a slit throat or bullet wounds, or an accident victim might be disfigured.

- They showed no sign of having been in a hellish purgatory—no blackened faces, no singed clothing.

◆ They were aware of goings-on on Earth, especially of events in their own family and society.

From Enlightenment to Romance

The Enlightenment of the eighteenth century led to a rise in skepticism and disbelief in ghosts. Free thinkers openly debated religious doctrine and the existence of an afterlife.

During the Romantic era of the late eighteenth and early nineteenth centuries, society once again embraced the emotional and the spiritual.

Thus, as humanity's beliefs about science and religion changed, so, too, did their beliefs about the soul, the possibility of survival after death, the existence of ghosts, and the ability to communicate with the dead.

Mystical Visions

It was against this backdrop that Emanuel Swedenborg (1688–1772) was born in Sweden. A scientist and scholar, he had no particular interest in the paranormal, although he did believe in the existence of the soul.

But in 1743, Swedenborg had a series of dreams and trances in which he claimed he experienced visions of an Unseen World. He claimed that he had conversations with "angels," which is what he called the spirits of the dead. Among those Swedenborg said he talked with were Aristotle, Plato, and Napoleon. He began to deliver messages from the dead by *automatic writing*, a technique in which you hold a pencil to paper and allow the "spirits" to move your hand.

Phantom Phrases

Automatic writing is a form of automatism, which is any unconscious and spontaneous muscular movement caused by the spirits. Automatisms are especially impressive if they're skills such as painting, creative writing, singing, or the playing of a musical instrument.

Swedenborg proclaimed that a person exists simultaneously in the physical and the spirit worlds. The spirit survives death intact, with complete knowledge of its life on Earth. After death, the soul enters an astral plane where the dead meets deceased friends and relatives. Then, after a period of reflection, the soul moves onto a sort of heaven or hell, an afterworld created by the soul's own memories from Earth. (Swedenborg didn't believe in redemption through Christ, nor did he believe in Satan.)

Needless to say, Swedenborg's announcements didn't endear him to the Christian Church. Even many of Swedenborg's friends and colleagues thought that he was insane. Eventually, Swedenborg moved to London, where he died in 1772.

Swedenborg's mystical teachings and revelations had gained a foothold during his lifetime, but the Swedenborgian movement, based on his writings, started up after his death. It evolved into a religion that is still practiced today.

But what does Swedenborg have to do with ghosts? Well, his teachings would have a great impact on the soon-to-be-born spiritualism movement. Many of his ideas, such as the belief that the spirit survives death intact along with all its earthly memories, were wholeheartedly embraced by spiritualists. Also, his pioneering use of automatic writing was adopted by mediums as a great improvement over the tedious rappings used up to that time for spirit communication.

Mesmerize Me

The work of an Austrian-born physician named Friedrich (sometimes seen as Franz) Anton Mesmer (1734–1815) proved to be the next big step in the attempt to communicate with the Other World. Around the beginning of the nineteenth century, Mesmer was successful in putting his patients into a trance state as he treated them. (And, yes, you're getting ahead of me: That's where the word "mesmerize" comes from!)

Mesmer's methods were dubious at best, because he attempted to heal patients primarily by placing magnets on the affected parts of their bodies. Traditional medicine was quick to dismiss Mesmer as a quack. However, one of Mesmer's students, the Marquis de Puységur (1751–1825), discovered that once mesmerized, some of his patients were able to diagnose and heal themselves.

Before long, physicians across Europe were experimenting with patients in mesmerized states. In the 1840s, British surgeon James Braid (1795–1860) coined a new term for the induction of a trance state: hypnotism (from the Greek *hypnos*, meaning "sleep"). Braid discovered that while in an hypnotic state, the subject was especially responsive to suggestion. Some of the other phenomena exhibited by hypnotized subjects included the ability to perform seemingly impossible physical feats, tolerance to pain, and extraordinary recall of

Phantastic Tips

Hypnotism is a fascinating subject, and the induction technique can be learned by almost anyone. Your eyelids are getting heavy! Sleep! Sleep! See how easy that was? If you want to learn more about how to hypnotize and otherwise mesmerize, check out *The Complete Idiot's Guide to Hypnosis* (Alpha Books, 1999).

past events. Rumors soon surfaced that some hypnotized people showed telepathic or other extrasensory powers.

Mesmerists discovered that if two or more people—hypnotized or not—sat with their fingers lightly resting on a tabletop, the table would often begin to move or tilt. They explained that "table-tipping," as this phenomenon became known, was caused by magnetism, even if the table were made of wood.

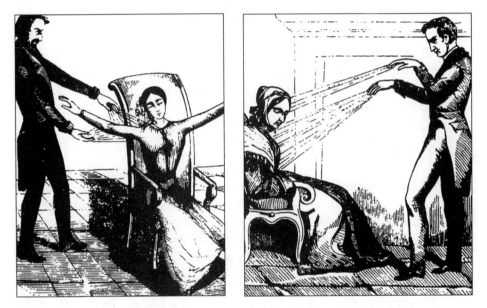

These fanciful engravings show subjects being hypnotized. Sleep rays don't come out of a hypnotist's fingers during induction, of course. However, Mesmer, from whose name we get "mesmerize," believed he could cure people by passing "animal magnetism" out through his hands.

It was only a matter of time before occultists began to speculate whether putting people into trances would allow the subjects to see into the spirit realm—or whether the spirits could use someone in a trance as a way back to this world. Mesmer's work even seemed to make such an attempt "scientific." Soon there were numerous reports of people who had been able to contact the spirit world while mesmerized.

The Poughkeepsie Seer

Andrew Jackson Davis (1826–1910), born in upstate New York, is remembered for helping to bridge the gap between mesmerism and spiritualism. He was put into a trance for the first time in December 1843 and soon showed an ability to diagnose people's illnesses while mesmerized. Before long, he became known as the Pough-keepsie Seer.

In March 1844, Davis experienced a series of life-transforming visions while walking in the Catskills Mountains in a semi-trancelike state. This led to his book, *The Divine Revelations*, in which he wrote of spirits of the deceased residing in a realm called the Summer-Land:

> It is a truth that spirits commune with one another while one is in the body and the other is in the higher spheres … and this truth will ere long present itself in the form of a living demonstration. And the world will hail with delight the ushering in of that era when the interiors of men will be opened, and the spiritual communion will be established …

Did I read that right? "This truth will ere long present itself in the form of a living demonstration"? Perhaps without even knowing it, Davis had predicted the arrival of spiritualism!

Soon, the lights would be lowered. Wait a second! Did you hear something? Did you feel the table move? The spiritualist movement was about to be born!

But first, let's take a breather from these theorists and thinkers. By taking a look at the variety of things people actually have *experienced* over the centuries we might be able to make our own conclusions about the nature of ghosts.

The Least You Need to Know

- Seers such as the Biblical Witch of Endor tried to foretell the future with necromancy—consulting the spirits of the dead.

- Ghosts have appeared in even the earliest Greek and Roman literature.

- The early Christian Church accepted many pagan beliefs about ghosts, then added the concept of Purgatory to the mix.

- Catholics and early Protestants differed in their beliefs about ghosts, with the latter denying their existence entirely.

- Several important collections of ghost stories were assembled in the seventeenth century, including those by Joseph Glanvil; however, belief in ghosts waned during the Enlightenment of the eighteenth century.

- The work of Friedrich Anton Mesmer and his followers, along with mystics such as Emanuel Swedenborg and Andrew Jackson Davis, laid the path for the spiritualism movement.

Do the Dead Return?

In This Chapter

- ◆ The connection between the body and the soul
- ◆ The search for the soul by Edison and other scientists
- ◆ Out-of-body experiences: the astral body and astral projection
- ◆ Near-death experiences
- ◆ Deathbed visitations

Is there any evidence that some part of us—*something*—survives death? Those of you who've seen and possibly recognized a ghost have probably already made up your minds. Others believe in survival after death because of otherwise-unexplainable type of paranormal experiences. These include out-of-body experiences, crisis apparitions, and near-death experiences, all of which we'll examine in this chapter.

Many researchers, not wanting to define the soul in religious terms, say that anything that continues after death would have to be some elemental force, such as energy. Some scientists will only concede the existence of the soul if they can take quantitative measurements.

Do you need proof? Read on. Maybe one of these stories will make you believe in ghosts.

Purgatorial Proof

As far as we know for certain, no one has ever gotten as far as heaven or hell and come back to tell us about it. But how about those who made it halfway? Has anyone ever come back from Purgatory? Some people seem to think so, and they've housed their evidence in a church just blocks away from St. Peter's Basilica in Rome!

Near the end of the nineteenth century, Father Vittore Jouet of the Sacro Cuore del Suffragio Church in Rome took it upon himself to investigate the many stories he had heard about spirits returning from the Beyond to visit their loved ones. Often, the souls asked their nearest and dearest to offer prayers and extra masses so that their souls could be released from Purgatory.

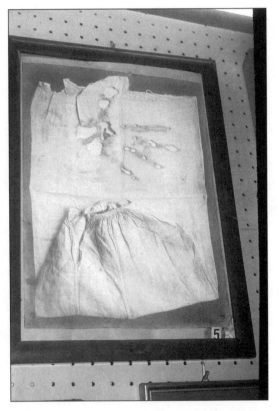

The Purgatory Museum is housed in an annex off the nave of the Sacro Cuore del Suffragio Church in Rome, just blocks away from the Vatican.

(Photo by author)

The ghost of Mrs. Leleux burned her palm print into the sleeve of her son Joseph's shirt on a visitation during the night of June 21, 1789 in Wodecq, Belgium.

(Photo by author)

In many instances, the bereaved asked the spectres to leave some physical evidence behind to prove that they'd been there; otherwise, how could they convince people that the visitation had occurred? Sometimes the spirits complied by burning a palm print or the fingerprints into a prayer book or a piece of clothing. More than one phantom caller seared the sign of a cross into wood.

These burnt offerings were the tangible relics that Father Jouet collected and, with the blessing of Pope Pius X and Pope Benedict XV, put on display. Father Gilla Gremigni, Jouet's successor, closed the museum in 1920 to give him time to authenticate the pieces. It remained shut for 30 years. Today, all of the remaining exhibits, about a dozen or so, are housed behind glass in a hallway next to the church nave, where they can be viewed by visitors.

Ghostly Pursuits

According to Christian Church doctrine, apparitions of ecclesiastical figures (such as visitations of the Virgin Mary said to occurred at Lourdes in 1858 and Fatima in 1917) are not ghosts. Likewise, sacred images (such as the likeness of a crucified man on the Shroud of Turin) are considered holy relics rather than evidence of spectral visitations. They are extraordinary religious phenomena produced by the hand of God.

You Mean You Don't Have to Die First?

Many paranormal believers think that the soul or spirit can separate from and return to the body even while a person is alive, allowing an out-of-body experience (OBE) or a near-death experience (NDE). (We'll take a closer look at these phenomena in a moment.) Paranormal hair-splitters suggest that what actually departs from the physical body during an OBE or NDE is an *astral body*, which acts as a vehicle to carry the soul on its journeys.

For some, this is an important distinction, because they claim that the actual soul stays in the still-living person or in whatever realm it has traveled to after death. The ghost or apparition is merely its astral body.

Phantom Phrases

The **astral body** is a spiritual life force that's sometimes able to separate from and return to the corporeal, living body. Some paranormal experts use the term synonymously with the soul; others think of them as two distinct entities.

A Weighty Matter

Scientists have long wondered whether there might be a controllable, objective way to observe the soul. Some have attempted to detect or prove the existence of the soul by comparing a person's body weight just immediately prior to and after death. If there were any observable, measurable weight loss within those few moments, is it possible that the difference—the change in ounces or pounds—could have been caused by the soul having departed from the body?

Is this an actual photo of a soul leaving a woman's body at the moment of death?

(Photo from the author's collection)

In one very limited 1907 study, researcher Duncan McDougall attempted to measure the soul by weighing five patients as they died. In two of the patients, there was a sudden weight loss of a half-ounce, followed by another sudden one-ounce weight loss within three minutes of the time of death. A third patient's weight fluctuated just after death, first dropping a bit, followed by an abrupt large weight gain(!), then another loss. There was no discernable change on the other patients. Needless to say, the results were inconclusive.

If you want to become a star in the paranormal world, all you have to do is come up with a test that proves the soul exists. Duncan McDougall experimented with body weight. What else might change in a person's body at the moment of death? How could it be measured? Could that measurement be evidence of a soul?

Edison's Search for the Soul

Albert Einstein (1879–1955), the great German-born physicist, theorized that energy, like matter, could be neither created nor destroyed. It could merely be converted or transformed, from one state to another.

Perhaps this had also been the thinking of inventor Thomas Edison (1847–1931) when, late in his career, he began work on a device to detect and communicate with the dead. Edison believed that the soul, or whatever survived death, was comprised of what he called "life units." According to Edison:

- Humans—indeed, all life forms—are made up of microscopic life units that could arrange themselves in any variety of forms, from a starfish to a human.

- The life units had a memory. (Edison used this argument to explain skin regeneration, for example.)

- If the life units had a strong enough memory to remain together after the death of the body, perhaps the person's personality would remain intact. (But, Edison was quick to caution, he didn't think that the survival of an actual personality had been proved—as yet.)

- If the life units were not strong enough to stay together, they would disperse and reformulate into other beings.

- There's a fixed quantity of life units on this planet, and the number could never be increased or decreased.

- Life units are indestructible, so they definitely survived the death of the body.

Edison worked for years to create a piece of scientific apparatus that could detect these life units and act as a sort of megaphone or amplifier. Used correctly, he reasoned, the machine would register even the smallest life unit, even after the death of the body.

Edison operated on the presumption that the personality continued to exist after death. He pointed out that it was only reasonable to conclude that those who leave this earth would like to keep in touch with those they left behind. Accordingly, the thing to do was to furnish the best conceivable means to make it easy for them to open up communication with us, and then see what happens.

During his lifetime, Edison received hundreds of patents, and his laboratories created the first commercially viable electric light bulb, phonograph, and motion-picture projector. Unfortunately, Edison's life-unit detector and his ghost communication device remained uncompleted at the time of his death.

Do you think that this same genius, given enough resources and time, might have been able to provide us with the first positive proof of life after death? Only the spirits know.

Look at All the Pretty Colors

In 1937, Russian electrician Semyon Kirlian used the properties of electricity to create a series of stunning photographs. Kirlian set a piece of unexposed photographic film on a metal plate, then rested a small object on the film. Next, he grounded a high-voltage, high-frequency generator to the plate, and touched the other end of the wire to the object to be "photographed." As the film was exposed, a natural electrical discharge created a stunning, iridescent halo or corona on the photographic paper around the object, which appeared in silhouette. (The most famous example of these photographs is the often-seen picture of a hand, with fingers extended and rays shooting out in all directions.)

Paranormal believers immediately claimed that Kirlian photography, as this phenomenon became known, was scientific proof that the soul exists, and that it sometimes manifests itself in the form of an aura surrounding the body. Although amused by the photographs' novelty, scientists denied there was any connection whatsoever between Kirlian photography and an aura or the soul.

> **Boo!**
>
> Do not—repeat, do not!—rig up electric wires to a metal plate, place your hand on it, and take a photograph. You'll knock out a few fuses, burn down the house, and electrocute yourself. Besides, that's not how Kirlian photographs work. If you *must* have one done to see your aura, seek out a professional.

Even reproduced in black and white, this Kirlian photograph seems to reveal an aura surrounding the palm.

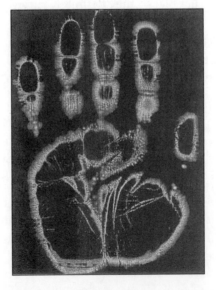

Leaving Your Body Behind

An *out-of-body experience* or *OBE* (also known as astral projection, bi-location, and, sometimes, ESP projection) is a paranormal phenomenon in which an astral body (or spirit double) of a person separates from the physical body.

The terms "OBE" and "astral projection" are often used interchangeably. If there's any difference between them, it's in connotation: "Out-of-body experience" creates the image of a spirit hovering over or near the body; astral projection seems to suggest it travels some distance.

Remember, in OBE, the actual person doesn't physically travel to another location. Only the astral body makes the journey. Sometimes, the astral body is able to bring back memories and information from the trip; on examination, this is often information that the person otherwise would not have known. This last sort of OBE, with experiences that can be verified, is perhaps the most valuable and the most credible in psychic research.

On occasion, the spirit double appears to another person. It might appear as an apparition, ghostlike, or it might appear to be solid flesh and blood. In his 1956 study "Six Theories About Apparitions," psychic researcher Hornell Norris Hart (1888–1967) concluded that astral projections and apparitions of the dead (that is, ghosts) are essentially the same in character and substance.

Some people who have experienced an OBE report having been transported to a different "world" similar to our own. Most of those who travel to such a dimension find it to be superior to ours in beauty and comfort. They also often report seeing friends and relatives who have died.

There have been some experiments in deliberately induced astral projection; that is, of a person trying to send an astral self to another place. Although there have been some claims of limited success, paranormal literature doesn't contain many case histories.

Like most paranormal activity, out-of-body experiences weren't seriously examined until the nineteenth century. Dr. Robert Crookall, one of the earliest paranormal investigators, dedicated most of his research to the OBE, and he wrote more than 10 books on the subject. Of course,

Ghostly Pursuits

Stories of astral projection appear throughout history. Puritan minister Increase Mather (1639–1723) chronicled the appearance of people in one location when, it was later discovered, they were actually in their homes at the time. His explanation was that Satan had created the doubles. He detailed this and other observances of paranormal phenomena in *An Essay for the Recording of Illustrious Providences* (1684).

his examples couldn't be verified. The cases he examined were once-in-a-lifetime events, and OBEs can't be corroborated by any outside observers. (No one else went along on the trip.)

The Wilmot Apparition

The so-called Wilmot Apparition is one of the most fascinating case histories of astral projection in the annals of paranormal research. In 1889 and 1890, the case was thoroughly examined by the Society for Psychical Research, a group of British investigators that you'll read about in Chapter 10. The occurrence remains a riddle.

S.R. Wilmot, a manufacturer from Bridgeport, Connecticut, sailed from England to New York on the *City of Limerick* steamship on October 3, 1863. A storm lashed the ship for nine days of the crossing. On the eighth day out, Wilmot dreamed that his wife (who was back in the United States) came to his berth and kissed him as he slept. The next morning, Wilmot's roommate, William J. Tait, kidded him about having had a lady visitor the previous night—before Wilmot told him about the dream! When they compared stories, they realized that Tait had been awake and had actually seen the astral body of Wilmot's wife!

Wilmot arrived in Connecticut, and before he could say anything to his wife about the strange experience, she asked him whether he had seen a vision of her at sea. News of the storm had reached her, and she had become alarmed. That night, she dreamed that she visited the ship to comfort her husband. The dream remained so vivid in her memory that, the next morning, she could swear she had actually been on board the ship.

The Wilmot case is notable because it involves both collective and reciprocal apparitions. A *collective apparition* occurs when more than one person sees the same spirit or ghost at the same time. A *reciprocal apparition*, in which both the spectral visitor and the person who is visited see and acknowledge each other, is exceedingly rare.

If I Knew You Were Coming, I'd Have Baked a Cake

One of the more unusual types of OBE is the "arrival case," in which an apparition of a person shows up at a destination before the actual person gets there. The apparition appears in the same clothing that the person is wearing during travel. In fact, the ghost looks so real that people often talk to it—and sometimes, the phantom even answers! The doppelgänger apparition is always gone by the time the living person shows up.

Mark Twain recalled having once experienced an arrival case while attending a large reception. He spotted a female acquaintance across the room, then met her later that evening at dinner. As it turned out, she had never been at the party. Her train was delayed, so she was still traveling when the soirée was held.

Your Friend in a Crisis

A *crisis apparition* is a specific type of astral projection in which the astral body is released at the time of illness, trauma, accident, or impending death to warn or inform another person, usually a loved one. Often, the person whose spirit travels is unconscious or heavily medicated at the time.

There is continuing study and controversy concerning crisis apparitions. Because the exact moment of death is hard to pinpoint, there's debate about whether the apparition actually appears just *before*, *as*, or immediately *after* death occurs. Is the person seeing the ghost of someone's who's dead or the astral body of a living person? Regardless, the phenomenon itself is well documented. Here are just three of the hundreds of crisis apparitions recorded by the Society for Psychical Research:

- ♦ On the evening of January 3, 1840, Mrs. Sabine Baring-Gould of Exeter, England, was sitting at the dining room table reading her Bible when her seaman brother Henry appeared across from her. After a few minutes, he faded from sight. Knowing that he was serving the Royal Navy in the South Atlantic, Mrs. Baring-Gould noted the time and date: A month later she found out that her brother had died at sea at that exact time.

- ♦ On January 3, 1856, Mrs. Anne Collyer of Camden, New Jersey, awoke to see her son Joseph standing in her bedroom doorway, his face battered and bandaged. She was surprised because he was the captain of a steamboat on the Mississippi River and was supposed to be a thousand miles away. Soon, his image slipped from sight. Two weeks later, she learned that her son had died in a steamboat collision at the very moment she had seen his apparition.

- ♦ On March 19, 1917, Capt. Eldred Bowyer-Bower, a British aviator, was shot down and killed over France. At the time of his death, he appeared simultaneously to his half-sister in Calcutta and to his niece in England. He was clearly recognized by both and disappeared after only a few moments.

Wow! That Was Close!

Sometimes a person who clinically dies (or comes very close to actual death) and is revived sometimes undergoes a *near-death experience* (NDE). The person might recall leaving the body and extraordinary, even paranormal, visions of an afterlife. An

American physician, Dr. Raymond Moody, coined the phrase "near-death experience" in the 1970s, to describe the phenomena that his patients said they had experienced while "dead."

People who have had an NDE describe many of the same experiences, including:

◆ A realization that he or she is undergoing an out-of-body experience.

◆ The sensation of floating above one's own body and looking down at it.

◆ An unconcerned and objective, almost detached, view of the situation.

◆ An end of pain.

◆ A feeling of happiness.

◆ The sensation of passing down a long, lighted tunnel or pathway.

◆ Meeting apparitions such as deceased friends or relatives, unknown individuals, or religious figures. They often are dressed in white and seem to be glowing.

◆ Hearing a voice from the spirit world tell them that it's not their "time" yet and that they must return to the world of the living.

About 97 percent of those surveyed who have had an NDE said that it was a positive and life-affirming experience. Most lose their fear of death and develop a belief in survival after death. Many become more religious or have a stronger belief in God.

> **CAUTION**
>
> **Boo!**
>
> Okay, this shouldn't have to be said, but as neat as a near-death experience might be to undergo, it's not worth trying to induce one just to see what it's like. (If you don't believe me, rent the 1990 movie *Flatliners* and see what happened to those people!) Besides, what if you got to the end of the long, bright tunnel and no one tells you to turn back? Wait your turn: It'll come soon enough all on its own without any help from you.

Of course, there's no evidence to prove what a person who has undergone an NDE actually experienced. The scientific explanation most often proffered for NDE is that it's all a hallucination caused by their medication or possibly a lack of oxygen to the brain.

But this scientific theory doesn't explain why so many who have had an NDE see the same things, such as white lights and the long tunnel. Until someone actually dies and returns from the dead, the NDE phenomenon will probably remain an unsolved mystery.

> **Ghostly Pursuits**
>
> Perhaps the most famous person to tell of her own near-death experience is actress Elizabeth Taylor, who fell ill from pneumonia in 1961 during a break in the filming of *Cleopatra*. Her health deteriorated, and she slipped in and out of a coma. At one point, her heart stopped and for a brief time she was clinically dead. Fortunately, doctors were able to revive her. Taylor later spoke at a fundraiser for the hospital that treated her and described having undergone an NDE. She described the sensation of hovering over her bed, then going down a long tunnel with a light at the end, and then hearing voices urging her to return to her body.

To learn more about NDE and other types of out-of-body experiences, you might want to read *The Complete Idiot's Guide to Near-Death Experiences* (Alpha Books, 2000). It really does cover just about everything you've ever wanted to know about the phenomenon.

As I Lay Dying

There are thousands of reports of people who have seen apparitions leading up to or at the moment of their deaths. It stands to reason, too, that the phenomenon occurs much more often than is reported: After all, many times the person who sees the ghost dies before being able to tell anyone about it.

In *Deathbed Visions* (1926), Sir William Barrett described case after case in which the dying seemed to see dead relatives who came to greet them and to help them on their passage to the next world. Needless to say, if these visions were what the observers claimed, it would be remarkable proof of an Afterlife.

To prepare his study *Deathbed Observations by Physicians and Nurses* (1951), Dr. Karlis Osis surveyed 5,000 doctors and 5,000 nurses about their experiences regarding apparitions that appeared to their dying patients. He concluded that dying persons in full possession of their faculties and in normal consciousness *frequently* "see" spirits of the dead, including those of friends, relatives, and—in a convincing proof of survival after death—people who the patients didn't know had already died.

Sometimes, it's not only the person who's about to die who sees the ghosts. There have been numerous instances in which those seated beside the deathbed reported seeing spectral entities as well.

People will continue to debate the existence of the soul. Scientists and paranormal investigators will continue to look for evidence. And all the while, people will keep seeing ghosts—perhaps the best possible proof.

Myths about ghosts have been with us for thousands of years. Some have been heard so often that they've evolved into so-called "urban legends." In the next chapter, we'll look at some of these ghosts that inhabit our folklore and traditions.

First-Person Phantoms

I know what I saw, but I don't know what I saw. On one of my last visits with my mom, I realized that she was looking toward the foot of her bed, a listless and unfocused gaze at a spot slightly above her and to the left. I asked her what she was staring at. She said that she saw my father, who had died nine years earlier. Uncomfortable at the implications, I quietly changed the subject. But now, more than a decade later, I wish I hadn't.

I saw that same look in my younger sister's eyes during the last week of her life. In fact, her gaze was so intense at one point that I turned to see who was standing behind me in the hospital room. No one was there. My sister wasn't able to speak those final days, so I never asked …

Both were on heavy medications; both slipped in and out of sleep. Were they seeing anything at all? And, if they were, was what they were seeing really there? Or was I just imagining the whole thing?

The Least You Need to Know

- The existence of ghosts is linked to the belief in the existence of the soul or, at least, to the survival of *some* part of us after death.

- Scientists have tried to detect, measure, and communicate with the soul; so far, they've been unsuccessful.

- Out-of-body and near-death experiences seem to offer proof of survival after death and, therefore, the possibility that ghosts might exist.

- People near death often have visions of deceased friends and relatives.

4

Ghostly Urban Legends

In This Chapter

- Phantom travelers and hitchhikers take to the road
- Gray ladies in waiting
- Magic mirrors on the wall
- Mysterious ghost lights
- Spectres unique to specific nations
- Charms and amulets to ward off ghosts and evil spirits

Some ghost stories have been repeated so many times that no one can pinpoint when or where they started. After scores of variations, some of these so-called "urban legends" have taken on lives of their own.

In this chapter, we'll investigate a few of the most common—mysterious ghost lights, phantom hitchhikers, spirit faces appearing in mirrors, and more. Then, to wrap it all up, we'll look at some of the charms and lucky amulets different cultures have used to ward against spectres of evil.

Did you hear the one about …?

Going My Way? Phantom Travelers

Phantom travelers are ghosts of humans or even animals that haunt roads, way stations, or vehicles. They haunt a specific location, route, or type of transportation due to some tragedy or other strong emotional connection. Sometimes they're doomed to journey the route forever for committing some sin or transgression. (The story of the *Flying Dutchman*, which we'll look at in Chapter 19, is a perfect example.)

The earliest known recorded stories about phantom travelers date to around 1600 in Europe and Russia. The legends were certainly well-known in the United States by the time Washington Irving wrote his tale about a headless horseman in 1819 and 1820 (see Chapter 24). Phantom travelers almost always seem solid and substantial—that is to say, real. They often appear from nowhere and can just as suddenly disappear.

Stick Out Your Thumb: Phantom Hitchhikers

The best-known urban legends of phantom travelers involve phantom hitchhikers. Such stories were well-established in the United States before the end of the nineteenth century.

In most variations of the basic tale, the phantom hitchhiker is a girl or young woman—a damsel in distress—who is seen by a male driver, late at night along a remote stretch of highway. She suddenly appears in the headlights, usually dressed in white. Often she is soaking wet, even if it's not raining or there is no body of water nearby.

The driver stops and asks if he can help or can offer her a ride to her destination. She tells him where she's going: It's always to the next town or in the direction that he's heading. She quietly gets into the back seat. Sometimes she gives her name, but only rarely. He might give her his coat to wear to warm her. He constantly checks his rearview mirror, noticing how beautiful she is.

When they reach her destination, he stops the car and turns to discover that the back seat is empty. The girl is gone! If the girl's clothes were wet when she got into the car, the car seat is still damp, or there may be a puddle of water on the floor. Sometimes she leaves behind some object, such as a scarf or a book.

The driver goes to the door of the house she had indicated, where he's greeted by a woman, or sometimes a man and wife. They tell him that this has often happened before—in fact, every year. It's the anniversary of their daughter's death. She was either murdered or died in an accident at the location where the driver first saw her. Every year, on that date, the girl tries to make it home, but she never succeeds. The disbelieving driver is shown a photograph of their daughter. It is, indeed, the woman he helped, wearing the same clothing. And here's the kicker: The man later visits her grave, and, if she disappeared wearing his jacket, it's draped over the tombstone.

Oooh! Spooky!

Can You Give Me a Lift to the Cemetery?

The most famous phantom hitchhiker known by name is Resurrection Mary, who haunts the town of Justice, a suburb of Chicago. She takes her name from the district's Resurrection Cemetery, where she is thought to be buried. Mary is most often described as a beautiful blonde with blue eyes and dressed in white. (There's no definite record of anyone having been buried in Resurrection Cemetery that matches her description. The closest in age is a young Polish woman named Mary, but there are no further details in the cemetery register.)

According to legend, Mary was killed in 1934 in a car accident after an evening of dancing at the O. Henry Ballroom (later the Willowbrook Ballroom). Her ghost began appearing on Archer Road about five years later. The phantom would suddenly come into view in the middle of the road in front of an oncoming car or would jump onto its side running board. The spectre would ask to be taken to the O. Henry, where she would dance all night. Then, at closing time, she would catch a ride with a stranger back toward Resurrection Cemetery.

Usually Mary would disappear from the car as it neared or passed the cemetery. Sometimes she would ask the driver to stop in front of the graveyard. She would get out of the car and then vanish as she melted through the closed gates of the cemetery.

Boo! _____

Remember how your parents always warned you not to pick up strangers in your car? If you see a female hitchhiker near a cemetery outside Chicago, you might want to think twice before you offer her a ride. It might be Resurrection Mary.

Resurrection Mary also has been seen standing inside the cemetery. There were an especially large number of sightings while the cemetery was being renovated in the 1970s. Since that time, she's been sighted all over the Chicago area, but she always returns to Resurrection Cemetery.

In the past few decades, there have been varied reports of phantom hitchhikers attached to other cemeteries. For example, in the 1980s the ghost of a young brunette girl was frequently seen hitchhiking in the area of the Evergreen Cemetery in west Chicago, where she is believed to be buried. The spirit was tangible enough to be mistaken for being corporeal. One time, she even boarded a CTA bus headed for downtown. When the driver approached her for payment, she disappeared right before his eyes.

Now You See It, Now You Don't

A classic variation of the phantom hitchhiker story involves a person (actually an apparition) that suddenly appears in the middle of a roadway. A speeding driver sees the person too late, swerves to avoid an accident, and winds up crashing the car. When the driver checks the road, there's no one there.

In yet another version, the driver actually hits the person standing in the road. The driver hears and feels the impact. Yet when the driver stops to check under the vehicle, there's no one there, nor are there any marks on the vehicle.

You're Giving Me Gray Hair!

Gray ladies are ghosts of women who have died for their love. Either they've pined away while waiting for their beloved to return from afar, have been murdered by their lovers, or have otherwise died as a result of their love. They're called gray ladies because they usually appear dressed in gray. But "gray" also refers to their ashen, mournful expressions. (There are also brown ladies and white ladies, who usually dress in … but you're ahead of me, aren't you?)

The reason that a gray lady returns to haunt the world of the living is simple: She's still hoping to be united with the person she loves. Gray ladies have been reported all over the world, but the majority of sightings have been in England.

Mirror, Mirror, on the Wall …

One of the most unusual types of apparitional manifestation is the appearance of a phantom's face or figure in a mirror. Perhaps the best-known example of a spirit-infested mirror is the one belonging to the Evil Queen in the story of Snow White and the Seven Dwarfs.

Apparitions have also been seen on other types of shiny or reflective surfaces, such as tabletops, and on wooden wardrobes and cabinets. Interestingly, there don't seem to be many reports of ghost reflections appearing on windowpanes.

Here's the typical haunted mirror scenario: You look into a mirror, and the reflection of a ghost appears behind you, looking over your shoulder into the mirror. When you turn, no one's standing there. In other cases, you might be walking by a mirror and glimpse the reflection of someone besides you in it. When you turn full face to the mirror, the image of the other person is no longer in the glass.

First-Person Phantoms

Several years ago in Buenos Aires, I met a well-educated, nonsuperstitious woman who was attached to the U.S. Embassy, and, somehow, the subject came around to ghosts. She became quite agitated and confided that she owned a haunted mirror. It had belonged to her grandmother, and when she inherited it, she proudly hung the large mirror in her home.

At first, she would sometimes glimpse the figure of an elderly woman reflected in the mirror as she passed by. But sometimes she would see the unmistakable face of her grandmother peering out at her. The ghost didn't try to communicate with her in any way and expressed no emotion—neither happiness, sorrow, nor pain.

Well, the granddaughter freaked! Her first thought was to smash the mirror, but what if her grandmother's ghost was trapped in there? Would smashing the glass somehow extinguish the spirit? Was the mirror some sort of portal between the worlds of the living and the dearly departed? She couldn't sell the mirror: Sell her grandmother to a stranger? But she couldn't stand having the mirror hanging in her house. It was just too creepy! So she carefully and lovingly wrapped up the haunted mirror and placed it in storage, where it remains today.

Perhaps the best-known haunted mirror can be found in the Roosevelt Hotel in Hollywood, California. It's famous not for the glass itself but for who appears in it: Marilyn Monroe! You'll read more about Marilyn's apparition when we visit the landmark hotel she frequents in Chapter 21.

Hi, How Are You? I'm Dead

Since the beginning of the electronic age, messages from the dead have been received from every form of communications device. Voices have come through telegraph and wireless, phonograph records, and loudspeakers. So many spirit voices have been heard coming over the radio that the paranormal activity has been given a name: *radio voice phenomena*, or *RVP*. The term *electronic voice phenomena* (*EVP*) is usually reserved for ghost voices picked up on magnetic (audio) tape.

Phone calls have actually been made from the living to the dead. People have reported calling and talking to someone whom they later discover was already dead by the time they chatted.

But phone calls *from* the dead must be among the most shocking type of ghost phenomena possible. Imagine hearing the phone ring, picking up the receiver, and hearing the voice of someone you know to be dead! Such calls have been reported time and again. The calls generally have several similarities:

♦ The recipient of the call is tranquil or relaxed when the call arrives; then, after the initial shock, the call is soothing rather than disturbing and stressful.

♦ The voice of the deceased sounds exactly the same as when the person was alive, although it may sound distant, progressively fading, or mixed with static or other voices in the background.

♦ The call is usually brief—a few seconds to a few minutes—although some have been reported as lasting up to half an hour. At the end of the call, the spirit may hang up, or the line may simply go dead.

♦ Most phone messages from the dead have a purpose: to impart information, to make a warning, or to say goodbye.

♦ Many occur on emotionally laden days, such as birthdays, Mother's Day, or the anniversary of the death.

♦ Most occur within 24 hours of the death of the person. Short calls usually come from people who have been dead less than a week; people who have been dead longer generally make lengthier calls. (I guess they have more to catch up on.) The longest recorded interval between a death and the receipt of a phone call from the deceased has been two years.

Phantom Phrases

Electronic voice phenomenon (EVP) is the reception of the voice of someone who's dead through any type of electronic equipment. Usually, the term is reserved for ghost voices recorded on magnetic tape that are inaudible until playback. **Radio voice phenomenon (RVP)** is a form of EVP in which the spirit voice comes through the speakers of an ordinary radio.

Ghostly Pursuits

A phone call from the dead featured prominently in "Night Call," an episode of *The Twilight Zone* that first aired on television in 1964. It's also a crucial plot element in the 1998 Conor McPherson play, *The Weir*.

Very few phone calls from the dead actually arrive person-to-person. Upon later investigation, it's discovered that the telephone company has no record of any of their operators having placed the call. Occasionally, spirit phone calls come from a stranger on behalf of a third party.

The current most popular explanations for phone calls from the dead are:

◆ They're a prank or bad joke, although some think it may be a playful spirit and not a human being pulling the gag.

◆ The whole experience, including the telephone ringing and the recognition of the voice, is hallucinatory or produced by the subconscious.

◆ They really *do* come from the dead.

Let There Be Light

Ghost lights have been seen and recorded in every country and civilization. These spectral lights are usually seen as ball-shaped or irregular, glowing patches, though occasionally they appear as floating candles. The most common colors are white, blue, and yellow, but some are red or orange. Ghost lights almost always occur in remote areas, and they can only be seen from certain angles or distances. If pursued, they can't be reached.

There have been attempts, of course, to trap a ghost light for examination, but when chased, they always seem to be just out of reach. At some point, they acquired the Latin name *ignis fatuus*, meaning "foolish fire," because it's considered foolish to try to follow or to capture such a phantom light.

Needless to say, most have spawned their own local legends. Perhaps because the appearance of spectral lights is so mysterious, folklore has traditionally suggested that ghost lights are souls of the dead. The appearance of the lights is sometimes said to signal an upcoming death or disaster.

So far, no definitive natural source has ever been discovered for the lights, although paranormal skeptics and some scientists have suggested that the lights might be caused by a number of things, such as:

◆ Swamp gas

◆ Electricity

◆ Magnetism

◆ Phosphorescent gas or material

◆ Car headlights or some other reflected or refracted light

◆ Practical jokes or hoaxes

The legend of the jack-o'-lantern and other ghost lights is celebrated on Halloween by carving out vegetables and using candles to make them into lanterns. In the United States, the pumpkin has been the vegetable of choice for jack-o'-lanterns since the latter half of the nineteenth century.

According to some legends, the light of an *ignis fatuus* is the ghost of a sinner who is condemned to wander the world for eternity. As always, there are many variations to the tale. In German folklore, the *Irrlicht* is a forest spirit or a soul following a funeral procession. In Sweden, it's the soul of an unbaptized baby roaming the earth in search of water. In Finland, the *liekko* (literally "flaming one") is the soul of a child who was buried in the woods. In parts of Britain, it's sometimes called the will-o'-the-wisp and is a death omen.

Sometimes the lights are playful beings, trying to lure travelers to follow them in the dark to get them lost. This type of *ignis fatuus* is often known, especially in Britain, as the jack-o'-lantern. Legend has it that the light is the soul of a person named Jack who was so ornery in life that heaven wouldn't take him and the devil didn't want him. Shut out of both heaven and hell, he must roam the earth endlessly.

The most famous locations for regular sightings of ghost lights in the United States include:

♦ Marfa lights, named for their appearance outside Marfa, Texas. The lights were first reported in 1883. Spectral lights are also regularly seen in Anson and Abilene, Texas.

♦ Joplin lights, near Joplin, Missouri. They're been visible almost every night from dusk until dawn since they were first seen around the time of the Civil War.

♦ Brown Mountain lights, in the Brown Mountains (especially in Linville Gorge) near Morgan, North Carolina. They've been reported since 1913. Legends associated with the Brown Mountain lights say that they are the spirit of a Native American maiden seeking her brave or a slave searching for his master.

Luminescence is not limited to *ignis fatuus*. Frequently, balls of light are reported at haunted places. Other times, there have been reports of ghosts appearing to glow, such as the "radiant boys" you'll read about later in this chapter. Or the phantom might appear inside a circle of light.

Of course, as we'll see in Chapter 8, luminous patches and shapes were common manifestations in séances. Spirit faces and hands often appeared bathed in a low light. Sometimes the entire figure might appear, glowing in the dark.

Ghostly Pursuits

In 1907, Dr. Hippolyte Baraduc produced supposed photographic evidence of astral lights leaving the body of his recently deceased son. Six months later, the doctor's wife died, and he photographed globular mists and streaks of light departing her body almost immediately after her death. Even though the photographs themselves are suspect, his descriptions of the phenomenon match numerous accounts by people who've reported seeing mists and luminescence being emitted from a dying person's body.

Ghosts from Around the World

Many ghosts are specific to a particular country or culture. Perhaps they like to stay close to home.

But just because you may not have heard of them, that doesn't mean they're not real. Here's a primer of world spirits, just in case you'll be going on vacation any time soon. Sometimes it's nice to know in advance who, or what, you might bump into when you're traveling.

The Cry of the Banshee

Everyone's heard of the "cry of the banshee." According to ancient Gaelic (primarily Irish and Scottish) tradition, a banshee is a female death spirit that appears to a household just before someone in the family is about to die. Often, no apparition appears; only her mournful singing or crying is heard.

Folklore gives us several types of banshees. Some are spirit entities but not necessarily thought to be the ghost of a deceased person.

The Bean-Nighe or Little-Washer-by-the-Ford of the Scottish Highlands and parts of Ireland, however, is supposedly the spectre of a young woman who died during childbirth. She's doomed to wash clothes in a stream until the time she would otherwise have died. Legend suggests that the bloody clothes she washes are the burial clothes of the soon-to-be departed. The Bean-Nighe is hideously ugly, with only one nostril, a single front tooth, long sagging breasts, and webbed feet.

Boo!

Irish and Scottish folklore claims that if you can bring yourself to suck a bit at the breast of a Bean-Nighe, she'll grant you a wish. (I wonder who found this out? And how?) If you try your luck, your wish better be to stay alive. Banshees are notorious omens of impending death.

The Ghosts of Murdered Boys

Radiant boys are the ghosts of boys who have been murdered by their mothers. As their name suggests, they glow in the darkness. The sighting of a radiant boy is often an omen of a violent death or at least very bad luck.

A medieval engraving of a radiant boy.

For a description of a radiant boy, let's turn to the rector of Greystoke, who encountered one in Corby Castle in Cumberland, England in 1824:

> Between one and two in the morning … I saw a glimmer in the middle of the room, which suddenly increased to a bright flame. … I beheld a beautiful boy clothed in white, with bright locks resembling gold, standing by my bedside. … He then glided gently toward the side of the chimney … and entirely disappeared.

Fortunately for the rector, this radiant boy brought no ill tidings. It was also, apparently, a unique experience. The boy was never identified, and his ghost has never appeared to haunt Corby Castle since.

Wild, Baby!

A "Wild Hunt" is a group of ghost huntsmen, horses, and hounds in procession, almost always seen at night. The legend is most prevalent in the British Isles. A Wild Hunt led by Herne the Hunter haunts the grounds of Windsor Castle in England. (You'll read much more about this particular story in Chapter 15.) The ghost of Sir Francis Drake has been seen leading another Wild Hunt (see Chapter 17).

Screaming Skulls

Ghosts living in—or acting through—skulls, haunt a number of places, most of them in England. Once it's placed in a house, the skull seems to become comfy with its surroundings. Any attempt to remove the skull from the building, even to bury it in its rightful grave, results in loud screaming from the skull. Many times, poltergeistlike activity, such as bangs and thumping noises, accompany the shrieking.

Some of the skulls belong to people who were, in some way, attached to the house during their lifetimes. Most of the people died by murder or some other violent means. The two most famous screaming skulls are located at Wardley Hall, outside Manchester, England; and at Bettiscombe Manor, outside Dorset, England.

Don't Go Near the Water!

In Russian folklore, Rusalka is the ghost of a virginal lass who drowns, either by accident or by violence, and is fated to haunt the spot of her death for eternity.

In most versions of the story, the spectre is a benevolent water nymph. But, like a siren, Rusalka is so beautiful and bewitching that she may inadvertently (or sometimes deliberately) entice a young man to join her, entering the waters to his doom.

The Weeping Walker

La Llorona is a ghost figure of Mexican and Mexican-American cultures. According to folklore, La Llorona was a woman who already had several children when she fell in love with a man who didn't want a family. In order to attract him, she drowned her own children. But then, overcome with grief and guilt, she killed herself.

She's seen at night, usually along a river, a forest, or a deserted road, crying and looking for her lost children. On some occasions, she is offered a ride; if she accepts, like all phantom hitchhikers, she vanishes from the car.

Boo! _____

To some, La Llorona is a death omen: Anyone who sees her will die within a year. In less extreme versions of the tale, the person will merely have bad luck for a year. So if you meet a mysterious sobbing woman dressed all in black down some dark road in Mexico, be careful. That unearthly encounter could be your last.

La Llorona is usually dressed all in black, but she is sometimes seen in white. She usually has long black hair and long fingernails. Under normal circumstances, she would be considered sexy or at least seductive. But she has a dark side: To some, she appears without a face, or with the face of a bat or a horse.

Even in modern-day Mexico, some parents use the La Llorona legend to scare their children into behaving: If the children are rowdy at bedtime, the mother might tell them to settle down or La Llorona will come for them!

Let's Face It!

A chance encounter with Oiwa on the streets of Tokyo can be a terrifying experience. Japan's most famous ghost, Oiwa appears as a spectral woman dressed all in white. But don't look too closely: Her long tresses hide a ghoulish, disfigured face.

This ghost story is based on a true event. In the nineteenth century, a man named Iyemon poisoned his wife Oiwa so that he could be with his new lover. He also killed an accomplice who had helped him murder the wife. Iyemon nailed the two corpses to opposite sides of a door and threw the door into a river.

Before long, Oiwa's ghost began to haunt Iyemon, day and night. Finally, in desperation and delirium, he took his sword and struck the phantom—only to discover that he had actually beheaded his young lover.

Ghostly Pursuits

In Shinto, an ancient religion in Japan, it's believed that after death, the spirit does live on in another, eternal world. But before reaching that final reward, the spirit might be trapped halfway, in a sort of netherland. It's thought that unhappy and vengeful spirits can return to Earth to harass the living, so Shinto priests conduct rituals to ease and hasten the passage of the deceased on to Eternity. Compare this to Catholic doctrine on Purgatory.

Tell Me Moai!

Famous for its giant basalt sculptures of rough heads and torsos (called *moai*, meaning "statue"), Easter Island lies 2,200 miles off the coast of Chile. According to tradition, the ancient King Tuu-ko-ihu, who ruled sometime after 450 C.E., saw two *aku aku* (or "sleeping ghosts") in Puna Pau, one of the island's stone quarries. The ghosts had beards, long hooked noses, and earlobes that reached down to their necks. Their ribs stuck out so much that they looked emaciated. Tuu-ko-ihu knew that disturbing the ghosts might make them angry, so he crept away and hurried home. To remember what the ghosts looked like, the king immediately carved wooden sculptures of them. Ever since, islanders have made *moai kavakava* (or "statue of ribs"), as the wooden replicas are called, to recall the encounter for future generations.

A moai kavakava, or "statue of ribs," portraying the aku aku, or "sleeping ghosts," of Easter Island.

(Photo by author)

Bad to the Bone

There's no getting around it: Some ghosts and spirits are just plain evil. They're always bad news. Many are found only in a particular country or region.

For example, there are at least four types of evil ghosts that haunt the living in India. The *bhut* (or *bhuta*) is the ghost of a man who has died by suicide, accident, or execution. The *airi*, the spectre of a man who was killed while out hunting, is just as nasty. A *churl* is the ghost of a woman (typically from a lower caste) who died in childbirth or in some impure ritual. They have no mouth and their feet face the wrong direction. And an *acheri* is the spirit of a little girl who causes disease, especially to other children. It can spread the malady simply by casting its shadow over the victim.

Here are just a few more ghastly ghosts, each unique to its culture:

◆ In Arab legends, the *afrit* is the spirit of a murdered man who aimlessly seeks revenge by killing the living.

◆ In ancient Assyria, an *ekimmu* is the ghost of a man who died a violent or unpleasant death. The spirit was denied entrance to the underworld and therefore has to haunt the earth.

♦ In Ireland, a *fetch* (called a "co-walker" in England) is an astral double or apparition of a living person. Generally, seeing one means bad luck; when seen at night, it's a death omen.

♦ Among Native Americans, *whirlwinds* are sometimes thought to be evil spirits of the dead.

Charmed, I'm Sure

Every culture has had *amulets* or charms. Some are thought to provide good luck. Others provide protection from harm, such as a defense against curses, black magic, and evil ghosts or spirits. Pure, natural objects, such as crystals and gemstones, were believed to be especially effective. Salt, for instance, could be carried in the pocket or sewn in the lining of one's clothes to help keep away ghosts.

Certain metals have always been associated with the occult. Silver was thought to have magical powers against all sorts of supernatural creatures, including ghosts. Using silver nails to close a coffin, for example, would prevent the spirit of the dead from escaping.

Phantom Phrases

An **amulet** is any man-made or natural object that's thought to be endowed with supernatural powers to bring good luck or ward off harm from ghosts, evil spirits, or black magic.

The ancient Egyptians used chalcedony, a type of quartz, to scare away ghosts and other spectral visitors, particularly at night. Usually cloudy blue, yellow, or white in color, this mineral was most often used to coat scarabs, beetle-shaped protective amulets that were carried or placed in tombs.

In classical Greece, it was believed that sharp or pointed objects, such as knives, swords, or even thorns, could frighten away ghosts. Building a cairn (a pyramid or pile of rocks) over a grave was thought to keep the ghosts in the grave.

Several tribal cultures have carved amulets for protection from the spirit world. The Arawaks of the Caribbean sculpted wood and stone idols called *zemi*, which they believed could protect themselves, their families, homes, and villages from destructive spirits of the dead. Some *zemi* were small enough to be worn or carried. The charms took their name from Zemi, the Arawak god of death.

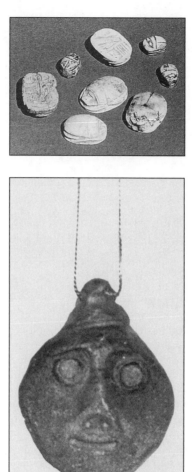

Scarabs—small, beetle-shaped, carved, and coated stones—were used in ancient Egypt to ward off evil spirits.

(Photo by author)

A small zemi amulet, meant to be worn or carried.

(Photo by author)

One of the most common folkloric traditions is a belief in the "evil eye," the ability of a witch, sorcerer, or other enchanter to curse you merely by his or her glare. The fear of "being eyed" is still prevalent today among certain cultures. Various amulets have been fashioned to ward off the evil eye, and it's believed that they're just as powerful against ghosts and bad spirits. Most of the charms incorporate some stylized rendering of an eye.

There you have it: all sorts of ghosts and spirits whose appearances are so common that their stories have entered the realm of urban legend. It's impossible today to tell when the stories began, but it's certain that more, similar tales—and sightings—will be told in the future.

Two versions of amulets able to protect against the evil eye. They are also thought to ward off ghosts and spirits.

(Photos by author)

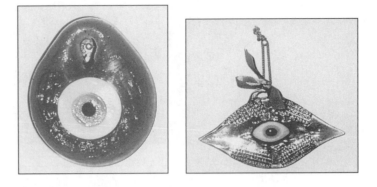

When you think of evil ghosts and spirits, you gotta think poltergeists. There are so many poltergeist stories that I've saved them for a chapter all their own. And it's coming up next!

The Least You Need to Know

♦ Ghost legends, such as the phantom traveler, magic mirrors, and spirit lights, transcend countries and civilizations.

♦ Ghost communications have been received through every type of electronic device, including phone calls from (and to) the dead.

♦ Every culture has unique legends about ghosts and spirits. Among them are banshees, wild hunts, and radiant boys.

♦ Every society has had its amulets and charms to ward off evil sorcery, ghosts, or other harmful phenomena.

Poltergeists: They're Here!

In This Chapter

- The differences between a ghost and a poltergeist
- A look at traditional poltergeist activity
- Stone-throwers and phantom drummers
- Modern books and movies based on poltergeist activity

Any examination of ghost phenomena must include a discussion of poltergeists. For many, poltergeists are proof of a nonphysical or nonmaterial world, a realm occupied by spirits.

Poltergeists are not ghosts, at least not as we commonly use the word "ghost," because a poltergeist is not an apparition of a dead human being. On rare occasions, poltergeists have been seen, but usually they are described as invisible spirits. They're playful, simple, fun, annoying, teasing, and mischievous, but, at times, they can also be malicious, malevolent, vicious, or even dangerous.

In his 1945 book *Poltergeist over England*, paranormal investigator Harry Price variously calls a poltergeist a spirit, an entity, and a secondary personality. He notes that a poltergeist is usually cruel, destructive, purposeless, and has noisy behavior, among other undesirable traits. But he never calls it a ghost.

What's the Difference?

Sometimes it's hard to tell whether a ghost or a poltergeist is haunting you because many of their activities are so similar. For example, both ghosts and poltergeists are known for their thumping and rappings. Indeed, the word *poltergeist*, from its Greek roots, literally means "noisy ghost."

Poltergeists tend to be more destructive in their behavior than ghosts. They're especially known for throwing stones (or making them appear to rain from the air) and for starting spontaneous fires. Ghosts are not known for either.

Secret Identity

Since poltergeist activity usually doesn't seem to originate from any specific event or deceased person, the identity of the poltergeist is usually unknown. It's an unexplained force, possibly of pure disembodied energy, which plants itself in a particular place.

Why a poltergeist chooses to haunt a specific location or person, and why it will often start and cease activity quite suddenly, are mysteries as well.

Quiet Down!

Nandor Fodor and Hereward Carrington were two of the most active paranormal investigators in the first half of the twentieth century. In their 1951 book *Haunted People* (published in 1953 in the United Kingdom as *The Story of Poltergeist Down the Centuries*), they define poltergeists by the stereotypically violent type of activity they produce. Carrington also points out a seeming connection between the poltergeist and a psychical energy emanating from a human's body at the time of puberty. Among the activities produced by poltergeists, Carrington noted:

- ◆ Kitchenware being smashed
- ◆ Bells ringing
- ◆ Various loud noises, including footsteps, knocks, raps, and crashes
- ◆ Objects tossed about by unseen forces
- ◆ Objects levitating or moving slowly through the air

Phantastic Tips

If a baseball comes through your window, it's probably from the kids playing in the sandlot next door. But if stones start materializing above you in a closed room and drop to the floor, or if your chair suddenly bursts into flames all on its own, chances are you're dealing with a poltergeist—not pranksters, not the kids down the street. And almost *definitely* not a ghost.

- Flying objects changing course in midair (not traveling in a straight line)
- Spontaneous fires
- Stone-throwing
- Passage of solid objects through a wall or closed door
- Sprinkling or falling water
- Voices
- On rare occasions, visible apparitions

How many of these unexplainable episodes have occurred in your house? Maybe it's not your little brother. You might be playing host to a poltergeist!

What Causes Poltergeists?

Currently, a popular explanation for poltergeist activity suggests that it's actually caused by a secondary personality or agent (in other words, a human being) who is unknowingly using paranormal abilities to produce the phenomena. It's been noted that many instances of poltergeist activity occur in households in which there is a child, especially ones in which a female is just entering puberty. Some researchers have advanced theories suggesting that, if the adolescent is undergoing mental or physical trauma, it might somehow unconsciously reveal itself in the guise of bombastic poltergeist behavior.

Interesting as this hypothesis may be, there is a notable absence of children in many well-documented cases of poltergeist disturbances. Therefore, the theory is certainly no catch-all explanation. Also, if the theory is true, why aren't there *more* poltergeists terrorizing households everywhere? Surely there are lots of adolescent kids harboring all kinds of hidden frustrations.

Sticks and Stones May Break My Bones

Stone-throwing or falling stones is probably the single type of activity most associated with poltergeists. The phenomenon is usually noted for its sudden appearance, severity, and abrupt cessation. The activity is also distinguished by the seemingly impossible nature: Sometimes the stones seem to float or drop slowly; often they appear and fall within a closed room, without coming through a window or hole in the ceiling.

Although apocryphal accounts date to ancient Egypt, Greece, and Rome, the first recorded eyewitness report of unexplained rocks hailing from the skies was in 335 C.E. Early Christian saints and writers also experienced paranormal stone-throwing; for example, in 1170 C.E., the hermitage of St. Godric was inundated with falling rocks.

Unfortunately, most occurrences are isolated or one-time incidents and, therefore, can't be investigated. For example, one night in 1903 on the island of Sumatra, W. D. Grottendieck of Dordrecht, Holland, woke around 1 A.M. to see stones slowly dropping to the floor around his bed, even though there were no holes in the thatched roof of his hut. He even caught one of the rocks, but it rose and floated out of his hand. He woke his young male servant to help him check all around the hut to make sure that some of the mischievous local laborers weren't responsible. Panicked, the boy fled; soon after, the stone-throwing suddenly stopped. Most investigators of the incident point to the boy, even though he appeared to be sleeping through most of the event. The case remained unsolved.

A half century later, beginning on April 12, 1959, a well-documented poltergeist stone-thrower attacked the family and home of Don Cid de Ulhoa Centro in Sao Paulo, Brazil. The first volley consisted of only two stones, which fell into a hallway where three of Don Cid's children were playing. Soon, dozens of rocks were falling within rooms all over the hacienda. As is often the case with such disturbances, no one was hit by any of the stones.

Over the next 48 hours, several neighbors witnessed the activity. In addition to the stones, other household objects such as pots, pans, eating utensils, and food began levitating, flying, and crashing around the kitchen and dining room. Finally, Don Cid called in a priest, Father Henrique de Morais Matos, to cast out the evil spirit. Three exorcisms slowed the poltergeist activity but failed to end it.

The rain of terror continued for 40 days and 40 nights, then suddenly stopped. Immediately, suspicion shifted from the supernatural to the natural. Even though she was never seen throwing any objects, a teenage maid named Francesca was accused of causing the stone-throwing by somehow attracting the pesky entity to the house. Paranormal investigators who later reviewed the case agreed that, indeed, she may have had latent paranormal abilities, or she may have unconsciously released what is sometimes referred to as *repressed psychokinetic energy* to cause the activity.

> ### Boo!
>
> There have been few recorded instances when poltergeists deliberately seek to hurt or kill an individual. Nevertheless, if you ever suspect you're the target or victim of a poltergeist get away from the surroundings immediately! Even if you aren't directly harmed by the poltergeist, you might be hurt from ricocheting rocks, flying objects, fires, or other activity.

> ### Phantom Phrases
>
> Some paranormals theorize that a person undergoing physical or mental trauma may unconsciously produce a force called **repressed psychokinetic energy.** This power, if released, might cause paranormal happenings such as poltergeist activity.

The Little Drummer Boy

Another form of poltergeist infestation is that of phantom drummers. The first famous case is the Drummer of Tedworth, who appeared in Tedworth, England, in 1661. The incident was touched off when a real drummer (whose name is unknown) presented the town bailiff with a suspicious promissory note supposedly signed by a Colonel Ayliff. The drummer banged on his instrument nonstop and threatened to continue until he was paid. Although everyone in the town was annoyed, it wasn't until John Mompesson, an important and well-respected resident, complained that the sheriff arrested the drummer and confiscated his drum.

The drummer was soon released, but the drum was given to Mompesson. Within days, almost incomprehensible poltergeist activity began to occur at Mompesson's house. It started with the spectral sound of loud drumming, but soon more extraordinary phenomena erupted:

- Rude animal noises and unintelligible human voices were heard.

- Objects levitated and flew about the rooms.

- The children sometimes floated off their beds.

- Doors opened and shut by themselves.

- Chamber pots overturned onto beds.

- An unidentifiable apparition with glowing red eyes appeared to a servant and in the children's bedroom.

A rendering of a ghostly drummer by artist George Cruikshank, from Barham's Ingoldsby Legends.

And, through it all, the drum beating continued. The poltergeist activity continued for two years.

Occurring as it did while the witchcraft hysteria was in full swing in England, most locals believed that the events were the work of the devil. Some people blamed Mompesson and his family, saying that they must have been sinful and brought the curse upon themselves. The poltergeist case was personally investigated by one of the first paranormal researchers, the Reverend Joseph Glanvil, who you read about in Chapter 2.

The same drummer was later arrested elsewhere for similar fraud and disturbing the peace. While jailed in Gloucester Goal, he confessed, "Do you not hear of the drumming at [the] gentleman's house in Tedworth? That I do enough, I have plagued him … and he shall never be quiet, 'til he hath made me satisfaction for taking away my drum." His words were used against him in court, and he was expelled from the area. The drummer returned to the region from time to time, however, and it was noted that during the periods he was nearby—and *only* then—the poltergeist activity started up again at the Mompessons' house.

Coincidence or poltergeist? Certainly the drummer could have hidden away and created a ruckus, but how about all that other stuff?

The Drummer of Tedworth, from Joseph Glanvil's Sadiucismus Triumphatus *(1661).*

Some Things Never Change

There have been so many reports of poltergeists over the past few centuries that it would be impossible to list them all. Some have been unusual enough to warrant special attention, including the next few examples.

Epworth Rectory

For about two months in the early eighteenth century, Epworth Rectory in Lincoln-shire, England, was the site of daily poltergeist disruption. Queen Mary gave over the rectory to the Reverend Samuel Wesley, but his family (especially his daughter Hetty) was not happy with the move into the faraway rural village. The local townsfolk were not particularly welcoming to the stern and severe new clergyman either: They set fire to the rectory in 1709 and injured his cattle. Wesley decided to rebuild the rec-tory, however, and stay on.

On December 1, 1719 (although some accounts say 1716), poltergeist activity started at the Epworth Rectory. Groans, knockings, and foot-stomping on the floorboards overhead, as well as other noises, were heard. The sounds of bottles smashing and pewter plates crashing could be heard in adjoining rooms; but when the rooms were checked, nothing had been disturbed. On at least one occasion, the bed of a daughter, Nancy, levitated with her on it.

Poltergeist activity became a nightly event, usually starting about 9:45 P.M. Once, Mrs. Wesley tried to scare the ghost away by blowing a loud horn throughout the house. The poltergeist responded by doubling its efforts to both day and night.

CAUTION Boo!

If you're a teenager reading this book, or can remember when you were a teenager, you know how difficult those years can be—mentally, physically, and emo-tionally. Take comfort in the knowledge that you're not alone in these feelings. If you're a parent, friend, or adult caregiver, offer special concern to those who may need your attention most. And who knows? In the process, you may prevent poltergeist activity (caused by all that otherwise-repressed psychokinetic energy) from breaking out in your home.

The children blamed the manifestations on an invisible spirit whom they nicknamed "Old Jeffrey." Some people believed the culprit to be the ghost of "Old Ferries," which was the name of someone who had died in the rectory. No apparitions were ever seen, but some thought that a rabbitlike creature seen one night and a badger spotted on another evening were actually spirits in animal form. Also, no real com-munication was ever established with the poltergeist.

As suddenly as the poltergeist activity started, it abruptly stopped at the end of January 1720.

Paranormal experts suggest that the poltergeist phenomena were actually caused by the unleashing of pent-up psychic energy, either on the part of the frustrated Mrs. Wesley (who was kept in an almost constant state of pregnancy—19 births in 20 years, only five children of which lived past infancy), or of the daughter Hetty (who hated the rectory and was at that poltergeist-triggering age somewhere between 14 and 19 years old). There is also the possibility that villagers who wanted to drive the rector and his family out of town perpetrated some of the activity.

The Smurl Haunting

In a spectacular case history, the home of Jack and Janet Smurl in West Pittston, Pennsylvania, was purportedly haunted by poltergeists or possibly evil spirits from 1974 to 1989. Over the course of a decade, the spirit activity escalated from minor annoyance to life-threatening. The Smurls contacted two well-respected paranormal researchers from Connecticut, Ed and Lorraine Warren. (See the New England Society for Psychic Research listing in Appendix A.) With the help of Rosemary Frueh, a nurse and psychic, they identified four evil spirits, one of which, they felt, was most likely a demon. The investigators decided that the entities probably had been in the house for years (it was built in 1896) but were psychically spurred into action by the onset of puberty in the daughters.

Phantastic Tips

If you've eliminated all other possibilities and still suspect that it's poltergeists or ghosts that are haunting your house, you'll probably want to call in a professional ghost investigator. Check out Appendix A for the names and addresses of some of the most respected paranormal researchers in the United States.

The Warrens brought in an exorcist, Father (later Bishop) Robert F. McKenna, but the poltergeist activity continued. In all, McKenna eventually performed three full exorcisms to no avail. The Smurls decided to go public with their appeal for help, appearing on a talk show and in the newspapers.

Paul Kurtz, chairman of the Committee for the Scientific Investigation of Claims of the Paranormal (CSICOP), asked to look into the hauntings, but the Smurls and the Warrens refused, claiming that CSICOP, a skeptic society, was too prejudiced to make a fair assessment.

Indeed, without inspecting the premises, Kurtz published an article in CSICOP's journal, *Skeptical Inquirer*, musing on some of the possible causes of the Smurl haunting. He cited:

◆ Ground settling over the underground coal mines

◆ Leaky sewer pipes

- ◆ Antics by local teenagers

- ◆ Fanciful imagination, even delusion

Kurtz pointed out discrepancies in several of the Smurls' accounts and pondered their motivation in going public.

Press coverage picked up, prompting the Catholic diocese to take over the case. Shortly after the Smurls moved to a new town, Robert Curran's book about their ordeal, *The Haunted: One Family's Nightmare* (St. Martin's Press, 1988), was published. A film version of the book came out in 1991. A final exorcism by the Catholic Church in 1989 seemed to put the house's poltergeists or demons to rest.

CAUTION | **Boo!**

Don't rent the movie *Poltergeist* if you think you're gonna see the little critters in action. The movie is not about poltergeists at all. Rather, it's the story of a modern suburban house that, unbeknownst to its owners, was built on top of an old cemetery—and the unhappy ghosts that haunt it in retribution. And the poltergeist activity that supposedly disrupted the home in *The Amityville Horror* (both in the book and film) wasn't based on actual events. As you'll see in Chapter 12, the entire episode was a money-making hoax from the start.

The Mount Ranier Poltergeist

In January 1949, poltergeist activity started in the home of a 13-year-old boy (noted in case histories as "Roland") in Mount Ranier, a Maryland suburb of Washington, D.C. At first, overhead scratching noises were heard in the boy's bedroom at night. Later, the boy's bed shook and his bedclothes were torn off. Soon, activity was occurring day and night. Other noises, such as invisible squeaky shoes, were heard, and dishes and furniture sometimes moved on their own.

The parents were convinced that the boy was possessed by an evil spirit. They called in their Lutheran minister, Luther Schulze, who prayed over the boy and commanded the demon to leave.

The activity worsened. Messages in scratched letters appeared on the boy's skin. A mental examination was considered, but instead, the parents moved the boy to a hospital. The scratchings continued to appear, and the boy began to spit up phlegm. For 35 days, a team including a Lutheran minister, an Episcopal priest, and some Jesuit priests took turns performing at least 20 exorcisms over the boy. Soon, the activity slowed. By April, the attacks had ended completely, and the boy returned home.

If this story sounds somewhat familiar, it's because author William Peter Blatty used the incident as the basis and inspiration for his 1969 book (and later the film) *The Exorcist*. Blatty was a student at Georgetown University in August 1949 when he read a newspaper report on the events.

So there you have it, some of the best-known ghosts and poltergeists in legend and folklore. But so far, we've only looked at what happens when ghosts come to haunt you. What do you do if you want to go to them? Part 2 awaits to answer that very question.

The Least You Need to Know

- Poltergeists are not ghosts. They are nonhuman entities, not the returned spirits of the deceased.

- Ghosts and poltergeists are often confused or misidentified because they both produce phenomena such as unidentifiable rapping, footsteps, voices, and levitating objects.

- In general, poltergeists tend to be more malicious and destructive than ghosts.

- Poltergeist activity has been recorded since at least 335 C.E.; some of the more spectacular twentieth-century accounts have been transformed into popular books and films.

Part 2

Don't Call Us, We'll Call You

Let's say you want to talk to the dearly departed. You can't just pick up a phone. Well, maybe you could, but chances are no one from the sprit world would answer at the other end.

If the ghosts won't come to you, maybe you could go to them. Communication with the Beyond had always been the dominion of the shamans, priests, and oracles. It was sort of a religious monopoly of the highway to heaven—or wherever the spirit called home. But with the advent of mediums and spiritualism changed all that!

In these chapters, we'll investigate what takes place behind those closed doors to the séance room and—if you dare—how you can try to contact the spirits for yourself!

Chapter 6

Spirit, Move Me: The Birth of Spiritualism

In This Chapter

- ◆ Spiritualism gets its start
- ◆ The Fox sisters, Spiritualism's first mediums
- ◆ The rising popularity of séances in the United States and England
- ◆ The founding of the Spiritualist Church

People have been trying to communicate with the dead since ancient times. As we've seen, necromancers and early wizards claimed that they could raise the spirits of the dead as part of their stock in trade. It was still an age of wonders in the mid-1800s when Spiritualism began. People were performing impossible feats while mesmerized or entranced. Tables miraculously tipped by pure magnetism.

By 1848, the climate was ripe for a new religion—Spiritualism—to be born. It would all start with two young girls in a rural village, but by the end of the nineteenth century, belief in the controversial faith would spread to England and much of the Western world. Journey with me now to another time, a step back, as we take a look at the humble beginnings of the Spiritualism movement.

The Stage Is Set for Spiritualism

It began in a small wood-frame house in Hydesville, New York—a tiny town of no more than three or four dozen homes, just southwest of Rochester. John D. and Margaret Fox moved into their one-and-half-story house on December 11, 1847. Two of their four children, the youngest, Catherine (Kate) and Margaretta (Margaret), lived at home. (There is some discrepancy as to the girls' ages. Reports have them as young as six-and-a-half and eight, respectively; Margaret later told a newspaper they had been eight and nine-and-a-half years old at the time; Rochester records show them as having been 12 and 14.) An older daughter, Leah Fox Fish, whom Margaret later said was 30 at the time, had been recently widowed and was supporting herself as a music teacher in Rochester. A son, David, lived on a farm in nearby Auburn.

Almost as soon as the family settled in, they began hearing unusual rappings and thumping sounds. When Mr. Fox could find no natural source for the noises, neighbors confided that the cottage already had a reputation for being haunted. Similar noises as well as footsteps had been heard by a former resident, John Bell, as well as by his employee, Lucretia Pulver, in 1843 and 1844. Michael and Hannah Weekman lived there for the two years before the Fox family and often heard knocking at the front door. When the door was opened, no one was ever there!

CAUTION

Boo! _____

Be careful what you wish for—it may come true! The Fox sisters supposedly asked "Mr. Splitfoot" to answer them. Next thing they knew, the devil (or so some people thought) was at their door. If you start calling on spirits, be careful—you never know who might answer!

One evening, on March 31, 1848, young Kate responded to the ethereal tappings by snapping her fingers and asking "Mr. Splitfoot" (a common nickname for the Devil) to repeat her actions. To the amazement of her mother, an identical number of raps was heard. Kate asked the invisible spirit to try again, but this time she only pretended to snap her fingers. Nevertheless, the correct number of taps sounded, and Kate delightedly informed her mother that the spirit must be able to *see* as well as *hear* her! Within two days, the thumpings were occurring during the day as well as the night.

As word spread among the neighbors that an intelligent spectral presence was haunting the Fox house, the girls worked out a tapping code to communicate with it. The spirit supposedly told them that he was the ghost of Charles B. Rosma, a peddler, who had been murdered some years before and buried in the basement of the house. This prompted a lot of discussion but no agreement over whether a traveling salesman had ever vanished from the area. Nor were any human remains found in the Fox cellar.

Nevertheless, some people claimed that John Bell must have been a murderer, though no charges were ever filed.

Ghostly Pursuits

Ghosts generally don't follow people from one location to another. They haunt a specific location. It would be very unusual for a murder victim to move on to not just one but two new haunts. So doesn't it seem odd that, once the Fox sisters left Hydesville, the ghost activity stopped there, but then the rappings suddenly appeared at their new homes? Now I'm not going to tell you what *I* think was going on. (But then, I know how the story ends.) I'll let you decide for yourself.

Imagine the sensation these events caused! Proof had been established that there was life after death, and that the living can communicate with the spirits—perhaps even with loved ones!

Soon crowds were descending on Hydesville to hear the sounds for themselves. To restore some semblance of order to their lives, the Fox parents decided to send Kate to live with her brother, David; young Margaret moved in with her sister, Leah. Interestingly, the sounds stopped in the Hydesville house, but they started up in the Rochester and Auburn homes where David and Leah lived!

Taking Their Show on the Road

The girls began to invite visitors to experience the phenomena for themselves. Kate conducted "sittings," as she called her gatherings in Auburn; Margaret often referred to her get-togethers as "spirit circles." In time, such assemblies came to be known as *séances*. The word "séance" is derived from the Old French *seoir* and Latin *sedere*, meaning "to sit."

In November 1849, Margaret announced she had received a spectral message that she was to provide a large public demonstration. Her sister Leah rented the Corinthian auditorium, the largest in Rochester, and spectators paid one dollar apiece to see and hear a spirit visitation.

More séances followed. On three separate nights during Margaret's presentations in Rochester, committees selected by the audience took part in the sittings on stage. None of the spectators was able to detect any fraud.

With Leah as their manager, Kate and Margaret went on tour across the United States. In the spring of 1850, Horace Greeley, the powerful owner and publisher of the *New York Tribune*, invited the three sisters to his home in New York City. They held sittings for his society friends and celebrities, and many of them were converted to this new belief called *Spiritualism*. The Fox sisters' lifelong careers as mediums were launched.

Phantom Phrases

A **séance** (also known as a "sitting," "spirit circle," or "circle") is a gathering of individuals, usually led by a medium, for the purpose of receiving spirit manifestations or to establish communication with the dead. Séances performed in a person's house, with or without the assistance of a medium, are known as "home circles" or "home sittings." **Spiritualism** is the belief system that spirits of the dead can (and do) communicate with living humans. Usually this contact is made through a medium.

The Best of Times, the Worst of Times

During their heyday, the Fox sisters held séances for the great and the near great. Kate held at least one séance for Mary Todd Lincoln, who wanted to contact her late husband, President Abraham Lincoln. Margaret's famous clients included William Cullen Bryant, James Fenimore Cooper, and Harriet Beecher Stowe.

Ironically, many attendees were convinced that the Fox demonstrations validated rather than opposed their Christian beliefs: The séances proved that there was, indeed, a resurrection after death. More conservative Christians, however, thought that the work of the Fox sisters was demonic. Some participants were merely amused and dismissed it all as pure theatrical entertainment. Still others considered it to be deliberate fraud.

Boo!

It's amazing what people will say and do when there's money involved. Always be wary of people who profit in some way by their claims of seeing ghosts or experiencing other paranormal activity. The most reliable sources are often those who have nothing to gain and perhaps even something to lose (such as their reputation) by the telling.

There were two early accusations of trickery. In January 1850, a committee of doctors investigating Margaret Fox discovered that spirit sounds wouldn't appear as long as they held tightly onto her legs during the sitting. Then, on April 17, 1851, Mrs. Norman Culver, a relative by marriage of the Fox sisters, told the *New York Tribune* that Kate had confessed that she secretly produced the snapping sounds by cracking the joints of her toes. Despite these semi-exposures, Spiritualists refused to believe that they were being duped.

In the end, life was not terribly kind to the Fox sisters. In 1852, Margaret Fox became involved with a surgeon and Arctic explorer, Dr. Elisha Kent Kane. He departed on an expedition in 1856 and died unexpectedly in Cuba on February 16 the following year. During settlement of the estate, Margaret claimed that she and Kane had a common-law marriage. (To the end of her life, she frequently called herself Margaret Fox Kane.) Dr. Kane's brother challenged her in court. A financial agreement was reached, but the brother defaulted on the payments. Margaret, by necessity, returned to her life as a medium.

At first, Kate fared better. In 1854, the Society for the Diffusion of Spiritual Knowledge engaged her for a full year to conduct free public séances. She perfected the art of producing automatic writing (see Chapter 2) that was *also* mirror-writing: That is, the script was written backward and had to be held up to a mirror to be read. Then, in 1861, Kate Fox became the first Spiritualist medium to produce a *materialization*—a physical manifestation of a spirit.

Phantom Phrases

A **materialization** is the manifestation or production of some physical object or person from the spirit world. The most difficult and impressive materialization, of course, was a complete human form.

From 1861 to 1866, Kate was hired by New York banker Charles F. Livermore to hold private séances for him in an attempt to contact his recently deceased wife, Estelle. In 1871, Livermore sent Kate to London, where she sat for physicist William Crookes and held séances with fellow mediums D. D. Home and Mrs. Agnes Guppy. (You'll be hearing a lot more about these folks in upcoming chapters.)

While in London, Kate married Henry Jencken in 1872. They had two sons. The first, Ferdinand, born in 1873, was proclaimed a medium by the age of three. Mr. Jencken died of a stroke in 1885, and Kate returned to the United States with her sons.

By the 1880s, both Margaret and Kate Fox were drinking heavily. Relations between them and Leah deteriorated. It's speculated that Leah feared her younger sisters would reveal their deceptions. Also, she was increasingly embarrassed by the sisters in front of her society guests.

In January 1888, the Society for the Prevention of Cruelty to Children had Kate's young sons taken from her because of her alcoholism, and Kate apparently suspected that Leah was somehow to blame. With Margaret's help, Kate obtained the release of the boys, and mother and sons departed for England.

So *That's* How It's Done!

On September 24, 1888, Margaret Fox admitted in an interview published in the *New York Herald* that "every effect produced by us was absolute fraud." They had produced the first thumps while in bed at night by tying an apple to a string and bumping it on the floor. When people began to flock to the house to see the children and hear the knockings, the girls became frightened that they would be punished and kept up the ruse for "self-preservation." Margaret explained that Kate first discovered that she could produce noises with her knuckles and joints "by swishing her fingers … and that the same sound could be made with the toes."

Margaret went on to implicate Leah, claiming the elder sister had secretly fed the young mediums information about the people who participated in the séances. Margaret said that she believed Leah wanted to use the girls to help found a new religion; Margaret maintained that she was making her belated confession in an attempt to save her own soul, as well as those of her sisters. Leah, happily married for the third time to a wealthy husband, dismissed Margaret's claims. Kate, in England, at first made no response.

Just a month later, on October 21, she confessed in the *New York World* that she and her sister started the tappings as a game to terrify their mother. That same day, Margaret and Kate took the stage of the New York Academy of Music and showed how they produced their spirit rappings. (Kate had returned from England for the occasion but did not speak at the demonstration.) Their disclosure did not change many people's opinions.

Spiritualists came up with several possible explanations for the confessions:

- ◆ The Catholic Church had coerced the sisters.

- ◆ Newspapers had bribed them.

- ◆ The confession couldn't be believed because the sisters' alcoholism had made them delusional.

- ◆ The Fox sisters were *real* mediums and didn't even know it. (As you'll see in Chapter 23, famed writer Sir Arthur Conan Doyle believed this about Houdini!)

Indeed, many Spiritualists who reluctantly accepted the Fox sisters' confessions argued that just because *they* were fakes, that didn't mean that *all* mediums were fakes.

The sisters set out on an exposé tour, but it soon faltered. Kate recanted her testimony and started to perform séances again. In 1891, penniless and abandoned by her wealthy clients, Margaret also withdrew her confession and returned to the séance table.

Ghostly Pursuits

Located in Chautauqua County on the shore of Cassadaga Lake in upstate New York, Lily Dale was founded as a Spiritualist retreat in 1879. It's only 123 miles from Hydesville, where the Fox sisters made their first contact with the spirit world. In the last century the village has played host to a diverse group of guests including Sir Arthur Conan Doyle, Mae West, Mahatma Gandhi, Franklin and Eleanor Roosevelt, and Susan B. Anthony. Visitors enter the town today by passing under a large sign proclaiming Lily Dale to be "The Largest Center for the Religion of Spiritualism in America." Lily Dale still thrives as a haven for spiritualism and has daily activities from late June through Labor Day.

How was it possible for the Fox sisters to find any clients after their admission? Well, some spiritualists were more than willing to accept the sisters' retraction. Perhaps they just didn't want to admit they'd been duped. People believe what they want to believe. Still, neither sister ever again enjoyed great success.

Leah Fox Fish Brown Underhill died in 1890. Kate Fox Jencken died on July 2, 1892, and Margaret Fox Kane died in poverty in a rooming house on March 8, 1893. The original Fox house was moved from Hydesville to a Spiritualists' retreat in Lily Dale, New York, in 1915. The camp is still there today, but a fire destroyed the original cottage in the 1950s.

The Spiritualist Church continues as an active religion, with churches and congregations worldwide. There are also a number of Spiritualist retreats in addition to Lilly Dale. The most notable are Cassadaga Spiritualist Camp outside Orlando, Florida; and Harmony Grove, near Escondido in San Diego County, California.

Belief in Spiritualism encompasses much more than mediums and séances. Many of the churches in the United States are members of the National Spiritualist Association of Churches (N.S.A.C.), the oldest organization for the science, philosophy, and religion of modern Spiritualism. (The organization was founded on September 27, 1893.) For more information on the Spiritualist Church in America, contact the National Spiritualist Association of Churches, P.O. Box 217, Lily Dale, New York 14752; phone: 716-595-2000; fax: 716-595-2020; website: www.nsac.org. There's also an International Spiritualist Federation with a website at www.isfederation.org.

So that's how Spiritualism all began. Now let's go inside a séance room to meet some of the movement's most famous mediums, along with their contacts in the spirit world. Most of the séance activity you'll be reading about normally takes place with the lights out, so I hope you're not scared of the dark.

The Least You Need to Know

◆ In 1848, the Fox Sisters, Kate and Margaret, triggered the movement known as Spiritualism by claiming they could receive messages from the dead.

◆ Spiritualism grew worldwide, spurred on by spirit manifestations at sittings known as séances.

◆ Forty years after it all began, Margaret Fox confessed to having faked the original spirit rappings and revealed her methods.

◆ The Spiritualist Church continues to be an active religion with churches as well as campsites and retreats.

Striking a Happy Medium

In This Chapter

- ◆ Public séances give way to private home circles
- ◆ The Davenport brothers—mediums or magicians?—introduce the spirit cabinet
- ◆ D. D. Home, the Brown Circle, and the Ashley Place Levitation
- ◆ Florence Cook materializes full-figured spirits
- ◆ Spirit photography: Ghosts captured on film
- ◆ Channelers and mediums still talking to the spirits today

Who could follow an act like the Fox Sisters? Who indeed?

Several important mediums gained a large following. Some, like D. D. Home and Florence Cook, made significant contributions to the repertoire of their craft. Along the way, another important development was the discovery that spirits could be photographed! Even in modern times, the medium mania hasn't died—it's just changed names. Today there are channelers and celebrity mediums like James Van Praagh and John Edward who claim to be able to talk to the dead.

You might want to lower the lights while you read this chapter. Spirits prefer the dark.

In the Closet: The Davenport Brothers

As we've seen, the heyday of spiritualism was from the mid-to-late 1800s. Almost from the start, mediums were frequently accused of using magicians' tricks to produce their spirit phenomena.

As it turns out, two of spiritualism's first stars were, indeed, magicians, although they never called themselves such. But then, they never claimed to be mediums either. During their 20-year career, the Davenport brothers created a sensation—and controversy—wherever they traveled.

The Brothers Start to Rap

Ira Erastus (1830–1911) and William Henry (1841–1877) Davenport, from Buffalo, New York, performed one of the most celebrated séance acts of the nineteenth century.

The Davenport brothers.

Having heard reports of spirit noises in Rochester (perhaps produced by the young Margaret Fox, who was living there with her sister Leah at the time), the Davenport boys' father decided to try a sitting around the family table. Rapping began almost immediately. At one gathering, Ira shot a pistol in the dark, and the surprised spectators briefly saw a flash of a ghost. It was John King, a spirit guide or *control* who was to manifest himself for the brothers for the rest of their career.

The King Family Takes Control

King claimed to have been Henry Owen Morgan in life, the seventeenth-century English pirate who ransacked Jamaica before being knighted and made its governor by Charles II. (King's daughter, Annie Owen Morgan, nicknamed Katie, sometimes appeared as a spirit control at a few later Davenport séances. She reportedly died young, at 23, after murdering her own two children.)

Phantom Phrases

A **control** is a spirit of the dead who acts as a medium's guide or intermediary to the Other World. The control can take possession of the medium, at least enough to communicate through ouija boards, script (automatic writing), or speech (direct voice phenomenon).

According to the Davenports, in 1855 John King ordered the boys, then aged 14 and 16, to "go public," so the family rented an auditorium to perform a séance before a paying audience. Their professional debut included spirit rappings and table-tipping, musical instruments being played by invisible ghosts, and spectral hands touching the sitters at the table.

Ghostly Pursuits

Some controls were very popular, appearing for many different mediums. John King, first produced by the Davenport brothers, was especially in demand, appearing for many of the top nineteenth-century mediums, including Mrs. Guppy and Eusapia Palladino. (You'll hear more about them in Chapter 8.) This wasn't unusual: Contemporary mediums often usurped each other's best-known and most colorful controls. For example, although first materialized by the Davenports, Katie King became the main control for famed medium Florence Cook. Not surprisingly, the same control often spoke in different accents or changed in appearance, depending on which medium summoned it. Katie King was much more beautiful when manifested by Cook, for example, than when she appeared for the Davenport brothers. Any surprise there?

Out of Bounds

They staged their first public show in 1855, just seven years after the Fox sisters rose to prominence in nearby Hydesville (see Chapter 6). By the end of the year, the Davenport brothers were appearing in New York City, where, for the first time, they had themselves bound in ropes as proof that they didn't perform the spirit shenanigans themselves. An audience member suggested that the brothers also be enclosed in a box to prevent any outside assistance. Realizing that anything could be accomplished if they were out of the sight of the audience, the Davenport brothers immediately embraced this new condition.

The first *spirit cabinet* (or simply, *cabinet*), as such armoirelike enclosures came to be known, measured seven feet by six feet by two feet and sat on three sawhorses up off the floor. It had three doors on the front. The two brothers, bound separately in ropes, sat facing each other from opposite ends of the cabinet. A low bench holding musical instruments sat between them. The center door had a diamond-shaped window to let in air and to allow the audience to see the spirit manifestations.

Phantom Phrases

A **spirit cabinet**, or **cabinet**, is a solid or curtained enclosure within which the medium sits to allow the spirits to appear unimpeded. The first spirit cabinet was introduced in New York City by the Davenport brothers, and its use was quickly adopted by many of the leading mediums of the day.

During a séance, the brothers, tied tightly, would be shut inside the cabinet. Instantly, music was heard from within. Phantom hands waved through the window. No matter how often the doors were opened, the Davenport brothers were always still securely bound. Sometimes audience members were invited to sit in the center section of the cabinet, but they had to allow themselves to be tied to the brothers for protection from the spirits. At the end of the séance, the audience had to untie the Davenports to release them.

A Sudden End; a Final Farewell Visit

During a tour of England in 1865, the Davenport brothers were bound so painfully at a Liverpool engagement that they refused to perform. A riot ensued. Similar violence met them in Hudersfield and Leeds, so the brothers quickly moved on to France. A four-year tour of Europe followed, during which they performed before many of the crowned heads of state.

In 1876, the Davenport brothers traveled to Australia to perform, where, the following year, William died suddenly in Sydney. Ira attempted to bury William beneath a gravestone engraved with a rendering of their spirit cabinet, ropes, and musical instruments, but church officials refused to allow the memorial to Spiritualism on sacred grounds. Devastated, Ira buried William outside the hallowed walls of the cemetery, and returned home to New York to retire.

There's No Place—and No *One*—Like Home

By the end of the 1850s, spiritualism had taken on a successful life of its own, independent of the Fox sisters. The Davenport brothers were just two of the hundreds of mediums sprouting up all across the United States and England. It was discovered that spirit contact could be made in any number of situations. People everywhere seemed to be meeting informally in their homes, trying to contact spirits for themselves. Home circles reached their peak in popularity in the late nineteenth and early twentieth centuries.

The Amazing Physical Feats of D. D. Home

D. D. Home was particularly noted for the physical feats he performed at his séances. He usually materialized spirits, sometimes levitated or elongated and shrank his body, and made inanimate objects move (such as the obligatory tipping table) without touching them.

A Young Medium Emerges

One of the most famous mediums of the late nineteenth century was D. D. Home (1833–1873). Home (pronounced *hume*) was born in Edinburgh, Scotland, and supposedly showed paranormal abilities from an early age:

- His cradle rocked without assistance.

- At four years of age, he predicted a cousin's death.

- He later claimed to have known three days in advance that his mother would die.

- At 13, he had a vision as his boyhood friend died in a faraway location.

Home was adopted by his mother's sister, Mary Cook, when he was still a baby, and they moved to the United States when Home was nine years old. Home was 15, living with his aunt in Connecticut, when the rappings began in the Fox household in neighboring New York. Soon, similar sounds began to manifest themselves for Home. His aunt asked local preachers to help rid the house (and the boy) of demons. When, in 1850, the lad told his aunt that he had seen a vision of his dead mother, kindly Mary Cook tossed the boy out.

Trademarks and Trickery

Home attended séances, although he was usually unimpressed and considered most mediums to be frauds. He began to hold his own séances—usually in dimly lit rooms, rather than in the customary complete darkness. He often asked sitters to hold his hands and feet to prove that he wasn't using trickery.

Home quickly impressed his sitters with the manifestations he was able to produce: ghost lights and knockings, disembodied ghost hands that shook with those present, and phantom guitars that played music. He received messages from spirits, which he delivered by pointing at letters on alphabet cards. Home worked through different controls, the most common being a spirit named Bryan.

In addition to materializing spirits and moving inanimate objects (such as the obligatory tipping table), Home had three signature pieces that really put him on the map:

◆ **A spirit-played accordion.** Home would place an accordion under the séance table, and before long, its music began to play.

Phantastic Tips

Learn from the best. Build on their success, and eliminate their mistakes. D. D. Home was a quick study and learned how to perform a more entertaining and mystifying séance than his peers. You can take the advice of early ghost investigators to hone your skills as a ghost hunter.

◆ **His stretching and shrinking body.** Home had the ability to stretch (sometimes as much as 11 inches to 6½ feet in height) or shrink (as much as 7 inches to 5 feet tall).

◆ **Levitation.** Home would levitate séance-goers as they sat in their chairs, and he would also occasionally float himself! His first self-levitation occurred spontaneously during a Connecticut séance when Home was 19 years old. He appeared to rise about twelve inches and hover before rising all the way to the ceiling. In later séances, he was reportedly able to fly about the room.

Although often accused of trickery, D. D. Home was never actually caught in the act of fraud. Two of the most famous magicians of the era, John Nevil Maskelyne and Harry Houdini, swore that Home was little more than a very clever illusionist. Houdini probably best expressed the reason why Home was never exposed: The medium never gave public demonstrations. Home led séances in people's homes, where it would have been exceedingly impolite, if not downright rude, to suggest that their house guest was cheating. (My, how times have changed!)

Circle Home

For the next decade, Home was in his heyday. His séances caused a sensation in England, especially the one conducted for a gathering of 14 people that included poets Robert and Elizabeth Barrett Browning. The Browning circle, as the group was known, held the séance in the London residence of John S. Rymer, a well-to-do solicitor, and his wife in 1855.

At the Browning séance, the sitters gathered around a large table in a room lit only by a dim lamp. After a series of the usual raps, taps, and table-tilts, the Rymers' deceased son Wat began to speak to his parents but suddenly stopped. Without explanation, Home asked five uncooperative sitters to leave the room. Then the séance resumed. The table tilted, and the ghost of Wat Rymer touched his parents. The spirit seemed especially interested in Elizabeth Browning, rustling her dress and placing a wreath on her head. Even the skeptical Robert Browning felt a spectral hand on his knees. (This was hardly the first appearance of the boy's spirit. Home was staying with the Rymers, and he had made the ghost materialize at previous private séances.) As a conclusion to the Browning circle sitting, ghostly hands played the trademark accordion.

Elizabeth Browning was convinced that Home had genuine powers. Her husband found Home to be smarmy and, worse, a fraud. His nickname for the medium was "Dungball" (a wordplay on Home's middle name, Dunglas). Although Robert Browning couldn't prove any specific chicanery, he pointed out that Home wore loose clothes that could conceal strings and fake "spirit hands." The poets' argument over Home was one of their few public disagreements, and Elizabeth soon dropped her patronage and all discussion of Home. For his part, Robert Browning became such an anti-Spiritualist that he wrote a lengthy satirical poem, "Mr. Sludge, the Medium," in which he attacked all mediums, but especially a thinly disguised D. D. Home.

Behind Every Good Man ...

Home continued on to Europe. In France, during séances for Napoleon II and Empress Eugenie, he manifested the ghost of Napoleon I. While in Russia, Home married a wealthy noblewoman named Alexandria; she soon died, but the courts cut off the medium from the estate.

Then, in 1866, Home became the spiritual advisor to a 75-year old widow, a Mrs. Lyon. Two years later, she became disenchanted with Home (according to some, after her romantic advances were rejected) and demanded the return of about £30,000, which she claimed she loaned him while under his spell. Despite her rambling and raving during the subsequent trial, the court found in her favor. It addition, the judge denounced Spiritualism as "mischievous nonsense, well calculated on the one hand to delude the vain, the weak, the foolish, and the superstitious."

The Ashley Place Levitation

Interestingly, the trial seemed to spur Home to new heights, figuratively and literally. In 1867, Home performed several stunts to prove that he was impervious to fire: He stuck his head into a lit fireplace without even singeing his hair. He handled hot coals and enabled others to do so as well.

Then, in December 1868, came the famous Ashley Place levitation. Three sitters at a séance held in a London manor claimed that, while in a trance, Home rose, walked into the next room, opened the window there, levitated up and out the window, then floated back in through the window of the room in which they sat. The three witnesses (the Master of Lindsay, later the Earl of Crawford; Viscount Adare, later the Earl of Dunraven; and Captain Charles Wynne, a cousin to Adare) gave varying accounts. None of them claimed to have actually *seen* Home open the window in the next room, nor float out; even the circumstances of Home's reentry were reported inconsistently. Nevertheless, the levitation resulted in a media frenzy.

> **Boo!**
>
> Here's a double whammy: Don't jump to conclusions, and don't believe everything you hear. Home's Ashley Place levitation became accepted as fact even though no one really saw him do it. But because three reputable people gave the same account, it was accepted as being true. Also, check out all ghost claims for yourself before blindly believing.

D. D. Home and the Ashley Place levitation.

The End Games

In 1871, Home was subjected to a number of scientific tests devised by Sir William Crookes (1832–1919), a brilliant nineteenth-century chemist, physicist, and investigator of mediums. Home passed the tests with flying colors, making an untouched accordion play, despite its being enclosed in an electrified cage. (Crookes had hypothesized that Home used some sort of electromagnetic force to move the instrument's keys.)

In October 1871, Home was back in Russia, where he married the wealthy Julie de Gloumeline. Home retired in 1873. He died that year of tuberculosis in Auteuil, France, and was buried at St. Germain-en-Laye. His widow wrote two biographies about him, which augmented the two editions of Home's autobiography, *Incidents in My Life* (1862 and 1872).

Florence Cook Meets Katie King

British medium Florence Cook (1856–1904) was renowned for the number and variety of spirits that she materialized at her séances, especially full-form spirit figures. Born in London, Cook discovered her powers to tip tables at an early age. Her family introduced her to a local spiritualist group, the Dalston Association, in 1871. The following year, she drew the attention of Frank Herne and his partner Charles Williams, the British mediums that were famed for teleporting their mentor, Mrs. Guppy, across London. (You'll read more about the feat in Chapter 8.) Herne's spirit guide was John King, and it was during Cook's apprenticeship with Herne that she discovered her own control: King's daughter, Katie.

Katie King, Cook's most frequent control and the daughter of spirit control John King, materialized at a séance.

Let the (Spirit) Show Begin!

Cook was young, beautiful, and talented, so she drew a large, dedicated following. In 1873, Mr. Charles Blackburn, a wealthy spiritualist from Manchester, became her patron.

From her earliest séances, Cook specialized in materializations. At first, she only produced spirit faces. They would appear in a window cut out of the door of a large cupboard that she used as her spirit cabinet. Before long, Cook was manifesting the complete bodies of spirits, rather than just a ghostly face or hand.

Cook's standard séance began with her being placed in the cabinet with a rope draped across her lap. The door to the cupboard was closed, then immediately reopened. Cook was found to be tied to the chair at her neck, waist, and wrists. The door would be shut again, and the lights would be lowered. Soon, spirit faces would appear in a window in the door. (Detractors claimed the face always seemed to look a lot like Cook draped in white gauze.)

Later in the séance, the cabinet door would be flung open wide, and Katie emerged. Cook would be heard moaning inside the cabinet, though hidden behind a curtain. At first, Katie only smiled and nodded; before long, she was walking among the sitters, shaking her solid hand with theirs, and answering questions. Katie would return to the cabinet, her portal back to the Spirit World. The cupboard doors would be re-opened, and Cook, still bound and exhausted, was released.

Crookes Checks Out Cook

During a Cook séance in December 1873, one participant, Mr. William Volckman, grabbed Katie King's arm. Some sitters restrained Volckman, while others helped Katie back into the cabinet. When the doors were reopened, Florence Cook was still bound. Nevertheless, Volckman swore that Katie King had actually been Cook in disguise. (Indeed, many people had commented that King bore an amazing resemblance to Cook.) If Volckman was fiercely opposed to Spiritualism, however, it didn't last. He later married medium Agnes Guppy.)

British scientist and paranormal researcher Sir William Crookes, who had only recently investigated Home, publicly defended Cook. She subsequently allowed herself to be fully tested by him, starting in December 1873. In his preliminary report, issued in

> **CAUTION**
>
> **Boo!** _____
>
> It's not a good idea to grab a ghost. You never know what kind of spirit you might be snatching. Volckman's behavior at the Cook séance was a real no-no: It was considered terribly bad-mannered for sitters to hang onto mediums or their controls in the dark.

February 1874, Crookes endorsed Cook, although he admitted that the only way to prove that the manifestation of King was genuine was to have both ladies be seen together. Cook soon moved into the home of Crookes and his wife to continue being tested. Crookes was allowed to see King and the draped figure of Cook resting in the cabinet at the same time, and he was permitted to take photographs. (Only a few survive, and most show Katie only. When Cook and Katie are seen together, one of their faces is always obscured.)

In the spring of 1874, the séances moved back to Cook's home. There, Cook would materialize King in the privacy of her bedroom. Sitters were allowed to enter the darkened room to see and touch both figures. That was enough for Crookes to certify Cook as a genuine medium.

It's often been speculated that Sir William Crookes became Florence Cook's lover at some point during his investigations, which might have compromised his neutrality. Or perhaps Crookes had been totally duped by her, or he was merely naive. Then again, perhaps Florence Cook was the real thing.

Though Crookes obviously was sympathetic to Spiritualists, he never really joined their ranks until three years before his death. He made the announcement of his conversion to Spiritualism in the December 9, 1916, issue of *Light*, a Spiritualist magazine. Apparently, another medium, Anna Eva Fay, and photographs of spirits taken by a Mr. Hope had removed any lingering doubts—despite the fact that both of them had been previously exposed as frauds.

A New Control Takes Control

In May 1874, in a sad farewell held behind a curtain, Katie King said goodbye to "dear Florrie." The next month, Cook's secret marriage to Edward Elgie Corner was revealed. Within months, Crookes, Cook's great supporter, and Blackburn, her patron, lost all interest in her.

Subsequently, Florence Cook was often caught in trickery. Fellow medium D. D. Home (perhaps out of professional jealousy, to further his own career, or to divert attention from his own suspicious actions) called Cook a "skillful trickster" and an "outright cheat." Nevertheless, she maintained a loyal following.

Cook replaced Katie King with a new spirit control, Marie. In 1880, Cook sat for Sir George Sitwell, who grabbed Marie during the séance

Phantastic Tips

If you're thinking of trying your luck as a medium, start today, before you age another minute! It's been observed that the psychic powers of mediums, both female and male, seem to wane as they grow older.

and wouldn't let go. He inspected the cabinet and found that Cook was no longer inside. Cook's supporters claimed that she was walking in her sleep and had never intended to deceive her public.

After two such shattering incidents, however, Cook took the unusual step of requiring that a sitter be bound in the cabinet beside her. Before long, Cook retired from the séance biz. She conducted one last séance as a test for the Sphinx Society in Berlin in 1899, where she materialized Marie as part of the examination. Cook died penniless in London on April 22, 1904.

Say "Cheese": Spirit Photography

Photography, perfected around 1839, was less than a decade old when the Fox sisters first heard the tappings in Hydesville, New York. It was only a matter of time before mediums began to use photographs to prove the existence of ghosts and spirits.

Phantom Phrases

A **spirit photograph** shows a spirit or ghost on film. Spirit photography was originally used in posed sittings to capture the image of a deceased person, usually a loved one, next to the subject of the portrait. In modern times, spirit photography is used in ghost hunting to try to catch a spectral image on film.

Technically, a *spirit photograph* is any ghost, phantom, or spirit of the dead captured on film, although the term is usually reserved for photos in which a ghost appears beside a living person. There's never been an authenticated spirit photograph. Most are obvious fakes, optical oddities created when the photo was taken, or flaws in its development. Still, about 10 percent of the pictures that have been examined by photographic and paranormal experts cannot automatically be dismissed as fraudulent or caused by natural means.

Mumler's the Word!

Spirit photography is generally credited to William Mumler, a jewelry engraver and amateur photographer in nineteenth-century Boston. Mumler took a self-portrait in 1861, and when he developed the plate, he noticed what seemed to be a ghostly face next to his. Upon careful examination, he realized that it was, of course, a double exposure. But, with interest in Spiritualism at its zenith, Mumler immediately realized the financial potential of his discovery.

He began working as a medium, specializing in spirit photography. Mumler photographed his subject, then added the shadowy likeness of a loved one or a deceased celebrity. Needless to say, sitters paid high prices for such visible proof that the spirits of their dearly departed still surrounded them.

Spirit photographs helped spread belief in spiritualism worldwide, and Mumler had many imitators. Mumler's trickery was soon found out, however, because he made the mistake of inserting identifiable *living* fellow Bostonians as ghosts in some of his photographs. He left town in a hurry and set up shop in New York, but he was arrested there and tried for fraud in 1869. He was found not guilty, in part because of the flattering testimony of Judge John Edmonds from the U.S. Court of Appeals (who also just happened to be a Spiritualist).

Abraham Lincoln appears to hover over his widow, Mary Todd Lincoln, in this famous spirit photograph, probably taken by Mumler.

The Crewe Crew

William Hope, another spirit photographer, claimed to have captured more than 2,500 "extras" (as he called the spirit faces). He headed an early 1920s group of spirit photographers in Crewe, England, that called themselves the "Crewe Circle." They actively invited inspection of their cameras, film, and equipment. They even allowed sitters to bring their own. They would start a sitting with prayers and hymns, followed by the taking of photographs.

In his 1924 book, *A Magician Among the Spirits*, Harry Houdini debunked the Crewe Circle. He pointed out that if the sitter wanted to supply the photographic plates, the Circle demanded that they receive them several days in advance in order to "magnetize" them. In that time, the plates could easily be doctored or switched.

> **Ghostly Pursuits**
>
> Sometimes William Hope didn't even bother to use a camera to take the spirit photo-graph. He would simply hold the sealed plate up to his forehead to imprint a mental picture. Spirit writing has also allegedly appeared on photographs; British medium Reverend William Stainton Moses coined the term "psychography" to describe this phe-nomenon. In the 1960s, Ted Serios of Kansas City, Missouri, created a stir when he allegedly used "thoughtography" to create images on Polaroid film simply by staring into the camera.

On one occasion, a sitter secretly marked the plates he gave to the Crewe Circle. But the plates that were returned had no markings. Another sitter reported that when he brought plates to the sitting unannounced, he caught members of the Crewe Circle trying to switch them while passing out the hymnals.

Despite frequent exposure, spirit photography remained popular well into the twenti-eth century.

Now I'm not saying that all spirit photographs are phony. Remember, at least 10 per-cent go unexplained. But if you want to try to make some spirit photos for yourself, you can see the best ways to do it in Chapter 9.

Don't Touch That Dial!

In the 1970s and 1980s, a new type of mediumship called *channeling* became popular, especially in the United States. Rather than produce manifestations, a channeler allows a spirit to take complete possession of his or her body so that it may impart spiritual guidance, healing, growth, or wisdom through automatic writing or direct speech.

Channelers don't limit themselves to spirits of the dead, however. Most often, they claim to be in touch with angels, guardian spirits, demons, nature spirits (including those of animals), a Higher Self, or the Universal Mind.

One of the first famous channelers was Jane Roberts, whose writings became best-sellers. She claimed that some of them were actually authored by an entity named Seth as she channeled the spirit.

Kevin Ryerson, from California, became famous as the channeler for actress Shirley MacLaine, who later recounted her experiences in *Out on a Limb*. Ryerson even played himself in the TV movie version of the popular book.

The belief in channeling is far from over, however. Even former First Lady Hillary Rodham Clinton is said to have met in the White House with a channeler, who allowed her to chat with the spirit of Eleanor Roosevelt.

Hello, Heaven?

There will always be people claiming to be able to communicate with the dead as long as there are people willing to believe that it's possible. Let's look at three of the most well-known psychics today.

According to her website (www.sylvia.org), Sylvia Browne first showed psychic ability at the age of three in her hometown of Kansas City, Missouri. Her success in private readings led to her founding the Nirvana Foundation for Psychic Research, a nonprofit organization (now known as the Society of Novus Spiritus) in 1974. Its mission is based in Christian Gnostic teachings, which includes a belief in life after death. A popular lecturer and guest on TV talk shows, Browne has also authored several books, including *Journey of the Soul*, *Conversations With the Other Side*, *Astrology Through the Eyes of a Psychic*, *Adventures of a Psychic*, and *The Other Side and Back*. Her most recent book, *Visits from the Afterlife*, looks at the differences between ghosts and other types of spirits, discusses paranormal terms such as "visitation" and "astral travel," and ends with her favorite ghost story.

One of the newest media sensations in paranormal circles is medium and best-selling author, lecturer, and television personality James Van Praagh, who claims to be able to contact the Other World and chat with its residents. He says that after death, our souls travel to a "different dimension" where our thoughts and emotions move on a "higher frequency." Van Praagh says he's able to tap into "vibrations" and "pure thought" as he makes his "spirit readings." In his book, *Talking to Heaven*, he claims that anyone can do it! The books *Reaching to Heaven*, *Healing Grief*, *Heaven and Earth*, and *Looking Beyond* have followed.

On his syndicated television program *Beyond With James Van Praagh*, which is no longer airing, Van Praagh demonstrated his ability to talk to the deceased loved ones of members of the audience, and some of these readings have been amazingly accurate. Juliet Mills is among the celebrities who have had readings on his program. During her appearance, she was contacted by the spirits of Sir Laurence Olivier, who was a family friend, and Josh Ryan Evans, a boy who had co-starred with her on the television soap opera *Passions*. For more information on James Van Praagh, go to www.vanpraagh.com.

John Edward, another well-known medium, author, and lecturer, first became popular with the publication of his book *Crossing Over*. Like Van Praagh, Edward claims to be able to talk to spirits of the dead. Numerous TV guest appearances and a television series called *Crossing Over* (currently airing on the Sci Fi Channel) followed. Recent books include *After Life: Answers from the Other Side*, *One Last Time: A Psychic Medium Speaks to Those We Have Loved and Lost*, and *Unleashing Your Psychic Potential*. Check with www.johnedward.net for details.

Ghostly Pursuits

Paranormal skeptics point out that many mediums obtain their information through a technique known as "cold reading," in which the pseudo-psychic fishes for (and obtains) clues by asking leading questions or making vague statements. For example, the medium makes an innocent remark such as "I sense a long trip," and immediately follows it with a generalized question, such as "Does that make sense?" The reading continues with a series of questions, answers, and declarations, as the medium makes a calculated reading according to the sitter's answers and body language. The technique is called cold reading because the medium meets the subject "cold," without any advance knowledge about the individual.

Paranormal investigators suggest the possibility of a mundane explanation for the apparent success of television psychics. Secret assistants could mingle with members of the studio audience, either while they wait in line before the show or in the seats before taping begins. Likewise, hidden microphones could easily pick up casual conversation. And it's amazing how much can be learned just from the names on a guest list. Any of these methods could provide the psychic with more than enough information to make startling revelations once on camera. Also, few shows are aired live: Detractors wonder how many hours are taped in order to get 30 minutes of impressive television-worthy "contacts" and reaction shots.

Perhaps there is a World Beyond, and perhaps there are mediums, channelers, and psychics who can peer through that veil. And maybe, one day, those of us on the mortal side of eternity will receive clear, indisputable proof. Until that time, there will be skeptics, scoffers, and paranormal investigators.

The Least You Need to Know

- The Davenport brothers, magicians acting as mediums, introduced the spirit cabinet, one of spiritualism's greatest tools.
- D. D. Home, who was able to produce amazing physical phenomena during his séances, was one of Spiritualism's most popular mediums.
- Florence Cook, attended by the spirit control Katie King, was perhaps the best-known female medium in the second half of the nineteenth century.
- A spirit photography purports to capture the image of a ghost on regular camera film, often in the same photo as a living person.
- Sylvia Browne, James Van Praagh, and John Edward are three of the more visible contemporary psychic-mediums who claim to be able to communicate with the Other Side.

Chapter 8

Things That Go Bump in the Night

In This Chapter

- The spooky goings-on at séances
- Controls: spirits returning from the Beyond
- The ouija board: the first form of spirit communications?
- Spirit handwriting appears on slates
- Disembodied voices speak in the dark
- Gooey, ghostly slime emerges as ectoplasm

So what actually happens at a séance? Do people just sit around in the dark, hoping to be grabbed by a ghost? Well, not exactly, but pretty close!

Over the years, mediums developed some incredible ways to talk with those on the Other Side. Sure, the spirits still tapped out messages, but they started using Ouija boards, too. Before long, the ghosts were writing notes, talking away, and, eventually, appearing right in front of the sitters' eyes. Let's take a peek for ourselves.

Getting the Most Out of Your Séance

Not everyone felt the need to engage a professional medium to hold a séance. Conducting or attending home circles became such a popular pastime in the 1870s that *The Spiritualist*, a weekly magazine in England, actually published suggestions on how to set up a proper home sitting, including:

♦ Pick the right person to lead your séance. There's probably at least one person in every household who has the talent to be a medium. The best mediums are persons who are genial, impulsive, and affectionate.

♦ Never invite people who don't like each other to take part in the same sitting: The bad vibrations inhibit spirit materialization.

♦ Spirits most often appear in rooms that are kept cool.

Mediums offered some of their own tips for successful séances:

♦ Many mediums felt the number of participants should be strictly limited (usually to a maximum of 10 or so).

♦ Some thought that there should be an equal number of men and women present, alternated in their seating around the circle.

♦ Mediums claimed that spirits preferred dark rooms; needless to say, that's where the best results were always produced.

♦ The spirits are much more likely to appear at séances held in the medium's own home. If repeated sittings are going to be held in a home elsewhere, the same room should be used every time. That way the spirits would feel more comfortable and be more likely to appear. (Paranormal skeptics would point out that the mediums would also get to know their way around.)

Usually séances were held at night. The lights were extinguished or dimmed; sometimes the séance was conducted by candlelight or by moonlight streaming through a window.

The parties would gather around a table and hold hands or place their palms on the tabletop. Many groups simply sat in chairs that had been arranged in a circle.

Trusted or cooperative sitters were placed to the immediate left and right of the medium. To prevent dishonesty, they were often invited to hold the medium's hands, to place their hands on the medium's legs or in the medium's lap, and to rest their feet on top of the medium's shoes. As we've seen, some mediums had themselves tied up to prove that they were not using their own hands and feet to produce the spirit activity.

Once the Davenport brothers introduced their spirit cabinet in the 1850s, many mediums welcomed this new tool as a means to prove that they were totally removed from any ghostly phenomenon. Unfortunately, dishonest mediums also embraced the new technology: They realized that once they were hidden away in a cabinet, away from the prying eyes of the audience, they could get away with just about anything!

In the early years, some mediums began their sittings with the singing of hymns or the recitation of prayers. Besides having a calming effect on the attendees, it reassured them that attending a séance was a perfectly acceptable activity for a Christian. Next, the medium called on the spirits to show themselves or to give a sign that they were present.

Take Control

You may have noticed that almost every medium worked through a spirit, called a control, which acted as a guide or intermediary to the Other World. Some controls became as famous in the spiritualist world as their mediums.

Mediums usually employed one control repeatedly, although some had many different controls. Spiritualists pointed to the existence of controls as proof of survival after death, although some mediums thought their controls were actually produced from their own subconscious minds. Regardless, controls always seemed to have unique personalities, separate and distinct from those of their mediums.

Drop by Sometime

An unexpected phenomenon at some séances was the *drop-in communicator*, a spirit or entity that suddenly made itself known, uninvited by the medium. As opposed to a control, the drop-in communicator was usually a stranger to the medium and all of the sitters.

Because the participants didn't know the identity of the spirit, it would often give information that didn't mean anything to the sitters. Occasionally the spirit spoke in a foreign language.

Most times the drop-in communicator had no ulterior motive in showing up; it was simply lonely or was even unaware that it was no longer alive.

Phantom Phrases

A **drop-in communicator** is an uninvited spirit that suddenly makes its presence known at a séance. Its identity is almost always unknown to the medium and the sitters.

Other times, the spirit would convey a message. Regardless, the spirit usually departed as quickly as it had arrived. Few drop-in communicators returned, so it was particularly difficult for paranormal researchers to investigate them.

One of the oddest cases of a drop-in communicator involved the spirit of Runolfur Runolfsson, who barged into a series of séances conducted by Iceland's most famous medium, Hafsteinn Bjornsson, between 1937 and 1940. Runolfsson wanted his leg back! The spirit claimed to have died in October 1879: He had gotten drunk, passed out on a beach, and was swept out to sea and drowned. His decomposed remains finally washed ashore a year later; they were buried, but the thighbone was missing. Runolfsson claimed that a local fish merchant named Ludvik Gudmundsson had the bone at his house. Upon inquiry, Gudmundsson discovered that the carpenter who built his house had placed a bone between two of the walls—why, no one knows. The wall was torn open, the leg bone was found, and it was given a proper burial. Runolfsson later "dropped in" to a séance to express his thanks, and eventually he became a regular control for Bjornsson.

Tapping at the Table

Back in the séance room, table-tipping was standard fare. Mediums claimed that ghosts moved the table. But it wasn't enough. People wanted the spirits to talk to them. To keep one step ahead of the competition, mediums had to devise more and more ingenious ways to keep the lines of spirit communication open. Each new method marked one small step for a medium, one giant leap for mediumkind.

In Hydesville, the Fox sisters had worked out a rapping code for the spirit to communicate with them. No raps meant "no," one rap meant "yes," and a series of raps indicated that a numerical answer was coming. Five quick raps meant the spirit wanted to answer in alphabetic letters. The medium would call out the letters one at a time, A to Z, and the spirit would rap again when the medium reached the correct letter.

Needless to say, this was tedious going. By the time of Margaret Fox's public demonstrations in Rochester, a streamlined code had been devised. One rap indicated "no," three raps meant "yes," and two raps meant the question couldn't be answered. But the biggest improvement was Margaret's introduction of automatic writing into the séance room (see Chapter 2). She would hold a pencil and let the spirits "take possession" of her hand to write their answers to questions. This was certainly much quicker than the old rapping alphabet code!

First-Person Phantoms

Shreeyash Palshikar, an illusionist and authority on the magic of India, wanted to conduct a fun but spooky Halloween séance for friends while at college. To finish the pseudo-séance, he was going to re-create a trick he had learned from his uncle in India, in which smoke and fire would issue from a pile of bones after water was poured on them. To make the trick even more effective, Shreeyash borrowed a human skull from friends in the biology department. Indeed, as he started the séance, smoke billowed from the eyes of the skull— which set off a fire alarm and forced the evacuation of the dorm.

Undaunted, Shreeyash decided to finish the séance outside and chose a spot near the monument for a man whose spirit he pretended to summon. But when Shreeyash poured water over the skull this time, there was a blinding flash and the skull exploded in his face. He was temporarily blinded and rushed to a hospital; fortunately, he completely recovered his vision by morning.

Had pressure from the smoke and fire built up inside the skull, causing it to split apart? Or was the conjured spirit showing his displeasure at being disturbed? Or was it something even more extraordinary? Shreeyash later learned that his uncle, the magician whose ceremonial skulls he had played with as a child, had died in India the very night of that séance. Was his uncle taking a last bow before the final curtain fell?

The Ouija Board

Sometimes, in lieu of automatic writing, the medium would receive answers to questions through the use a board preprinted with letters and words. The earliest board of this type dates to ancient China. The sixth-century B.C.E. Greek philosopher Pythagoras and his followers used a similar board, in which a wheeled table moved across a stone slab engraved with mystic symbols. Today, this device is commonly known as a *ouija (pronounced WEE-juh) board.*

Mediums were using "talking boards" printed with letters and numbers with moveable pointers by the middle of the nineteenth century. In 1853, a French spiritualist created the *planchette,*

Phantom Phrases

A **ouija board** is a small piece of wood or card preprinted with letters, numerals, and words, used by mediums to receive spirit communications. Usually the fingers do not contact the board directly but lightly rest on a raised pointer called a **planchette.**

a small triangular board—planchette is literally "little board" in French—with legs, sometimes with wheels on the end, at each corner. A pencil would be attached to one corner, and the planchette was set onto paper.

One or more people would rest their fingertips on the planchette, and someone asked the spirits a question. Usually, the planchette would begin to move, spelling out a message—supposedly animated by impulses from the spirit world.

By 1868, the planchette was a popular mass-marketed "toy" in the United States.

William Fuld of Baltimore, Maryland, patented what we know today as the ouija board as a fortune-telling game in 1892. He said he got its name by combining the French and German words for "yes" (*oui* and *ja*, respectively.) But Fuld also claimed that the board actually named itself by spelling out the letters to him.)

In 1966, Parker Brothers marketed OUIJA® as a game for entertainment purposes only. Today, Hasbro distributes their design of the board.

First-Person Phantoms

Katy Dickinson, a family friend, tells about a time she stayed overnight at her grandmother's and decided to play with a ouija board. She tried to contact her late grandfather and asked for a sign of his presence. At first, she was disappointed. The only word that the planchette spelled out was "candles," but she decided that her own subconscious hand motion might have written the word. After all, she had started her ouija "ceremony" by lighting candles at the four corners of the board.

Katy, finished with the spirit world for the evening (or so she thought!), blew out the candles as she had promised her grandmother she would, and went to sleep. The next morning Katy awoke to find all four candles burning brightly. Her grandmother hadn't lit them. Had the grandfather told Katy through the ouija board the night before that he'd use the candles to give her a sign? Only the spirits know for sure.

Mediums claim that spirits move the planchette, but most nonbelievers dismiss ouija-board phenomena as unconscious muscular motion moving the planchette. Its direction, the skeptics say, as well as the answers to the questions, are supplied subliminally by the sitters themselves.

So is the ouija board a doorway to the spirit world? Decide for yourself by enlarging a copy of the miniature ouija board and following the directions printed in Chapter 9.

CAUTION **Boo!**

Beware! Even though ouija boards are supposed to be simply for amusement purposes, some people have been known to become psychologically dependent on them. They need to "consult the board" for advice or to make decisions. In addition, many respected paranormalists believe that ouija boards work by opening a portal to the Other Side, from which any spirit can enter our world—even the evil ones. If you do get a message through a ouija board, just remember: It may not be coming from a friend!

The Spirit Writes; and Having Writ, Moves On

Direct writing was an even greater leap forward than rapping codes, automatic writing, or ouija boards. With direct writing, the script simply appeared on a piece of paper or some other surface. It didn't take forever to get long messages anymore. Needless to say, direct writing became a favorite tool among mediums.

In the 1800s, small chalkboards such as the portable slates used by schoolchildren became the most popular surface for direct writing to appear on, perhaps because they were so common at the time and seemingly free of trickery. In fact, William E. Robinson wrote in his book, *Spirit Slate Writing and Kindred Phenomena* (1898), that nothing converted more people to spiritualism in the nineteenth century than direct writing appearing on slates.

Phantom Phrases

Direct writing is a paranormal phenomenon, usually seen in a séance, in which spirit handwriting (without the use of the medium's hand) appears directly on a previously unmarked surface.

Ghostly Pursuits

Slate writing is credited to the medium "Dr." Henry Slade (1825–1905), who claimed to have discovered slate writing in the 1860s. Slade's new way to communicate with spirits was an immediate success, and mediums everywhere soon adopted the method. Perhaps Slade did produce real spirit phenomenon on occasion, but he also was exposed regularly for trickery. (It turns out Slade was able to secretly write with tiny pieces of chalk held in his mouth, in either hand, or between the toes of either foot.) In 1876, he fled London after a court found him guilty of fraud. By 1892, with his reputation and clients gone, Slade's career was finished.

Although a single slate was sometimes used, usually two were employed. All sides of the slates would be shown free of writing. They would be strapped together, sometimes with a small piece of chalk between. Later, when the slates were inspected, there would be a message in "spirit" handwriting on one or more sides of the slates.

Talk to Me

Soon, mediums discovered that they could speed up communications as well as captivate the audience if the spirits were able to speak instead of having to write everything down.

At first, mediums allowed their controls to speak *through* them. The spirit took possession of the medium—or, at least, of the medium's vocal chords. Then the spirit talked through the medium's mouth, almost always sounding different than the medium's voice.

This was fine, if the control had a lot to say. But if the medium tried to have a conversation with the spirit, well, you can imagine it sounded somewhat schizophrenic.

That's when mediums began to produce *direct voice phenomenon (DVP)*, speech from a spirit that didn't seem to emanate from the medium. Usually, the ghost's voice would seem to come from a point slightly above or to the side of the medium's head. This so-called "independent direct voice" phenomenon was possible, according to mediums, because the phantom had somehow constructed and spoken through an invisible, artificial larynx. (Huh?) Skeptics dismissed the stunt as mere ventriloquism or it was accomplished through the use of hidden assistants.

Phantom Phrases

In **direct voice phenomenon (DVP)**, a spirit speaks from no natural source. Usually the sound appears to come from some point near the medium (usually above or to one side) but not from the medium's mouth. Sometimes the voice has to be amplified through a spirit horn or trumpet.

Sometimes, especially in the early days of séances, mediums introduced a megaphone-shaped horn known as a spirit trumpet. During the séance, the spirit would levitate the trumpet and speak through it as the horn floated around the room. Supposedly, the spirit needed the trumpet to condense its vocal energy and amplify its volume.

DVP was introduced in the 1850s in séances led by an Ohio farmer/medium, Jonathan Koons. Although other unintelligible spectral voices were also heard at Koon's sittings, his primary control, John King (yes, him again), was quite articulate—and loud: King spoke through a floating tin horn. (Koon's séances were also musical events. During a sitting, Koons and his wife filled the room with musical instruments. Once the lights were dimmed, the instruments flew around the room while being played by invisible spirits.)

Whatever Possessed You?

People have believed since ancient times that a person's mind, body, and soul can be taken over—possessed—by a spirit, god, or demon.

Many mediums actually wanted to have their controls take possession of their hands (for automatic writing) or even their whole bodies. The spirits usually seemed quite willing to cooperate, and, unlike demons, they would depart on command.

On rare occasions, drop-in communicators take possession of a medium. Such was the case with a spirit named Patience Worth, who first took possession of Pearl Curran on July 8, 1913, while the St. Louis housewife was playing with a ouija board. (See, I warned you!)

The spirit claimed to have been born in 1649 in Dorsetshire, England, to a poor family. Unmarried, she traveled to the American colonies, where she was killed by Indians. From 1913 until around 1922, Worth, through Curran, dictated poems, plays, epigrams, allegories, short stories, and historical novels—more than four million words in 29 volumes.

Literary experts who have examined the writings are divided in their opinions of whether Curran, who left school at 14 years of age, could have produced the works on her own.

Appearing Out of Thin Air

But written words and voices in the dark weren't enough for sitters at séances. They wanted more! Soon, some mediums began to manifest or materialize real, solid objects. At first, the spirits didn't personally appear. Instead, they simply dropped their spectral gifts, such as flowers or fruit, into the laps of the surprised and delighted sitters.

An object that appears from nowhere in the presence of a medium is called an *apport*, from the French word *apporter*, meaning "to bring." The opposite of an apport—that is, an object that's made to vanish or is *teleported* to another location—was known as an *asport*. Needless to say, asports were not as popular as apports. After all, who wants to have their toys taken away?

Phantom Phrases _____

An **apport** is a solid object that seemingly appears from nowhere in the presence of a medium. Spirits supposedly assembled some apports from invisible matter; other apports are simply teleported from another location. The opposite of an apport—something that disappears or is teleported to another location—is called an **asport**. **Teleportation** is a kind of paranormal transportation in which an object is moved from one location to another, sometimes through a solid barrier such as a door, wall, or closed window.

Two nineteenth-century mediums who were especially known for their ability at producing apports were Mrs. Agnes Guppy and Eusapia Palladino. Not all apports were pleasant: Palladino sometimes produced repulsive objects such as dead rats. Mrs. Guppy herself became an apport at one of the most celebrated spiritualist events of the nineteenth century. Frank Herne and his partner Charles Williams, who were protégés of Mrs. Guppy, were conducting a séance in their home in London in July 1871 when one of the sitters, Mr. W. H. Harrison, jokingly challenged them to teleport Mrs. Guppy to their séance room. Before three minutes had passed, the lights came up. There, sitting in the center of the séance table, was a seemingly surprised Mrs. Guppy, dressed only in her night robe and holding her pen and account books. The very large Mrs. Guppy had apparently teleported from her own home, two or three miles away, into the center of their circle.

Spiritualists had various theories about what apports were and where they came from:

- The spirits brought them from another dimension.

- The medium used magnetism and psychic power to bring them from another dimension.

- Apports were previously existing objects that the spirit or medium disintegrated, teleported, then reassembled in the presence of the medium.

- Apports were created from the material matter called *ectoplasm* excreted from the medium. (There's more about ectoplasm coming up in the next section.)

"I've Been Slimed!"

"I've been slimed!" Remember that catchphrase from the movie *Ghost Busters*? In spiritualist jargon, the icky goop that covered the ghost hunter in the film is called ectoplasm—a materialization of spirit essence or matter. It usually appears as a shapeless, gelatinlike material oozing from one or more of the medium's orifices. The production of ectoplasm was pretty impressive stuff, especially if it shaped itself into human form.

The word ectoplasm was coined in 1894 by French physiologist Charles Richet to describe the third "arm" (actually a false limb, or pseudopod) that sometimes emerged from medium Eusapia Palladino during her séances. The word comes from the Greek *ektos*, meaning "exteriorized," and *plasma*, meaning "substance."

Phantom Phrases

Ectoplasm is spirit substance or matter that usually exudes from the medium's body. Ectoplasm is dense but liquid and milky white, often with the scent of ozone. Although fluid and shapeless at first, ectoplasm can mold itself into spirit limbs, faces, or entire bodies.

Was ectoplasm a true manifestation of a spirit's essence? Sitters weren't allowed to touch or examine it too closely—if at all, and no early samples have been preserved. And, even though séances are still performed today, the vogue for the production of ectoplasm has passed. Perhaps we'll never know what it really was.

But we *do* know that *fraudulent* mediums produced phony ectoplasm, because some of them were caught at it. The fake ectoplasm was constructed in advance from cheesecloth or netting and was often covered with luminous paint so that it would glow in the dark. It was a simple matter for secret assistants to make the "ectoplasm" appear at the proper time and place in the pitch-black room. How did ectoplasm come out of a medium's nose? Well, maybe that wasn't a trick. But miracles can be pulled off in the dark.

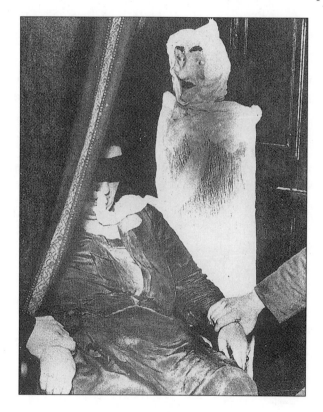

A spirit forms from the ectoplasm oozing from the nose of medium Mrs. Duncan.

(Photo from the author's collection)

Ectoplasm was exciting, but soon came the *pièce de résistance*. Sitters actually got to *see* the spirits! At first, only the spirits' faces appeared, but, before long, "full-form" (complete head-to-toe) materializations of spirits were becoming common at séances everywhere. After all, what could be more exciting than the appearance of an actual, entire ghost? Remember, the first medium to regularly produce full-form spirits was Florence Cook, and it made her a star!

As the séance field became saturated with mediums, only those with the best "shows" drew followings large enough to find fame and fortune.

So do you think you have what it takes? In the next chapter, you'll learn some of the "tricks of the trade"—ways in which you can fool your friends into thinking you can talk to the Other Side.

The Least You Need to Know

◆ Mediums often drew up their own rules of engagement to maximize their chances of producing spirit phenomena.

◆ Mediums developed a variety of ways to allow a spirit to communicate with them, including table-tipping, rapping codes, automatic writing, slate-writing, ouija boards, and direct voice phenomenon (DVP).

◆ Other proofs that spirits were present at séances included teleportation, apports and asports, the production of ectoplasm, and materializations.

◆ Some mediums impressed (and entertained) the participants at their séances by materializing ghosts and other phantom phenomena.

◆ Séances were entertaining as well as amazing—from musical instruments that played themselves to glowing spirits that appeared in the dark.

Chapter 9

Haunting Your House

In This Chapter

◆ Tips and tricks for taking convincing ghost photos

◆ Testing the Bloody Mary mirror

◆ Parlor tricks: tipping the tables, making a ghost detector, working the ouija

◆ Be a ghost host

Let's say you're sitting around with friends, talking about how cool it would be to have a ghost pop in to visit. Or you'd like to scare the pants off that bratty little cousin of yours. Perhaps it's getting close to Halloween, and you want to creep out a few of your friends.

Well, you've come to the right chapter! It's time to learn some of the "tricks of the trade" so that you, too, can conjure spirits.

Now, don't be scared. We're not talking about black magic here. You won't *really* be calling up the dead. Instead, I'm gonna show you some ways to create the *illusion* that you have ghosts at your command. These are simple, "entry level" methods to duplicate many of the effects performed by fraudulent mediums and spiritualists.

Say Cheese: Taking Ghost Photos

Remember William Mumler from Chapter 7? He's the guy who started the ghost photo craze in 1861 by "capturing" spirit images on film. Within just a few years, his methods were exposed—actually *double* exposed, if you catch my drift.

Now I'm not saying that all spirit photographs are phony. Some are obvious fakes. Others "give up the ghost" after a little close inspection. But, if you recall, at least 10 percent of all spirit photographs go unexplained. If you want to try to make a bogus spirit photograph to fool your friends, here are five great techniques to put a phantom in your photo.

Two Exposures Are Better Than One

If you have a camera that allows you to manually forward the film, you can create a spirit photograph by making a double exposure. Simply take two photos without winding the film between exposures.

First, shoot the image that you want to look like a ghost against (or suspended in front of) a flat, featureless black surface. Alternately, the shot could be taken outside at night against an empty horizon. For best results, you should aim a focused light—even if it's only a flashlight—directly on the "ghost."

When you look through the camera viewfinder to take the picture, position the "ghost" off-center so that the person you're going to photograph later does not block it.

Phantastic Tips

You might want to shoot the "ghost" image slightly out of focus. That way, it'll be less obvious that it's a fake in the final photograph. Compare the picture of Abraham Lincoln's ghost hovering above his widow's head in Chapter 7 with the photo of the spirit over Harry Price's shoulder in Chapter 11. Which spectre looks more "real" to you?

Take Your Time

Would you like to create the image of a shimmering ghost as it glides across the room? Sure you would. You can do it by taking a time-exposure photograph. "Point-and-shoot" cameras are designed to stop or freeze the action in perfect focus and lighting. So you'll need a programmable camera that allows you to override those automatic settings.

Set your camera for a slow shutter speed, which will keep the shutter open longer. (Shuttle speed appears as a fraction or whole number followed by " marks, which indicate seconds. For example, the setting .5" means the shutter will stay open for half a second; a 5" setting will keep the shutter open for a full five seconds.)

Houdini chats with the ghost of President Lincoln in this early twentieth-century double-exposure photograph.

(Photo from the author's collection)

Place the camera on a tripod to keep it still, because the slightest movement will blur the entire photograph. When you snap the photo, have your "ghost" sway back and forth or walk through the field of view.

When the film is developed, the stationary objects will be crisp, but anything that moved will be fuzzy. It will look like a ghost floated through the scene.

Ghostly Pursuits

Professional, albeit fraudulent, ghost photographers may not use double or time exposures. Their images might have been—in fact, probably were—created in the darkroom. By taking separate shots of the spirit image and the living person's portrait, the photographer can control the opacity of the ghost and its position in the photo. The negatives or plates could be layered or combined in any number of ways to produce the finished product. (Today, all of this can be done digitally, but more about that later in the chapter.)

Bear in mind that with a time-exposure photo, the spectral image won't be translucent. It will be hazy, but will look solid. To compensate, whatever or (whoever) you want to appear as a ghost should wear white or dress in very light colors when the photo is taken. The clothing will reflect more light and make it seem to glow.

And don't use a flash! If you do, the camera will freeze onto film whatever it "sees" at the moment of the brightest light, regardless of your shutter setting. As a result, your "ghost" will be distinct, not blurry.

Instead, set your camera to use available light. You can boost the level of light in the room, of course, but it must remain constant during the time exposure. This will take a lot of experimentation to avoid an over-exposed or washed-out photo. With success, you'll have a sharp, focused photograph of a room or vista that just happens to have a ghost walking through it.

A fuzzy spectral image can be produced by taking a time-exposure photograph in which the "ghost" subject moves in an otherwise-still setting.

(Photo from the author's collection)

The Camera Strap Ploy

Let your camera strap (or any other object) dangle in front of and close to the lens. As you shoot your photo, make sure the lens is focused on the distant objects or person, not the strap. (This will happen automatically with point-and-shoot cameras.) On the finished photo, the out-of-focus camera strap will look like a ghostly white streak.

You can test this optical illusion by holding a small object, such as a pen or a shoelace, close to your eyes while focusing on something farther away.

Why does this work? Well, it's a visual "trick" inherent in the nature of lenses (including those in your eyes). In simple terms, the lens spreads out or disperses the out-of-focus object in an attempt to capture as much of the image as it can. Thus, if you're focused on something 20 feet away, something that's only an inch away from the lens will appear cloudy or indistinct—making it appear ghostlike.

Into the Light

Have you ever taken a photograph with the sun to your side or directly in front of you? Then, when you develop the photos, you have little balls of light ruining the picture?

Don't be upset: Those phantom lights aren't necessarily a bad thing—not if you want to make ghost photos. Who says you goofed up? Maybe those spots aren't reflections from the sun at all but are one of those mysterious ghost lights we talked about in Chapter 4.

If the distortion appears as a vertical streak of light, you might be able to claim that the anomaly is actually a ghost floating through your photo!

If life gives you lemons, make lemonade. If life gives you gaffs on your photos, make them ghosts!

Is that a ghost rising out of the Chase Vault in Christ Church, Barbados? Or was it just a photograph taken facing into the sun?

(Photo by author)

Right Place, Right Time

Sometimes you get lucky without even knowing it. You take a photo, and when you get it developed there's something odd—something that looks like a ghost—in the picture. You were just in the right place at the right time.

Here's a personal example: Jan Kok built a landhus (Dutch for plantation house) on the island of Curaçao in 1750. Until 1863, when slavery was abolished, his estate produced salt by drying out artificial ponds filled with water from nearby St. Marie Bay. At one time, Kok had more than 100 slaves working the flats, and he was reportedly rather cruel to his workers. His ghost is said to return to oversee the plantation.

While visiting the property, I took a series of photographs of the main house where Kok lived. When I had the pictures developed, I discovered that in one of the shots, I had captured the dark silhouette of a human form in the otherwise-empty doorway.

Did I fail to notice someone briefly passing through the doorframe? Or had I caught an image of Jan Kok's ghost? You decide.

Can the ghost of John Kok be seen in one of these photographs of his plantation house in Curaçao?

(Photos by author)

It's a Digital Ghost World

I know. You're thinking, "I have a camera. But what's film?" It's a new world in photography. Digital cameras make it much easier to create special effects. And you can check your results before you print them out as photos, e-mail them to friends, or file them away on your hard drive.

That's the upside. The downside is that everyone *knows* that you can do miracles digitally. And if you don't get it right when you first take the photograph, you can always "Photoshop it" later to get the results you want.

It really doesn't matter whether you make your ghost photos on film or digitally. But if you want to fool your friends with them, they'll be less likely to suspect trickery if the ghosts show up on actual film processed in a lab.

So here's my advice: Try creating your phantom photos with your digital camera first. You can practice with little cost, because you won't be using up rolls of film (plus the cost of developing them) while you experiment.

Play around with different settings for your shutter speed, aperture (the amount of light that's allowed in the lens), and the ISO (film speed). Rehearse in the same lighting conditions that you'll be shooting in later.

Then, when you've figured out all that technical photography stuff, switch to a film camera and use the same settings. That way, you can hand the exposed roll of film to your friend and say, "Here, *you* take this and get it developed. I can't wait to see how the photos come out!"

> ### Ghostly Pursuits
>
> For help with your camera settings, check with a professional photographer, a camera shop, or (if all else fails) the manual for your camera. Or you might want to look into one of the books in *The Complete Idiot's Guide* series: *Photography* (R. Dodge Woodson), *Photography Like a Pro* (Mike Stensvold et al), *Portrait Photography* (Kathleen Tracy), or *Digital Photography* (Steven Greenberg).

The Bloody Mary Mirror

Remember those haunted mirror stories in Chapter 4? Well, here's yet another version of that apocryphal urban legend, but this one you can test for yourself to see if it's true.

Bloody Mary was either executed centuries ago for being a witch or she died in a car crash in the twentieth century, depending on which version of the story you hear. (Janet Langlois published one take on the story in 1978, and the myth was depicted in the 1999 movie *Urban Legends*.)

According to the tale, if you recite "Bloody Mary" over and over in front of a mirror, her spirit will appear, reflected in the glass.

Here's how you and your friends can try it:

1. Pick a mirror in a room that will be completely dark when the lights are turned out. (Bathrooms seem to be especially good for this.)

2. Light a candle in front of the mirror.

3. Turn off all of the other lights in the room.

 Boo!

Be forewarned before you decide to call on Bloody Mary. It's been said that, if she appears, she might pull you into the mirror with her, blind you, make you go crazy, or even kill you.

4. Stare into the mirror and chant "Bloody Mary" 13 times.

5. Pay close attention: The thirteenth time you say her name, Bloody Mary is supposed to appear in the mirror, seemingly standing behind your left shoulder.

Of course, it's only a legend. Don't be too disappointed if she's too busy elsewhere to show up.

Unconsciously Yours

We breathe without thinking. Our hearts beat without thinking. Some of us even talk without thinking.

Well, we also occasionally have bodily movements—miniscule twitches or jerks—that are triggered unconsciously. In medicine, these are called ideomotor responses. They can explain a lot! Especially in the spirit world.

Take a Tip from Me

Remember those mesmerists in Chapter 2 who tilted tables using "animal magnetism?" Then later, mediums added the stunt to their repertoires but claimed that invisible spirits were moving the furniture?

You can try table-tipping for yourself! Have four or more people stand or sit, spread evenly around a table. Everyone lightly rests his or her palms on the edge of the tabletop. Ask one and all to concentrate as you command the spirits to show their presence by lifting the table into the air. Before long, the table will probably begin to shift, vibrate, or tilt. Sometimes, the table actually rises and moves around the room as it clings to the hands.

How does this work? Are ghosts really lifting the table? No, it's those sneaky ideomotor responses you just heard about moments ago.

In 1853, the English chemist and physicist Michael Faraday (1791–1867) dismissed Mesmer's "magnetic" explanation for table-tipping. (And Faraday should know: He discovered electromagnetism.) Instead, the scientist suggested that the expectations of the people sitting around the table produced unconscious muscular pressures in their hands that moved the table.

So when you tell your group that their table will levitate, you actually plant the suggestion in their minds. This causes an unconscious muscular response: Even if they try to keep perfectly still, they have tiny, unnoticeable reactions in their hands that, taken all together, move the table!

If you want to make *sure* the table will move, there *is* a secret method sometimes used by magicians! Promise you won't tell? You'll need to have an assistant help you, and it'll require special preparation and practice.

Before you're going to "perform," strap a ruler to each forearm using rubber bands, wristbands, or bracelets. Cover these with a long-sleeved shirt or blouse and make sure that others can't see the rulers. Your helper has to do the same. When you get ready for the séance, you and your partner have to sit down on opposite sides of the table, facing each other. With your hands under the table, pull out the rulers so that a few inches of each protrude from your cuffs. Then, place your hands palm-down on the top of the table, but let the ends of the rulers slide under its edge. (Be careful that you don't accidentally clack the rulers against the table and give away the secret!) As you and your assistant (who has done the same secret maneuvers) raise your arms, the table will seem to lift on its own!

The Ghost Detector

Here's an old parlor game all dressed up in spirit clothing. Usually you see this performed as a lie detector test, but it's adaptable for use as a ghost detector as well.

Bring out a piece of thread or string with a finger ring tied to one end. Ask someone to hold the free end of the string, pinched between the thumb and forefinger so that the ring hangs down.

Tell the person that this makeshift pendulum is a "ghost detector" and that if you ask a question, the spirits will respond. If the answer is "yes," the ring will spin in a circle. If the answer is "no," the ring will move back and forth in a straight line. If it stays still, the answer is uncertain. When it stops for good, the spirit has departed.

Anyone asks a question. After a few moments, the weighted string will start to swing one way or the other! As more questions are asked, it may change direction, continue going the same way, or stop.

Why does this happen? Once again we have to thank Faraday for the explanation. Believe it or not, the person's mind will unconsciously trigger imperceptible muscular responses in the fingers and arms, causing the string to move.

That's the bare bones of how to present the ghost detector. But you can make this a genuine piece of spirit theater by dressing it up with an atmospheric story. Of course, any kind of small weight could be attached to the end of the string, depending on the tale you want to tell. It could be a gem or a birthstone, or perhaps a Celtic or other mystic-looking amulet of some sort. You might want to borrow the finger ring, especially if it once belonged to someone's who has crossed over.

Here's the kind of story you might want to weave to introduce the ghost detector:

> The ring on the end of this cord is very special to me. It belonged to my grandmother, who died exactly three years ago tonight. I always felt comfortable and safe when I was around her, and I really miss her. But even now, even though she's passed on, sometimes I still feel her presence. Especially when I hold something that was hers. Take this ring, for example: It was one of her favorites. I discovered that when I hold it or make any kind of physical connection with it, it's almost as if her spirit were in the room.

Trust me, with a story like that, you're bound to cause a few shivers down the spine when that string starts to spin!

Bored of Ouija Yet?

Ready to try a ouija board for yourself? You'll find a miniature ouija board printed on the following pages. Open the book flat and photocopy both pages onto one large sheet of paper. (It's designed to be printed on legal size, 11" × 14", paper.) Alternately, you can use the artwork in the book as a guide to draw your own, even larger ouija on a piece of poster board. The spirits won't mind if the board is homemade: In fact, it may be a plus because it's more personal!

You can use your hand as the planchette. Close one hand into a loose fist. Lightly rest it on the ouija board, or hold it just an inch or two above it. Extend your forefinger; this will act as the pointer. Think of a question or ask it out loud. If you feel your hand or arm wanting to move, let it. As your forefinger points to or nears consecutive letters, write them down.

If the spirits are with you, they'll spell out words to answer your question. Sometimes they'll make a shortcut by guiding your hand to "yes," "no," or the numbers to reply. Hopefully, before long, a message will emerge. (Remember, when working with the spirits, spelling and grammar don't always count.)

Skeptics, of course, suggest that your mind is unconsciously making you move your hand, that it's just another ideomotor response. But we know better, don't we?

Invite the Spirits In

In the previous chapter, we read how mediums claimed that ghosts are more likely to show up if their séances are held in the same place every time—and preferably in the medium's own home or lodging.

Maybe. But skeptics would say they had an ulterior motive. If the ghost-caller has time to—how can I put this delicately?—"prepare" for the spirits' arrival, it would be surprising if ghosts and spectral phenomena *didn't* appear!

It's finally time for us to look at ways that you can get your own home ready for a haunting.

Let the Games Begin

When some victims—I mean, friends—are over visiting and you're ready for some frighteningly good fun, start out by setting the mood for a haunting.

I suppose you *could* put on some hokey Phantom-of-the-Opera-type pipe organ music, like Bach's "Toccata and Fugue in D Minor." But I don't recommend it. Anything too melodramatic at this point will just seem silly.

Instead, start out by tossing out a simple question, like "Do you believe in ghosts?" This will immediately grab their attention and get them involved.

Mention a well-known ghost story. One of the urban legends from Chapter 4 would be perfect, especially if your audience is already somewhat familiar with the tale. How about those hitchhiking ghosts? Do you think they could be real?

What do *they* think?

By now your friends will be more than ready to share their own experiences. Casually ask if any of them has ever seen, heard, or felt a ghost. You may be surprised by how anxious they are to tell you.

1 2 3 4 5

oui

A B C D E

K L M N O

U V W

yes

6 7 8 9 0

ja

F G H I J

P Q R S T

X Y Z

no

At some point, you might want to throw in a personal ghost story, something that happened to *you*. Or maybe something that happened locally—perhaps in the very house you're in at that moment. Remember, the story doesn't have to be true. It just has to *sound* true.

Time for some parlor tricks! How about bringing out a ghost detector or a ouija board? Or passing around a photo you took that has some sort of a weird image in it? Do they think that ball of light in the picture could be a ghost?

Why not try a séance? "How do you do that?" they ask. Well, everyone sits around a table and—wait!—why not get that small table over in the corner, and you'll show them? Do you think that, if you asked nicely, the spirits would give you a sign of their presence by, oh, moving the table?

Finally it's time for the really scary part: the "dark" séance. Sit around the table and join hands. Lights out.

CAUTION **Boo!** _____

Even though you know it's all in fun, you still have to be very careful about safety in a dark room. If it's your house, you may know your way around in the dark. But others won't. If they move around, they might stumble or fall. And some people panic in the dark. (That's why they invented night lights.) If you perform your ouija board or séance by candlelight, be very aware of the danger of fire. Always know where everyone's sitting, know where the exits are located, and be ready to switch the lights back on at any time. Most of all, be ready to expect the unexpected.

Did You Hear That?

Ask the spirits to show themselves. To speak. Or to let you know that they're in the room. Then wait.

It's hard to believe until you experience it, but one of the scariest things in the dark is silence. That's right: When the room is quiet and you're sitting in the dark, even the smallest sound can be deafening.

Your mind starts playing tricks, especially if you can't immediately recognize the sound. What was that noise? Who or *what* made it? How close was it? Is it near *me*?

Here's a trick to make sure that your friends experience some sounds from the dead during your séance: Before the night of your haunting, record with a few, short unusual sounds on an audiotape. Leave a few minutes blank at the beginning of the tape, then space out the noises about three or five minutes apart.

> *First-Person Phantoms*
>
> When Lynn Northrup, my development editor, was about 11 years old, she and her friends tried to hold a séance. They crowded into a small, pitch-black furnace room, and everyone held hands. When they asked for that all-important sign that the spirit was with them, lo and behold, the furnace kicked in! It turned on regularly, of course, but because of the timing, she and the rest of the kids got a good scare out of it. Ah, the power of the dark!

Now, don't use any obvious or exaggerated sounds, such as screams or rattling chains. Instead, you want to find noises that will fire your friends' imaginations in the dark. Record subtle, unidentifiable sounds, like whispers or shuffling. Maybe a coin dropping onto the floor. A sudden thud, a door slamming, or a coffee cup breaking will make everyone jump in his or her seat.

Have the tape player in the next room or hidden somewhere some distance from where you'll be setting up the séance table. Your friends shouldn't be able to tell what direction the sound is coming from.

Of course, you have to be able to turn on the tape player without anyone knowing you're doing it. Perhaps the easiest way is to have the plug or on/off control located next to the lamp or light switch in the room. When you turn off the light, start the tape. The unrecorded space at the beginning will give you time to make your way back to table, join hands, and quiet everyone down.

The Big Chill

Want to make your friends feel the cold, clammy hands of the spirits in the dark? Actually, they'll be feeling a fan blowing air on their faces. But given the way you've prepared them with all of those strange stories, in their mind's eye it won't be a fan at all. It will be a ghost! All you need is a timer switch—one of those special adapter plugs that turns on the lights while you're away to fool burglars.

Needless to say, for this ruse to work, the fan has to be hidden or disguised. It should be noiseless and put on its lowest setting. Ideally, the fan should be one of those that move back and forth so there's no steady breeze coming from a single, detectable direction.

This effect should be used sparingly and done very briefly. You don't want to give your friends enough time to realize that it's just a fan that they're feeling. They're supposed to imagine that it's a ghost breathing down their necks or perhaps floating by.

Phantastic Tips _____

This "special effect" works best if you've psychologically prepared your friends in advance. When you're swapping stories, tell them how ghosts are often "felt" rather than seen. The most common experience, you tell, is a sudden chill, a cold spot in the room, or a rapid drop in temperature with no apparent cause. You don't have to worry about making these stories up: You'll find plenty of real-life examples throughout this book.

The Secret Assistant

Mediums usually ask people to join hands in the dark. They say it connects the sitters not only physically but also psychically. It also supposedly keeps the medium honest. How could anything sneaky be going on if all the people around the table are holding onto each other? (And, although the medium never points it out, holding hands also prevents anyone else from interfering with the "spirits" if they do turn up.)

As you've seen in earlier chapters, fraudulent spiritualists developed many ways to get their hands and bodies free to do their dirty work. As you'll see in Chapter 23, stage illusionists used many of the same methods in their acts. Houdini, for instance, made a career out of escaping from ropes and other restraints. He never revealed his own secrets, but in later years he frequently exposed those of fake mediums.

Escaping from such bindings is a specialized skill and requires years of practice. So, for most people, the easiest way to produce spectral sights and sounds in the séance room is by using a secret assistant. The professionals did it; why shouldn't you?

Phantastic Tips _____

Here's a sneaky alternative to having a secret assistant at the table. It's risky, but you can do wonders when it works. After sitting at the table but before you turn out the lights, have everyone put both hands palm-down on the table. Ask them to spread out their fingers and lightly touch their little fingers with those of the people sitting immediately next to them. Then, get up and turn out the lights. When you return to the table, place only one hand back onto the tabletop. Remind all the people to keep their fingers touching. The friends on both sides of you will move their hands in closer to yours. One of the people will actually touch your thumb, thinking it's your little finger. Your other hand will be free to produce spirit phenomena.

The aide in your adventures could be someone already in the room—a mole among your guests. It's just that the others can't know that you and one of your friends are in cahoots.

When you sit down at the séance table, make sure that your helper sits next to you and will be holding one of your hands. Once the lights go out, you can let go. Just think what you two can pull out of your pockets in the dark!

It's also possible to have a helper or two, separate from the group at the table, who can sneak into the room in the dark. They should dress in black and cover their hands and faces with black gloves and hoods so that they can't be seen. They have to be able to enter and exit the room secretly and silently. But when they're there, what marvels they can make!

Here are just a few of the ethereal miracles they can produce:

♦ A secret assistant could be the one to turn that fan on or start your audiotape recording of spectral sounds.

♦ A black thread slid along people's skin will feel like a spirit has touched them.

♦ A gentle spray from a water bottle mister (like the ones used to dampen the leaves of house plants) feels like the insubstantial essence of a spirit, as if the ghost passed right through you.

♦ Objects could fall off a bookshelf.

♦ Ghostly ectoplasm could appear or float through the air. (Of course, this would actually be gauze treated with luminous paint that the assistant has kept hidden inside a black bag or in a pocket. The light must be very faint so that the helper won't be seen in its glow. In the dark, a little luminous paint goes a long way!)

♦ When the lights later come up, it's discovered that a framed picture on the wall has tilted. Perhaps it was a photograph of the person whose spirit showed up in the dark?

Not only that: Look to the center of the table. It seems the spirits have left behind presents for everyone! (Remember those apports you read about in the last chapter?) What better way to finish our séance and leave our haunted house than by receiving a few parting gifts?

You know, it's all well and good to be able to call up the spirits. But how do you track them down on someone else's turf? And what do you do if phantoms show up when you don't want them? Time to call out the ghost hunters and the ghostbusters!

The Least You Need to Know

- ◆ Ghost photographs can be made by a variety of methods, such as double exposures, time-lapse photography, and the creative use of focus and light.

- ◆ Table-tipping, ghost detectors, and ouija boards can be explained by unconscious muscular movements known as ideomotor responses.

- ◆ Secret assistants can help create otherworldly effects in a darkened séance room.

- ◆ With special preparation, any house can appear to be haunted!

Part 3

Who Ya Gonna Call?

Quicker than you can say, "Boo!" spirit and paranormal researchers began to examine the extraordinary claims of mediums. Before long, haunted houses were being staked out. Ghost sightings were studied. Some ghost hunters (and a ghostbuster or two) founded highly respected societies for psychical investigation.

And why not? If you have to track down or get rid of a ghost, you might want to try what that old movie suggested: "Who ya gonna call? *Ghost-busters*!" Sounds like good advice to me. But what about you? Could you be a ghost hunter? Once you learn the methods of the professional ghost stalkers, you'll be ready to start out on your own—if you dare!

Can your trust your own senses? How do you interpret what you've seen and heard on your nocturnal stakeout? How can you tell if that noise was a ghost or just a creaky floorboard? If the apparition or phenomenon you experienced wasn't a ghost, and you can't explain it away by some natural cause, what else could it have been? Finally, what do you do if you find a ghost but you really don't want it around? What if the spirit turns out to be just plain evil? It might be time to call in an exorcist!

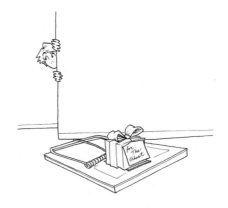

10

Ghost Hunters and Ghostbusters

In This Chapter

- ◆ The Society for Psychical Research gets its start
- ◆ Early psychic and paranormal investigation
- ◆ Paranormal associations
- ◆ Ghost hunters Harry Price and Hans Holzer
- ◆ Ghostbusters and exorcists

The study of ghosts, apparitions, and paranormal phenomena began in earnest in the first half of the nineteenth century. Up until that time, ghosts were variously considered to be the spirits of the dead, demons, angels, or a combination of all three, depending upon the culture or civilization in which you lived.

The impetus for serious investigation was the claim that mediums were producing spirits in the séance room. The spectres weren't just showing up: They were being summoned—and on a regular basis!

What better time to try to find out if ghosts were real?

The Beginnings of the Society for Psychical Research

The Society for Psychical Research, or SPR, was founded in London in 1882. It was the most important early association dedicated to the systematic study of ghost activity. It grew out of the Spiritualism craze that swept England in the 1870s, but its purpose was to examine spirit activity in the light of scientific knowledge and religious beliefs. In addition to ghost and poltergeist phenomena, the SPR also involved itself in the study of hypnosis, ESP, and other paranormal topics.

The key members of the original organization were Henry Sidgwick, Frederic W. H. Myers, and Edmund Gurney, all of whom were Fellows of Trinity College at Cambridge. Myers was fascinated by an appearance of the control John King at an 1873 séance, and he asked Sidgwick and Gurney to help him investigate. Soon after, Myers put together an informal association of friends and intellectuals for the purpose of examining ghosts. Other original members of this Sidgwick Group, as it became known, were Arthur Balfour and his sister Eleanor (who married Sidgwick in 1876).

Ghostly Pursuits

One of the goals of paranormal investigators has always been to come up with one workable theory that can accommodate all types of apparitional and spectral phenomena, including ghosts, poltergeists, spirit communications through mediums, hauntings, and so on.

In 1882, Sir William Barrett, several spiritualists, and others expanded the Sidgwick Group to form the Society for Psychical Research, with Sidgwick as its first president. Among the SPR's other early leading members was G. N. M. Tyrrell, who became known for his theoretical work on apparitions. Chemist/physicist Sir William Crookes (see Chapter 7) and author Sir Arthur Conan Doyle, both confirmed Spiritualists, also joined. Years later, psychoanalyst Sigmund Freud and psychiatrist Carl G. Jung became members as well.

How Do You Characterize a Ghost? An Early SPR Survey

Well, where do you start? First, the SPR had to define a ghost or apparition. Here's a simplified explanation of their thinking: Imagine a material, nonphysical "being" from which all corporeal components (flesh and bones) have been removed. Yet all other characteristics by which we perceive that person (including their personality or soul) has survived. What you'd have remaining would be a ghost or apparition.

One of the first studies undertaken by the SPR was an investigation that they called a Census of Hallucinations. Their initial survey split ghosts into three broad categories:

◆ Apparitions of people who were still alive

◆ Apparitions of the dying (including those that appeared to others at the moment of death)

◆ Apparitions of the dead

The first question of the survey was: "Have you ever, when believing yourself to be completely awake, had a vivid impression of seeing or being touched by a [spectral] being or inanimate object, or of hearing a voice; which impression, as far as you could discover, was not due to any external physical cause?" Approximately 9.9 percent of 17,000 people sampled replied yes; the clear majority of those were women.

As a result of their research, the society came up with a list of more than 20 general characteristics of ghosts, most of which clearly distinguish them from living human beings. Ghosts …

◆ Can pass through walls, closed doors, or other solid objects.

◆ Often perceive and react to objects around them. They sometimes behave as if they were totally aware of their surroundings, coming in through doors, not walls. They move around furniture, not pass through it. If the ghost moves through a house, it uses staircases and hallways, established pathways or routes taken by the living.

◆ Can be perceived by multiple viewers (a so-called "collective" case), although sometimes the ghost appears to some but not all of the people in the group.

◆ Are visible and audible only to certain people.

◆ Sometimes, though rarely, feel solid to the touch.

◆ Are sometimes, though rarely, reflected in mirrors.

◆ Sometimes cast shadows or block the light if they pass in front of a candle or lamp.

◆ Can be penetrated. You can walk or pass your hands through them without meeting any physical resistance.

◆ Appear and disappear in unexplainable ways, even in locked rooms.

◆ Disappear while you're watching them.

◆ Sometimes become transparent and fade away.

◆ Leave behind no physical evidence or traces, such as footprints.

◆ Are often perceived by animals, especially family or domesticated pets, even if any humans in the room don't sense anything out of the ordinary.

◆ Almost always occupy the center of your field of vision.

- Appear three-dimensional, not like a flat projection. You could walk all around the apparition and see it from all angles.

- Are often accompanied by a feeling of cold. Either the room temperature drops, there is an icy breeze or wind, or, if the ghost touches you, the apparition feels cold.

- Sometimes first appear as a "presence": You wake up with a start or you "feel" some entity in the room. Often, you sense someone or something staring at you from behind.

- Can create the physical sensation of pressure weighing against your body.

- Usually won't show up on photographs, film, or video.

- Are often silent. If they do speak or make noise, the sound usually won't record on audiotape.

- Might glow.

- Sometimes change their appearance as you're looking at them.

First-Person Phantoms

While attending UCLA, Ronna Kajikawa moved with her family to an apartment near campus. One evening, their dog Auggie Doggie, a mixed breed—collie, shepherd, and chow—started barking and wouldn't stop. This was unusual because Auggie was usually a quiet creature. The family noticed that the dog's eyes were fixated at the top of the front door, as if someone or something was perched above it. Auggie continued to bark until he was taken outside. This happened at least a half dozen times in the next few weeks. Each time, the dog directed his barking at the emptiness above at the door. Then, one day the barking stopped as suddenly as it had started. The family was convinced that Auggie had scared off a poltergeist or ghost who was visiting their home.

It's All in How You Perceive It

The SPR survey probably raised more questions than it answered. Many of the characteristics appeared to conflict with one another. How could they all be true?

The answer lay in the person who sees the ghost. Our senses deliver information to our brain, which then sorts and analyzes the data to make a perception. For example, we see something red with a long green tube attached; we touch it and feel a prick; we smell an attractive scent. Our brain decides that it's a rose.

Thus, each person who comes in contact with a ghost perceives it through the five— and some would say more—senses. Some people see it; others might hear it; others experience some combination of these or other senses. Our brains analyze these sense responses to identify that what we're seeing is a ghost.

Phantastic Tips

Ghost researchers made an interesting discovery that might "prove" ghosts are real rather than being mere hallucinations. In all reported cases, if the people closed their eyes, they no longer saw the ghost. Perceiving the ghost depended on their being able to *see* it.

Ever See a Naked Ghost?

One of the earliest quandaries to puzzle investigators was, "Why do ghosts wear clothing?" A ghost is thought to be the spirit of a human being, but the clothing was never alive. Cloth has no soul, so it can't come back from the dead. Is the apparition wearing ghost pants?

This query, of course, immediately brings up the larger question, "Is it possible for *any* inanimate object to become a ghost?" After all, phantom horses, carriages, or other nonhuman objects have frequently been reported. Where do these objects come from?

Paranormals theorized that apparitions are perceived as complete entities. The only way the mind can identify the spirit is in a recognizable human form, which would include all of its usual trappings.

Tyrrell suggested that ghosts are seen as part of a hallucinatory drama or theme; the person who sees a ghost fills in any missing parts of the vision. Thus, you might see a ghost approach a door, open it, and pass through it, even though the actual physical door never moves. You "see" what is dramatically appropriate, whether or not it actually happens.

Baby, It's Cold Inside

Another question that still baffles investigators today is why haunted rooms have cold spots, icy breezes, or temperature shifts.

Some researchers, including Tyrrell, have hypothesized that the mental shock of seeing or sensing a ghost might cause a physical reaction in the viewer in such a way that the body produces a chill. Others have suggested that the reduced temperature is caused by a temporary opening of a portal to the Other Realm. Or maybe ghosts are just unpleasantly cold.

Other Research Organizations

The Society for Psychical Research was not the only group investigating paranormal activity in the nineteenth century. The London Dialectical Society, for example, was formed in the late 1860s to conduct inquiries similar to those of the SPR.

The Ghost Club, a private organization in London that looks into ghost phenomena, actually predates the SPR. It's been around in one form or another since 1862. The Ghost Club is the oldest existing organization to research paranormal matters, having been predated only by the now-defunct Cambridge Ghost Club. The Ghost Club was originally established primarily to scrutinize the Davenport brothers (see Chapter 7). Over the years, the Ghost Club has shared many members with the SPR, but currently membership is by invitation only.

In late 1884 or early 1885, the SPR helped found the American Society for Psychical Research, or ASPR, in Boston. After the first few years, the ASPR has operated independently of the SPR, although they share almost identical goals. Originally, their main difference was that the majority of the ASPR's members were Spiritualists, not scientists. In 1925, arguments over the investigation of the fraudulent medium Margery (Mina Stinson Crandon) led several members to break away and form a splinter group, the Boston Society for Psychical Research; but the organization merged with the ASPR in 1941.

> **Ghostly Pursuits**
>
> The Ghost Research Society has found that 70 to 85 percent of ghostly phenomena have explainable natural causes. But what about the rest?

In the 1950s, the ASPR became more involved with the study of extrasensory perception (ESP) and psychic phenomena other than ghosts. Much of their analysis focused on the laboratory trials being performed by J. B. Rhine at Duke University.

The Price Is Right: Harry Price

Harry Price (1881–1948) was, perhaps, the most famous ghost hunter of the first half of the twentieth century. In his 1942 autobiography, *Search for Truth: My Life for Psychical Research*, he claimed to have had his first paranormal experience in a haunted house at the age of 15. He became interested in magic at an early age, and it was partly because of this that the SPR, which he had joined in 1920, sent him to investigate the spirit photographer William Hope (see Chapter 7). Price's findings were inconclusive;

some accused Price, not Hope, of trickery. Price also investigated Dorothy Stella Cranshaw, who worked as a medium under the name "Stella C." Price was actually quite impressed with her work, which caused consternation among both his magician friends and SPR associates.

Price started the National Laboratory of Psychical Research, which is now part of London University, and he wrote voluminously about his investigations. Throughout his career, his methods, conclusions, and even his honesty, frequently came under fire.

Price is best known, however, for his high-profile investigation of "the most haunted house in England," the Borley Rectory, from 1929 until 1944. (We'll take a closer look at the Borley Rectory case in Chapter 14.)

Price died suddenly of a heart attack on March 29, 1948. After his death, there were reports for a time that his spirit had returned. He supposedly appeared in Sweden by the bedside of a man whom the case histories call Erson. Erson spoke no English, but somehow he was able to figure out that the solid-looking phantom was named Price. The spectre began to appear regularly to Erson, his wife, and daughter. The young Swede attempted to take photographs of the ghost, but no image ever appeared. The phantom Price advised Erson to go to a particular hospital for a health problem. While he was there, Erson talked to a doctor who was interested in the paranormal. From Erson's description of the elderly phantom, the doctor was able to identify him as the British ghost investigator Harry Price. Now, why the ghost of Price would want to travel to a different country, materialize for someone who didn't speak English and who had no interest in the paranormal ... well, no one knows. It's just one of those mysteries.

The Ghost Hunter Himself: Hans Holzer

No list of ghost hunters and ghostbusters would be complete without a mention of Hans Holzer (b. 1920). His investigations often rely on the use of mediums at haunted sites.

Holzer's first book, *Ghost Hunter*, led to numerous television and radio appearances, so he took the book's title as his nickname. A ubiquitous personality in paranormal investigation, Holzer has published more than a hundred books and other works on ghosts, paranormal phenomena, and related activities. He's also produced and narrated several television and film documentaries on the Spirit World.

Holzer studied at Columbia University and the University of Vienna, and received a doctorate from the London College of Applied Science. For eight years, he taught parapsychology at the New York Institute of Technology. Currently, he heads the Center for Paranormal Studies and lives in New York.

You're Busted

Most people who call in a ghost hunter do so because they want to know who or what is haunting them; often they want to get rid of the spirit—or at least they want the haunting to stop!

Frequently, a ghost hunter can act as a ghostbuster as well. Many ghosts leave on their own accord as soon as they:

◆ Are asked to go. (It's amazing how polite some ghosts can be.)

◆ Are told to leave. (You just have to be a little more firm with some of them.)

◆ Find out they're dead. (Some aren't aware they're no longer alive, especially those who died suddenly or unexpectedly.)

◆ Have the "situation" properly explained to them. (The ghost is dead and belongs among its own kind, not among the living. It's time to move on to their rest and reward on the Other Side.)

◆ Have their corporeal remains properly buried.

◆ Complete an unfinished deed or action they returned (or stayed) to do.

Exorcise Your Demons

If the ghostbuster is unsuccessful after trying these civilized methods of ghost removal, or if the spirit seems to be truly evil, then it might be time to consider bringing in the big guns: an exorcist!

Exorcists are the ultimate ghostbusters. But an *exorcism* is usually reserved for a worst-case scenario—an extreme situation in which a person or place is possessed by a demon rather than by your everyday mild-mannered ghost.

Phantom Phrases

Exorcism is the expulsion of demons, spirits, ghosts, or other entities thought to be possessing a human being or haunting a location.

Exorcists have existed since ancient times. The word "exorcism" comes from the Greek *exousia* (meaning "oath") and the Latin *adjuro* (meaning "demands.") Hence, an exorcist makes an oath to (calls on) a Higher Power, asking for the spirit's removal and adjures (commands) the devilish or troublesome spectre to follow the exorcist's orders.

Exorcists usually work within the doctrine and rites of an established religion, because their work is often perceived as a battle of Good versus Evil and a fight for a person's soul. Exorcisms are performed in almost all cultures and faiths, including Judaism, Christianity, Islam, Hinduism, Buddhism, and Taoism—even among animistic societies.

Roman Catholicism is the only Christian sect to have a formal rite of exorcism. Called the *Rituale Romanum*, the ceremony dates to 1614 and was updated for the first time in January 1999. (Protestant ministers perform exorcisms as well, but there's no established ritual.)

So what does an exorcist actually say and do? To prepare for the Catholic ritual, a priest says prayers and blessings, sprinkles holy water, and makes the sign of the cross over the possessed person. According to Father Amorth, currently the official exorcist for the diocese of Rome, contact with the sacred objects often provokes an immediate physical—sometimes violent—reaction from the afflicted individual.

Whether sacred or secular, the exorcism culminates with the evil spirit being commanded to leave the person's body.

Exorcism rituals are used to "dispossess" a demon from its human host. But there's no established rite for removing ghosts from haunted *places*. In such situations, ghostbusters and exorcists perform the ceremony at the haunted site. Some paranormals like to conduct the ritual while standing inside the safety of a "magic circle" that they've drawn on the floor or ground.

Whether it's removing an unwanted spirit from a person, place, or thing, ghostbusting and exorcism don't always work. Sometimes it must be repeated a number of times before the hauntings end. Even when ghostbusters are seemingly successful, the spirits may return. Occasionally several exorcisms are required to completely eliminate the unwanted presence.

Chances are slim that you'll ever come up against evil or demonic entities on a ghost hunt. Chances are even more remote that you'll ever need the services of an exorcist. Still, it's comforting to know what to do and who to call if you need one.

The future of paranormal investigation may be *you!* Continue on to the next chapter to learn the guidelines set down by other researchers, and get ready to put together your own ghost-hunting gear!

 Boo!

> If you ever suspect that you, someone you know, or a location is haunted or possessed by a demon, poltergeist, or other malignant being, do not attempt to exorcise the spirit by yourself! Seek out an expert, whether it's a professional ghost investigator or a religious advisor. You may be dealing with forces you aren't equipped to handle alone.

The Least You Need to Know

- ◆ Although predated by other paranormal associations, the Society for Psychical Research was the first major institution dedicated to the scientific investigation of ghost and spirit phenomena.

- ◆ Part of the early research process was defining an apparition and delineating its characteristics from those of living human beings.

- ◆ Harry Price was one of the best-known paranormal investigators of the first half of the twentieth century.

- ◆ Author/investigator Hans Holzer, nicknamed the Ghost Hunter, has published more than a hundred works on ghosts, paranormal phenomena, and related activities.

- ◆ Ghostbusters remove unwelcome ghosts and spirit entities. In extreme cases, exorcists are brought onto the scene, especially when demonic possession is suspected.

Chapter 11

A Method to the Madness: Conducting a Ghost Hunt

In This Chapter

♦ Ghosts investigations vs. ghost hunts

♦ Advice from the pros on conducting a ghost hunt

♦ The importance of doing your research

♦ What to take along in your ghost hunter's field kit

♦ Sorting through the data

Ready to go on a ghost hunt? Let's take a look at the techniques of some of the pioneers in paranormal investigation, then apply their methods and discoveries to modern-day ghost detection.

In the next few pages, you'll find tips to help you during all three parts of a ghost hunt: What you have to know and what preparations to make before you go, what to look for and what to do while you're out there in the dark, and what to do with all the data you collect. Hopefully, by the time you finish this chapter you'll be prepared to join a ghost investigation or set out on a ghost hunt of your own.

What's the Difference?

Although the terms are sometimes used interchangeably, ghost investigations and ghost hunts are very different things, even though they have the same goal: to sight and record spectral activity. A ghost investigation is a carefully controlled, scientific research project of a location known, reported, or presumed (though usually with probable cause) to be haunted. Most investigations are instigated at the request of the owner or resident of the property, although researchers sometimes ask the owner or resident for permission to investigate properties that are reputed to be haunted.

A ghost hunt, on the other hand, is simply an attempt to sight or sense a ghost, often in a location where there's been no previously reported paranormal activity. Ghost hunters usually choose a location just because there are rumors that it's haunted or similar sites have been haunted (such as cemeteries or decrepit buildings).

Call in the Troops

You know how, when you get a leaky pipe, you crawl down under the sink with your wrench and pliers and you sorta get it fixed, then suddenly the whole pipe bursts open and you get soaking wet? So you wind up calling a professional plumber, which is what you should have done in the first place?

It's kind of like that with ghost hunting. You can set up your own cameras, tape recorders, and booby traps. But if you're really serious about tracking down a ghost, you'll probably need the services of a professional.

The Society for Psychical Research set the standard for paranormal investigations way back at the end of the nineteenth century. They, and other societies like them, have conducted field studies of thousands of sites for more than a century. Many of the organizations you might consider contacting were profiled in the last chapter. You can find their names and addresses, along with those of some independent ghost hunters, in Appendix A.

First-Person Phantoms

In 1998, Bryan Wood was a member of the Australian Skeptics. Although everyone in the Melbourne club knew it was unlikely that Bryan would ever be convinced that ghosts exist, he was challenged to visit a particular house that was said to be haunted. It had been empty for a long time, so the house was both foul-smelling and very dirty. A group of around eight people came along for the evening.

Bryan says, "Even now I do not believe in ghosts. I live just across the road from a cemetery; believing in ghosts would be far too time consuming! But I can tell you that there's *nothing* scarier than walking through a dark, old house with a group of people who are all convinced that *everything* is a ghost."

If the wind blew, it was a ghost. A car drove past; that was a ghost, too. Everyone was screaming and jumping up and down so much that any spooks in the area would have been scared off long before the ghost hunters got to them.

They walked through the place for about an hour. One person brought a ouija board and tried to contact the "dearly departed." But the spirits remained silent. Paranormals might blame the ghosts' nonappearance on Bryan's disbelief; he would say that spirits can't show up if they don't even exist. The moral of the story? Go on a ghost hunt with an open mind. Try not to carry preconceptions about whether a site is actually haunted or not.

Do Your Homework Before You Start

Just for the fun of it, let's say you want to stake out someplace on your own and conduct a ghost hunt. How do you begin?

First, I can't stress enough the importance of prior, and proper, research before you begin a ghost hunt. Your first tool as a psychic investigator is always research. It helps you to know exactly what you're looking for and makes it easier for you to recognize phantom phenomena when you do find (or see) it.

Although most of the tidbits you learn during your pre-hunt inquiries will probably lead nowhere, you might find that one piece of information that helps everything else fall into place. In addition, with a stack of documents under your arm, you'll boost your credibility with others and make your own findings harder to dispute or contradict later on.

It's also a good idea to ascertain who's already researched the site. Have other investigators been there before you, and if so, what did they discover? Were their methods reliable? Do you agree with their findings?

Don't automatically assume the current resident is also the owner. Find out everything you can about the property and its history: the address, former residents, former owners, current resident, current owner (including liens on the property).

Where can you find all of this information?

- The County Registrar-Recorder office keeps records of deeds, real estate transactions and voting rolls, as well as birth, death, marriage, and divorce certificates for that county. Look under the government pages in the local phone book.

- Public Utilities and Motor Vehicle Registration offices. (Privacy laws are being enacted in some areas to prevent the release of this information.)

- The public library.

- Historical societies (city, county, and state).

- Church and cemetery records.

- Current and former residents.

- Current and former owners.

- Current and former neighbors.

Sometimes finding out all the information is as easy as knocking on the door of the house you want to investigate. If you want to do a ghost hunt on the property, you're going to have to talk to the residents at some point anyway. They can usually provide you with almost everything you need to know. And, if they can't, a nosy neighbor probably can.

Phantastic Tips

While you're pumping the residents, neighbors, and owners for information on the history of the buildings and property, don't forget to ask them whether they've ever seen any ghosts or other paranormal activity. You might be surprised by what you hear—and it may make your job a whole lot easier!

Why is it so important to establish the identities of all the owners and residents of the property throughout the years? Because many times these are the people whose ghosts are haunting it. Sometimes paranormal activity is attached to an event that took place on the site before the structure was built.

Also find out *how* and *why* the property changed hands. This is especially useful if it's thought that a spirit is haunting the grounds to right a wrong or to complete some activity—hence, the need to find out as much of the personal histories of all the current and former owners and residents as possible.

Whenever you can, double-check and crosscheck your information. Again, this will increase your credibility as a researcher among your peers, interested parties, and skeptics. It will also make the results of your investigation stronger and more valid.

Look Before You Leap

Two words: permission and safety. For starters, you need permission just to go on private property. Some public areas, such as parks or cemeteries, may have restricted visiting hours. It may be unlawful to park on the shoulder of the haunted highway you want to stake out. Always check ahead of time.

Play it safe! The archetypal haunted house is old and has rickety stairs and rotted, easy-to-fall-through floors. If the house is in a state of decay, there will probably be lots of opportunities to step on rusty nails or get cut with shards of glass, so have your tetanus shot up-to-date.

Boo!

You don't want to be accused of trespassing on private property. Look for "No Trespassing" signs. And obey them! You want to protect yourself legally, especially should there be any damage or injuries during the ghost hunt. If a "Stay Out" sign is posted, you could still ask the owner to make an exception.

You might be surprised to find a transient living, finding temporary shelter, or hiding there. The building might be infested with all sorts of other living creatures, like bats and raccoons, both of which have large rabies populations. Oh, then there are the spiders, and rats, and snakes, oh, my! Again, always be careful for your own physical well-being. You're trying to see a ghost, not become one.

Ghost-Hunting Advice from a Pro

Let's look to the experts for advice. Harry Price, who you read about in the last chapter, wrote one of the first "how to" guides on investigating haunted houses. The pamphlet, called "The Blue Book," was issued in conjunction with his examination of the Borley Rectory in 1937 and 1938. Among his many suggestions were the following:

♦ Establish a base in one room and keep all of your equipment there when it's not in use. This will prevent having to search for an item when it's needed.

♦ Keep a working flashlight in your pocket at all times.

♦ Be careful with flammable objects, such as matches, candles, and cigarettes.

◆ Always observe the area in question for the half-hour before and after dusk. These are especially active times for spirit phenomena.

◆ If you're part of a team and you experience a very strong phenomenon, or if a succession of phenomena occur, immediately contact the rest of your group (or a partner with whom you made previously arrangements) to also record the activities in detail. Others may be able to assist you or corroborate your sightings.

◆ Be courteous to strangers and personal friends if they meet you on site, but don't allow untrained assistants to help or join you. They may do more harm than good.

◆ Check measurements on your instruments regularly to be sure they're in working condition. Record all readings and the times at which they're taken. Note anything that appears unusual when you first notice it.

◆ Spend at least part of the day and night prior to an investigation in a totally dark room. This will get you accustomed to periods in the dark and will make your eyes sensitive to even the dimmest light.

The very-much-alive Harry Price (seated) is visited by a spectral female being. Though Price believed in spirit photography, he rejected this example as a double exposure.

(Author's collection)

In the same guide, Price pointed out some possible phenomena ghost hunters might experience, along with his recommendations on what to do if they occur:

◆ **Noises.** Try to judge where they came from. Record in a notebook at what time and for what duration they were heard. If the sound seems to move, try to determine its origin, the direction in which it travels, and how long it continues. If you can determine the type of sound, make descriptive observations. For example, in the case of footsteps, were they soft, heavy, or shuffling? Did they sound like shoes, high heels, boots, or slippers? Were the steps regular, did they start and stop, or did it sound like limping?

◆ **Moving objects.** If an object is seen or heard to move, identify the room in which it occurred, what item moved, and in which direction it moved. Draw a rough map of the room, noting the path of the motion. Estimate how much force must have been needed to move it. Did the object float? Did it crash? If the object is seen in motion, record its speed, direction, force, and trajectory. In any case, examine the object after the motion for any changes it may have undergone, and return it to its original position.

Phantastic Tips

Take the guesswork out of your ghost investigation. Use chalk to outline moveable objects so that, later, you'll have proof that they actually did shift. Put marks around anything you suspect the ghost might want to play around with. Two good bets: anything that was owned by a deceased person or anything that's been reported as having moved on its own in the past.

◆ **Forms or apparitions.** If you see a ghost, don't move. Remain absolutely silent, try to control the rate and loudness of your breathing, and, most important, don't approach the spectre. Note at what time and for what duration it appears. Record everything it does, including any mannerisms and gestures, that might help you identify the spirit later. Determine its path and the speed at which it travels. Observe its characteristics, such as height, shape, size, color, density, wardrobe or costume, accoutrements such as a cane, attendant animals or vehicles, speech, or sounds. If you have a camera, take as many photos as possible, being careful to minimize noise (such as that of the lens shutter).

In the Shadows: Tips from a Shadow Lord

Dave Juliano, who as Shadow Lord manages "The Shadowlands" website (see Appendix A), has had more than 30 years of experience investigating hauntings. He discourages untrained amateurs from conducting their own ghost hunts and directs them to several groups established for that purpose.

The following are among his many tips for those who insist on ghost hunting on their own:

♦ Do an initial daytime reconnaissance so you will know the area in the dark.

♦ Do your ghost hunt between 9 P.M. and 6 A.M. Historically, that's the most active time for ghost phenomena to take place, although it's possible for spirit behavior to occur at any time. Juliano notes that the best ghost photographs have also been taken in the dark.

♦ *Never go alone!* If there are several people going on the hunt, break off into pairs or small groups.

Boo! _____

Recycling is a good thing. But always work with brand-new audio, video, and film materials every time you do any ghost hunting. You want to avoid the possibility of accidental double-exposures or accusations of having fabricated evidence.

Boo! _____

Don't smoke while on a ghost hunt. First of all, fire, burning ash, and still-burning butts are safety hazards, especially if you're in an old building or a dry field. Plus, others may wrongly perceive the dim glow of a cigarette to be spectral phenomena. And no alcohol: You want to be in complete control of your senses!

♦ Always take photo identification with you in case you're stopped and questioned by police, owners, or other authorities.

♦ Carry a log to record all activity. Record the date, the time, and the weather at the start of your ghost hunt, and enter any changes that occur.

♦ Be sure you're working with clean, fresh materials (film, audiotape, plastic bags) and, to prevent contamination, wait until you're on site to open and load your film, videotape, and audiotape. Juliano suggests though that this will alert "aware" spirits of your intentions, which I suppose could be a good or a bad thing depending upon whether the ghosts feel in the mood to cooperate.

♦ Make a quick walk of the area immediately before setting up shop, noting conditions so that you can recognize any changes or activity when it does occur.

♦ Take videotape and still photos, and keep a tape recorder going continuously during the hunt. Be quiet. Don't even whisper. You don't want your voice picked up on tape and have it be mistaken later for electronic voice phenomena (EVP).

Remember, we're talking ghosts here. Just because you don't sense, see, or hear anything, doesn't mean a ghost's not there and recordable. Quite often, ghost activity isn't discovered until much later, when the sound recording is listened to, the film is developed, or the videotape is watched.

Dave Juliano adds two personal, optional tips. He recommends that you start any ghost hunt or investigation by asking for protection from whatever Higher Power you believe in. He also suggests that, as you finish up a ghost hunt, you ask any ghosts and spirits present to stay there and not follow you home!

Call me old-fashioned, but I'd also take a silver cross and some holy water.

Your Ghost-Hunting Bag of Tricks

In your attempt to see a ghost, you're going to be sitting out or walking for hours, probably at night. In such situations, few things could be worse than needing something and knowing that you left it at home.

You carry a first-aid kit on camping trips. What kind of kit should you be carrying with you on your ghost hunt?

Some of these are commonsense items. Others have been recommended by ghost-hunting experts. There are probably other things that you'll want to take along that are important just to you. When it's time to do the final packing for the ghost hunt, you'll have to decide for yourself what to take.

This only makes sense, but you should always wear appropriate clothing to keep warm and dry, and your ghost hunter's field kit should always contain food and water. With your basic physical needs out of the way, you'll also want to bring:

♦ A watch. (And a stop watch, if you're obsessive or just want to be precise about timing the duration of phenomena.)

♦ At least one 35 mm camera with high-speed film (at *least* 400 ASA) for shooting in low light. You might consider a second camera loaded with high-speed black-and-white film.

♦ Video camera. Bring a tripod if you can't hold your camera steady or if it doesn't have gyroscopic correction for shakiness. Trust me, if you actually do see a ghost, chances are good you'll start trembling.

Phantastic Tips

Some ghost hunters have had success taking photographs with infrared film, or simply by placing a red gel over the flash unit. If you're using anything other than a point-and-shoot camera, learn how to set your camera to snap shots in available light without the use of a flash.

- Audio recorder with an external (not built-in) microphone, with a wind cover over the head of the mike. Some experts recommend using high-grade metal tape. Regardless, you should only record on one side of the audiotape to prevent any sounds from bleeding over from one side of the tape to the other. You may also want to carry a small, cheap, but reliable back-up tape recorder with a built-in microphone for when your expensive, hotshot unit fails.

- More film and tape than you think you'll ever need. What if you finally see a ghost, and you're out of film?

- A flashlight (and an extra, for when you drop and break the first one), with lots of batteries.

- Candles and matches. (For when you drop and break the second flashlight.) Or, if you prefer, a kerosene lantern for warmth as well as light. But always keep in mind the dangers of an open flame!

- A basic first-aid kit.

- A cellular phone in case of emergency or to contact other team members in a hurry.

- A log or notebook, with sufficient pens and/or pencils. In addition to noting all phenomena and the times that things occur, you'll want to record the *unseen*—what you feel and sense. Also, sketch floor plans of the haunted site and, if you can, draw a quick likeness of any apparitions you see.

- Clean, uncontaminated containers or plastic bags to hold evidence that you collect.

- Chalk, to outline objects and mark paths.

- A compass. Some researchers claim that ghost activity can shift magnetic fields; an unexplained change in the compass needle might indicate a spectral presence. A compass also comes in handy for navigation on back roads and to mark directions on maps you've made.

- A thermometer, to record temperature changes. Icy blasts and cold spots have been reported in almost all ghost literature; temperature shifts of up to 6 to 20 degrees have been reported. Use a standard mercury thermometer. It's thought that some electronic gadgets might be disrupted by those unaccountable changes in magnetic fields.

Good luck catching a ghost! Heck, good luck just trying to carry all that gear out to the car.

Who Goes There?

If you do run into a ghost, it'll probably be just as surprised to see you as vice versa (if it acknowledges you at all). Remember that it was once a living human, and it has chosen or been forced to visit or remain in the material world at that specific location for some reason probably unknown to you.

Ghosts usually aren't dangerous to mortals. They're attending to their own business. But, like humans, ghosts can be good or bad, so be as wary as you would be of any stranger that you're meeting for the first time in a dark room.

 Boo!

Although rare, it's possible that you'll run into a poltergeist or other nonhuman spirit on a ghost hunt. Since many of these spirits are malicious, if not downright malevolent, it's best to avoid them if at all possible. If you do suspect the apparition is a poltergeist or some demonic entity, get outta there as quickly as possible.

After the Hunt: Sorting Through Your Data

Let's say you spent all night staring into the inky darkness, and you didn't see or hear a thing. What do you do with all the data you've collected when you get home? Just throw it out?

No! That could be a big mistake!

When you have your 35 mm film developed, be sure to ask the lab to give you all of the negatives and make prints of all the exposures. Some photography studios don't bother to print what they consider to be dark, under- or overexposures, or otherwise "bad" photos. But that spot or streak that looks *to them* like light leakage or poor photography might be a ghost light or other spectral evidence you're looking for.

Watch those endless hours of video. You may have captured something without knowing it. Scan the entire screen: Not all ghosts automatically take center stage. If you see something odd or unusual, freeze-frame the picture. If you're set up to do so, generate a computer printout of the image. Have you captured a ghost on camera?

Likewise, listen to all of your audiotapes, even if you didn't hear anything while you were recording. You'll be amazed to find out how much ambient noise you've picked up on even the quietest of nights. First of all, identify what sounds you can. To assist you, check your log. You should have made a record of any identifiable sounds (such as a dog barking or a car horn) as they occurred and the time at which you heard them. That'll probably leave only a few unidentifiable noises on the tape.

Almost everything you see or hear, regardless of how unusual it seems, will have a natural explanation. So if you have a recorded sound that you can't explain or pinpoint, don't jump to the conclusion that it's electronic voice phenomenon (see Chapter 4). EVP is very, very rare! If you've been lucky enough to capture a spirit voice, it'll probably have a rasping or grating sound, little more than a hoarse whisper. It may be only one or two words, probably less than a full sentence.

> ### CAUTION Boo!
>
> Listen to any unusual sounds you've captured on tape over and over before you claim that you've recorded a talking ghost. EVP believers contend that the sounds are the voices of the dead, but skeptics insist they're signals from radio, telephone, or television, or that the listener imagines hearing words formed from the static or white noise. I usually chalk up such sounds to the little voices talking to me from inside my head.

So now you know how to get ready for a ghost hunt, how to collect your data, and how to analyze your results with logic, if not a healthy dose of skepticism. Part of that process is asking yourself, "If this spirit activity wasn't caused by a ghost, what did cause it?" So for those of you who still refuse to believe in spirits, let's take a look in our next chapter at what other people have suggested might explain all this spooky, paranormal phenomena.

The Least You Need to Know

◆ Ghost investigations are serious, scientific attempts to locate, identify, and deal with ghosts. Ghost hunts usually are much more informal, and often much more fun!

◆ Always thoroughly research the site at which you plan to set up a ghost investigation or hunt. Even a slight detail might help you track down a ghost.

◆ Always secure permission before walking onto private property.

◆ Safety should be a primary concern when out on a ghost hunt.

◆ Be meticulous in collecting your data, and never discard it until it's been thoroughly examined.

12

If Not a Ghost, Then What?

In This Chapter

- ◆ Telepathic projection as a cause for hallucinogenic ghosts
- ◆ Super-ESP spreads around the spirit phenomena
- ◆ Alternate explanations for ghost activity
- ◆ When ghosts turn out to be fake
- ◆ The Cock Lane Ghost, the Cottingley Fairies, and the Amityville Horror

Reports of apparitions and ghost activity number in the hundreds of thousands, if not millions. Some are so solidly investigated and firmly established that the phenomena itself cannot be questioned. *Something* happened. All that remains is the explanation. *How* or *why* did it happen?

Now a lot of people, and probably most of the people reading this book, would like to believe that all of the weird things we see out there are ghosts, or at least caused by ghosts. But—and I don't know how to break this to you—a lot of it isn't. So let's look at other things paranormal researchers have suggested might cause some of the apparent ghost activity.

What Are Your Thoughts on That?

We have Frederic W. H. Myers and Edmund Gurney, founding members of the Society for Psychical Research (see Chapter 10) to thank for much of the early modern theoretical work on the issue of spirits returning from the Beyond. At first, they both decided that there were no such things as ghosts.

Let me rephrase that. Both Myers and Gurney believed that people saw what they *thought* were ghosts. But, they said, the apparitions were not actual physical entities. They believed that what people were experiencing were only hallucinations caused by the dead. That's right: They thought the spirits of the dead somehow sent a *telepathic projection* of themselves into the minds of a living person. That person then formed a hallucination (the ghost) from the telepathically induced message. (As you'll see in Chapter 19, Myers originally explained sightings of the ghost ship the *Flying Dutchman* as *telepathic projection*.)

Phantom Phrases

The now-discredited theory of **telepathic projection**, first proposed by Frederic W. H. Myers, suggested that spirits of the dead merely sent mental messages to the living rather than physically returning as ghosts. The person's brain then interpreted the psychic impression and used it to produce an external hallucination that resembled a ghost.

In their 1886 work *Phantasms of the Living*, Myers and Gurney were joined by fellow researcher Frank Podmore in suggesting that there was an underlying telepathic explanation for most, if not all, apparitions. They felt this was especially true for spectres of the living, such as crisis apparitions that appear at a time of stress or the moment of death. How could such a vision be a ghost, they reasoned, if the person wasn't even dead yet? In 1888, Myers theorized that *all* apparitions (those of the living *and* the dead) were telepathic in origin.

The Collective Dilemma: A Ghost for All People

If a phantom is a personal hallucination as Myers and Gurney suggested, than how can more than one person sometimes see the same ghost? Even if a spirit *were* able to send out simultaneous thought waves, why would the ghost look the same to everyone? Wouldn't each individual create a unique hallucination?

Myers believed that telepathic projection could be used to explain collective apparitions, as such sightings are called (see Chapter 3). The spirit could be sending a telepathic projection to several people at the same time.

Edmund Gurney's main area of interest was this so-called "collective dilemma." Gurney rejected Myers's explanation out of hand. For it to be true, the spirit would have to send out simultaneous, identical messages to several people, each of whom would then have to psychically transform the "broadcast" into that person's own personal apparition.

Instead, Gurney proposed a telepathic "infection" solution. The spirit would emit a telepathic message to only one specific person. He or she would receive the impulse and would, in turn, send it on to another person who would then also see the ghost.

Myers was quick to object to this idea. He pointed out that there was no research or evidence to suggest that any "normal or nonparanormal hallucinations spread in this fashion."

Doubters of "telepathic projection" and "infection" theories have problems with all of these explanations:

- If the ghost's image is being transmitted by one person, why doesn't it look exactly the same (including the same angle, distance, and perspective) to everyone else who sees it?

- If the ghost is only a hallucination, how can some of them move solid objects? Or do we also have to assume that hallucinations have telekinesis (the ability to move solid objects without touching them, using only the power of the mind)?

- Why do animals react when there are ghosts in the room? Do animals receive and react to telepathic messages as well? Animals often seem to notice invisible presences in the room before humans do—in fact, many times, they respond even though the people present sense nothing. Are the spirits of the dead sending telepathic projections to animals? And, if so, why?

  For that matter, how do we know that animals aren't reacting to a ghost when they snarl, bark, or hiss at empty air? Unless we see or otherwise sense the same ghostly activity at the same time as the animals, there's really no way for us to know for certain. The subject will no doubt continue to be discussed until animals learn to talk—but that's a whole different issue.

- In order to believe in telepathic projection, you must first believe that telepathy itself exists. So far, there's been no documented proof of extrasensory perception (ESP). So pick your poison: Which is easier for you to believe in, telepathic communication or ghosts?

> *First-Person Phantoms*
>
> The night after her father's funeral, Bambi Burnes was sitting in her parents' home in West Holyoke, Massachusetts. The family dog startled barking and howling, loudly and incessantly. Suddenly, Bambi was startled to hear the distinct voice of her father hushing the animal. The dog immediately stopped. When Bambi went to check on their pet the next morning, the gate to its pen was open. After a search, the dog was found dead, curled up inside a patio fireplace that Bambi's father had built. Her only explanation for the events was that her father had indeed returned, quieted the dog, and for whatever reason, opened the gate. Then her father either called his lonely pet to him, or the sad creature had somehow willed itself to join him.

Eventually, all of the arguments against telepathic projection proved persuasive. By the time he wrote *Human Personality and the Survival of Bodily Death* (1903), Myers had abandoned his theory in favor of belief in actual apparitions. He suggested that the ghosts probably were made up of some sort of energy coalescing and focusing into a kind of "phantasmogenic center."

More Than Your Ordinary ESP

In the late 1950s, American sociologist and psychical researcher Hornell Hart (1888–1967) coined the term super-ESP for a theoretical ability that's been debated since the earliest days of paranormal investigation. Essentially, super-ESP is an extraordinarily powerful form of telepathy that would allow mediums to mentally pick up information about the deceased from other living beings, even from great distances. Likewise, mediums possessing super-ESP could mentally project this information in the form of a hallucination that could be perceived by others in the form of a ghost. Not only that, the medium might be doing this without even knowing it!

If, indeed, super-ESP exists, then apparitions would not necessarily be the returning spirits of the dead. They could be hallucinations formed from information mentally gathered from people who knew the deceased. Super-ESP doesn't disprove or negate the question of survival after death, but its existence could explain many ghost sightings.

The concept of super-ESP has generally been rejected by modern paranormal thinkers. After all, they argue, super-ESP requires that you believe people can actually read minds! As with telepathic projection, defenders of super-ESP respond, "Which is harder to believe, that our brains are capable of communicating without speech or that ghosts are real?"

In the 1800s, people believed that proof of the afterlife was provided by *cross correspondences*, a rare but potent phenomenon in which separate mediums at different times and locations received the same or interrelated bits of information from one or more spirits. The catch was that these messages had to be joined together to form a complete and understandable spirit communication.

Those who believe that these messages are coming from the Other Side say that cross correspondences prove that there's life after death. How else could different mediums receive parts of a full message unless a spirit is delivering them piecemeal from Beyond?

Any Other Bright Ideas?

If ghosts aren't real, and even the paranormal experts are backing away from their theories of telepathic contagion, what else could be causing all the apparitions and spectral phenomena?

Here are just a few more alternate explanations:

- **Mental illness.** You could be delusional or deranged—you know, just plain "seeing things."

- **Legend.** A folktale, told often enough, sometimes comes to be believed or accepted as truth.

- **General inaccuracy or distortion of the facts to make a better story.** And if the account is ever published, it's even more likely to be believed. Because, as everyone knows, if it's in print, it has to be true.

- **Indifference to the truth.** Many times, even after the ghostly phenomenon has been investigated and explained away, the ghost legend continues to be recycled because it's more interesting than the truth.

- **Hysterical mistakes.** The mind plays tricks. It's as simple as that. Under momentary mental or physical stress, you can mistake innocent objects and events as being ghosts and spectral phenomena.

> **CAUTION**
>
> **Boo!**
> Are you beginning to get the idea that paranormal skeptics are grasping at straws for some explanation—*any* explanation—for a spectral activity, just so long as it isn't a ghost? Make sure any explanation *you* come up with for spirit activity isn't more outlandish than the possibility that you actually *have* seen a ghost.

◆ **Honest error due to illusion.** A shadow on the wall becomes a monster under the bed. A white curtain fluttering in the moonlight becomes a ghost. The settling of an old house becomes the creaky footsteps of a phantom. A sudden, short breeze becomes the breath of the bogeyman. Need I go on?

◆ **A hoax or deliberate fraud.** Unfortunately, this is one of the more common causes.

In the rest of this chapter, we'll take a closer took at this last possibility.

Why Resort to Fraud?

The reasons for fraud may be as varied as those who perpetrate the deception. But here are some of the most common:

◆ Attention

◆ Excitement

◆ Publicity

◆ Games, just for fun, especially by children fooling their parents and friends

◆ To frighten people away from the area

◆ To destroy property values

◆ For money, especially by those who hope to write about their experiences or sell their story

---

First-Person Phantoms

Australian ghost skeptic Bryan Wood can attest to what happens in the economic decision-making process of otherwise sane people when property they're considering buying has a reputation for being haunted. When the "haunted" estate was put on the market, it remained there for years. In the end, the owners had to tear down the building in order to sell the land. No one would buy the acreage while a haunted house was on it! The site eventually sold to the church next door, but even today it's still just an open field. Bryan says it's the old story: "People say they don't believe in ghosts, but they won't buy a house that has one."

A Real Cock-and-Bull Story: The Cock Lane Ghost

Some researchers date the modern age of ghost hunting—and ghost hoaxes—to 1762, when paranormal events started occurring in a house on Cock Lane in London.

According to legend, around 1760, a parish clerk named Mr. Parsons leased his house on Cock Lane to a stockbroker named Kent. After Kent's wife died, his sister-in-law, Miss Fanny, came to serve as his housekeeper. Kent and Miss Fanny became close and named each other beneficiaries in their wills.

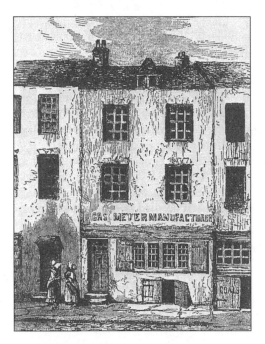

A 1762 engraving of the haunted Parsons house on Cock Lane in London.

Parsons borrowed money from Kent, which may have led to a disagreement over repayment. Regardless, for whatever reason, Kent moved out and soon sued Parsons for the money he was owed. Within two years, Miss Fanny died of smallpox, but Parsons spread the rumor that Kent may have poisoned her.

At the beginning of 1762, people were saying that Miss Fanny had returned to the Cock Lane house to haunt the Parsons family. Elizabeth Parsons, the 12-year-old daughter, swore that she had seen the ghost and that the apparition itself said Kent had poisoned her.

Although no one else actually saw the spectre, many people heard the knockings and scratchings that are so often associated with ghosts. Soon, Elizabeth worked out a rapping code for the ghost to answer questions. Everyone wanted to hear the ghost, and Parsons was more than happy to admit them to his home—for a small fee, of course.

A committee of local residents listened to Miss Fanny's ghost. It accused Kent of her murder and suggested that he be arrested and hanged for the crime. One of the members of the group was the Reverend Aldrich of Clerkenwell, who was pastor of Saint John's Church, where Miss Fanny's body was buried. The pastor refused to believe that the knocks he was hearing were actually being made by Fanny's ghost, so the spectre offered to travel to her crypt (in the company of young Elizabeth, of course) and knock on her coffin lid to prove that she—the ghost—was real. (After all, if sounds came from inside the vault, didn't they have to be made by the person "living" there?)

Elizabeth stayed at the pastor's house the night before the ghostly visit was scheduled to occur. No one openly accused Elizabeth of making the noises, but she had once been discovered knocking on a piece of wood she had hidden under her dress. So, just to prevent any trickery, the pastor had Elizabeth's bedclothes searched. There's no report whether anything out of the ordinary was found, but no rappings were heard in the clergyman's household that night, and, needless to say, the ghost also didn't appear in the vault the next morning. Nor were there any knockings on the coffin.

> **Ghostly Pursuits**
>
> Elizabeth Parsons worked out the knocking code—one rap for "yes" and two for "no"—86 years before the Fox sisters in Hydesville, New York, used a similar system to communicate with the spirit in their home. The Cock Lane incident was declared a fraud by most, whereas the events of the Fox sisters marked the birth of Spiritualism and sparked a worldwide craze for holding séances.

But that wasn't enough proof of fraud for some people. Kent was dragged in front of the coffin so Fanny's ghost could accuse him directly. Still, no knocking was heard. But rumors die hard. Someone suggested that the reason the ghost wasn't making any noise was because the coffin was empty. The body must have been stolen! So the coffin was opened and what was left of poor Fanny was still there for all to see.

Kent reacted by suing Parsons, his wife, daughter, and several others for defamation. The trial was held on July 10, 1762, and the judge Lord Chief Justice Mansfield found in favor of Kent on all counts. In addition to monetary restitution, Parsons was sentenced to stand in the public pillory, then be imprisoned for two years.

> **Ghostly Pursuits**
>
> According to local legend, some years after the Cock Lane incident, a man named J. W. Archer visited Saint John's Church, entered the crypt, and opened the coffin said to be that of Miss Fanny. By the light of a lantern, the corpse still seemed perfectly preserved. Archer noted that there were no smallpox scars on the remaining bits of flesh. Could some ingredients in a poison have helped preserve the body? Perhaps we'll never know the whole story unless Miss Fanny comes back a-knocking.

Why had the people of Cock Lane been so slow to suspect Elizabeth? Even though Elizabeth had once been "caught in the act," as they say, most people didn't think that isolated incident could explain all of the rappings and other sounds they had heard. Or perhaps they just wanted to believe in ghosts.

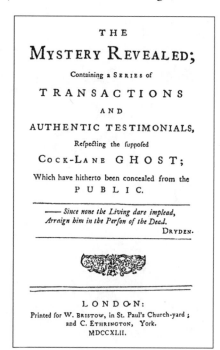

THE

MYSTERY REVEALED;

Containing a SERIES of

TRANSACTIONS

AND

AUTHENTIC TESTIMONIALS,

Respecting the supposed

COCK-LANE GHOST;

Which have hitherto been concealed from the
PUBLIC.

—— Since none the Living dare implead,
Arraign him in the Person of the Dead.
DRYDEN.

LONDON:
Printed for W. BRISTOW, in St. Paul's Church-yard;
and C. ETHRINGTON, York.
MDCCXLII.

Frontispiece of a 1762 book detailing the "transactions and authentic testimonials respecting the supposed Cock-Lane Ghost."

Seeing Is Not Always Believing: The Cottingley Fairies

Although this tale from the age of Spiritualism is not about ghosts, it shows how easily the naive and believing public can be fooled, even by their own eyes.

In 1917 Cottingley, England, two little girls, Elsie Wright and her cousin Frances Griffiths, claimed that they had seen fairies in Cottingley Glen—and that they had taken photographs to prove it!

Hundreds of people believed that the photographs were real. Among those duped was author Sir Arthur Conan Doyle, a devoted Spiritualist and the creator of the oh-so-logical detective Sherlock Holmes.

Finally, someone noticed that the fairies in the girls' photos bore a remarkable resemblance to those pictured in *Princess Mary's Gift*, a popular children's book of the time. In later years, Elsie Wright said she never understood how so many people could have been fooled by their "little joke."

The story of the Cottingley Fairies was the subject of *Fairy Tale*, a 1997 film starring Peter O'Toole as Arthur Conan Doyle and Harvey Keitel as his friendly nemesis Harry Houdini. (You'll hear about how these two argued over mediums, Spiritualism, and the existence of ghosts in Chapter 23.)

One of the photographs taken by the girls of the Cottingley Fairies.

Ghostly Pursuits

As a child, did you have an invisible playmate? Some paranormal theorists suggest that some of those imaginary companions may actually be ghosts! It's long been thought that children are much more sensitive to spirit entities than practical, literal-minded adults. Isn't it a pity that we may lose our invisible friends simply because we're taught and come to believe that such things can't—and therefore don't—exist?

The Amityville Horror

Perhaps the most famous hoax haunting of them all is known simply as "The Amityville Horror." On December 18, 1975, George and Kathleen Lutz and their three children moved into a large house in Amityville on Long Island, New York. The enormous house was priced exceedingly low because it had been the site of an infamous murder the year before: 23-year-old Ronald DeFeo had killed his father, mother, and four younger siblings on November 13, 1974. Legend had it that the house was also sitting on an area that the Shinnecock Indians believed was beset by evil spirits.

By January 14, 1976, the Lutz family had left their new home, leaving all of their possessions behind. The Lutzs claimed that they'd been the victims of unnatural and severe poltergeist and ghost activity for 28 consecutive days. They said that they had seen hooded apparitions and that swarms of flies had attacked them in the children's room. There were wide temperature shifts, green goo appeared on the stairs, scratches appeared on Kathleen's body, objects were seen floating, and they heard sounds of a marching band. The Lutzs claimed that people who visited the house later had troubles befall them, including a local priest, Father Ralph Pecararo, who had blessed the house before they moved in. Supposedly, Pecararo fell deathly ill and did not recover until he was moved to another parish.

Boo!

> Don't believe everything you read or see on TV or in the movies. It's especially difficult to separate fact from fiction these days when so-called docudramas and re-creations of historical events sprinkle facts among half-truths and fabrications. Even the most convincing tale should be taken with a grain of salt, and require extraordinary proof, if it's asking you to believe unbelievable events.

In 1976, *The Amityville Horror*, a nonfiction book written by Jay Anson about the Lutzs' experiences, became a bestseller. Anson wrote the book in three or four months entirely from taped telephone interviews with the Lutzs. It spawned a successful 1979 movie of the same name, followed by two movie sequels inspired by subsequent books penned by John G. Jones that supposedly told of the further adventures of the Lutz family.

In January 1976, George Lutz contacted Jerry Solfvin of the Psychical Research Foundation to investigate the activity. Solfvin found no definite proof that poltergeist activity had occurred, so he brought in members of the American Society for Psychical Research. All were skeptical. Besides, there were some major discrepancies between actual occurrences and those chronicled in what was supposed to be a non-fictional account. Then, in 1979, William Weber, Ronald DeFeo's lawyer, claimed that he and the Lutzs had co-conceived the idea of inventing a story about poltergeist activity in the house in order to obtain book and movie deals. He sued for part of the profits. The Lutzs counter-sued. But the lawsuits didn't stop there. The owners that followed the Lutzs into the house (who experienced no demonic activity) sued the

Lutzs, author Jay Anson, and the book's publisher because of problems caused by curious thrill-seekers who constantly overran their property. Even Father Pecararo sued the Lutzs and the publisher for invasion of privacy and for making false claims about him.

The new residents of the house and Pecararo prevailed in their suits. As for Weber, the judge stated while hearing his case that "the evidence shows fairly clearly that the Lutzs during this entire period were considering and acting with the thought of having a book published."

Paranormal researchers will continue their investigations as long as people keep seeing ghosts. Fortunately, ghost hunters and ghostbusters are able to discover the natural causes for just about every sighting.

But then, there are the others.

It's time for more than 100 pages of ghost stories—ghosts haunting houses and castles, battlefields and forts, theaters, schools, and libraries—you name it! Are you ready? That's the spirit!

The Least You Need to Know

- ◆ Frederic W. H. Myers and others suggested that ghosts are caused by telepathic projection from the spirit world.

- ◆ Edmund Gurney suggested that collective apparitions were caused by the telepathic sharing of information from one medium to all of the people who see the ghost.

- ◆ In theory, super-ESP is a powerful form of telepathy that allows a medium to obtain information about the deceased from living people and to mentally create apparitions that others can see.

- ◆ A great deal of spirit phenomena has been explained away by intentional fraud.

Part 4

Make Yourself at Home: The Hauntings

Here's what you've been waiting for: dozens of ghost stories to knock your socks off. Some of these are pretty creepy, so you may not want to read them alone. And keep those lights turned up bright. I got goosepimply just writing about these ghosts.

If you're a ghost-story addict, you've come to the right place. I've collected some of the most celebrated ghost tales in history, and I've thrown in lots more that are obscure but equally fascinating. After all, ghosts don't haunt only the big cities or famous places, like the Tower of London or the battlefields at Gettysburg. They might haunt a roadway that goes right by your door!

Remember: Ghosts tend to haunt *places*, not *people*. So I thought it might be fun—and bit different—to look at the kinds of places ghosts feel at home. As a result, I've separated this enormous section into haunted houses, castles, churches and cemeteries, battlegrounds, theaters, schools, modes of transportation, and many more. And there's a whole chapter on Haunted Hollywood. Are you ready for your close-up?

I don't mind the haunting, but this is getting out of hand...

This Old House: Haunted Homes in America

In This Chapter

- ◆ A tour of America's most infamous haunted houses

- ◆ New Orleans—one of America's most haunted cities

- ◆ Ghosts governing the nation's capital

- ◆ Abraham Lincoln, the White House's busiest phantom

Can you tell if a house is haunted just by looking at it? Is it the one down the street that's boarded up and decaying? Or maybe it's one of those brooding New Englanders with a widow's walk and towering gables?

The majority of houses that are reported as haunted, however, don't fit any of these stereotypes. True, some are deserted; most have what might be called a "history." But many are occupied by spectres side-by-side with their human hosts. For many people, it's an acceptable, if unusual, arrangement in cohabitation!

Believe it or not, a number of these homes are open to the public—see Appendix C for details. So here's a sampling of some of my favorite haunted houses and cities found in the old U.S. of A. Hop in your ghostmobile, and let's go ghost hunting.

Haunted Houses of the East

Perhaps the phantoms that haunt the Northeastern United States do so out of a sense of history and patriotism. People were living—and dying—in this part of the country long before the settlements out West. Some of the former residents were never able to pull up stakes and move away from the East Coast in life, death—or the Afterlife!

Edgar Allan Poe House

The Baltimore, Maryland, home of the mystery and horror author Edgar Allan Poe is reportedly haunted, but not by Poe himself. Poe lived there from 1832 to 1835 with his grandmother Elizabeth Poe, his aunt Maria Clemm, and his cousin (and later his wife) Virginia Clemm. Elizabeth died there in 1835. The house changed hands many times during the next hundred years, and it remained empty from 1922 to 1949. Since then it has been a museum, open to the public.

> **Boo!**
>
> Remember, many of the sites mentioned throughout this book, even some haunted houses, are private residences. Never trespass on private property without the express permission of the owners or residents. Even when viewing a site from the road, be aware of possible loitering, trespassing, or invasion of privacy violations.

In the 1960s, visitors began reporting strange goings-on, especially in what were Virginia's bedroom and Poe's room in the attic. Spectral activity includes guests being tapped on their shoulders by invisible hands, voices, sounds, lights going on when no one is inside, and windows that open and close by themselves. Some have reported seeing the ghost of an elderly, overweight, gray-haired lady, dressed in gray nineteenth-century clothing. No positive identification of the phantom has ever been made.

First-Person Phantoms

All of his friends said that Wayne Wiswesser was just cantankerous enough that, if *anyone* could come back to haunt you, Wayne could—and would!

Wayne's daughter Michelle and her husband, Joe Amos, moved into her father's house in Reading, Pennsylvania, after his death. But strange things started happening:

- Several times, when Joe was working on his motorcycle in the basement garage where Wayne used to park his roadster, he heard a door open upstairs, followed by footsteps—from boots like the ones Wayne had worn.

- While Joe and Michelle were away, the curtains in the living room would somehow lift themselves off the rod and drape themselves neatly over the couch. It wasn't until they hung them just the way Wayne liked them that the phenomenon stopped.

- Without warning, a portrait of Wayne that was hanging in the stairwell crashed to the floor while the family was arguing. In order to fall, the photo would have had to be lifted off its wall mounting.

- Joe sometimes saw a dark shadow on the landing; Michelle's sister saw the shade of a human shape on the stairs.

- One of Joe and Michelle's friends—one whom Wayne hadn't particularly liked—stayed overnight on the living room couch, but he couldn't get to sleep; something or someone kept lifting the pillow.

It was several months after Wayne's death before Michelle finally came to terms with her father's death and was able to let go. She told him, aloud, that she loved him, but it was really time for him to move on. After that, except for a few minor quirky incidents now and then, all ghost activity in the house stopped.

The Mount

Several ghosts are said to haunt the country home of author Edith Wharton (1862–1937), in Lenox, Massachusetts. Wharton built the neo-Georgian mansion between 1900 and 1902, moved out in 1908, and sold the property in 1912. Later it became Foxhollow School for Girls. The Mount is currently owned by an acting troupe, Shakespeare & Company, which performs plays on its three indoor and outdoor stages. In the summer months, it opens the house to tourists.

Visitors in the house have heard unexplained thumps, footsteps, and girlish laughter. Apparitions have been seen both day and night. A female ghost has been seen alone, and on another occasion accompanied by a male ghost; they were later identified as Wharton and author Henry James, who was a frequent guest in the house. The spectre of a pony-tailed man (James?) has been glimpsed in the so-called Henry James Room, and a phantom thought to be Wharton has been seen walking the terrace. An unidentified man, in a cloak and hood, has appeared at bedsides, pressing down on the person lying there. The ghost of Edith's husband, Edward, among other phantoms, has also been reported.

Boo!

Sometimes it's better not to kid around with curses! It's said that anyone who sits in Amelia's chair at Baleroy in Philadelphia will die within a year. So far, four deaths have been attributed to the curse coming true!

First-Person Phantoms

My brother-in-law, Randy Eagle, tells of the hauntings at his boyhood home in Pottstown, Pennsylvania. His grandmother wanted a particular set of phosphorescent rosary beads that had been blessed buried with her, but they couldn't be found the day of her funeral.

A few months later, Randy's older brother Terry, who was about 17 at the time, found the rosary beads and put them around his neck. He was startled to feel something tugging at the beads. Terry tore off the rosary beads and tossed them aside.

Some days later, Randy told the story to his girlfriend and showed her the rosary beads. As he spoke, the beads were yanked out of his hand by some invisible force. Randy glanced toward the window and saw a strange, translucent blue aura. Was it his grandmother returning for her rosary?

Philly Phantoms

Pennsylvania played a pivotal role in colonial and Civil War-era America. It only makes sense that ghosts haunt this Keystone state. One of the most haunted mansions in the greater Philadelphia area is Baleroy. The splendidly restored and furnished mansion was owned by descendants of Civil War general George Meade. Thomas Jefferson's ghost has appeared standing by a large clock in the dining room. A monk dressed in a brown habit has been seen in the master bedroom on the second floor, and a cranky, old woman with a cane has been spotted in the second floor hallway.

A 200-year-old wing chair located in the Blue Room is sometimes occupied by the ghost of a woman named Amelia. There's even an unexplainable cold spot in the corridor between the Reception Room and the Blue Room. Still more ghosts have materialized at séances held at Baleroy over the years.

First-Person Phantoms

Cathy Calabrese vividly remembers one night when she was five or six years old and living in Sanatoga, Pennsylvania. She woke up in the middle of the night to see the greenish-colored apparition of a human head floating above the bed, watching her. She watched it for a minute, then reached to switch on the light by her bed. When she turned back, the spirit face was gone. When Cathy later mentioned the ghost to her parents, her father told her about an incident that had occurred when she was even younger. Her parents woke up in the middle of the night to find Cathy in their bed, hysterically screaming about a green lady in her room. When they investigated, no ghost was found. But Cathy's father believed that it was the ghost of his late mother, popping in to see her grandchild (whom she had never seen while she was alive).

The Left Coast

People can hardly resist the sun and sizzle of California when they're alive. No wonder so many of them want to stay there after they're dead! Here are just a few of California's famous phantoms.

Winchester House

Located in San Jose, the Winchester House is a 160-room Victorian-style mansion, built by Sarah Winchester beginning in 1884. She was still building onto the house when she died almost 40 years later.

Sarah was the daughter-in-law of Fisher Winchester, who manufactured the popular rifle that bore his name. She was interested in the paranormal but became even more so after the death of her only child, Annie Pardee, when the baby was a month old. Her husband, William Wirt Winchester, died from tuberculosis just 15 months later, leaving her with a fortune of $20 million.

Sarah consulted a medium in Boston who told her the spirits of those who had been killed by the Winchester rifle wanted her to sell her home in New Haven, Connecticut and move out West. There, she was to build a home large enough to house all of the ghosts. If Sarah didn't, the spirits said they would kill her.

In 1884, she purchased a large mansion already under construction in California. She employed up to 20 carpenters at a time to continue adding on to the house. She would placate the spirits, she reasoned, but she would have the rooms built in confusing designs to make it impossible for them to find her. As an added precaution, she slept in a different bedroom every night. Likewise, her massive gardens included trails leading to nowhere, and trees were planted closely together so that she could hide behind them to spy on approaching phantoms.

> ### Ghostly Pursuits
>
> Sarah Winchester seemingly became obsessed with the number 13: In her house there were 13 bathrooms, 13 windows and doors in the sewing room, and a staircase of 13 steps that led to a dead-end ceiling. Even her Last Will and Testament was divided into 13 sections, and she signed it 13 times.

Sarah Winchester was especially proud of her grand ballroom, in which she played the piano or an organ each night (despite severe arthritis in her hands) so the spirits could dance. She also entertained at dinner each night, serving 12 empty places besides her own at the table. She personally descended to the wine cellar to choose each night's vintage, but, after seeing a black handprint on the door to the cellar one evening, she had the room walled up forever.

Except for her eccentric behavior regarding her house and her belief in vengeful ghosts, Sarah was as sane as you and I. (Hmmm …) She was a recluse, however, and usually stayed indoors. Sarah Winchester died of natural causes at the age of 82 in 1922. She willed her house to a niece with the stipulation that "the ghosts continue to be welcomed and provided for." Or was she actually providing for herself?

Since Sarah's death, the Winchester House has acquired a reputation for actually being haunted. Witnesses have heard unexplainable footsteps and doors slamming on their own. The house is filled with cold spots in odd places, and floating auras have been reported. Sometimes lights turn on or doors become unlocked by themselves. Piano music is sometimes heard, even though the instrument in the ballroom is no longer playable. The kitchen also seems to be haunted: There's often a strong odor of chicken soup, and at least one tour group has seen the apparition of a lady seated at a kitchen table. And some staff members have seen a gray-haired female ghost drifting down the halls.

Could it be the ghost of Sarah herself that's haunting the Winchester Mansion? No one's really sure.

Today, the Winchester House is open to the public and is a popular California tourist attraction.

First-Person Phantoms

The childhood home of Michael Gingras, manager and night host at the Magic Castle in Hollywood, was haunted from the time he was around 11 years old until he moved out at around the age of 18. The house in Grand Terrace, California, still has ghostly visitors, but only on rare occasions. Among the many phenomena Michael and others experienced are the following:

♦ Michael's first encounter was the ghost of a tall, hazy, male figure that appeared at the end of his bed. It bent down to pet the family cat, which immediately jumped up and started walking in circles.

♦ Lights and water taps turned on and off by themselves.

♦ Toilets flushed by themselves.

♦ Invisible hands shook Michael, his Aunt Michelle, and others from their sleep.

♦ One night as Michael slept, the closed door to his room repeatedly rattled in its frame, then couldn't be opened, as if something were pushing it shut from the inside. When Michael's father forced the door open, he was met with a blast of cold air.

♦ While in the bathroom of the game room, one of Michael's friends heard someone walking behind him. He turned to just catch a glimpse of a ghost walking out the door. Another friend felt an invisible force push him away from the refrigerator in an adjacent room.

♦ Bedding was pulled off Michael's 2-year-old cousin as the child slept otherwise undisturbed in Michael's bedroom.

♦ A collection of ceramic souvenir bells that Michael's mother kept in the living room fell off their shelves, one by one.

♦ Michael's jacket, accidentally left in a friend's car, reappeared on its own a few days later. Michael found the clothes in his closet parted, with the missing jacket hanging right in the center.

♦ As Michael's grandmother was taking a bath, something made a splash in the tub. Concentric rings appeared on the surface of the water, then something grabbed her under the water and slid a hand up the inside of her leg. The woman jumped out of the tub and ran out of the bathroom, soap-suds flying everywhere.

The source of the hauntings at the Gingras home has never been discovered. The house did have a previous owner, however, who had built the place himself, and who died less than a year after Michael's family moved in. Has the former inhabitant returned?

Hart Mansion

The home of the silent film star William S. Hart is located in Santa Clarita in southern California. The actor lived there with his sister, their nurse, and several dogs. All of them haunt the house, which today is a museum. Hart's ghost seems to recognize certain people and materializes primarily to those he likes—mostly the docents. For some unknown reason, the spectral scent of coffee often wafts through the building.

Whaley House

The Whaley House, built in San Diego by Thomas Whaley for his wife Anna Eloise deLaunay, was completed in 1857. The home was constructed on the site of an 1852 botched hanging: The gallows had been too low, and instead of dying immediately of a broken neck, "Yankee Jim" Robinson slowly strangled to death.

Family members believed from the start that Robinson's ghost haunted the house, and the Whaley children frequently claimed to hear his footsteps!

Lillian Whaley, the last of the daughters, lived in the house until her death in 1953, after which the house rapidly deteriorated. It was saved as a historic monument and has since been refurbished with period furnishings and opened to the public. Visitors have identified the ghost of Anna Eloise Whaley, carrying a candle as she strolls from room to room. Nonapparitional activity including footsteps, windows opening and closing by themselves, a cradle rocking without assistance, cold breezes, and tripped burglar alarms has also been reported.

The Windy (and Ghostly) City

Chicago has more than its share of fascinating ghosts and spirits blowing through. Perhaps it's the brisk night air that draws them to the shores of Lake Michigan.

Several of Chicago's historic homes seem to be haunted:

- Allerton Mansion, by a "lady in white"
- Beverly Unitarian Church, formerly a home known as the Irish Castle, by a young woman
- The bedrooms of Schweppe Mansion, by Mr. And Mrs. Schweppe, who both committed suicide; and a servant

But far and away, the most famous haunted location in Chicago is historic Hull House, but, ironically, it probably is *not* haunted in the slightest. Its reputation comes from a 1913 rumor that claimed a "Devil Baby" with a tail, cloven hooves, scales, and pointed ears was being cared for in the house.

To this day, some passersby say they have spotted the Devil Baby in a left-side attic window. Others have seen luminous ectoplasm ascend the staircase to the attic. The glowing mist has supposedly been caught on film, as have four monklike apparitions ascending the staircase to the second floor.

Hull House is now a museum and is still on the itinerary of "Haunted Chicago" tours.

The South Shall Rise Again

Mysterious Charleston, South Carolina, lays claim to being the most haunted city in the Southeast. And why not? Can't you just imagine ghosts haunting the antebellum homes of the city? Take a look at these four representative haunted houses:

- **Heyward House.** The young James Heyward accidentally shot himself to death in a hunting accident in 1805. Later owners and residents have spotted his ghost, dressed in hunting clothes, in the library of his house.

- **Ladd House.** Dr. Joseph Brown Ladd, who lived here in the 1780s and died in a 1786 duel, haunts this 1732 house. His ghost is sometimes preceded by a cold draft, footsteps, and whistling. The ghost of a little girl who lived in the house in the 1830s is sometimes felt on the second floor.

- **Medway.** Jan Van Arrsens built Medway, the oldest building still standing in South Carolina, in 1686. The scent of his ghost smoking a pipe can be detected in the upstairs south bedroom. The spectre of a later resident, a young bride, sometimes appears standing at a downstairs window. She's waiting for her husband, unaware that he has died in a hunting accident.

- **Yeoman's Hall.** In its latter years, the Goose Creek Plantation in Charleston was haunted by one of its early residents, an old Irish woman named Mary Hyrne. She often appeared whenever someone living there swore, missed church, or worked on a Sunday. A tract of luxury homes was built on the site, but Mary has materialized in the development's clubhouse, Yeoman's Hall. She appears as a frowning old woman, wearing a white hat and period black dress.

Phantastic Tips

Why not go on an "organized" ghost hunt? In many places, nighttime ghost tours allow guests to visit a city's most haunted hideaways. Visitors to Charleston and Key West can enjoy popular walking tours through haunted areas. In cities such as Chicago and Hollywood, where the sites are more spread out, the ghost hunts are usually by van or bus. (See Appendix B for more information.)

Key West, Florida, is a bit further down the coast—well, actually as far south as you can go. Many ghosts call the once-remote town home. Author Ernest Hemingway is, perhaps, the community's most famous phantom. He made Key West his home from 1928 to 1940, and some of his happiest times were spent there.

Caretakers of the Hemingway house, which is now open to the public as a museum, began to see the author's ghost soon after his suicide by shotgun in 1961. They've also heard him moving about the house overhead and sometimes hear his ghost clicking away at his old manual typewriter. Neighbors have occasionally seen his phantom: It appears at a second-story window around midnight, sometimes waving at passersby.

The Hemingway house in Key West, Florida.

(Photo by author)

Way Down Yonder

New Orleans, with its night air stirred by the rhythm of jazz and the chants of voo-doo rituals, is uniquely qualified to stake its claim as the most haunted city in the United States. Dotted with aboveground tombs and sepulchers, all of the Cajun and Bayou country seems to be under the spectral spell of hauntings. Here are the stories of just four of the haunted houses in New Orleans.

Beauregard-Keyes House

Gen. Pierre Gustave Toutant de Beauregard, the commander of the Confederate soldiers at the calamitous Battle of Shiloh, stayed in this home built by Joseph Le Carpentier, a wealthy New Orleans auctioneer, for 18 months beginning in 1865. It was later the winter home of novelist Frances Parkinson Keyes for about a quarter century starting in 1944.

The home is now a museum, with heirloom pieces from the general and his family exhibited in the bedroom he used during his stay. It's said that sometimes, around 2:00 A.M., the ghosts of Beauregard and his soldiers appear in full military uniform outside the ballroom. According to some accounts, their uniforms then visibly change into torn and bloody rags.

The Beauregard-Keyes house is haunted by the ghosts of a Confederate general and his soldiers.

(Photo by author)

Gardette-LePrêtre House

In the 1790s, the brother of a Turkish sultan was living in this mansion located at the corner of Dauphine and Orlean streets. Enemies of the ruler murdered the entire household (including the wives and servants), and buried the brother's corpse under a date tree (now nicknamed the Death Tree) in the courtyard. For years, apparitions were seen and ghostly Turkish music was heard near the tree, but, for some unexplained reason, the phenomena stopped after the rooms surrounding the enclosed court were converted into apartments.

Lalaurie House

Dr. Louis Lalaurie and his wife Delphine moved into their mansion on Royal Street in 1832. The wealthy socialite secretly kept her slaves chained; some were imprisoned in the attic. In 1833, one slave girl escaped. Madame Lalaurie chased her across the roof with a whip, and the terrified girl jumped to her death. The ensuing scandal led to authorities forcing Lalaurie to sell her slaves, but friends bought them and returned them to her.

On April 24, 1834, a cook accidentally set the kitchen on fire. Firemen found the charred remains of the slave chained to the floor; the bodies of seven other slaves were found on torture devices in the attic. Lalaurie and her husband were driven out of town, and she was later fatally gored by a wild boar in southern France.

Around 1900, her New Orleans house was converted into apartments. Residents have reported seeing the ghost of Madame Lalaurie, a tall black man on the staircase, and various hooded figures. Spectral sounds include the classic rattling chains being dragged down the stairs, screams in the attic, and the cries of a young girl in the courtyard.

Laveau House

Born an illegitimate mulatto in 1794, Marie Laveau was the undisputed "Voodoo Queen" of New Orleans in the nineteenth century. She sold charms and medicines, led voodoo dances in Congo Square, and held pagan rites at St. John's Bayou at nearby Lake Ponchartrain. She seemed to stay eternally young. (Many speculated that there were really *two* Marie Laveaus, a mother and daughter. There are actually two tombs said to be hers in the old French Quarter cemetery—see Chapter 16.)

> **Ghostly Pursuits**
>
> St. John's Eve celebrates the summer solstice, the beginning of summer. The event can occur anywhere between June 20 and 26, but when the early Catholic Church adopted the pagan festival as a Christian holy day, they named it for John the Baptist and fixed the date at June 24. Festivities are traditionally held the night before, on St. John's Eve. Likewise, the real revels for All Saints' Day usually take place on All Hallow's Eve, or Halloween.

After her death around 1895, Laveau's ghost continued to practice voodoo, along with her phantom followers, in her home on St. Ann Street. Her apparition has also been spotted strolling down St. Ann Street in a long white dress with her trademark seven-knotted handkerchief around her neck. On at least one occasion, she was seen to slap a man in a French Quarter pharmacy and then float to the ceiling. Laveau's voice also can be heard singing at St. John's Bayou on St. John's Eve, which marks the summer solstice.

D.C. Denizens of the Dark

Finally, the homes in the nation's capital contain some of the most famous haunts in the nation located everywhere from Georgetown to the White House itself. The ghosts include military heroes and even presidents!

The Octagon

This three-story house was built on an oddly shaped plot of land near the White House in the early 1800s for Col. John Tayloe, a planter from Virginia. It's said to be the most haunted private home in Washington, D.C.

The first apparition to haunt the property was one of Tayloe's daughters. She died after falling over a railing and down a stairwell. (Some say she actually committed suicide, because the tragedy occurred shortly after an argument with her father about an unsuitable suitor.) Sometimes, the daughter's ghost doesn't appear; instead, the shadow of a candle floats up the steps, followed by a scream, then a thud at the bottom of the stairs.

Tayloe and his family moved out during the War of 1812. Miraculously, the British didn't burn down the house during their assault on the capital, but the White House wasn't so fortunate. Tayloe loaned his home to President James Madison and his wife Dolly during the renovation of the Executive Mansion. They stayed there from 1814 to 1817.

After the Tayloes returned, the father had an argument at the top of the stairs with a second daughter, who had eloped. Tayloe brushed her aside to pass, and she, like her sister, fell to her death. Her ghost is said to haunt the house as well.

A gambler, accused of cheating, was killed in one of the house's upstairs rooms during the Civil War. As he slumped to his death, he clutched the bell cord that was used to summon the servants. Ever since, the gambler's ghost has been seen falling and grasping at the sash.

The house's most famous phantom is that of Dolly Madison herself, whose ghost first appeared in the late nineteenth century, dressed in period wardrobe and perfumed with lilac. Other spectres and phenomena at the Octagon include carriages and footmen, various unrecognizable human shadows moving up the staircase and out the back door to the gardens, footprints left behind in dust, the clashing of swords, the aroma of food, and groans and cries. Rumor has it that loud thumping, heard throughout the house for more than a century, is caused by …

Boo!

It should go without saying, but never get into a rough-and-tumble argument with someone at the top of a staircase. Chances are good that at least one of you is going to wind up being a ghost!

- Ghosts of runaway slaves (from when the house purportedly acted as a station of the Underground Railroad).

- Union soldiers who died there (from when the house acted as a rooming house/hospital).

- A slave girl who was murdered by her lover, a British soldier, who then walled up her corpse within the house.

Today the Octagon is open to the public as a museum.

The Capitol Building

The Capitol Building, "home" of the federal government's legislative branch, is haunted by numerous ghosts, including spirits of congressional rivals Joseph G. Cannon and Champ Clark. Both former speakers of the House of Representatives have been spotted late at night debating in the House chambers. The rap of the speaker's gavel often accompanies their materialization.

Dark stains on the steps outside the House gallery mark the spot where Kentucky congressman William Taulbee was shot and killed in the winter of 1890 by newspaperman Charles Kincaid. All attempts over the years to remove the stains have been futile. Staff workers say they've seen and heard the murdered congressman near the steps whenever a reporter slips on the slick stairs. Is Taulbee's ghost taking revenge on journalists?

The apparition of a stonemason is seen in the Senate chambers. Legend has it that he was struck with a brick during an argument with a carpenter, who then sealed up the mason in a wall while he was still alive. A ghost of another worker, carrying a tray, is sometimes seen floating in the rotunda, where he was accidentally killed.

Other spectres haunting the Capitol include presidents John Quincy Adams and James Garfield, World War I's Unknown Soldier, and a large cat. Also, the marble figures in Statuary Hall are rumored to come to life on New Year's Eve.

The White House

Several rooms of the Executive Mansion (or White House), built to serve as the residence for the president of the United States while in office, are haunted. Many of the spirits are those of former U.S. presidents. The ghost of William Henry Harrison is frequently heard in the attic. Andrew Jackson revisits his bed in what is now called the Queen's Bedroom, and his guttural laughter has been heard there for more than a century. Thomas Jefferson is heard practicing his violin in the Yellow Oval Room.

The ghost of Abraham Lincoln also reportedly haunts the White House. Phantom footsteps on the second floor have long been attributed to him. Supposedly, the first person to report seeing his spirit was Grace Coolidge, the wife of President Calvin Coolidge. She saw Lincoln's silhouette standing at one of the windows in the Oval Office, dolefully looking out over the Potomac. Many, including poet Carl Sandburg, have since reported seeing or sensing Lincoln in that same pose.

Lincoln is said to haunt his old bedroom, now called the Lincoln Room, as well. Overnight guests in the chamber have heard spectral footsteps in the hall; one has seen Lincoln sit on the bed to put on his boots. Queen Wilhelmina of the Netherlands stayed in the Lincoln Room while on a state visit to President Franklin D. Roosevelt. One evening she heard footsteps and a knock at the door. She opened it to see Abraham Lincoln standing before her, dressed in a frock coat and top hat! Like any respectable lady of her generation who found herself in such a situation, she fainted.

Eleanor Roosevelt said that she often sensed Lincoln's presence late at night, and her dog, Fala, often barked for no reason, seemingly at an invisible presence. President Harry Truman also heard footsteps that he attributed to Lincoln. During Ronald Reagan's tenancy, his daughter Maureen saw Lincoln's ghost in the Lincoln Room.

To paraphrase the old adage, you can't keep a good ghost down. Lincoln's spirit hasn't been restricted to the White House. He's been seen at a number of sites around the country, including the Loudon Cottage (now Eamonn's restaurant) in Loundonville, New York. The house was once owned by one of the women sitting in the president's box when he was assassinated in Ford's Theatre.

Lincoln's spectral footsteps have been heard at his gravesite in Springfield, Illinois, where popular lore says his tomb is actually empty. His image appeared in a portrait taken of his widow Mary Todd Lincoln, when she sat under an assumed name for spirit photographer William Mumler (see it in Chapter 7). And the phantom Lincoln funeral train is seen every year on the anniversary of its cortege from Washington, D.C. to Springfield, Illinois (see Chapter 19).

Yes, ghosts haunt houses in every corner of the United States. But many owners and residents of these homes have denied the rumors of hauntings. Only recently have a few begun to admit to one and all that they have spirits as houseguests. England, on the other hand, embraces its distinction of being, perhaps, the most haunted country in the world. Great Britain touts its ghosts with pride, so let's cross the pond to tour the haunted houses of the British Isles.

The Least You Need to Know

- Every state in America has houses that are reputed to be haunted.

- New Orleans, Chicago, and Charleston are just three cities claiming to be the nation's most haunted.

- Today, many historic haunted houses are museums that can be visited by the public.

- Some politicians can never be voted out; they just haunt the halls of the District of Columbia forever.

There'll Always Be an England

In This Chapter

- Great Britain, the world's most haunted country
- Borley Rectory, England's most haunted house
- Ghostly tales of the great manors of England
- The haunted village of Pluckley

Perhaps no country on Earth is as haunted as Great Britain. For as far back as anyone can remember, any castle or venerable manor worth its salt had at least one resident ghost. Remember, this is a country where children *and* adults commonly believed in the existence of fairies, leprechauns, and other elfin spirits.

When Spiritualism first reached British shores from America in the 1850s, it started a craze of mediums, séances, and ghost sightings unmatched anywhere else in the world. It's no accident that one of the first serious groups to investigate the paranormal and ghostly phenomena, the Society for Psychical Research, was founded in London.

Here are just a few of the more famous examples of haunted houses found in England, Scotland, and Ireland. We'll start off with one of the most intense paranormal investigations ever of a haunted house: the Borley Rectory.

The Most Haunted House in England

Located in the small village of Borley, Essex County, about 60 miles northeast of London, the Borley Rectory was dubbed "the most haunted house in England" by paranormal expert Harry Price. Although spectral activity was considerable and supposedly occurred for more than 50 years, ghostly goings-on at the Borley Rectory were really rather ordinary: the usual rappings, footsteps, levitations, and so on. What made the case sensational was the incredibly thorough investigation by Price between 1929 and 1944 as well as the massive amount of publicity his research generated. (Although the bulk of Price's work was done by 1938, he was still digging about in 1943; and in April 1944 he accompanied a photographer from *Life* magazine, who shot a famous, though controversial, snapshot of a brick seemingly floating in midair in the rectory ruins.)

The Borley Rectory.

(Photo from the collection of Vincent O'Neil)

The rectory, a somber if commonplace redbrick structure, was built in 1863 by the Reverend Henry Bull. He and his family lived there until 1927. When Henry died, his son Harry was made rector.

It was during the Bull family's residency that the house obtained its reputation for being haunted. A phantom nun often floated over the property, especially down one path the Bulls nicknamed "the Nun's Walk." Once, she was spotted at the same time by four of Henry Bull's daughters. The ghost nun was usually seen at dusk (an especially active time of day for paranormal activity), but she was also seen at night and in broad daylight. A phantom horse-drawn coach also haunted the grounds.

Ghostly Pursuits

Legend has it that the hauntings at the Borley Rectory were related to a monastery that occupied the site in medieval times, although historical records dating back to the twelfth century show no monastery on the property. According to folklore, a nun from a nearby convent eloped with a monk from the monastery, and they escaped by carriage with the aid of a brother monk. All were caught. As punishment, the nun was buried alive in a monastery wall; her lover and his aide were hanged. There are multiple variations on the tragic tale.

After Harry Bull's death, Borley Rectory sat vacant for a number of months, from June 1927 to October 1928. Because of the house's notoriety, a dozen clergymen declined the position at Borley before the Reverend G. E. Smith accepted it. Neither he nor his wife believed in the paranormal.

Enter Harry Price

Harry Price entered the picture in 1929 after reading several articles about the rectory in the *Daily Mail*. He and his secretary, Lucie Kaye, visited the estate on June 12, 1929. According to Price, the Smiths confided that they'd been experiencing ghostly phenomena ever since they arrived, including …

◆ Footsteps.

◆ Whispers and murmurs.

◆ Harry Bull's ghost.

◆ Black, irregularly shaped figures.

Phantastic Tips

If you even suspect that you may have experienced paranormal activity, make a record of the activity. Write down as much as you can remember, in as much detail as possible. Include *what* you saw or felt, *where* it happened, and *when*. You never know when someone like Harry Price will come along years later asking what you experienced.

- The phantom nun (also seen by two maids).

- Lights seen in the windows of unused rooms.

- A woman moaning, followed by her pleading, "Don't, Carlos, don't!" (Her words were no louder than normal conversation. It's not known who Carlos was—or the woman, for that matter.)

British ghost hunter Harry Price.

(Photo from the collection of Vincent O'Neil)

During Price's years of investigation, various people associated with the house reported such things as banging doors, bells ringing, sudden temperature changes, spontaneous combustion, unexplained odors, frightened animals, moving objects, broken pottery, writing on the walls, spectral music, choirs singing, and the sounds of invisible horses and coaches. In all, Price claimed to have interviewed more than a hundred eyewitnesses to ghostly activity. During subsequent visits, Price himself experienced poltergeist-type phenomena, especially the bell-ringing and objects flying about room.

Phantastic Tips

Harry Price advertised for ghost hunters; he trained those he selected on the spot. Interested in becoming part of a team yourself? Consider offering your services to an established, bona fide ghost hunter who's already out in the field. You'll find the names and contact information for several in Appendix A.

On July 15, 1929, the Smiths moved out of the rectory. They claimed not to have changed their disbelief in the paranormal; rather, they left because they found the rectory uncomfortable. Three months later, on October 16, 1930, the Reverend Lionel Algernon Foyster (who was related to the Bulls) and his wife Marianne moved into the rectory.

Within a year, Price received word that the poltergeist activity had picked up and had become increasingly violent. According to Price, the most important manifestations were notes addressed to Marianne, written in strange, tiny lettering on the rectory walls. Price called these the "Marianne messages." (At one point Price thought that Marianne somehow subconsciously evoked the poltergeist that wrote the messages. But the Foysters left Borley in 1935. Price's team subsequently saw various marks on the walls during his lease of the rectory from May 1937 to May 1938.)

The spectral "Marianne messages" on the walls of the Borley Rectory.

(Photo from the collection of Vincent O'Neil)

Price Moves In

In 1937, Price rented the Borley Rectory so that he could conduct a detailed, controlled investigation. He advertised in *The Times* in London for research assistants. Of the 200 respondents, Price selected 40 men to help. He drew up a master plan to document all spectral phenomena, using technical equipment such as movie and still cameras. He circled all moveable objects with chalk outlines to measure any changes in their positions.

There were three amateur mediums on Price's team: S. H. Glanville, his son Roger, and his daughter Helen. They were allowed to conduct séances in the rectory in an attempt to contact any spirits present. During one sitting, Harry Bull allegedly appeared to disclose that a nun and a monk, named either Fadenoch or Father Enoch, were buried in the garden.

On another occasion, the spirit of a nun named Marie Lairre explained through a planchette that she had been convinced to break her vows and marry. Her fiancé murdered her on May 17, 1667, and he buried her in the cellar. (Price discovered fragments of a skull and jaw bone during an exploration of the basement on August 17, 1943, but it was never determined whose remains they were.) The nun said that she would haunt the rectory until she received a Mass and Christian burial.

On March 27, 1938, medium Helen Glanville received a spirit message with her planchette that "Sunex Amures and one of his men" would start a fire over the hall and burn down the rectory that night at 9:00 P.M. The deadline came and went, but no fire materialized.

Price finished his investigation and left the rectory on May 19, 1938. While activity had been recorded, most of it was minor or mundane. Price claimed that the phantom nun was seen in February 1938, and there were reports of apports; however, none of the evidence was indisputable.

Nevertheless, in his book *The Most Haunted House in England* (1940), Price called Borley Rectory "the best authenticated case in the annals of psychical research." Although most of the activity seemed to suggest a poltergeist, there were also many sightings of ghosts. Price concluded that the phenomena he experienced were caused by lingering mental impressions of former occupants. He conceded that readers could label these remnants "spirits," if they wished.

Within a year of the planchette warning to Helen Glanville, the rectory did burn down, at midnight on February 27, 1939, but the cause was not supernatural in origin. Capt. W. H. Gregson had begun living in the rectory (or Borley Priory, as he called it) in December 1938. He accidentally dropped a paraffin lamp in the hallway, which started a blaze that eventually engulfed the house. Completely destroyed by the fire, it was razed in 1944.

Although the rectory itself is long gone, curiosity seekers still journey to Borley, at all hours of the day and night, in the hopes of catching a glimpse of a ghost.

Boo!

If you're absolutely resolved to visit Borley yourself and can't be dissuaded, please don't disturb those living in the small community. Avoid doing anything that might cause undue hardship, embarrassment, or discomfort to the present residents of Borley, *especially* at night. As the old adage goes: "Take nothing but photographs, leave nothing but footprints." And even then it shouldn't be on anyone's private property.

Finding Fault with the Master

Price's methods—and the authenticity and conclusions of his research—have been debated by parapsychics ever since his book about the investigation was published. For example, all of his researchers were untrained nonprofessionals. There was no common logbook to record activity and compare data. And the claims made by mediums, while interesting, were certainly neither scientific nor reliable.

Criticism picked up in earnest after Price's death in 1948. Psychical researchers Eric Dingwall and Kathleen M. Goldney, along with paranormal skeptic Trevor H. Hall, revisited Price's observations and conclusions.

They discovered Charles Sutton, a *Daily Mail* reporter, who claimed to have caught Price with his pockets full of pebbles, faking a stone-throwing activity that hit him on the head. Lucie Kaye noted that stone-throwing poltergeist activity never seemed to occur when Price wasn't around.

In 1949, Mrs. Smith came forward, saying that she believed Price had caused all the paranormal activity during her tenure at the rectory. She claimed nothing out of the ordinary had ever happened to them before Price's arrival, and that she and her husband were overwhelmed by all that occurred when Price was there. The Smiths had only asked the *Daily Mail* for the name of a reliable psychic research society so that she and her husband could put the rumors about the rectory being haunted to rest. Instead, the articles in the *Mail* flamed interest in the ghost stories.

> **Boo!**
> Be careful what you wish for: It may come true with a vengeance. If you request the services of a ghost hunter, be prepared for your life and your property to be turned upside down. Thorough ghost researchers will investigate every nook and cranny of your house. They won't hesitate to ask questions, no matter how personal, to get the information they need to help them catch the ghost.

In their book *Haunting of Borley Rectory* (1956), Dingwall, Goldney, and Hall concluded that all of Price's data, even if true, was too unreliable. None of his observances was corroborated, and all of them were subject to interpretation. As an example, they noted a time that the Reverend G. E. Smith mistook a column of smoke for an apparition. Price reported only the paranormal interpretation, not the possible (and probable) natural cause.

But the debate was far from over. Robert Hastings countered their criticisms in 1969 in an almost forgotten rebuttal published by the SPR as "An Examination of the 'Borley Report.'"

Speculation about the Borley Rectory has refused to die. In 1953 and 1954, newspapers reported ghosts on the grounds. It's said that a phantom nun still haunts the nearby church. Also, a newspaper reported that playful boys removed some bricks from the ruined rectory and buried them in the playground of their school in Willingborough; soon after, one of the boys reported seeing a ghost at the school.

Even if all of the poltergeist activity during Price's visits had been faked, that leaves decades of previous sightings unaccounted for. The truth about the Borley Rectory may never be known.

Cheery-OH!: Ghosts of the British Isles

Ghosts flourish throughout the British Isles. Just imagine yourself walking down a cobblestone street in a heavy London fog, or perhaps you're wandering alone across a Scottish moor as clouds drift past the face of a blood-red moon. It's not so hard to imagine a ghost or two in jolly old England now, is it? Here are just two of the best-documented haunted houses in Britain.

Chingle Hall

Located at Goosnargh, Lancashire, England, six miles north of Preston, Chingle Hall was built in the thirteenth century. In the 1600s, the Wall family owned Chingle Hall. St. John Wall, who was hanged as a religious martyr in 1679, was born there. Legend has it that his head was removed, returned to the Hall, and buried in the basement. His ghost has been seen and heard (rappings, scratching sounds, footsteps) in the house and over the property. Several Benedictine monks who were reportedly murdered there during the sixteenth and seventeenth centuries have taken up residence at Chingle Hall, too. Some spirits have shown up in photographs.

In addition to the apparitions, visitors have reported seeing table objects and pictures on the wall move on their own. They've also been touched and pushed by invisible spirit hands. Visitors sometimes experience sudden chills and "flashbacks" from the manor's past. (You'll learn more about this type of residual haunting in the next chapter.) Chingle Hall is open to guests for several months a year (see Appendix C); you can even arrange to spend the night!

The Brown Lady of Raynham Hall

Located near Fakenham, Norfolk, in England, Raynham Hall has been haunted by the apparition of a "Brown Lady" for more than 250 years. The mansion is the family seat of the Marquises of Townshend. The ghost is thought to be that of Lady Dorothy Townshend, wife of the second Marquis, because of its resemblance to her official portrait, in which she's dressed in brown.

Dorothy married Lord Charles Townshend, her childhood sweetheart, about a year after the death of his first wife in 1711. Some say Lord Townshend later learned that, prior to his marriage to Dorothy, she had been a mistress to Lord Wharton; in a fit of rage and jealousy, Townshend locked Dorothy in her own section of Raynham Hall. There, it's said, she died either of a broken heart, smallpox, or a fall down a stairwell.

Numerous reputable people have seen the Brown Lady, including:

Phantastic Tips

Consider the source. A ghost sighting is more believable if the person who claims to have seen a ghost (or had some other paranormal experience) has an excellent reputation for telling the truth and, indeed, no reason to lie. The story is even more credible if the observer has nothing to gain (and in some cases, much to lose) by telling the story.

- ◆ Then-regent George IV, in the early nineteenth century.

- ◆ A Colonel Loftus, around Christmas 1835. The ghost visited him on two successive evenings.

- ◆ Novelist Captain Frederick Marryat, also in December 1835 or early 1836.

Marryat saw the ghost while accompanied by two of Lord Charles's nephews. He fired his gun at the phantom, but the spectre immediately disappeared. His bullet was found in the wall the next morning.

The apparition wasn't seen again for almost a hundred years, reappearing next in 1926 to the Marquis Townshend, then to a boy, and to one of his friends. Ten years later, Lady Townshend hired Indra Shira and his assistant, Mr. Provand, to photograph the rooms of Raynham Hall. As they shot the staircase, Shira saw a white form appear on the steps. At his instruction, Provand took a photo of what, to him, appeared to be an empty staircase. When the film was developed, an image of the Brown Lady, dressed in white and wearing a veil, appeared. The spirit photograph, published in the December 1, 1936 edition of *Country Life* magazine, has never been proven to be a fake.

The ghost of Raynham Hall. This spirit photograph, taken in 1936 for Country Life *magazine, is of the Brown Lady of Raynham Hall. Many experts think it's authentic, and it's one of the most famous ghost photos ever taken.*

(Photo by Captain Provand, courtesy of Country Life *Photo Library)*

The Brown Lady has also been reported at Houghton Hall, which was owned by Lady Townsend's brother. She spent much of her happy childhood in Houghton, so perhaps it's only natural that her spirit would want to return there as well.

Plucky Pluckley Phantoms

Finally, there's one town near Dover in County Kent that has so many ghosts it's crowned itself "the most haunted village in England." Yes, I know—*another* "most haunted" location. Yet Pluckley may deserve the title. Consider this …

One residence known as Dering House has two ghosts: A White Lady frequents its library. A Red Lady seen in the house is said to be a woman who died in the twelfth century and was buried in a red gown, holding a red rose. (She also occasionally haunts the graveyard where she was laid to—well, apparently *not* to rest.) A former owner of Dering House committed suicide by eating poisoned berries; her ghost has returned to haunt the estate's Rose Court—but only between four and five o'clock in the afternoon, which was the time she died.

And that's just the beginning! A phantom monk inhabits Greystones, a neighboring house, but sometimes he can be seen walking outside with the woman from Dering House who killed herself. Other ghosts and apparitions in and around Pluckley include a gypsy woman, a highway robber, and a spectral stagecoach.

What a whirlwind visit to the great haunted manors of the British Isles—with plenty of ghosts to boot, from kitchen maids to queens! No wonder many people think that England's the most haunted country on Earth. In fact, in the next chapter, we'll visit some of the most famous haunted castles in Great Britain—and even one across the Channel in France.

The Least You Need to Know

- Spirits and ghosts are considered commonplace in England, perhaps the most haunted country in the world.

- No part of the British Isles is immune from haunting.

- Borley Rectory, once called "the most haunted house in England," was the site of one of the most thorough, if imperfect and inconclusive, paranormal investigations.

- The spirit photograph of the Brown Lady of Raynham Hall has never been discredited. Many experts think it's the real thing.

- The small town of Pluckley, located in County Kent, claims to be the "most haunted village in England."

Castles in the Air

In This Chapter

- ◆ The haunted castles of England
- ◆ Glamis Castle, Scotland's most famous haunted castle
- ◆ Spectral sightings in Irish castles
- ◆ A step into the past at France's palace of Versailles

I don't know about you, but when I hear "castle," I automatically think "ghost." It's easy to imagine spirits haunting those dark, torch-lit, drafty corridors—not to mention the dank, subterranean dungeons and torture chambers.

Europe is dotted with hundreds of ancient castles, many in total or partial ruin or decay. Still others have been restored, refurbished, or modernized. But no amount of renovation can keep out a ghost if it wants to live there!

It would be impossible to tell the tales of all the haunted castles, towers, and palaces in Great Britain and the rest of Europe, but here are some of my favorites.

Apparitional England

From the time of the Norman Conquest up to today, castles and palaces have housed royalty and noblemen throughout England. Odd thing about the British: They pride themselves on their resident ghosts. But why not? One of these tantalizing stories may make you want to have a live-in ghost of your own!

"Welcome to Henry's Haunted House!"

Several ghosts are said to haunt Hampton Court Palace, which lies on the Thames about 15 miles southwest of London. This famous castle was built as a private residence by Cardinal Thomas Wolsey, who later made it a gift to King Henry VIII to secure the monarch's favor. (It was Henry VIII, king of England from 1509 to 1547, who replaced the Catholic Church throughout the realm with the Church of England.) But Wolsey apparently still walks the grounds. His ghost was seen under an archway in 1966.

Hampton Court Palace.

(Photo by author)

The sound of footsteps and other paranormal phenomena experienced in the adjoining Old Court House are thought to come from the ghost of the famous architect Sir Christopher Wren (1632–1723) because they occur on the anniversary of his death.

Wren lived there while overseeing renovation of the palace, and he died there on February 26, 1723.

King Henry VIII lived at Hampton Court with five of his six wives. Two of them still haunt the palace grounds. Jane Seymour, who was the sovereign's third wife, died there a week after giving birth to the boy who would become King Edward VI. Seymour's spectre is frequently seen carrying a lit torch or candle through one of the courtyards.

Catherine Howard was the fifth wife of Henry VIII, but she was beheaded for adultery in 1542. Her ghost is frequently seen in the so-called Haunted Gallery, the walkway down which she ran to plead her case to her husband. (Another version of the legend says she was trying to escape.) Her spirit often materializes on the anniversary of her arrest. An apparition of Howard's ringed hand has also been seen hovering in front of her official portrait in the gallery.

Catherine Howard, the fifth wife of Henry VIII.

After Catherine's death, her son Prince Edward was nursed by Sibell Penn. She died in 1562 and was buried on castle property. Her spirit lay peacefully until 1829, when her grave was accidentally disturbed during renovations. Almost immediately, people began to hear an odd humming noise behind a brick wall in the southwest wing of the castle. The wall was torn down to reveal a hidden chamber: It held an old-fashioned spinning wheel, just like the ones used in the days of Sibell Penn. Had it been hers?

Two sentries as well as Princess Frederica of Hanover spotted the apparition of an old woman wearing a hooded gray robe in the area of the secret room. The ghost, thought by some to be Penn, was promptly nicknamed the Lady in Gray (no relation to any of the other gray ladies we've discussed).

Among the other numerous ghosts that haunt Hampton Court are:

◆ A mysterious White Lady.

◆ The headless Archbishop Laud.

◆ A spectral party of two men and seven women (reported by a police officer during World War II).

◆ Two officers from King Charles I's army. Until their remains were given a proper burial, the ghosts haunted the Fountain Court by making loud noises throughout the night.

Boo! _____

The Lady in Gray was a common name for any of the dozens of gray ladies who've been spotted over the centuries. Some ghosts do get around. They've been known to haunt more than one location. So you have to be careful when you identify a ghost who's called a Lady in Gray. It may or may not be the same spirit you've already met at some other haunting.

And now there might be another ghost to add to the list. For some time, guards had been finding one of the palace's emergency exit doors left open. When, in December 2003, they reviewed video from the closed-security camera directed at that area of the castle, they were stunned at what they saw: the image of a man wearing a monklike robe. Though blurry, a skeletal white face could be seen under his hood as the spectre stepped into the doorframe and grabbed the handle of the door. Does Hampton Court have a new inhabitant?

The Wraiths of Windsor Castle

Windsor Castle lies 20 miles outside London and has been the summer residence of England's royal family for 900 years. William the Conqueror built a wooden castle on the site around 1078, but nothing of it remains. Henry I began building the first stone castle there around 1110.

Windsor Castle is haunted by the ghosts of three of the English rulers who are buried there:

◆ Henry VIII

◆ Charles I

◆ George III

Other spirits of nonroyals—thought to be courtiers, soldiers, and servants—have been sighted there as well. Among the most recent of these apparitions is the ghost of a royal guard who committed suicide in 1927.

Henry VIII is sometimes seen walking along the castle ramparts, but he is more often spotted in the cloisters. Percipients often report that they can hear his moans as he drags his ulcerated leg behind him. Queen Elizabeth I, who was Henry's daughter and the last of the Tudor monarchs, has haunted the library since her death in 1603. Her phantom has been seen there by no less than Her Royal Highness Princess Margaret and the Empress Frederick of Germany, among others.

Two other royal spirits haunt the Windsor Castle library as well: King Charles I, who was beheaded in 1649 at the end of the English Civil War; and King George III, who ruled England from 1760 to 1820 and spent the final years of his life within the castle walls.

Finally, here's that story about a Wild Hunt that I promised you way back in Chapter 4. The most famous Wild Hunt haunts Hampton Court Palace, and it's led by the ghost of Herne the Hunter. According to popular lore, Herne was a royal huntsman of Richard II, who reigned from 1377 to 1399, or possibly of Henry VII or Henry VIII. Herne saved the life of his king by throwing himself in front of a wounded stag that was charging the monarch. A wizard suddenly appeared and told the king that he could prevent Herne's death by cutting off the stag's antlers and tying them to the hunter's head. Miraculously, Herne recovered. The king felt indebted to the hunter, so he showered Herne with attention and rewards. His fellow woodsmen became jealous and eventually convinced the king to oust Herne from the court. Cast out and in despair, the loyal hunter hanged himself from an oak tree on the grounds.

Herne's ghost has been seen there ever since. He usually appears in the nearby forest of Windsor Great Park, riding on a phantom black horse, accompanied by spectral baying hounds. The spectre can't be mistaken: He wears chains and has stag's antlers growing from his head.

Henry VIII was among the first to report seeing the apparition. When the oak tree from which Herne purportedly hanged himself blew down in 1863, Queen Victoria ordered that the wood from the tree be burned in order to release the hunter's spirit.

The ghost of Herne the Hunter is still said to materialize whenever England is in crisis, as he did before the 1931 Depression and again before the outbreak of World War II.

Changing of the Ghostly Guards

Then there's the primary residence of the royal family. Buckingham Palace is haunted by at least two ghosts, one ancient, and one a bit more modern. A phantom monk, wrapped in chains, occasionally appears in the castle, most frequently on Christmas Day. He's said to have been imprisoned in a priory that once stood where the palace is now located.

The other spirit is that of Major John Gwynne, a private secretary of King Edward VII. During a contentious divorce, the aide shot himself at his desk on the first floor of the palace. Although his ghost hasn't been seen, his presence is sometimes felt in the room to this day. Some people have reported hearing a spectral gunshot come from inside the room at night.

A Palace for a Princess

Today, Kensington Palace is probably best known as the last royal residence of Lady Diana, Princess of Wales. King William III originally bought the castle palace and had it converted into his residence in 1689. It remained the royal palace until 1760, when King George II died there.

At least three ghosts haunt the mansion. The most famous is King George II himself, who's been seen on the roof near the weather vane; his voice is heard on occasion as well. Another spirit, that of an elderly lady sitting at a spinning wheel, is thought to be an aunt of Queen Victoria, who was born in the palace. Finally, an unidentified man wearing period white breeches haunts the courtyard.

And, before you ask, no; no one has reported seeing Lady Diana's spirit in the palace.

> **CAUTION** **Boo!**
>
> If you become famous, don't expect to be left alone—even after you've gone on to your supposedly final reward. On March 9, 2003, American television aired a pay-per-view special entitled *The Spirit of Diana: A Worldwide Séance*. The show featured psychics in London, Paris, and elsewhere attempting to contact the spirit of the late Princess of Wales. It's not surprising that no provable contact was made, but that didn't stop the mediums from trying.

The White Ghosts of Dover

Dover Castle, the twelfth century fortress built high on the seaside white cliffs overlooking—what else?—Dover Harbor, is home to a gaggle of ghosts.

There have been reports of visible apparitions and spectral sounds haunting the castle for centuries. The phenomena include:

- A headless drummer boy on the ramparts. (Usually he isn't seen; only the beating of the drum is heard. He's thought to have lived during the time of Napoleon. The reason for his beheading is unknown.)

- ◆ A phantom horse galloping on the grounds (reported by groundskeepers and night security).

- ◆ Wailing and moaning of a woman who's said to have been walled up alive in the castle.

One more ghost story about Dover Castle: A Canadian group was in the underground casement rooms that had been used as a communications center during World War II. A man in a naval uniform approached a female member of the tour and asked whether she had seen a Miss Gumm. She said no, and he walked off. When the woman later asked the tour guide about the stranger, the leader was perplexed. It turned out that one of the other visitors had also seen the ghost but had assumed that it was an actor in wardrobe. But, no, the tour guide assured them, although the castle did employ costumed actors elsewhere on the grounds, none were working in the casements. When wartime records were later checked, the name that the mysterious man had asked for was found: She had been a Wren stationed there during the war.

Dover Castle on the cliffs above Dover, England.

(Photo by author)

Spooks in Your Sporrans

Along the dark moors and the Highland heath, the Scottish landscape is dotted with scores of castles, some still standing, many a shell of their former selves. Most served as the ancestral homes of the various northern tartan-clad clans.

Shades of Shakespeare

Perhaps the most famous castle in Scotland is the notorious Glamis Castle, the setting of Shakespeare's *Macbeth*. Is it any surprise that Glamis has been haunted for as long as anyone can remember?

Glamis Castle is the oldest inhabited castle in Scotland and easily one of the most impressive. The historic home of the Earls of Strathmore and Kinghorne, Glamis Castle has been a royal residence since 1372 and is the family home of Her Majesty Queen Elizabeth and the late Queen Mother.

Among the many apparitions said to haunt Glamis Castle are:

- A small, unidentified Gray Lady (yes, yet *another* Gray Lady), who has been seen most often in the chapel.

- Shadowy figures near the Blue Room.

- A woman without a tongue, madly pointing toward her mouth as she darts across the grounds.

- A thin man nicknamed "Jack the Runner," dashing up the driveway.

- A young black boy thought to have been a servant, who appears near the Queen Mother's bedroom.

- A wild man seen on dark and stormy nights bounding across a section of the roof known as "Mad Earl's Walk."

- A female figure bathed in a red glow, floating above the clock tower. (She's thought to be the Lady Glamis who was burned at the stake for witchcraft and for attempting to poison King James V.)

- A tall, unidentified figure, dressed in a long cloak.

- An unidentified woman looking out an upper window, with a pale face and sad eyes.

> **Ghostly Pursuits**
>
> Don't believe every ghost legend you hear. Glamis Castle is probably best known as the site of Macbeth's assassination of King Duncan; but this legend is almost certainly the literary invention of playwright William Shakespeare. King Malcolm II *was* murdered in the castle, however, and a bloodstain is said to mark the spot. And the mark is permanent! If anyone washes it away, it mysteriously reappears.

Glamis Castle has its share of other paranormal phenomena. Invisible hands have removed the bed-clothes of some overnight guests. A door opens by itself every night, even when bolted. The sound of hammering and knocking is sometimes heard coming from a room in the oldest part of the castle.

Glamis Castle, which legend and literature (though not historical fact) identifies as the site of Macbeth's murder of King Duncan.

(Photo courtesy of the Strathmore Estates)

A local legend says that during the reign of James II of Scotland, Lord Glamis argued with Alexander, the fourth Earl of Crawford (known as "Earl Beardie"), over a game of dice. When they cursed God for their bad luck, the devil appeared and sentenced their souls to play dice in that room for eternity. To this day, the spectral sound of dice being rolled can be heard coming from an overhead tower. The ghost of Earl Beardie has also been seen in the castle, most often in the Blue Room.

The Haunted Harp of Inverary Castle

Inverary Castle has been the ancestral home of the Campbell clan since the end of the fifteenth century. Located in the hamlet of Inverary on Loch Fyne in western Scotland, the present castle was completed in 1789. A fire in 1877 caused extensive damage, and there have been many repairs and renovations since. The house, still the seat of the Duke of Argyll, was opened to the public in 1953.

The MacArthur Room, the state bedroom of the MacArthurs of Loch Awe, is found on the first floor—what Americans call the "second floor." The room is haunted by the ethereal sound of a phantom harp, thought to be played by a murdered servant boy. But beware: According to legend, if you hear the harp, you'll die within a year!

Inverary Castle, located on Loch Fyne in Scotland.

(Photo by author)

The Shamrock Shores of the Emerald Isle

When it comes to sprites and spirits, Ireland is best known for its leprechauns, the wee elves with pots of gold found at the ends of rainbows. But Irish stories include ghostly tales of terror as well.

Leap Castle is a perfect example. Overlooking the Slieve Bloom Mountains, it's the ancestral home of the O'Carrolls. The castle was built around a large, central square tower known as the Chapel. On the ground floor, a door opened at one end of the room into a secret chamber that was used as a dungeon. Wings were later added onto the tower; one of the hallways ended in the so-called Priest's House. The castle was almost completely destroyed by fire in 1923.

Several guests have described seeing what's been called an "It"—a phantom standing about four feet tall, with black holes for eyes, bony hands, and smelling of rotting flesh.

One overnight visitor awoke to feel a cold pressure against his heart. He turned to see a tall, spectral woman, dressed in red and illuminated from within. As he lit a match to see her better, the ghost disappeared.

Other ghosts seen at Leap Castle have included:

- ◆ A shaven monk, wearing a cowl, who floats out of a window in the Priest's House.

- ◆ A small elderly man, dressed in a green cutaway coat, brown breeches, and buckle shoes. An aged lady, also wearing period clothes, sometimes accompanies him. (Their attire suggests that they weren't royals. Perhaps they were servants or guests at the castle.)

- ◆ An invisible "bedmate," which lies down beside guests. The mortal visitors can feel the phantom's weight pressing into the mattress and against their night-clothes.

Fit for a King: The Palace of Versailles

Of course, Great Britain has no monopoly on haunted castles. In medieval France, as in all of Europe during the Middle Ages, every fiefdom was dominated by the lord's castle.

And then there were the palaces built by the kings. Versailles, outside Paris, is the most spectacular of these. Although there have been no reports of ghosts within the palace itself, some of the surrounding gardens and outer buildings have been reported as haunted for almost a hundred years.

One group of buildings is the Petit Trianon, which was allegedly the site of one of the most fascinating ghost materializations of the twentieth century. King Louis XV originally commissioned the buildings for his mistress, the Marquise de Pompadour, and construction started in 1762. The structures were enlarged over the years to accommodate the king's subsequent mistress, Madame Dubarry, and later, King Louis XVI's wife, Marie Antoinette.

Now to the spooky stuff. In 1901, two English scholars, Annie Moberly and Eleanor Jourdain, visited Versailles. As they approached the Petit Trianon, they felt the air become totally still, then oppressively thick. For about a half hour, they observed several men in late eighteenth-century garb working and strolling throughout the gardens. Moberly also saw a woman in period clothing sitting on the grass outside the main house.

The British women didn't discuss their strange experience with each other or compare notes for a week. Once they did, they decided that they had experienced a haunting. After a bit of research, they decided the phantom woman on the lawn that Moberly had seen was Marie Antoinette; one of the male ghosts was her friend the Comte de Vaudreuil. Somehow they even determined the exact date they had visited:

August 5, 1789. To test their theory, the ladies returned to the Petit Trianon. Jourdain visited in January 1902 and encountered phenomena similar to what the pair had experienced on their first visit. Moberly accompanied Jourdain on another visit in July 1904. This time, nothing paranormal occurred. Moberly and Jourdain wrote a book about their walk on the wild side titled *An Adventure*, which they published in 1911. They concluded that they had somehow traveled back to the time of Marie Antoinette.

Phantom Phrases

Retrocognition, also sometimes called postcognition or residual haunting, is a sudden shift or displacement in time in which you find yourself in the past, seeing or experiencing events of which you have no prior knowledge.

If the events did occur as they suggested, it would be a documented report of *retrocognition*. Also sometimes called postcognition or a residual haunting, this very rare phenomenon is a sudden displacement in time during which you find yourself standing in a three-dimensional past.

Retrocognition is not the same as déjà vu—in which you think you've seen, heard, or done something exactly the same way before. Rather, it feels as if somehow you have suddenly stepped into the past. Nor is retrocognition a case of regression of memory. Subjects experience events that have no connection to their personal lives or family history.

Think of it as an audio and video playback of an event from the past, except that you're in the middle of—but separate from—the occurrence. You remain disengaged, merely an observer. Most paranormal experts think that residual hauntings are not earthbound or returning ghosts. Rather, they feel, that those who experience it somehow tap into events that have somehow imprinted themselves onto some sort of atmospheric "ether."

Needless to say, as much as paranormal investigators may have wanted to believe Moberly and Jourdain, they just couldn't accept their story as being an authentic case of retrocognition. First of all, their sightings were totally uncorroborated. Also, the tale was considered unreliable because they had waited so long to write down what supposedly happened. Memory plays tricks, skeptics pointed out, and they dismissed the women's claims one by one by offering possible natural causes for each event. Even the Society for Psychical Research felt that there was insufficient proof that Moberly and Jourdain had experienced a true paranormal event.

Over the years, however, there have been other reports of spectral sightings near the Petit Trianon:

◆ In 1908, John Crooke, his wife, and son heard ethereal band music and watched at length as a phantom lady sketched on a piece of paper.

- In 1928, Clare M. Burrow and Ann Lambert felt the dense air and depression described by Moberly and Jourdain. They, too, then encountered phantom men and women in period wardrobe. At least one of the ghosts vanished suddenly.

- On October 10, 1949, Jack and Clara Wilkinson and their four-year-old son saw a woman in eighteenth-century costume that, although not initially appearing to be a ghost, disappeared in the blink of an eye.

- On May 21, 1955, a London lawyer and his wife saw two men and a woman in period wardrobe walking near the Petit Trianon. Within seconds, the three phantoms evaporated.

These and subsequent claims were all investigated by ghost hunters. Some suggested that the "ghosts" were actually living people dressed in eighteenth-century costumes, perhaps in rehearsal or as part of an historical pageant. Also, the researchers pointed out, it was once common for visitors to Versailles to dress in period wardrobe just for the fun of it.

Despite these healthy doses of skepticism, many spectral sightings at Versailles have continued into modern day.

Drop Dead!

Verdala Castle was built in 1585 by the French Grand Master Hugues Lourbenx de Verdalle. It's surrounded by a public park, the peaceful Buskett Gardens. Over the centuries, the mansion has acted as a government palace and visiting heads of state are often welcomed there.

One visitor who never leaves is the Blue Lady, thought to be the ghost of the niece of the aged Grand Master de Rohan, who was once in residence there. The man offered to marry his ward, but when she refused him, he held her captive in the castle. Trying to escape from an upper story window, she accidentally fell to her death. Her ghost has been seen tumbling down the side of the building, but just before the apparition hits the ground, it disappears. She's always wearing the same blue dress she had on when she died.

And now it's time to escape from those dusty dungeons and castle corridors. Do you hear that carillon out in the distance? For whom do those bells toll? They toll for thee! Let's get you to the church on time to meet the many ghosts who haunt cathedrals, monasteries, nunneries, and graveyards.

Verdala Castle, haunted by the ghost of a Blue Lady.

(Photo by author)

The Least You Need to Know

♦ Hampton Court, Windsor Castle, Kensington Palace, and Buckingham Palace are just four of England's best known haunted castles. All are visited by the phantoms of legendary kings and queens.

♦ Glamis Castle, the traditional (though not historical) setting for Shakespeare's *Macbeth*, is haunted by numerous apparitions.

♦ Ireland, known for its shamrocks and leprechauns, has a folk tradition that includes ghosts and other spirit phenomena.

♦ Haunted visions at Versailles have been attributed to retrocognition, a sense of seeing or being transported into the past.

Chapter

16

Get Me to the Church on Time

In This Chapter

- ◆ Old habits die hard: phantom monks and nuns
- ◆ The spookiest haunted churches and cathedrals
- ◆ Ghosts in the—where else?—graveyard
- ◆ Famous final destinations: Stonehenge, Machu Picchu, and more

Survival after death is a major belief of most of the world's more prominent religions. As you'll recall, as far back as the time of ancient Greece, it was believed that evil and dangerous ghosts haunted their burial places. Many people still believe that it's best not to get too close to graveyards, especially at night.

Is it any wonder, then, that churches, cathedrals, and cemeteries—especially those in ruins—have become prime targets for ghost hunters in their attempts to catch a glimpse of a spook? Let's take a look at some of the more infamous places worldwide.

Holy Ghosts!

Dozens of cases of hauntings by phantom monks and nuns have been reported throughout Great Britain and the United States. In almost all instances, the religious spectres haunt their former monasteries, abbeys, and cathedrals. The spectres return to haunt the ruins as well as modern structures built on ancient holy sites. It's believed that some phantom ghosts come back to the locations at which they were martyred for their beliefs; others return to a spot that they loved during their lives, such as the family homes in which they were born. Often, groups of ghosts are seen walking in procession, as if going to meals or vespers. Sometimes percipients hear chanting or singing. On rare occasions, phantom monks have been known to talk to those who see them.

Ghostly Monks and Nuns of the British Isles

We've already visited the so-called "Nun's Walk" at Borley Rectory (see Chapter 14). The apparition was no doubt surprising to those who saw (or see) it, but spectral nuns and monks are almost common in the United Kingdom. This is especially true at ancient Christian sites, though for some unknown reason there seem to be more ghostly monks running around than nuns. Here, then, are some of their favorite haunts in England and Scotland.

The Spirits Call You Home

The whole Isle of Iona seems to be haunted. Iona's one of the Inner Hebrides off the coast of Scotland, and it's dotted with ancient ruins and graveyards, plus the tombs of 60 Irish, Norwegian, and Scottish kings.

CAUTION | **Boo!**

The legendary "Call of the Island" beckons the unwary listeners who hear it, creating in them an overwhelming urge to travel to Iona. Many have heard the spirits beckoning them from halfway around the world before journeying there. For some, it's their last holiday: Either they choose to stay on Iona, or the spirits don't let them go—at least not alive. Many visitors have died under mysterious circumstances. If you hear the siren call from Iona, plug your ears. The trip could be your last!

A monastery founded in 563 by St. Columba was the home for the ghost monks now thought to roam the island, both singly and in procession. Reports of phantom monk sightings didn't begin until the Reformation, when many of the brothers' graves were defiled and crosses that had been used to mark their graves were thrown into the sea.

The monks have been seen indoors as well as outside, always dressed in brown robes with hemp rope belts. They never speak. In fact, they make *no* sound at all, but they're sometimes accompanied by twinkling blue lights. So many phantom monks have been spotted on Angels' Hill that many local residents fear going there after dark.

The Isle of Iona is also haunted by spectral music, invisible "presences," and phantom Viking longboats (especially on White Sands beach, where invading Danes landed on Christmas Eve 986).

The Three Ghosts of the Holy Trinity Church

Found in Micklegate, York, Holy Trinity Church is supposedly haunted by the ghost of an abbess. Soldiers who came to destroy the building during the Reformation killed the abbess, who was head of the Benedictine convent that was located there. As she lay dying, she swore to haunt the site. Indeed, her phantom did return to the ruins, and she moved in to haunt the new Holy Trinity Church when it was built on the location.

The church is also said to be haunted by the ghosts of an unidentified woman. She's thought to be the wife of a man who was buried near the organ within the church. Their child, whose ghost also appears, died of the plague, so it was buried outside the city walls. Soon after, the woman also died, but she was allowed to be buried next to her husband. It's said that the spirits of the mother and child cannot rest because they're buried apart. Also, it's believed that the phantom abbess sometimes leads the ghost child from its grave into the church to visit the mother.

Phantastic Tips

Before you call a ghost a ghost, make sure of what you're seeing. The victorious Normans, for example, called the site of the Battle of Hastings "Senlac," which means "Lake of Blood." The name probably comes from a natural phenomenon: After a rainstorm there, water in puddles appears red because it's colored by the iron content in the soil. To the ancients, this might have been mistaken for blood.

A Phantom Fountain of Blood

William I (William the Conqueror) built this now-haunted church and monastery on the site where he defeated King Harold at the Battle of Hastings in 1066. William placed the High Altar at the spot where Harold fell; now, a ghostly fountain of blood supposedly appears there on occasion.

In the nineteenth century, the ghost of an unidentified woman was frequently seen on the grounds. A phantom monk has also been spotted along the so-called Monk's Walk at the abbey. Some people think the apparition is that of a monk who cursed Sir Anthony

Browne after the nobleman accepted the abbey as a gift from Henry VIII in 1538. Others believe it's the ghost of the Duchess of Cleveland, who once rented the property.

Arthur Any More Ghosts Like You in the Abbey?

Glastonbury Abbey, the earliest Christian church in England, was built on Glastonbury Tor, a shelf of land towering five hundred feet above a plain that was once completely covered by water. According to tradition, the abbey was established in 166 C.E., but some experts claim it was founded as early as 47 C.E. Phantom monks are said to haunt the abbey grounds.

Legend has it that Glastonbury Abbey stands on the site of the island of Avalon, the final resting place of King Arthur and, in some versions of the tale, Queen Guinevere as well. According to Arthurian myths, the king was mortally wounded in battle against Modred, his illegitimate son and usurper of his throne. Arthur was whisked away on a boat by three fairies, where he waits in an enchanted, healing sleep. But he will triumphantly return when Britain is in its greatest hour of need. (Some claim, though, that his ghost already rises one night a year, on Christmas Eve, and that the spirit can be seen riding a horse into the courtyard of the abbey.)

The ruins of an ancient fortress on nearby South Cadbury Hill are thought by many Arthurian enthusiasts to have been part of Camelot as well. Some paranormals claim that on Midsummer's Eve the ghosts of the Knights of the Round Table appear in the fortress, where they're said to be buried. From there, the spectres make their way over to the Tor.

(Daniel Beard illustration from the first edition of Mark Twain's A Connecticut Yankee in King Arthur's Court, *1889)*

Canterbury Ghost Tales

Canterbury Cathedral, located in County Kent in southeastern England, is haunted by at least three ghosts.

St. Augustine, sent from Rome by Pope Gregory the Great, arrived on the shores of Kent, England in 597 C.E. The local ruler, King Ethelbert, gave the saint a church in Canterbury, where the clergyman was soon elevated to Archbishop. The cathedral was completely rebuilt beginning in 1070, and repairs and renovations have continued up to modern times. Canterbury Cathedral became a major pilgrimage site in medieval times (as immortalized in Chaucer's classic poem "The Canterbury Tales"), and it remains a popular religious and tourist center.

Perhaps its most famous Archbishop was Thomas Becket, who was murdered in the cathedral by four knights of King Henry II on December 29, 1170. There have been several sightings of Becket's ghost in the Crypt of the Cathedral, where he was originally entombed. (Becket's ghost is more often associated with the Tower of London, however, as you'll read in Chapter 22.)

A dark spectral figure in a hooded robe has been spotted in the Chapel of Our Lady Undercroft, also in the cathedral's crypt, but it has never been identified.

Then there's the story of Nell Cook, born Ellen Bean, who lived in the early 1500s during the reign of Henry VIII. She became a servant of a canon in the Priory of St. Saviour, who lived near the Dark Entry, a side entrance near the back of the cathedral. The friar gave her the playful nickname Nell or Nelly Cook because of her remarkable skill in the kitchen.

Shocked to discover that the friar was having a compromising relationship with a young lady who had moved in with him, Nell murdered the pair with a poisoned "Warden Pie." To prevent an inquiry and scandal, the other monks quickly buried the Canon and his "niece" (as the friar had called her) in the cathedral. But Nell Cook also vanished!

It's said that many years later three masons doing repairs discovered Nell's skeleton under a flagstone in the Dark Entry. The last crumbs of the notorious meat pie were found beside her.

Within a year, one of the masons was found dead, and the other two workers were hanged for his murder. But, according to rumor, they actually died as a result of a curse: They had seen the ghost of Nell Cook, who haunts the Dark Entry.

The legend grew, and over the years several other untimely deaths have been attributed to the victims of Nell Cook. Beware: She most often appears on Friday evenings, and it's said that anyone who sees her spectre will die within a year!

Stonehenge: Phantoms on the Salisbury Plain

We can't leave England without a visit to the most famous sacred site in the British Isles: Stonehenge (see Appendix C). The megalithic stone circle outside Avebury, Somerset, on the Salisbury Plain was constructed as a temple and astronomical observatory by unknown builders more than 5,000 years ago. The Druids, the priests of the ancient Celts, held rituals and ceremonies at Stonehenge soon after they arrived in the British Isles, but the stone circle predates them. To protect the monument, visitors are no longer allowed to walk within the circle itself, but this doesn't stop the spirits of Druid priests. Sometimes their ghosts are seen outside the entrance, near the standing stone called the Heelstone; others are occasionally seen at the Altar Stone in the center of the stone circle.

Stonehenge is not the only haunted ancient stone circle in England, by the way. Avebury Circle, located at Wiltshire Downs outside Marlborough, also in Somerset, is visited by ghostly, dancing figures; and ethereal music has been reported coming from within the ring. Spirit Druid priests are said to make the procession from Avebury, though Wiltshire Downs, to another, smaller stone circle on nearby Overton Hill.

Oh, and there are more modern ghosts haunting Avebury Circle, too. In the fourteenth century, the Catholic Church ordered that the pagan circle be dismantled and its stones dispersed or buried. A toppling stone crushed a barber, and his ghost soon began to appear near what became known as the "Barbers Stone." His skeleton was found beneath the stone during excavation and restoration of the site. Some people carted away the smaller stones to build houses, but a ghastly spirit that locals dubbed "the Haunt" soon began to haunt these homes.

Ghostly Monks and Nuns of the United States

Sacred spirits aren't exclusive to England, of course. The New World has plenty to go around. Wherever there are churches, there's the chance that you'll find ghost clerics—and phantom lay visitors as well.

Many churches throughout the United States have a reputation for being haunted, by everything from the ghost of a Confederate soldier to a businessman dressed in his coat and tie. Let's take an alphabetical romp through several states:

- **Alabama.** The chapel of the University of Alabama is haunted by the ghost of a Confederate soldier in uniform.

- **Connecticut.** The Church of Eternal Light, constructed around the end of the nineteenth century, was one of three churches built in Bristol by the Sessions family. Balls of ghost light have been filmed in the chapel, and an apparition has been seen in the bell tower.

- **Illinois.** There are at least three haunted churches in Chicago: Beverly Unitarian Church (see its earlier listing as a haunted house in Chapter 13); Holy Family Church (parishioners and clergy have seen an unidentified white apparition); and St. Turbius Church (an unexplained spectre has been seen near the altar).

  Also, the ghost of an unidentified man wearing a black business suit haunts the sanctuary of the First Methodist Church of Evanston. He's usually seen walking down the side aisle between the pillars and the wall. He often pauses behind the columns, as if hiding, but if you actually stop to look for him, he's never there.

- **Louisiana.** Sometimes on early rainy mornings, the ghost of Pere Dagobert can be heard singing a funeral mass in the St. Louis Cathedral in New Orleans. Legend has it that the phantom voice still continues from a service he conducted in 1769 for several townspeople executed for attempting to overthrow the Spanish occupation.

- **Maryland.** Featured on television's *Sightings: The Ghost Report*, Baltimore's Westminster Church dates back to the eighteenth century. Among those buried here is horror author Edgar Allen Poe. (Remember the Edgar Allen Poe house from Chapter 13?) Although no apparitions have been reported in the church or its graveyard, many people have heard voices or felt mysterious presences.

- **Montana.** The Bonanza Inn in Virginia City used to be a frontier hospital. The ghost of a nun who served there occasionally has been seen throughout the building.

- **Nevada.** In the Virginia City located in nearby Nevada, the spirit of an unidentified female spectre can be spotted in an upstairs window at St. Paul's Episcopal Church.

- **Ohio.** Collingwood Arts Center in Toledo used to serve as a dormitory for nuns, and several have apparently decided to stay on. One phantom nun is sometimes seen walking from the balcony down to a particular seat in the downstairs auditorium. Once she's settled, she vanishes. It's said that this spectre gives off negative and angry vibes and is,

Phantastic Tips

According to legend, a phantom "Pink Lady" appears on the night of June 15 every other year in the Yorba Family Cemetery in Yorba Linda, California. Ghost hunters from all over flock to the cemetery on that date, hoping to catch a glimpse of her. If you're in the area, why not drop by? You might get lucky!

therefore, very disturbing to encounter. A kinder, gentler phantom nun has been seen sewing in the attic.

The Arts Center is haunted by at least three other ghosts: There's a male spectre in the basement and another in one of the apartments, and the ghost of a bride who committed suicide after being left at the altar haunts the building's west hallway.

♦ **Virginia.** The ghost of a woman who was killed in the Aquia Church in Fredericksburg has been seen haunting its belfry.

♦ **Washington.** Monks once inhabited Monresa Castle in Port Townsend. It's said that one of the brothers committed suicide by hanging himself and that, on some nights, you can hear his phantom body swaying on an invisible rope.

♦ **Wyoming.** Likewise, the belfry of St. Mark's Episcopal Church in Cheyenne is haunted by the ghost of a man who was killed while building the tower.

First-Person Phantoms

Shortly after Lutheran minister Al Wagaman's arrival at Grace Church in Mt. Carmel, Pennsylvania, he was having coffee with the sexton in the parsonage when he heard a strange noise coming from upstairs in the church. It sounded like someone was pulling chains across the floor. He asked what it was. The sexton smiled and said, "Oh, that's the ghost of Grace Church." Certain that the elder was just playing games, Wagaman went upstairs to have a look for himself but saw and heard nothing. As soon as he went back downstairs, however, the sounds started again. The sexton flashed him a grin that said "I told you so."

Pastor Wagaman decided to tell the ghost story to some of the teens in the congregation, and of course they loved it! A haunted church? They decided that perhaps there was a homeless person living in one of the tower rooms of the church (a real possibility), but they went up into the tower and found nothing. So about six of the boys decided that they were going to "stake out" the place and find the ghost.

They went over to the church prepared to spend the night, sleeping bags and all. They arranged their quarters on the stage of the large adult Sunday school room and started to settle in. But within an hour, they all came running back to the parsonage, scared to death. Although they hadn't seen anything, they heard the invisible chains and "felt a presence." They never tried that again. Now retired from the ministry, Pastor Wagaman adds, "I heard the sounds, as did everyone else, and even though I believe there must be a rational explanation, none was ever found."

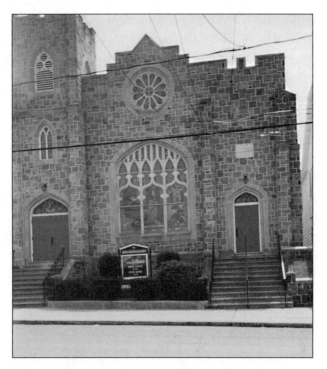

The haunted Grace Church in Mt. Carmel, Pennsylvania.
Is that aura in front of one of the towers actually a ghost?

(Photo courtesy of Diann Repko)

An International Assortment of Sacred Spectres

Let's see. We've visited churches in the United Kingdom and in the United States Only 200-plus countries to go. Don't worry: I've zeroed in on a half dozen of the spookiest haunted churches and temples. Some of them are among the world's top tourist destinations. Why not add a ghost hunt to your next vacation?

Les Phantomes de Notre-Dame

Work on the towering gothic Notre Dame Cathedral on the Ile de la Cite, a small island in the Seine River in Paris, France, was begun by Bishop Maurice de Sully in 1163. The cathedral was built on the foundations of two previous Christian churches and a still-earlier Roman temple. Its main structure was completed in 1250, but there have been constant additions ever since. A major renovation in 1845 resulted in the overall look we're familiar with today.

A spectral bishop is among the many spirits that haunt the interior of the cathedral. Hooded ghosts wearing tall ecclesiastical hats appear on the outside rear balcony underneath the rosette stained glass window. Hideous, troll-like shapes have been seen climbing the outside walls, but skeptics suggest that people are either mistaking the many decorative gargoyles as spirits or, in their imagination, are expecting to see the ghost of the famous (though fictional) Quasimodo from Victor Hugo's classic novel, *The Hunchback of Notre-Dame*.

The Bones of a Saint

Located on the Iberian Peninsula in Spain, the Cathedral of Santiago de Compostela is one of the great pilgrimage sites of the Catholic Church. According to legend, St. James the Elder, one of Christ's original 12 apostles, preached to the Celts in Iberia during his travels before he was martyred in Jerusalem around C.E. 44. Supposedly, his bones were returned to Iberia, where they were placed in a shrine, but they were lost during the years of Roman rule.

The Santiago de Compostela in Iberia, Spain.

(Photo by author)

Here's where the story gets good: It's said that a hermit, guided by a star and celestial music, discovered the buried relics in a large field around C.E. 813. A church was built over the spot just 16 years later. Then, in 844, it was claimed that Santiago Matomoro, known as St. James the Moorslayer, appeared on a white horse to lead Christian warriors against the Arab Moors, who were then occupying most of Iberia. The cathedral sent out storytellers to spread the good news: Healings and other miracles were taking place in Santiago de Compostela. By the twelfth century, the cathedral was the most-visited pilgrimage destination in all of medieval Christendom. (Jerusalem and Rome were #1 and #2 on everyone's list, of course, but they were too far away and too costly and dangerous to get to.)

No matter that St. James probably never reached what is today Spain. People don't claim to see *his* spirit at the cathedral, anyway. But through the years the ghost of Santiago Matomoro *has* been seen. And modern visitors have reported the apparitions of many of those long-ago pilgrims; still more have felt the ghosts' presence.

"Wat" Do the Ghosts Want?

The magnificent Hindu temples of Angkor, spread over 77 square miles in central Cambodia, were built by Khmer rulers between 879 and 1191 C.E. Angkor Wat, the largest and best-known temple area within the site, is just one of 10 major groupings, each with its own complex of monuments. Thai forces to the north frequently invaded territory in the Khmer Empire, but they made a major assault and captured Angkor in 1432. Rather than occupy Angkor, however, the Thai moved southward to establish their capital in Phnom Penh.

Although Hindu monks never completely abandoned Angkor, the temples were, for the most part, forgotten. Rumors persisted in the cities, however, about a mysterious sacred city in the north that had been swallowed up by the jungle. Angkor Wat was finally rediscovered and mapped in 1860 by a French naturalist, Henri Mouhot.

The presence of spirits can be felt everywhere in Angkor: It's been described as a deep repository of ancient energy. Many people report seeing actual apparitions, usually in the form of animals or Khmer warriors.

> **Ghostly Pursuits**
>
> How do ghost legends get started? Consider Angkor and Machu Picchu, both major cities that seemed to vanish into time. Yet tales about their existence persisted for centuries before they were finally rediscovered. It makes you wonder how many ghost stories that have been told and retold over the years also have that kernel of truth waiting to be proven.

Spirits dwell in the ruins of the Hindu temples of Angkor, Cambodia.

(Photo by author)

High-Flying Phantoms

Located high in the Andes Mountains of Peru, about 50 miles northwest of Cuzco, Machu Picchu is one of the most astonishing places on Earth. Modern scholars think that the city, most likely a royal citadel, was abandoned soon after the Spanish began their conquest in 1532. Remarkably, the conquistadors never found this "lost city." Over the centuries, the royal metropolis was completely overgrown by jungle. It wasn't discovered until 1911, by Hiram Bingham, an American explorer.

Shrouded in clouds, lost in time, Machu Picchu is only now giving up its secrets. In addition to the imperial buildings, there were layers of terraces to grow crops and, of course, temples to the gods.

Machu Picchu, the mystic Incan city in the Andes Mountains of Peru.

(Photo by author)

The ghosts seen at Machu Picchu today are those of fifteenth-century Incan priests wearing full religious regalia. They most frequently appear in the one of the temple areas or along the walkways between terraces.

A Place for All Ghosts to Gather

The Pantheon, with its immense unsupported dome, was completed by the Emperor Hadrian around 126 C.E. The temple was dedicated to the all of the Roman gods; in fact, the Greek word *pantheion* means "place for all gods." After the fall of the Roman Empire, the Pantheon was used as a Christian church from 609 to 1885. After that, it was converted into a national shrine and mausoleum for Italian heroes.

King Victor Emmanuel I and the painter Raphael are among those entombed in the Pantheon. But they're not the ghosts that haunt it. The apparitions are thought to be those of pagan priests from the Roman era. In addition, eerie balls of blue light can occasionally be seen under the dome.

A Phantom "Fisher of Men"

Father Charles was a dedicated priest at a small village church in Marsamxett, Malta. His parishioners were mostly families of fishers. In fact, he celebrated a 5 A.M. Mass every day so that the fishermen could attend before they set sail. As is common in the Catholic Church, many of the congregants asked the priest to perform special Masses for their loved ones who had passed on. Father Charles readily agreed, but he died before he could complete them all.

Marsamxett parish church was haunted by Father Charles, whose ghost returned to complete the Masses he had promised to perform.

(Photo by author)

Two years later, Father Simon was the new parish priest. He discovered that someone was opening a locked cabinet in the sacristy at nights and disturbing, though not stealing, items used during Holy Mass. At first, rather than accuse anyone, he simply changed the locks, but still he would find the items rearranged each morning. Finally, one night he hid in the church to try to catch the intruder. It turned out to be a ghost! A phantom priest emerged from the sacristy, moved to the altar, performed a Mass, and then left the nave—all in silence. When Father Simon followed the spectre into the sacristy to challenge it, no one was there. But, as usual, the cabinet door was wide open.

The priest shared his experience with some members of the congregation, who immediately recognized the description of the ghostly cleric. It was Father Charles! The new priest pledged to celebrate all of remaining special Masses and to perform one for Father Charles's spirit as well. When the services were completed, the ghost of Father Charles never returned, no doubt having moved on to his heavenly reward.

It's a Grave Situation

There's an old wives' tale that if you have to walk through a graveyard in the dark, you should whistle to keep away the ghosts. I've always thought it would take more than whistling to scare away a creature from the Beyond. But, hey, whatever works!

Given the great number of haunted churches in Great Britain, it's odd that there aren't more cemeteries there with the same reputation. Perhaps the United States has more than made up for that. Here are just a few of the dozens of (allegedly) ghostly graveyards right here in North America.

A Haunted Bachelor Party

Located on a one-acre plot near the Rubio Woods Forest Preserve in Midlothian, Illinois, Bachelor Grove Cemetery is one of greater Chicago's most paranormally active cemeteries. The graveyard got its name from the number of unmarried men who once lived in the area.

There have been more than a hundred ghost sightings at the cemetery between its opening in 1864 and 1965, when reports of apparitions and paranormal activity tapered off. Perhaps because of its ghostly reputation, the cemetery has experienced a great deal of vandalism, including gravestones being defaced or smashed and coffins being disinterred and opened.

Among the many ghosts and phenomena seen at Bachelor Grove have been:

- A hooded monk
- A so-called "White Lady"
- The "Madonna of Bachelor's Grove," seen on nights of the full moon carrying a phantom baby
- A farmer along with his horse and plow
- Various vehicles
- Men walking out of the lagoon adjacent to the cemetery, which was a common dumping place for bodies during the gang wars of the Prohibition Era
- A ghostly farmhouse, seen at various places on the property
- Ghost lights

CAUTION

Boo!

Don't always trust your eyes. More than a few people have mistaken statues for spirits, especially in moonlit cemeteries. In the soft, cool light of midnight, gleaming granite could easily appear to be the radiant glow of a ghost.

The Spirits Have Left the Building

Not to be confused with Elvis's estate, Graceland Cemetery is a Chicago graveyard opened in 1860 and home to numerous ghosts and haunted statues. Among the spirits is Inez Clarke, who died in 1880 but still roams the grounds. The glass-enclosed statue over her grave frequently disappears at night, especially during rainstorms, only to reappear the next morning. The area around the colossal tomb of Ludwig Wolff is haunted by a green-eyed monster that howls when there's a full moon. The statue of a seven-year-old girl seems to cry and has been seen walking through the cemetery.

The Tomb of the Voodoo Queen

St. Louis Cemetery, located in the French Quarter of New Orleans, hosts the ghost of Marie Laveau, the infamous nineteenth-century voodoo queen (see Chapter 13). Although Laveau doesn't haunt the cemetery in a recognizable human form, some say she flies over her tomb in the guise of a giant black crow. Others think she takes the shape of a large phantom black dog that's frequently seen on the grounds.

The tomb said to be that of Marie Laveau, the voodoo queen of New Orleans.

(Photo by author)

The Cavorting Coffins of Christ Church

Get ready to be freaked out! In the early 1800s, Thomas Chase, a wealthy gentleman in Bridgetown, Barbados, bought a crypt for his family in the Christ Church Parish cemetery. It's a small mausoleum, with a plain, undecorated interior. Half of the structure is underground. About a dozen steps lead down to the entrance, where you must duck your head to enter the empty vault. In place of the original rock and cement slab door that once closed the tomb, the entrance now has a metal door with open bars, but it always hangs open.

Mrs. Thomasina Goddard, a relative, was the first to be interred there, in July 1807. Chase's two-year-old daughter Mary Ann (or Anna), died a few months later, and her small coffin was added to the vault. His other daughter, teenage Dorcas, died in July 1812, and she, too, was placed in the tomb.

One month later, in August 1812, Thomas Chase died. Now it gets fun: When the cement seal of the crypt was broken and the slab was moved aside, it was discovered that the coffins inside had somehow moved around—*on their own!* This was particularly amazing because the lead coffins were incredibly heavy; it had taken several men to carry them into the vault.

Workers straightened the first three coffins and laid Thomas Chase's on top and across them to hold them in place. It was another four years before the mausoleum was opened again to add another family member. This time, all four coffins had moved, as if someone had lifted them up and tossed them about. Only two months later, in November 1816, the tomb was opened to inter Samuel Brewster. Again, the coffins had shifted.

By now, rumors were running rampant among the superstitious on the island. The vault was haunted! Remember, this was a time when the Caribbean was rife with tales of ghosts and voodoo. Chase had been a cruel and mean-tempered man, so some people concluded that his family spirits didn't want to be in the same tomb with him. They were just trying to get their coffins as far away from his as possible.

When it came time for another burial in the crypt, the British governor of Barbados, Lord Combermere, personally watched as the sepulcher was opened. Like before, the coffins were scattered everywhere!

Combermere ordered that the coffins be examined. The tomb was checked to ensure that there were no secret entrances or trap doors. The walls and doors were searched for cracks to make sure that the interior hadn't been temporarily flooded, which might have moved the coffins. The caskets were neatly arranged, the floor was dusted with sand (to show footprints if anyone sneaked inside), and the vault was sealed shut. The Governor pressed his personal stamp into the wet cement.

Nine months passed. On April 18, 1820, the tomb was re-opened in front of hundreds of spectators. Even though the cement, slab, and seals hadn't been disturbed, the Chase family coffins were again strewn about inside! Yet there was no evidence that anyone had entered in the intervening months.

To stop the terrifying phenomenon from recurring, the caskets were removed and separated to different graves. And to make certain that the tomb would never be haunted again, the crypt has been left empty and unused to this day.

Well, that's enough to keep me out of a cemetery at night. And if I do have to pass one, I'm gonna whistle a happy tune as I walk on by.

The haunted interior of the now-empty and abandoned Chase Vault, in Christ Church, Barbados.

(Photo by author)

All right, it's time to check out your battle gear. We're going to take a look at the ghosts of famous war heroes and haunted battlefields.

The Least You Need to Know

- For those fearful of ghosts, cemeteries have always been off limits at night. Reports of hauntings in graveyards date back to the ancient Greeks.

- Phantom monks and nuns have been seen in monasteries and convents throughout the world.

- England is perhaps the most haunted country on Earth; this is particularly true of its ancient cathedrals and abbeys, many of which are in ruins.

- The United States also has its share of ghost-ridden churches and phantom clerics. In fact, they can be found in every state of the Union.

Chapter 17

That These Honored Dead

In This Chapter

◆ Phantoms of military greats

◆ Phantom armies on the move

◆ Revolutionary and Civil War spirits

◆ Ghosts from the taming of the West

Some of the greatest tales of courage come out of war. And so do some of the spookiest ghost stories. Such tales date to at least the Sumerian civilization, which flourished in Mesopotamia (modern-day Iraq) from the fourth millennium B.C.E. to the mid-700s B.C.E. According to ancient myths, after some of the warrior-kings defeated a city in battle, they would order the graves of their fallen warriors opened so that their ghosts could hunt down any enemy soldiers that had escaped.

Apparently it's true: Old soldiers never die. Their ghosts continue to appear where they breathed their last. A few are famous phantoms; most are among the anonymous millions who have served their countries in the hours of need. It seems that the bloodier the battle, the more likely that ghosts will return to haunt the fields of glory. Let's walk across that Thin Red Line to see them for ourselves.

Hero Worship

Military heroes are often larger-than-life characters—if not during their careers, then certainly in legend. Sir Francis Drake and "Mad Anthony" Wayne are no exception. So when their ghosts come back, you know they mean business!

Sir Francis Drake: Spirit from the Sea

Sir Francis Drake (1540–1596) was an English navigator, and, perhaps because of his prowess in battle, many of his contemporaries thought that he was a wizard. He was the first Englishman to circumnavigate the globe (between 1570 and 1580). Along the way, he fought Spanish ships and sacked their settlements in the New World. In 1580, he was knighted by Queen Elizabeth I. Drake's enduring fame lies mainly in his defeat of the Spanish Armada in 1588.

Despite his seeming invincibility, Drake was eventually beaten by a Spanish force in the West Indies in 1595. He managed to escape capture, but the next year he fell ill and died aboard his ship off Puerto Bello, Panama.

Before his death, Drake ordered that his battle drum be taken back to his home, Buckland Abbey, in Devon, England. He swore that, should England face peril again, he would return from the dead, strike the drum, and lead his country into battle. (As you saw in Chapter 16, a similar legend surrounds King Arthur.)

Phantastic Tips

The sound of phantom drums beating is a recurrent theme in battleground and castle ghost stories. And don't forget the poltergeists: Along with stone-throwing and fire-starting, drumming was one of the most popular activities among pre-twentieth-century poltergeists. If, some spooky night, you hear a ratta-tat-tat coming from that toy drum in the kids' play chest, you might just be haunted.

Indeed, Drake's drum was supposedly heard beating throughout western England in 1914 as the country entered World War I. Some heard a single loud drum beat onboard the British ships surrounding the defeated German fleet at their surrender in 1919. Others claimed they heard the beating drum at the beginning of World War II.

Two final ghostly notes about Sir Drake: According to legend, Drake sometimes appears as the leader of a Wild Hunt (see Chapter 4.) Also, some occultists believe that, over the centuries, Drake's spirit has returned several times, reincarnated as various British admirals, including Viscount Horatio Nelson (1758–1805).

He's Mad, I Tell You: Major General Anthony Wayne

American Major General Anthony Wayne (1745–1796) was nicknamed "Mad Anthony" because of his single-minded determination in pursuing his enemies during the American Revolution. Apparently, he *is* tenacious, because his spirit has refused to depart this Earth.

His ghost is said to haunt Fort Ticonderoga, where he was commandant in 1771. The phantom most often appears in the dining room of his former quarters or sitting in a chair in front of the fireplace. He's usually seen smoking a long-stemmed pipe or drinking from a pewter mug.

While Wayne was stationed at Ticonderoga, he and Nancy Coates, a local woman, became lovers. Convinced that Wayne had turned his attentions to Penelope Haynes, another lady in the area, Coates drowned herself in nearby Lake Champlain. Nancy Coates's ghost is seen in and around the fort and floating in the lake. People often hear her crying as well.

Wayne's ghost also appears at Lake Memphremagog in Vermont, which he first visited in 1776 while hunting for bald eagles to capture and train. After Wayne's death, his spirit appeared at a log fort (by then a fur trader's post) next to the lake. The ghost also has been spotted on nearby paths with one eagle perched on each wrist. He's even been seen walking across the waters of the lake!

Ghostly Pursuits

In the mid-1800s, Major Duncan Campbell of Scotland was haunted by the ghost of his cousin Donald, because the major had unknowingly given sanctuary to Donald's murderer. Eventually, the phantom stopped his nocturnal visits, but not before warning his cousin that they would next "meet at Ticonderoga." Years later, while serving with the British forces at Fort Ticonderoga, the major was mortally wounded during a skirmish. Donald's spectre appeared one last time to wish his cousin farewell. People still claim to see the ghosts of both Campbells on the fort's old battlegrounds. The folktale served as the inspiration for Robert Louis Stevenson's 1889 novel *The Master of Ballantrae: A Winter's Tale*.

The ghost of Mad Anthony Wayne goes even further afield! In 1779, General George Washington ordered Wayne to warn the American troops of an upcoming attack by the British at Storm King Pass near Stony Point, New York. He made a daring ride during a stormy night on his horse, Nab, to alert the Continental soldiers. The spectral ride reoccurs to this day when storms approach the area. Wayne, with his cape rippling behind him, is seen hunkered over Nab. The horse's hooves and flanks spark fire as the duo gallop through the mountain passes.

Finally, Wayne's wraith is said to return to the ruins of a Georgian-style brick home located near Rogue's Road in Loudon County, Virginia, which the major general visited in 1779 when the house was owned by Philip Nolan. The reason for Wayne's haunting the site is uncertain. The former residence is also supposedly haunted by the ghosts of two Hessian soldiers who fled their nearby camp during the Revolutionary War. They hid in the house, but were found and executed. Their spectres haunt the basement, banging and scratching on the walls.

Tramp, Tramp, Tramp, the Boys Are Marching

Ghost soldiers haunt the places they defended worldwide. Out on the field of battle, as well, more than one living soldier has experienced visitations from spirits. Sometimes the apparitions are of humans; sometimes they're spectral angels.

Others have reported seeing entire phantom armies on the move. Often the ghosts pass by silently, but sometimes observers experience all of the noise and brouhaha of battle.

The Dieppe Raid Case

In late July and early August 1951, two Englishwomen (called Dorothy Norton and her sister-in-law Agenes Norton in later reports to conceal their identities) were on holiday with Dorothy's two children and a nurse at Puys, near Dieppe, France. On the morning of August 4 at about 4:20, the women were suddenly awakened by the sounds of war coming from the direction of the beach. The noises included gunfire, men shouting, screams, and, later, planes. The cacophony continued in various degrees of intensity for about two-and-a-half hours before disappearing completely. Throughout the disturbance, they saw no apparitions of men or machines.

The women were aware that a battle had taken place on that stretch of beach during World War II, but they knew none of the details. They also were familiar with the retrocognition that two other British women had undergone at the Petit Trianon in 1901 (see Chapter 15), so they understood the importance of independent verification of what had happened to them.

First, they surveyed the household to see if anyone else had heard the commotion. No one had, so the two ladies wrote down separate accounts of what they'd experienced and the times at which it had occurred. The accounts were almost identical. Upon further research, they discovered that the times and sounds nearly matched the events of the actual battle that had taken place on August 19, 1942. Dorothy Norton claimed that she also had heard the phenomena on August 3, but she had not wanted to alarm her sister-in-law, who had slept through the racket.

Psychical researchers G. W. Lambert and Kathleen Gray investigated their claims. They were impressed by the ladies' seeming honesty and conviction, but, of course, their stories couldn't be tested. Skeptics were quick to point out that there were several other possibilities to explain what the Nortons might have heard.

First-Person Phantoms

Richard Applegate of La Mesa, California, tells of having undergone an episode of retrocognition in England. Traveling with his wife and several friends, he visited a museum in Bewdley, about 100 miles northwest of London. As he was walking up a set of stairs, the wall beside him seemed to fade away. He plainly saw a battle taking place between two armies on an adjoining field. But these weren't modern soldiers. Being a student of military history, Applegate recognized the period battle gear. They were Cavaliers and Roundheads, who fought the English Civil War from 1642 to 1648. He says it was as if a window had opened, allowing him to peer into the mid-seventeenth century. In just a few seconds, the vision faded and the wall returned. Back in the United States, Applegate hesitantly wrote the curator to tell her of his unusual experience, but she had no problem believing his story at all. In fact, she had an explanation: It seems that his ancestors were from the region, and it's probable that many of them took part in the original battle, which had occurred at that same time of the year.

The Legend of the Legionnaires

An uninvestigated haunting appears in the records of Rene Dupre, who was stationed in Algeria with the French Foreign Legion. In May 1912, his company and two others were crossing the sands outside their fort when the warriors of an Arab tribe attacked them. They eventually repelled their assailants, but not before five Legionnaires, including two soldiers named Leduc and Schmidt, were killed. The men buried their comrades and returned to the blockhouse.

Two weeks later, Dupre was standing guard just after midnight. He saw a man in Legionnaire uniform staggering outside the fort across the sand. He seemed to be searching for something or someone. As the phantom drew closer to the fort, Dupre realized that he could see right through the figure. It was a ghost! Dupre called for others, who also saw the phantom. One man recognized it as Leduc. The ghost vanished, but it reappeared four nights later.

Three nights after that, Dupre was again on guard when he and others saw a different lone figure on the sands: the ghost of Schmidt. Like Leduc's ghost, he seemed to be moving along purposefully, as if looking for something. The ghost disappeared but, again, came back two nights later. One Legionnaire suggested that perhaps Schmidt was looking for Leduc, who was a friend as well as a comrade-in-arms.

Finally, on the fifteenth night after Dupre first spotted the ghost of Leduc, two phantom figures were seen walking together far out at a distance. The Legionnaires speculated that the ghosts were Leduc and Schmidt, and that they had finally found one another in the Other World. As the ghosts walked over the horizon, one raised a hand, as if in salute and farewell to their fellow Legionnaires back at the fort.

Touched by an Angel: The Angels of Mons

The appearance of spectral armies or angels over the battlefield of Mons is the most famous sighting of its type. Between August 26 and 28, 1914, British and French troops were overwhelmed by German forces in a fierce World War I battle at Mons, France. Before their eventual retreat, the British and French suffered more than 15,000 causalities.

On September 14, 1914, the *London Evening News* published "The Bowmen," an account of the clash by British journalist Arthur Machen. According to the tale, the British and French troops had seen spectral bowmen and other medieval soldiers holding back the German troops. The ghostly soldiers were thought to be from the fifteenth-century battle of Agincourt, which is located near Mons.

The story prompted sensational confessions from soldiers. Indeed, many claimed to have seen angels rather than soldiers. Some of the British had seen St. George. Many of the French identified the heavenly hosts as the archangel Michael or St. Joan of Arc. Soon, there were similar stories coming from other battlefields.

Then, in a devastating confession, Machen admitted that he had made up the entire story. No soldier had ever told him about seeing visions. Nevertheless, many soldiers continued to swear by their stories.

In 1930, Friedrich Hezenwirth, the former director of German espionage, put a new twist on the legend of the Angels of Mons. He claimed that during the battle,

German aviators had projected movies of angels onto the clouds. The intent was to convince the German soldiers that God was on their side. It was thought that if the soldiers were convinced of their moral right, they would fight even harder.

Who was telling the truth? Indeed, Machen had invented the story. But perhaps the troops had actually seen something but were afraid to admit it until after the newspaper article appeared. Was it a collective apparition?

CAUTION

Boo! _____

Can you believe your own eyes? Don't be so sure. Paranormals agreed with the soldiers at Mons, France, that they were seeing either angelic spirits, phantom soldiers from the past, or the mass departure of the souls of the dying. Skeptics explain it as hysteria, hallucination, or a desire to believe in the protection of a Higher Power. Or perhaps it was all a movie, as Friedrich Hezenwirth claimed. People believe what they want to believe, and, especially in cases like this, that's all that matters.

Gallipoli Ghosts

The Gallipoli Peninsula in southern Turkey is located at the mouth of the Dardanelles, where the strait meets the Mediterranean. Gallipoli was the site of some of the heaviest casualties in World War I. Allied forces made the first assault on April 25, 1915. United Kingdom and Russian troops landed near the tip of the peninsula; the Anzacs (the Australian and New Zealand corps) stormed a narrow beach 10 miles farther north, beneath tall cliffs that were heavily defended by the Ottoman army. At the time, it was the largest military landing in history.

The attempt to capture Gallipoli was a costly failure. Allied forces were never able to gain much of a foothold, and, finally, after severe losses, they withdrew in December 1915. The dead included 7,818 Australian soldiers and 2,721 from New Zealand.

After the war, the Gallipoli cemetery was established to honor all of the war's dead. Thousands from both sides are buried in graves in neat rows, with each nation having its own memorial area. A massive, austere white monument overlooks the battlefields on one of the highest hills along the Dardanelles.

It's impossible to view the Gallipoli beaches, graves, and monument and not be moved. It's almost as difficult to *not* run into a ghost there. Almost as soon as the campaign ended, people started seeing spectral soldiers, sometimes entire ghost armies, on the battlefields. Two of the ghosts that have been identified are—were?—Private John

Simpson Kirkpatrick, an English-born soldier, and his donkey! During the first weeks of the Gallipoli campaign, Kirkpatrick was one of the most daring rescuers in the corps. Rather than risk maneuvering a stretcher, Kirkpatrick retrieved a wounded comrade by draping the injured man over his donkey, then leading them to safety. Kirkpatrick himself was killed by shrapnel in May 1915 and was buried on the plains of Gallipoli.

The Gallipoli monument in Turkey.

(Photo by author)

Cape Town Castle

In 1665, a Dutch merchant built his home, Cape Town Castle, close to the waterfront in Cape Town, South Africa. To protect the mansion, he encircled it with ramparts and reinforced walls, with positions for guns and cannon. The citadel's cannons were never fired at an enemy during the owner's lifetime, but even after his death he seems disinclined to "surrender" his castle. For more than 300 years, his tall, glowing spirit has appeared, walking the battlements of his fortified home.

The battlements of Cape Town Castle, Cape Town, South Africa.

(Photo by author)

Haunted American Wartime Habitats

There are haunted spots throughout the United States—especially in the Northeast and Atlantic states—that date back to the years between the Revolutionary War and the War Between the States. Many of the spirits who haunt them were soldiers; the haunted buildings were connected to the military.

The Black Lady of Fort Warren

Fort Warren in Boston, Massachusetts, has been haunted since the Civil War by the ghost of the "Lady in Black," so-called because the spectre always appears dressed in black. She's thought to have been the wife of Lieutenant Andrew Lanier, who was imprisoned there. According to legend, she came to the fort disguised as a man to try to rescue him. During the attempt, Lanier's wife tried to shoot the fort commander but mortally wounded her own husband instead. She was captured and hanged, wearing a black dress.

The Spy House

The Spy House Museum in Port Monmouth, New Jersey, was an inn during the Revolutionary War era. It got its nickname because the owner welcomed British troops into the tavern, overheard their plans, then passed the information on to General Washington's troops. Prior to that, pirates had used the house to store their treasure, and they supposedly buried some of their murdered victims in the basement. There have been modern reports of the ghosts of pirates, soldiers, and a child thought to have died there.

Oh, Say Can You See Any Spectres?

The eighteenth-century star-shaped Fort McHenry stands guard over Baltimore harbor. Its bombardment by the British on September 13 to 14, 1814, during the War of 1812, inspired 35-year-old poet and lawyer Francis Scott Key to write the poem "The Star-Spangled Banner." The fort was never attacked again, but it remained an active military facility, on and off, for another century. During the Civil War, Union forces used it as a prison camp for Confederate soldiers and southern sympathizers. During World War I, it served as an army hospital, and the Coast Guard trained there as recently as World War II. Fort McHenry became part of the National Park Service in 1933.

Over the years, many ghosts and spectral activity have been sighted at the fort, including:

- A silhouetted figure moving on the parapets
- A malevolent spirit in the corridor leading to the public restrooms
- Furniture that levitates or moves on its own
- Spectral lights
- Disembodied voices heard by the staff after closing time

Spirits at the Inn

Many ghosts reportedly haunt the Farnsworth House Inn located in Gettysburg, Pennsylvania, including:

♦ Mary, a Civil War-era phantom, who walks the halls at night

♦ Three Confederate sharpshooters at their post in the attic

♦ Another soldier, singing to calm his wounded comrade, as he carries him to the basement to die

♦ A man carrying a child wrapped in a quilt (you can also hear him crying in a room upstairs)

♦ A midwife huddled over a woman in labor

Other spectral phenomena include cold spots throughout the inn. White balls of energy or "auras" have also been photographed. The Farnsworth House Inn has been investigated by psychic Carol Kirkpatrick and Ghost Hunters International, among others. The house has also been featured on TV's *Sightings* (Sci-Fi Channel) and *Unsolved Mysteries*.

How the West Was Won

One of the sorriest episodes of America's past is the treatment of Native Americans during the colonization of the West. As pioneers pushed toward the Pacific and were resisted by Indian forces, the settlers demanded government protection. Army troops were sent in to contain the native uprisings. Many times, this erupted into full-scale battle.

Fort Laramie

Fort Laramie in Wyoming was one of the great legendary Western frontier forts. From March 1834 to March 1890, it served to protect and assist settlers moving into the Pacific Northwest.

Apparently, many of its residents from those pioneer days have chosen to stay. In Quarters A (also known as the Captain's Quarters), bolted doors have unlocked and opened themselves. People have heard tromping on overhead wooden walkways and floorboards, and a security guard reported feeling himself grabbed and slapped on the back by invisible hands. The apparition of a man in a cavalry uniform also has been reported, and a ghostly woman dressed in green riding on a spectral black horse is said to appear on the grounds outside the fort every seven years.

Fort Sill

Fort Sill, an army base in Lawton, Oklahoma, was built on former Indian land. In fact, the grave of Geronimo, the great Apache chief, is located there. Lawton was the site of a bloody fight between Indians and settlers in the early 1800s. Strange noises are often heard at Fort Sill, and there have been apparitional sightings of Native American spirits.

Fort Abercrombie

Located in Abercrombie, North Dakota, about 25 miles south of Fargo, Fort Abercrombie Historical Site stands as a reminder of the bitter clashes between pioneers and Indians in the mid-nineteenth century.

The garrison was built in 1857 to protect settlers traveling westward against the native tribes already living in the region. There was relative calm for five years, until the Sioux began to attack the fort in earnest in 1862 as part of larger Indian uprisings throughout the Dakota Territory. To this day, ghosts of both the Indians and U.S. soldiers who lost their lives in the frequent battles are seen in the fort.

Skirmishes didn't end in the area until 1881 when Sitting Bull, the great Sioux chief, finally surrendered to U.S. troops. And speaking of Sitting Bull …

Custer's Last Stand

Perhaps the most famous personality of the Indian wars was General George Armstrong Custer (1839–1876). On June 24, 1876, he and his troops were killed by Sioux forces commanded by chiefs Crazy Horse and Sitting Bull at the Battle of the Little Bighorn (also called "Custer's Last Stand"). Some call Custer an American hero; others deride him as flamboyant, impetuous, and a glory seeker.

Say what you will about him, Custer commanded attention. And he still does! His ghost—and possibly that of his wife—has returned to the home they occupied prior to his traveling to Little Bighorn. The George Custer House was recently restored in Ft. Abraham Lincoln National Park, which stands on the Crow Indian Reservation southeast of Billings, Montana (see Appendix C).

There have also been many sightings of apparitions of unidentified soldiers in residential apartments located near Reno's Crossing, a bend in the Little Bighorn River where brutal fighting occurred. One ghost *has* been recognized by park personnel: that of Second Lieutenant Benjamin Hodgson. A stone house, formerly the park guard headquarters, located near the battlefield cemetery is also haunted.

Remember the Alamo

The Alamo, one of the most mythical structures in the United States, was built as a Catholic mission in 1718 in what is today San Antonio, Texas. In the winter of 1835-1836, the people of Texas decided to split from Mexican rule. To stop the independence movement, General Antonio Lopez de Santa Anna marched northward with about 4,000 soldiers. Badly outnumbered, Lieutenant Colonel William Barret Travis and about 150 men (including the woodsmen David "Davy" Crockett and Jim Bowie) retreated to the Alamo; another 39 men managed to join them later. It took 13 days, from February 23 to March 6, 1836, for Santa Anna to overrun the Alamo. At the end of the battle, all of the 189 Texan fighters were dead, although some historians believe that a few defenders (possibly including Crockett) were captured and later executed. There were a few other survivors from inside the Alamo, including an officer's wife named Susanna Dickinson, her baby and its Mexican nurse, and Travis's slave, Joe.

At least 1,200 Mexican soldiers also lost their lives fighting; few received proper burials. Needless to say, many of the spirits of the dead are thought to haunt the Alamo and its surroundings. No apparitions have been seen in the Alamo itself, but unexplained cold spots and a sometimes-overwhelming feeling of sadness pervade the mission.

Twenty-three years after the debacle at the Alamo, The Menger Hotel was built just steps away. Although none of its ghosts are connected with the famous battle, The Menger is one of the most haunted hotels in America (see Chapter 22).

Phantastic Tips

If you have your heart set on seeing a battlefield ghost, your best bet is probably one from the Civil War. Perhaps because it was such an emotionally trying time for the nation, a disproportionate number of phantoms seem to linger from that conflict.

Can't You Be Civil?

Abraham Lincoln, America's sixteenth president, is synonymous with the Civil War. You can't think of one without thinking of the other. A heroic and tragic man, Lincoln believed in the spirit world. During his tenure at the White House, Lincoln and his wife sat with several mediums.

Lincoln had several premonitions of his own death. The first occurred just before his first election in 1860. He saw two separate reflections of himself in a mirror at the same time: One face was hardy, the other pale. Ten days before his assassination, he had a more explicit foreshadowing. He reported that, in his dream, he had an out-of-body experience and saw his own corpse laid out in the East Room of the White House. The day of his murder, Lincoln told his bodyguard, W. H. Crook, that he had dreamt about being murdered for three straight nights.

Ghostly Pursuits

After her husband's death, Mary Todd Lincoln became even more involved in Spiritualism. She went to spirit photograph William Mumler under a pseudonym to have her portrait taken. The result was a now-famous photograph in which the faint shadow of the president can be seen over her shoulder (see Chapter 7).

As you'll see in Chapter 19, the ghost of Lincoln's funeral train can still be seen traveling the route from Washington, D.C., to Springfield, Illinois, on April evenings. And Lincoln's ghost has been witnessed many times throughout the residence area of the White House, most frequently in the so-called Lincoln Bedroom and the Oval Office (see Chapter 13).

Skirmishes during the Civil War were particularly acrimonious, pitting metaphorically—and sometimes literally—brother against brother. The pain and misery associated with the war have caused many spirits to remain behind, hoping to ease their psychic wounds.

Abraham Lincoln had several premonitions of his own death.

The town of Harpers Ferry, West Virginia, is home to many ghosts. The best known is John Brown, who conducted an unsuccessful raid on an arsenal there. His ghost is so lifelike that some modern tourists, thinking that he was a costumed actor, have asked him to have his picture taken with them. Most of the other Harpers Ferry ghosts are also from the Civil War era, although some have been identified as those of more recent residents.

First-Person Phantoms

Several years back, Bambi and Chuck Burnes were spending the night in a West Virginia motel, but they had trouble getting to sleep. They had chosen a room in the back, facing away from the road, for peace and quiet, but the sound of someone shoveling in the alleyway kept waking them up. After this happened several times, Bambi finally got up to look out the window. She saw three men in Civil War uniforms. One was watching his friend dig a hole. The other lay dead in a wheelbarrow. The next morning Bambi told the story to the desk clerk, who merely smiled knowingly.

Civil War soldiers haunt the environs of Mark's Mill in Warren, Arkansas. One ghost is that of a Rebel who was blinded from artillery fire while trying to keep a trainload of Confederate gold away from the Yankees. He later died from his injuries. Other phantoms belong to soldiers whose comrades hurriedly dumped their corpses down a well rather than burying them. Sometimes you can hear their cries coming from the well, begging to be given a decent burial.

Ghostly Pursuits

As the 20th Maine division approached Gettysburg during the Civil War to join the battle, a glowing phantom on horseback—an officer wearing a tri-cornered hat—suddenly appeared in front of them. The men soon recognized him: It was George Washington! The general spurred on the soldiers to the capture of Little Round Top, which they then successfully defended against Confederate advance. The story of Washington's ghost became so widespread that Edwin Stanton, Secretary of War, held an official investigation. Hundreds of soldiers, including General Oliver Hunt and several of his fellow officers, claimed to have seen and been able to identify the phantom as being Washington.

Almost every night, a strange fog rolls across the Chickamauga Battlefield in Chickamauga, Georgia. Oddly, the fog seldom extends beyond the boundaries of the park. The apparition who is most frequently seen is "Green Eyes," a Confederate soldier who was killed by his twin brother, who was a Yankee. The soldier's eyes often glow in the dark over Snodgrass Hill. Legend also has it that the ghost of a woman in a wedding gown haunts the battlefield in September and October. She's said to be visiting the grave of her fiancé, who was killed in action.

The most famous battlefield of the Civil War is located in Gettysburg, Pennsylvania. The apparitions of dozens of individual soldiers have been observed there over the past century, including Captain William Miller (who stopped haunting Gettysburg after his tombstone was inscribed to record his Medal of Honor). The ghost of a phantom cavalry officer—a headless horseman—is still seen today on Little Round Top. Some people have claimed to see (and sometimes hear) entire spectral battles! One of the most poignant visions is that of a dog, thought to have belonged to General William Barksdale. The dog was killed while trying to cross the battlefield to deliver a message from its owner to another general.

War is hell. There's no way to make war stories pretty and light. So let's take a break for a bit of R&R. It's time to play, or at least it's time to go *see* a play. It's curtains up on some of the most haunted theaters in the English-speaking world.

The Least You Need to Know

- All over the world, ghosts haunt the battlefields where they lost their lives.

- Although most battlefield spectres are strictly anonymous, some, like Generals "Mad Anthony" Wayne, George Washington, and George Custer, are famous phantoms.

- Paranormal sightings are not limited to individual ghosts: Entire phantom battles and armies have been reported.

- Phantom fighters from every American conflict have been reported, from the Revolutionary War of Independence through those of today.

Chapter 18

All the World's a Stage

In This Chapter

- ◆ Great ghosts of the British theater
- ◆ A tour of some of England's most haunted theaters
- ◆ Haunted theaters of the United States
- ◆ Ghostly apparitions in and around Ford's Theatre
- ◆ Leaving on a "ghost light"

The life of actors is unpredictable at best. They never know what their next role will be—or when it will come along. So who knows? Maybe a few of the theater ghosts decided that, once they got a gig in the theater, they'd just stay there, even if it meant hanging around after the final curtain.

But first, let's take a stroll on the other side of the footlights to meet some of the phantoms of the theater world. We'll start in ancient Rome, make a stop on London's West End, then head to the glittering lights of Broadway. Tickets ready? Curtain going up!

Ancient Hauntings

People love to be entertained. And one of the things that live theater does best is present spectacle. The Emperor Trajan certainly understood this when he constructed the Colosseum in Rome in 80 C.E. It was a monumental structure, capable of seating 80,000 spectators at one time.

The Colosseum was used to hold legitimate sporting events, but it just as often staged bloody battle-to-the-death combats. Five thousand exotic animals such as lions and bears were killed in the opening "ceremonies" alone; within the first four months, 9,000 gladiators and soldiers fought each other to the bitter end. These blood sports went on unabated, eventually claiming hundreds, if not thousands, of Christian martyrs, all for the glory and amusement of Rome.

Thankfully, those horrific days are long gone. Yet through the centuries, staff, work crew, and visitors have seen ghosts of many of those who suffered and died in the "games" held within the oval arena.

The ruins of the Colosseum in Rome, Italy.

(Photo by author)

Raising the Curtain on England's Haunted Theaters

England, home of William Shakespeare, has some of the world's most haunted theaters. Some activity, such as lights flickering, occurs in almost all of the West End theaters, but this is often attributed to their age rather than any paranormal activity. But some of the theaters are paid regular visits by their resident ghosts, and the phantoms are seen by cast, crew, and, occasionally, patrons.

Adelphi Theatre

The ghost of actor William Terriss haunts the famed Adelphi Theatre located on London's Strand. In December 1877, Terriss was stabbed to death as he exited the stage door. Among the phantom phenomena attributed to him have been …

- Unidentified footsteps backstage and in the stage door alley.
- Lights that turn on and off by themselves.
- Stage elevators that run without assistance.
- Furniture that moves by itself (including a famous 1928 incident in which many spectators saw the couch from Terriss's dressing room move on its own while a young lady was sitting on it).

From 1955 to at least 1972, Terriss's ghost, decked out in a gray suit and white gloves, was sighted on many occasions at the Covent Garden underground station. Several ticket takers, engineers, signalmen, and the like recognized him.

Drury Lane

The current Drury Lane, The Theatre Royal in London, is actually the fourth to stand on that site. It's one of the world's most haunted theaters and has had dozens of authenticated sightings.

Drury Lane's most famous ghost is the so-called "Man in Gray," who has been spotted by not only the actors but matinee audiences as well. He also appeared from time to time during World War II when the Entertainers National Services Association (ENSA) occupied the building.

It's said that the Man in Gray usually manifests in Drury Lane Theatre just before the theater is about to open a long-running hit. (Needless to say, he's a rather welcome spirit!) He appeared, for instance, during rehearsals—once to more than 70 cast members at one time—for the original London productions of *Oklahoma!*, *Carousel*, *South Pacific*, and *The King and I*.

The ghost is thought to be that of a nobleman from the 1770s. He appears with powdered hair, wearing a tri-corner hat, dress jacket, ruffled sleeves, riding boots, a cape or cloak, and a sword.

According to legend, the nobleman frequented the theater because he was in love with one of the company's leading ladies. A jealous rival stabbed the nobleman to death and walled his corpse into a seldom-used service passage on the left side of the stage. Skeletal remains were discovered there during renovation of the theater in 1848. Were they the bones of the Man in Gray?

Ghostly Pursuits

To avoid any confusion for non-British readers, any theater that received the Royal Patent to operate was able to call itself "Theatre Royal." It meant that the theater was under the patronage of the throne: Think of it as a "seal of approval" from the monarchy. Several theaters held and used the title concurrently because, once the honor was bestowed, it was theirs to keep and advertise unless or until the throne withdrew it.

No one seems to be able to get closer than about 40 feet to the Man in Gray. He's silent and undemonstrative. When he appears, he enters the auditorium in the stalls (the orchestra level) by walking through a wall, then passes through several doors without opening them, and walks up the stairs to the Dress Circle (the mezzanine). He crosses the front of the Dress Circle, descends the staircase at the other side, and leaves the theater by passing through the wall opposite where he entered.

Another spirit is that of actor Charles Macklin, who usually appears backstage. Although he lost his temper and killed fellow actor Thomas Hallam, he was never convicted for his crime. Macklin lived to be 107. It's said he's doomed for eternity to wander the corridor where the murder took place.

Other more pleasant ghosts have visited Drury Lane Theatre. Once, during the 1947 run of *Oklahoma!*, the spirit of King Charles II was spotted. Some say that the ghost of Joe Grimaldi, the celebrated clown and actor, also haunts the theater and occasionally gives an invisible "guiding hand" to help actors with their movements onstage. Grimaldi often played Drury Lane and was beloved for his willingness to encourage and assist new talent.

The Haymarket

The Haymarket, The Theatre Royal, is the second-oldest London theater still in use. Located between Piccadilly Circus and Buckingham Palace, the original theater was built in 1720 and replaced with the current structure a hundred and one years later. The theater is haunted by the ghost of John Buckstone, who spent 30 years with the theater, first as an actor for five years, then as manager (from 1853 to 1878). The first sighting of Buckstone's ghost in the theater occurred within a year of his death.

Buckstone appears in one of the theater boxes, dressed in a frock coat. The door of his old dressing room has also been seen to open and close by itself. Another ghost, an old man who walks the hallways, is thought to be that of Henry Field, an actor-manager of the theater in the early 1700s.

Ghostly Pursuits
Margaret Rutherford was among the notable actors who have seen the ghost of John Buckstone at the Haymarket. One night in 1963, the fog was so heavy after a performance of *School for Scandal* that she and her husband decided to stay the night in her dressing room. The next day, Rutherford claimed that in the middle of the night she had looked across the room and saw the hairy leg and calf-length breeches of a man. She then looked up to his face. It was Buckstone! She later gave a similar report to the magazine *Psychic News*.

Although Buckstone's apparition is rarely seen today, there are plenty of unusual occurrences in the theater of the type often associated with ghosts and poltergeists: lights going on and off by themselves, doorknobs jiggling, and props disappearing from one place and reappearing at another.

Her Majesty's Theatre

Also located between Piccadilly Circus and Buckingham Palace, Her Majesty's Theatre was built for actor-manager Sir Beerbohm Tree in 1897. After his death in 1917, Tree's ghost returned to the theater. His apparition was seldom seen, but one was often felt and presumed to be his. A drop in temperature always accompanied the presence. It usually appeared backstage on Fridays, or paydays. When the spirit was in the house, it usually occupied a top box on stage right, which was Tree's favorite seat in the theater. Audience members sitting there during a performance have complained of the door to the box opening by itself, then the air becoming icy cold.

On one celebrated occasion in the 1970s, many people saw Tree's ghost at one time (a collective apparition). During the run of Terence Rattingan's *Cause Célèbre*, the entire cast on the stage—including the show's star, Glynis Johns—saw Tree's ghost crossing at the back of the stalls.

Ghosts of the American Theater

British theaters have no patents on ghosts. More than a few theaters in the States are haunted. In fact, our phantoms aren't snobs: Some even haunt—shudder—movie theaters. For example, the Biograph Theater, a movie house on Clark Street in North Chicago, is haunted by the ghost of a man running down the alley next to the theater. It's thought to be the spectre of John Dillinger, who was ambushed there by police and died in a hail of bullets in 1934.

The Great Ghost-White Way

The Belasco Theatre in New York City, built by the Broadway impresario David Belasco, opened its doors on 44th Street between Broadway and 6th Avenue in 1907. It began its life as the Stuyvesant, but its name was changed to the Belasco three years later.

Boo!

Although the FBI certified that the corpse of the man shot outside the Biograph Theater was John Dillinger, some identified the body as that of another career criminal, Jimmy Lawrence. The FBI claimed that Dillinger's appearance had been altered by plastic surgery. The moral to the story: Always be certain about your corpses. You don't want to wind up being haunted by the wrong ghost!

Belasco himself was a creature of the theater—playwright, actor, director, producer, and set designer. His eccentric habit of dressing as a priest earned him the nickname the "bishop of Broadway." Belasco died in 1931 at the age of 71. But that doesn't mean he's left the building.

For years, actors and backstage staff have reported seeing the showman's ghost wearing his priestly garb. Often he appeared on opening nights, sitting in one of the empty theater boxes. Belasco had a private elevator to his office above the theater, and at least one stagehand has heard its gears and chains moving, even though the elevator isn't operational and hasn't been used in years. Belasco's phantom apparently isn't going anywhere anytime soon: He was seen as recently as 2003 by members of the cast of *Enchanted April*, which was playing in the theater.

First-Person Phantoms

How do you get to Carnegie Hall? Practice! And it doesn't hurt to take a tip or two from the ghosts of the hall. In the early 1970s, xylophonist extraordinaire Ian Finkel was making his debut at Carnegie Hall, soloing in Charles-Auguste de Bériot's "Scéne de ballet" with the 802 Senior Orchestra. But rehearsals were going badly; the orchestra seemed to be playing out of tune. Ian knew he was in trouble. He purposely arrived at Carnegie Hall early one day to walk around the empty stage, hoping to find some inspiration in that legendary space. He moved center stage and closed his eyes. After a few moments, he heard the sound of a note being played on a phantom oboe and felt a light tapping on his shoulder. Finkel opened his eyes to see the spirit of the great composer-pianist-conductor Sergey Rachmaninov standing before him. The spectre whispered in ghostly tones that, unfortunately, the concert would go very badly and that Ian should brace himself for the worst. The pitch of the ethereal oboe suddenly became very sharp, and the maestro vanished.

Why, Oh, Why Ohio?

Ohio can hold its own when it comes to claims on ghost-infested theaters. During renovations in the 1980s, it was discovered that the Music Hall in Cincinnati had been built over a pauper's cemetery. This might explain the strange paranormal activity that the theater staff experienced: Angry ghost whispering and ethereal female voices were overheard. A security guard investigated laughing coming from one of the ballrooms and was shocked to see the room filled with the ghosts of men and women dressed in 1880s period dress. Several women witnessed the same apparitions the next day.

Another Ohio theater, the Akron Civic Theatre, is protected by the ghost of Fred, its former long-time custodian. He returns during special events and frightens away would-be vandals. The phantom of a young, weeping woman is also seen near a water channel that once ran under the theater and much of the city. Although the style of her clothing offers no real clues, she's thought to be have lived during the heyday of canal boat travel.

California Dreaming

The Pasadena Playhouse, named the official State Theater of California in 1937, is haunted by its founder, Gilmor Brown.

Gilmor Brown.

(Photo courtesy of the Pasadena Playhouse)

Born in North Dakota in 1886, Gilmor had a diverse career in acting and theater company management, touring throughout the country and Canada before settling his troupe, "The Gilmor Brown Players," in Pasadena in 1916. His actors, newly dubbed the Community Players, performed in several facilities in the city. Finally, in 1924, the cornerstone was laid on a new theater, the Pasadena Community Playhouse, and the company moved in the following year.

Phantastic Tips _____

Staff members at the Pasadena Playhouse know that if the house ghost starts acting up, all they have to do is quietly chide him with a "Now, Gilmor, that's enough," or "Not now, Gilmor, I'm busy." And he'll go away! An example? After a very long day of brisk ticket sales, a box office employee couldn't get the transaction figures to balance. She finally told Gilmor out loud that it was no time to be playing tricks. On her next attempt, the numbers added up perfectly. Imagine that— a ghost with manners! Maybe that's all it takes to get a ghost to leave us alone: Ask it nicely to go away.

During its golden years from 1925 to 1937, the Playhouse produced more than 500 new plays, including 23 American and 277 world premieres. Being close to Hollywood, the Pasadena Playhouse often drew film stars to its casts. Over the years, many of today's stars—such as Dustin Hoffmann, Gene Hackman, Rue McClanahan,

Jamie Farr, and Sally Struthers—received some of their early training at the Playhouse's theater school. Following Gilmor's death in 1960, the Playhouse fell into decline, finally closing its doors in 1969. Restoration of the theater began in 1979, and in 1986 the Pasadena Playhouse once again started a full subscription season of plays and musicals.

Gilmor Brown's ghost has never been seen, but his presence is often felt. There have been reports for decades of his ghost playing pranks throughout the theater. The activity is so frequent that, these days, almost anything unusual that occurs at the Playhouse is blamed on Gilmor.

The interior of the haunted Pasadena Playhouse.

(Photo courtesy of the Pasadena Playhouse)

First-Person Phantoms

Cindy Freeling, an actress who worked at the old Montgomery Playhouse, now closed, which was located on Broadway near the Chinatown district in San Francisco, says that theater was also filled with phantoms. The ghosts were never malicious, but they liked to let the actors and crew know they were there. Freeling recalls the time that the actors were all backstage in line, ready for a curtain call. Every one of them, from the back to the front of the line, felt an invisible body elbow its way to the front in order to take its bow. On a few other occasions, Freeling had costumes or props invisibly pushed or yanked out of her arms. She mentioned the phenomena to some of the crew, who said, "Oh, don't you know? The theater's haunted. The building used to be a Chinese mortuary. If you go down into the basement you can still see the slabs."

First-Person Phantoms

Betty Jean Morris kept a journal of some of the ghost activity at the Pasadena Playhouse while she was one of the house managers in the 1980s and 1990s:

- Personal items of the actors and staff have disappeared. Morris's own binoculars once vanished from the lobby desk as she locked up the theater. No one else was in the building.

- Staff members have reported leaving some small item (such as a stack of papers) in one location, only to find it minutes later in another part of the theater.

- There were doors that couldn't be unlocked; minutes later, the same locks opened without any problem.

- In 1989, every Sunday matinee during the two-month run of *Groucho, A Life in Review*, the house lights in the theater would come up on their own at exactly the same time. Neither the technical crew nor the master electrician could find anything wrong with the equipment.

- For a time, whenever the tech crew came back to the sound and light booth after intermission, they would find the controls and earphones had been rearranged. This continued to happen even when an usher was posted to guard the booth or it was locked during the break. No one entered the room, yet the controls were somehow reset. Nothing was ever broken; things were just moved around.

- The backstage elevator frequently stops at the third floor, even if it's not the passenger's destination. For many years, Gilmor Brown kept his office on the third floor.

The Ghost of the Guthrie

In the mid-1960s Richard Miller was an 18-year-old shy loner who worked as an usher at the Guthrie Theater in Minneapolis, Minnesota. On Saturday, February 5, 1967, he committed suicide by shooting himself while sitting in his car in a parking lot on Lake Street. His body, still dressed in his usher's uniform, was not discovered until two days later.

Soon, patrons seated in Row 18 at the Guthrie (which had been part of Miller's assigned area) began complaining of a rude usher pacing the adjacent aisle and staring at them during performances. The young man never spoke or made any other sound. Their descriptions of the boy, which included a distinct mole on his cheek, matched Miller. Over time, dozens of staff members saw his apparition in the house, on the stage's catwalks, and in a seating area known as the Queen's Box. Sightings have tapered off since an exorcism was conducted in 1994.

From See to Shining See

Here are 10 thumbnail sketches of some other theaters from one coast to the other in which the spectres are the stars:

- **Maine.** A room on the second floor of the Boothbay Opera House in Boothbay Harbor is haunted by an unidentified spectre, and Revolutionary-era soldiers are sometimes seen at the Ogunquit Playhouse in Ogunquit.

- **New York.** At least two ghosts haunt the Cohoes Music Hall in Cohoes. The one most frequently seen is that of a woman, dressed in 1930s or 1940s apparel. She always appears to be angry. The other phantom is male and is thought to be a former stage manager who was crushed to death by a falling sandbag. His apparition has been seen and heard in the wings and on the stage. (You'd think he'd know better!)

- **Pennsylvania.** Many people have reported seeing the shade of an elderly woman walking across the balcony of the Majestic Theater in Reading. Unidentified ghosts also haunt the Pittsburgh Playhouse.

- **Maryland.** The old Opera House building in Westminster (today the home of the Opera House Printing Company) is supposedly haunted by an actor who was murdered outside the stage door after a performance. (Talk about critics! Could you get a worse review?)

- **Wisconsin.** A foglike apparition has been spotted in the balcony of the Majestic Theater in Milwaukee, and the ghost of a former theater manager has appeared in the Grand Theatre in Wausau.

- **Illinois.** The ghost of "One-armed Red" is seen and heard in the Lincoln Theatre in Decatur.

- **Tennessee.** The Orpheum Theatre in Memphis is home to the ghost of a little girl named Mary. People have sensed her presence as they sat in one particular seat in the theater: Obviously, it's her favorite. According to legend, she died in a fire that burned the original Orpheum Theatre, although some think she was actually killed on nearby Beale Street.

♦ **Iowa.** Ever since the renovation of the Grand Opera House in Dubuque in 1986, members of the theater staff have heard ghost voices and footsteps. Beginning in 1991, apparitions started appearing at the back of the auditorium.

♦ **Kansas.** The Purple Masque Theater on the campus of Kansas State University is haunted by several ghosts, including that of Nick, a football player who died in an accident while enrolled at KSU. He's a noisy one, banging objects and rearranging chairs. The ghost of a Confederate soldier also sometimes appears on the stage, seated in a phantom chair.

♦ **Wyoming.** At least two unknown ghosts haunt the Atlas Theatre in Cheyenne.

First-Person Phantoms

During a 1976 rehearsal of *A Midsummer Night's Dream* at New Mexico State University, Kim Roach and six other students looked up into the theater's fly gallery and were startled to see an eerie, green, glowing spectre standing on the catwalk. The ghost was of that a man, dressed in a nineteenth-century costume complete with top hat and opera cape. He had one hand on his hip and held the catwalk railing with the other.

Later at a restaurant, the students compared notes and decided to go back the next night to see if they could spot the spirit again. He didn't materialize—at least not visually. But while they were on the ghost hunt, the kids heard a series of loud crashes. Following the sound, they discovered that tools kept backstage had been scattered about inside of a locked room. They left the tools as they found them and relocked the storage area. The next day, when they returned, the tools were hanging and shelved, in their proper places. Upon relating their story to others, the students were told that the theater was known to be haunted. The ghost was probably that of an actor who had fallen from the catwalk to his death years before.

Ford's Theatre: A National Tragedy

Ford's Theatre in Washington, D.C., is perhaps the most famous—or infamous—theater in the United States. On April 14, 1865, during a performance of the play

Our American Cousin, John Wilkes Booth entered Box 7 and assassinated President Abraham Lincoln. After firing the fatal shot to Lincoln's head, Booth jumped from the president's box to the stage, breaking his leg in the fall. Booth managed to escape from the theater. Twelve days later, Booth was hiding in a barn on Richard Garret's farm near Bowling Green, Virginia, when soldiers surrounded him. They set the barn on fire, and Booth died either in the blaze or from the accompanying gunfire.

Shortly after Lincoln's assassination and Booth's death, noted photographer Matthew Brady shot several photos of the interior of Ford's Theatre. In one of his photographs, a hazy figure resembling Booth could be seen standing in the presidential box.

Congress forced the sale and closure of Ford's Theatre shortly after the assassination. It was eventually renovated by the National Park Service and reopened in 1968 as a museum and playhouse. Ever since, actors, audiences, and staff in the theater and museum have reported seeing Booth's ghost. In addition, actors often feel an icy presence, become ill at ease or nauseous, shudder, or forget lines when standing near the spot at left-center stage where Booth landed.

Lincoln's ghost hasn't appeared in the theater, but it has been seen across the street at Petersen's Boarding House, where the mortally wounded president was carried and subsequently died.

> ### Ghostly Pursuits
>
> Interestingly, because of damage to the corpse from the barn fire, Booth's body was never positively identified. Conspiracy theorists believe that Booth may have actually somehow escaped the carnage. Of course, if that's the case, how do you explain the sightings of his ghost almost immediately thereafter?

We'll Leave the Light on for You

Remember how when you were little, you used to keep on a night-light so that monsters wouldn't attack you in the dark? Then, as you grew up, that seemed so childish and silly? Well, maybe it wasn't so ridiculous after all.

No one knows exactly when or how the tradition of the so-called "ghost light" started, but many stage managers leave a single, dim light bulb shining all night on the stage of the theater. Sure, there are practical reasons: The lamp is a work light, and it helps keep people from stumbling in the dark. But there's a better reason why the light has to be kept on: Its glow scares away the theater's ghosts! It stops them from playing pranks and creating havoc when no one's there. Childish? Silly? Don't be so sure. Many theater folk have reported strange happenings in the theater when the ghost light wasn't left on overnight.

First-Person Phantoms

Bryan Lee is stage manager of the main theater at the Magic Castle, a private club in Hollywood, California. (You'll hear lots more about it in Chapter 23.) He notes that every time there's been a failure of the stage lighting or sound system backstage, it's been when he'd neglected to leave on a ghost light overnight. It's happened at least five times so far!

So there you have it. Next time you're sitting in a theater, and the lights go down, look carefully to your left, then to your right. Shakespeare wrote about the Seven Ages of Man. Who knows? Maybe you'll be seated next to someone who's in the Eighth.

If you'd like to investigate some of these theaters for yourself, check out Appendix C for more information. You may have to attend a performance to get inside a few of them, but many theaters are now offering backstage tours.

Now let's ease on down the road to look at some of the world's most famous haunted modes of transportation—by rail, sea, and air.

The Least You Need to Know

- Theaters have been haunted back to at least the time of the ancient Romans.
- England has more than its fair share of theater ghosts. Most are long-time owners, managers, or actors associated with their respective theaters.
- Both movie and legitimate theaters are haunted in the United States, and some of these hauntings are well documented.
- Ford's Theatre in Washington, D.C., may be haunted by John Wilkes Booth, but President Lincoln prefers to haunt the house next door where he died.
- A ghost light is left on all night in an otherwise-darkened theater to keep away the spirits.

Chapter 19

Trains and Boats and Planes

In This Chapter

- Haunted railways
- Lincoln's ghost train
- The *Flying Dutchman* and cruises to eternity
- Phantom pilots from flights of doom

You can't keep a good ghost down. As soon as a technological advance introduces a new form of transportation—boom!—it's haunted! First it was only phantoms on horseback, then in coaches and carriages. If we follow the natural—or perhaps supernatural—progression, we'll find that there are now haunted boats, railways, cars, and even planes. Sometimes the vehicles themselves turn into apparitions!

So far, paranormal researchers haven't come up with a good way to explain them. But they *have* come up with some great ghost stories. So fasten your seat belts: It's gonna be a bumpy night!

The Little Engine That Could: Railway Phantoms

Ghosts and phantoms have been reported on trains and along railroad tracks for as long as there has been an Iron Horse. During the golden age of railroads, steam-driven (and then early diesel) trains were fast, they were modern, but they could also be deadly. Collisions and derailments were a regular part of train travel.

At one time, British railways maintained a small makeshift morgue at many stations to house those who died on railway property until the corpses could be claimed. People have allegedly seen the ghosts of those whose bodies lay nearby in the "dead houses," as such structures were known.

Sometimes the spirits stay closer to the places where the tragedies occurred. Here in the United States, the Cody Road Railroad Bridge in Independence, Kentucky, is supposedly haunted by a woman who was killed by a train at the overpass. A ghost at the Old Depot House in New London, Minnesota, has been identified as passenger Ey Wtizke. There are endless examples of such hauntings by individuals.

Got a Light?

There's a whole genre of ghost lights that haunt railways. The so-called Summerville Light of Summerville, South Carolina, concerns a spirit. According to local lore, every night at midnight, a woman would meet her husband, a conductor on the rail line, carrying a lantern and a meal for him. One dreadful night, the train never arrived. The train had derailed, or crashed, and (according to most versions of the story) her husband was beheaded. The woman became deranged and never accepted the loss. She continued to show up at the station every night at midnight, swinging the lantern as she paced along the tracks.

Of course, eventually she, too, died. But that didn't stop her. They say that if you go to the old train stop at exactly midnight, all sounds of the evening (crickets, frogs, whatever) suddenly stop! (Perhaps they sense the presence of the woman's ghost.) Then, a light can be seen far off in the distance. It slowly comes toward you, and if you run, it chases you. Finally, it passes on and moves off into the night. You've seen the light of the sad, mad widow, waiting for her husband who will never arrive.

There are other ghost lamp stories from all across the United States. For example, television's *Unsolved Mysteries* retold the tale of a phantom man and his ghost lantern haunting the tracks outside Gurdon, Arizona. Ghosts have also been seen swinging lanterns by the train depot at Arcola, Illinois. A third legend has it that the shadow of a man appears, swinging a ghost lantern, every time a train stops at the Maco Station near Wilmington, North Carolina. It's thought to be the ghost of Joe Baldwin, a conductor who was run over by a train at the station one night in 1867.

Haunted Railroad Tracks in Texas

Before you drive onto a set of railroad tracks, be sure that a train isn't coming. Makes sense. But if you get stuck halfway, you better hope that ghosts push you across!

According to a famous legend, a loaded bus carrying school children stalled on some railroad tracks at a bend in the road outside San Antonio, Texas. Before the driver could restart the engine, a fast-moving train smashed into the bus, killing all of the students. No one can say exactly when the accident supposedly occurred, yet the rumor persists.

It's said that if you stop your car with the front tires just barely on those tracks today and set your car in neutral, the vehicle will roll up and over the tracks on its own. Purportedly, the ghosts of the children who died in the tragic accident push your car across the tracks so that a train won't hit it. It's also claimed that if you dust the back bumper of your car with talcum powder before driving it onto the tracks, small hand-prints will be seen in the powder when the car comes to rest on the other side.

Can the story be true? At first glance, there seems to be no other explanation. The tracks appear to be at the top of a ridge; from either side, you have to drive up a gentle grade to cross them. How could the cars roll forward on their own?

First-Person Phantoms

My nieces' stepmother, Marca Malick, actually tested the myth with friends when she lived in San Antonio—once in a car and once on a motorcycle. "We stopped at the tracks," she recalled, "put the vehicle in neutral, and turned it off. After a minute or two, we started to move and went uphill over the top of the tracks and down the other side without ever turning on the engine." She found the motorcycle trip to be scarier than being in a car, because she was riding on the back of the bike. How close must the ghost children have been?

Could there be a logical explanation? According to skeptical researchers, of *course* there is. In fact, some point out that the original story isn't even true. Discovery Channel researchers couldn't find any newspaper mention of the original bus accident having happened in the area. They *did* find a report of a nearly identical incident that took place on December 2, 1938, in Salt Lake City, Utah. The occurrence was so shocking that the story ran for days in surrounding states. Was this the true basis for the Texas legend of the haunted train tracks?

Jonathan Levit, host of Discovery Channel's *Miracle Hunters*, used GPS and surveyors to check out the railway crossing. According to his measurements, it's all an optical illusion. The landscaping makes it appear that there's a grade on both sides of the tracks, but it's really a continuous downward slope of one and a half feet over an incline of 100 feet. If the car were positioned correctly, gravity could eventually pull it across the tracks. Also, one of the local sheriffs confessed to Levit that, as a prank, he had occasionally put his own handprints on the talcum powder sprinkled on cars being used for ghost investigations.

Lincoln's Haunted Funeral Train

No doubt the most celebrated haunted locomotive—or at least the one that carries the most famous passenger—is the annual spectral visit of Abraham Lincoln's funeral train.

After President Lincoln's assassination on April 14, 1865, his body was transported for burial from Washington, D.C., through upstate New York to his home, Springfield, Illinois. The black-draped funeral cortege passed slowly on the tracks. All along the route, people stood to pay their final respects to the already-fabled leader.

Ever since, many people living along the New York Central rail line claim to see the funeral train pass by on April 27, the date that the cortege traveled that section of the route. The train's always described as being black, and some imaginative people have seen a crew of skeletons.

Abraham Lincoln's funeral train, at the Pennsylvania Railroad station in Harrisburg, Pennsylvania, 1865.

Ghostly Pursuits

It's not just kooks and crazies who see ghosts. Sometimes, apparitions are reported by legitimate news organizations. Here's one account of the Lincoln ghost train, as described by the *Albany Times*:

> It passes noiselessly. If it is moonlight, clouds cover over the moon as the phantom train goes by. After the pilot engine passes, the funeral train itself with flags and streamers rushes past. The track seems covered with black carpet and the coffin is seen in the center of the car, while all about it in the air and on the train behind are vast numbers of blue coated men, some with coffins on their backs, others leaning onto them.

My Body Lies Over the Ocean

There have probably been legends of phantom boats and ships as long as people have set sail on the waters. Here are just a few of the best-known nautical nightshades.

Come Fly with Me: The *Flying Dutchman*

Undoubtedly, the most famous ghost ship is the legendary *Flying Dutchman*. It's usually described as being a full-rigged ship, possibly seventeenth-century vintage, with all sails open. Spotting the ancient sailing vessel is supposed to be an omen of disaster.

The ship is said to appear during tempests off the Cape of Good Hope in South Africa. (The Cape is infamous for its sudden strong storms that can easily overpower and sink sailing vessels. In fact, it was originally named the Cape of Storms by Portuguese explorer Bartolomeu Dias, who discovered it in 1488.)

There are many variations of the *Flying Dutchman* story. Depending upon which account you hear, the ship is cursed to sail for eternity without reaching port because of …

   ◆ The captain's stubbornness and refusal to enter a safe harbor.

   ◆ The captain cursed God or some other spirit entity for bringing on the storm, then swore he could round the Cape without their assistance.

   ◆ Punishment for some sin.

   ◆ The captain had sold his soul to Satan in exchange for fast passage for his ship, and the devil was now taking his due.

   ◆ A pestilence onboard that makes ports turn them away.

Ghostly Pursuits

Sightings of the *Flying Dutchman* aren't exclusive to the waters around the Cape of Good Hope. In 1892 the phantom vessel was seen twice in Texas, both times at the south end of Galveston Bay.

Phantastic Tips

Always be on the lookout! In July 1881 a British midshipman on the HMS *Bacchante* reported seeing the *Flying Dutchman*. Just 16 years later, he ascended to the throne as King George V. So who knows? If you see the *Flying Dutchman*, you might be next!

The *Flying Dutchman* legend formed the basis for many works of art, including an 1855 short story by America's Washington Irving. The version written by Heinrich Heine (1797–1856), the nineteenth-century German Romantic poet, inspired German composer Richard Wagner (1813–1883) to write his opera *Der Fliegende Holländer* (1843).

Skeptics and scientists don't discount the sightings. They just deny that they're apparitions. The most probable cause, they say, is refraction, which casts the image of an actual ship, just over the horizon but not yet visible, up into the air and onto the clouds.

Please Be My *Palantine*

The lights of the blazing phantom ship *The Palantine*, which was variously said to have been Dutch or German, are supposedly seen near Block Island off Rhode Island. There are at least three different accounts of what actually happened to the ship.

In the first tale, the crew mutinied, killed the captain, robbed the passengers, and then deserted the ship. *The Palantine* ran aground on Block Island. Local pirates known as the Block Island Wreckers plundered the ship, but not before giving the passengers safe passage to shore. One woman who had gone mad refused to leave the ship, even though the pirates were going to set it on fire. As the ship was washed back out to sea, engulfed in flames, the woman's screams echoed to the shore.

In another version of the story, the ship was German, and the captain and crew deliberately wrecked and plundered their own vessel. In yet a third variation, the ship ran ashore because of pirates setting up decoy warning lights on the shore. In these last two tales, the passengers weren't rescued before the ship was set ablaze and sent back out to sea.

The Palantine light, as the apparition is known, has been seen on and off by residents of Block Island, usually just before stormy weather, from the late eighteenth century through the nineteenth century and, on rarer occasions, in the twentieth century. Many people believed that the light was God's punishment of the pirates who had killed *The Palantine*'s passengers and crew.

It was once thought that when the last pirate died, *The Palantine* light would never return. Yet return they do. Perhaps the ghosts of the pirates have come back, too. If so, *The Palantine* light might go on forever.

Watertown Wraiths

In December 1924, there was a fatal accident onboard the SS *Watertown*, a large oil tanker owned by Cities Service Company, as it steamed toward the Panama Canal from the Pacific Ocean. Two crew members, James Courtney and Michael Meehan, were cleaning one of the cargo tanks when they were overcome by toxic gas fumes and died. They were both accorded the traditional burial at sea.

The next day, the first mate saw two phantom faces in the trail of unsettled water behind the ship. He immediately pointed out the wavering images to Captain Keith Tracy. Soon, the whole crew was intrigued. Everyone agreed that the ghostly faces were those of Courtney and Meehan. The watery figures faces followed the ship for days, and virtually all of the crew saw them. When the ship reached port at New Orleans, the captain made a report of the strange occurrence. One company manager, S. J. Patton, gave Tracy a roll of film and told him to take some photos should the faces ever show up again.

Boo!

The SS *Watertown* incident demonstrates the importance of timely investigation. By the time paranormal investigators got to the case, eyewitnesses and evidence had long since dispersed or disappeared. Analyze any data from a ghost hunt as soon as possible after you collect it, when it's still fresh in your mind. The less time that elapses, the less chance there is for errors to creep in.

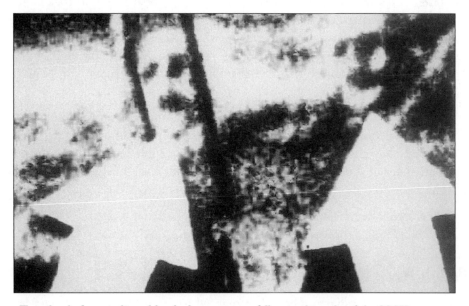

Two ghostly faces, indicated by the large arrows, follow in the wake of the SS Watertown.

(Photo from the author's collection)

Of course, such things never happen when you have a camera, do they? But this time, it did! The faces appeared during the very next sailing. The captain quickly got his camera, and he took six photographs. When the ship returned to port, the captain gave Patton the film. To prevent any chicanery, Patton took it to a commercial photographer to have it developed. Five of the shots showed nothing but waves. But on the sixth, there were outlines (possibly caused by light and shadow) that many swear are the faces of the dead seamen.

Although the story apparently was widely told within Cities Service circles, it didn't become public until the tale was published in the company magazine, *Service*, in 1934. The noted psychical researcher Hereward Carrington tried to investigate the sightings, but in the 10 years that had passed since the apparitions were last seen, both the first mate and Patton had died. The rest of the crew of the SS *Watertown* had split up, making firsthand documentation nearly impossible. The company couldn't even locate an original photo for Carrington, even though copies have since been published. To this day, the faces following the SS *Watertown* remain a mystery.

First-Person Phantoms

Boats don't have to be big to be ghost-infested. For many years, Dustin Stinett lived with his family on a boat moored in Dana Point, California. He recalls one unusually calm evening when, suddenly, the boat began to rock violently. Thinking perhaps that the vessel had been caught in the wake of a passing speedboat, Stinett went topside to see what had caused the disturbance. Not only was there no errant boat in sight, but the sea was smooth as glass. Nary a ripple. There wasn't even a wave from his own craft to show that it had been rocking.

He personally witnessed one other piece of paranormal activity onboard. The family was in the galley, cutting up a fresh pineapple. After each ring was removed, they always set the leafy top of the pineapple back in place to keep the remainder of the open fruit fresh. All of a sudden, as they watched, the top of the pineapple shot off and flew six to eight feet across the room.

The family never came up with a natural explanation for either occurrence.

The *Queen Mary* Mirages

Perhaps the best-known and best-documented haunted ship is the *Queen Mary*. When Britain's King George V and Queen Mary christened her at a Scottish shipyard in

1934, the *Queen Mary* was the largest ship in the world and the jewel of the Cunard Line. From 1936 to 1939, it sailed transatlantic voyages mostly between England and New York.

From 1940 to 1946, the ship was used for military service, acting primarily as a troop transport ship. Painted battleship gray to help camouflage her at sea, the *Queen Mary* was nicknamed "the Gray Ghost." Although she escaped harm from enemy vessels, on October 2, 1942, the *Queen Mary* had a tragic collision with one of her escort cruisers, the HMS *Curacoa*. The smaller ship was literally sliced in half, killing 338 of the sailors aboard.

From July 31, 1947, to December 9, 1967, the *Queen Mary* resumed service as a transoceanic cruise liner. Today, the ship is permanently moored in Long Beach, California, as a hotel and tourist attraction.

There have been literally hundreds of sightings of various ghosts throughout the ship, and they continue to the present day. Many of the ship's staff, tour guides, overnight guests, and visitors have reported seeing them.

One ghost who is regularly seen is that of 18-year-old John Pedder, who was trapped and crushed on July 10, 1966, when a watertight door in the engine room next to the propeller shaft closed on him. Because of the area he haunts, people call him "the Shaft Alley Spectre."

The ghost of Senior Second Officer W. E. Stark has been spotted in his former sleeping quarters as well as on deck. He, too, died in an accident. On September 18, 1949, he drank a mixture of carbon tetrachloride and lime juice: The deadly cleaning fluid had been stored without proper warning in an old gin bottle. At first, he treated his mistake lightly, but the next day he fell into a coma. He died three days later.

The phantom of a man in a mechanic's white boilersuit has also been seen and heard near the engine room. Likewise, a man in blue-gray overalls, with black hair and a long beard, has been spotted below deck.

> **CAUTION**
>
> **Boo!** _____
>
> So far there have been no ghosts reported from the discovery, examination, and excavation of the wreckage of the RMS *Titanic*. But don't be surprised if some of the passengers' spirits awaken from their unearthly sleep. They might not take too kindly to being disturbed.

In addition to the many ghosts sighted on the *Queen Mary*, there have been other haunting phenomena, such as unexplained voices and moving objects. Several séances have been held on the ship at which mediums claim to have contacted resident ghosts. The spirit most often mentioned is that of Lieutenant Carlo Giovetti, an Italian fighter pilot who was shot down by the British over North Africa. Giovetti died onboard the *Queen Mary* while being transported as a prisoner of war. He died primarily due to complications from injuries he suffered during the plane crash, and, like many others who died onboard during the War years, was most probably buried at sea. So far, his appearances have been confined to séances, but you never know …

Ghostly Pursuits

Several different phantoms have been seen around the *Queen Mary's* old indoor first-class swimming pool, including an elderly woman wearing an old-fashioned, one-piece swimsuit and bathing cap, as well as a young woman in a miniskirt. Their identities are unknown, but neither was a result of a reported drowning in the pool. The ghost of another unidentified woman, the so-called Lady in White, seems to be attached to a specific piano. When the instrument was in the Main Lounge, she was sometimes seen there, wearing a white evening gown and waltzing by herself. Sometimes she would stroll over to the piano. When the piano was moved to a different lounge, now called Sir Winston's Piano Bar, the ghost moved with it.

Dead in the Water

Who says death doesn't take a holiday? Rumors among Holland America Line crew members are that at least two cruise ships in their fleet are haunted.

While cleaning the officer's bar around 3 A.M., a staff member onboard the ms *Prinsendam* heard workout weights being used in the adjacent crew gym. When he went in to see who was there, the sounds stopped. The room was empty. On another occasion, a fire watchman making his rounds walked into the officer's bar and saw a blond man with his face in his hands, leaning on the bar. When asked who he was, the ghost vanished.

Even though the ms *Rotterdam* is one of the newest ships in the Holland America fleet, it's apparently already haunted. The ghost of a woman with long hair has been sighted at night swimming in the Lido Deck pool. (It's rumored that she's the ghost of a woman who drowned there, although no such death has ever been confirmed.)

Both ships are still in service and plying the high seas. Why not take a cruise on the wild side? Maybe you'll make a new friend—from the Beyond.

Fly the Scary Skies

Flying is frightening enough for some people. How can something as heavy as a plane stay up there? Well, sometimes it doesn't. And two crashes in particular have led to well-examined ghost stories.

Before you read this section, you better check to see where your two nearest exits are located. And don't forget, your seat cushion may also be used as a flotation device.

The Crash of British Dirigible *R-101*

The British dirigible *R-101* crashed on her maiden voyage in 1930. It lifted off in England on October 4, and fell to the ground the next day in France. Irish medium Eileen J. Garrett (1893–1970) knew it was going to happen! She received three visions of the airship, the first occurring four years before the disaster.

Three days after the crash of *R-101*, Garrett held a séance to try to contact the spirit of Sir Arthur Conan Doyle, who had died the previous July. Instead, Garrett's control Uvani started receiving messages from Flight Lieutenant H. Carmichael Irwin, who had been the captain of *R-101*. He gave very precise and detailed technical information about his craft. Ghost researcher Harry Price was at the séance; he was so convinced that the information was not only real but possibly top secret that he sent a transcript of the sitting to Sir John Simon, head of the Court of Inquiry that was investigating the airship disaster. Though fascinated, Simon said that ghost testimony was inadmissible in a court of law.

In a subsequent séance, several spirits of crew members who had died aboard *R-101* contacted Garrett. The ghosts explained that the accident had been caused by a gas leak that was ignited from a backfire from the engine. They also claimed that officials knew the dirigible was unsafe—it was too heavy to reach the proper altitude, and it had poorly made air and fuel pumps—but the maiden voyage was commanded to proceed as scheduled.

Phantastic Tips

If you start getting messages from the spirit world—maybe not just one, but two, three, or four—hey, pay attention! They're trying to tell you something! If they're coming all the way from the Other Side just to talk to you, it's probably important. And even if it's not, it'll sure be worth hearing.

The Ghost of Flight 401

On the night of December 19, 1972, Eastern Airline Flight 401 crashed in the Florida Everglades. A hundred passengers and crew, including Captain Bob Loft and second officer and flight engineer Dan Repo, died in or as a result of the crash. Loft and Repo both survived the impact, but Loft died about an hour later, before rescue crews could reach the plane. Repo died in the hospital about 30 hours after the crash.

The subsequent investigation concluded that the crash was caused by a combination of possible mechanical failure and human error. During take-off, instruments showed that the landing gear wasn't operating properly. As the two pilots checked the data,

Ghostly Pursuits

Two 1978 made-for-television movies dealt with incidents surrounding an L-1011 that crashed in the Everglades. Neither film mentioned people involved in the doomed Eastern Airlines flight by name. *Crash of Flight 401* told a straightforward story of the doomed flight, while *Ghost of Flight 401* focused on the ghostly aftermath of the crash.

they didn't realize that the plane was losing altitude. By the time they noticed, it was too late.

Eastern Airlines salvaged the wreck and allowed undamaged parts to be used for repair and maintenance on other L-1011s in the fleet. Before long, Loft's and Repo's ghosts began appearing on those planes, including several leased to other airlines and especially on Eastern's plane number 318. Sometimes, crews and passengers would experience paranormal activities such as cold spots, objects suddenly appearing, or the sensation of an invisible presence. Other people reported seeing, hearing, and receiving messages and warnings from the spectres.

Repo turned up more often than Loft, but both were frequently seen, recognized, and identified by crew members who had worked with them. Here are just a few of the reported sightings:

- Repo liked to visit the galley, where his face would appear reflected in the glass of the oven door. Even when Repo wasn't seen, flight attendants sometimes sensed his or some other presence, and the galley would feel cold and damp.

- A flight attendant watched as an engineer fixed an overloaded circuit on an oven before take-off. Only after later seeing Repo's photograph did the attendant realize she'd seen his ghost repairing the oven.

- Repo's ghost was particularly concerned about safety. He'd appear in the cockpit, sitting at the engineer's instrument panel or simply reflected in the instruments' glass. He even told one engineer he had already run the pre-flight inspection.

- Before one flight, Repo's ghost warned about an electrical failure. He alerted the crew to a problem with hydraulic fluid on another flight and about a fire onboard a third. His warnings were always found to be correct, and disaster was prevented in each case.

- Loft often appeared sitting, in uniform, in an unoccupied first-class seat. On at least one occasion, he was instantly recognized by the plane's captain. At that moment, the ghost simply disappeared.

- Loft also showed up from time to time in the small crew compartment. He even spoke over the public address system on flight safety, informing passengers on the proper use of the lap belt, etc.

First-Person Phantoms

In 1972, psychic entertainer Frances Willard (see Chapter 23) was living in Texas when she had a vivid dream of being a co-pilot on a commercial airline. The pilot said to her, "We are going to take off a little differently this time." To which she replied, "What do you mean?" And the pilot said, "Well, *look!*" And as Frances peered out the window of the cockpit, she realized that they were in water and surrounded by high grass.

Upon waking up, Frances went downstairs and shared the story with her family. She said it was the most vivid dream she'd ever had. Her husband said, "Well, that's interesting, because they just announced that an Eastern Airlines passenger jet crashed in the Everglades."

Just a dream? Merely a coincidence? Or was something or someone reaching out to her in a moment of crisis? Frances shares her opinion:

> I believe that when there is a disaster, sometimes the vibrations reach other points and other people. And if there is a collective consciousness—and there is!—perhaps in that flash, the soul of the pilot had made contact with me on its flight to wherever else it was going.

Do spirits feel guilt in the afterworld? Ghost experts say that they do, and that the spectres sometimes return to the mortal world to right wrongs and atone for their sins. That might explain why Repo, who carried the burden of the loss of a hundred lives under his care, returned to check the safety of other planes. He was not going to let such a crash happen again—not on *his* watch!

At first, the management of Eastern Airlines refused to believe the sightings. Besides, if they did acknowledge anything unusual, they knew the media would have a field day reporting that Eastern had planes that were haunted. The rumors became so plentiful and persistent, however, that eventually Eastern quietly removed all of the recycled Flight 401 parts. After they did, the ghosts were not sighted again.

As sad as some of these tales of vehicular hauntings may be, could anything possibly be more tragic than the loss of a school-age child to the Great Unknown? Perhaps that's why many student spirits have chosen to return to haunt the hallowed hallways of their demise. And, while we're talking about books and learning, let's stop by the library. Maybe the ghosts haunting *them* are simply returning their overdue books.

The Least You Need to Know

◆ There have been reports of hauntings on all forms of transportation.

◆ Most spirit legends of the railroads are connected to deaths caused by collisions, derailing, or other tragedies. A famous example is the ghostly appearance of Lincoln's funeral train.

◆ Legends of ghost ships on the Seven Seas include those of the *Flying Dutchman*, *The Palantine* light, the SS *Watertown*, and the *Queen Mary*.

◆ Spectral visits from the crew of the downed British dirigible *R-101* were discounted because the contact came through séances; the frequently seen apparitions from Eastern Airlines Flight 401 couldn't be dismissed so easily.

20

School Daze: America's Most Haunted Schools

In This Chapter

- ◆ Student ghosts stay after school
- ◆ Sshhh! Spirits in the library stacks
- ◆ Teachers who ignored the "final bell"
- ◆ Haunted halls of higher education

It was the best of times. It was the worst of times.

No, I'm not just quoting Dickens. I'm talking about being a kid. A *school* kid. It's possibly the most exhilarating time of life. Anything and everything in the world seems possible. If only there's time to do it all.

But sometimes, there's not.

It's a sad fact of life: People die every day. And, unfortunately, some of them are children and young adults. When they do return as ghosts, it's common for kids to haunt the happy (and, sometimes, not so happy) halls of their schools and dorms.

Let's take a class trip across the United States to look at some of America's haunted educational institutions, region by region. And, while we're at it, we'll hit some of the country's libraries as well. Maybe we can check out a few books on ghosts and hauntings. (That's 133.1 in the good old Dewey Decimal system.)

Hurry up, or you'll be late for homeroom.

Northern Nightshades

The Northeast region of colonial America is home to the nation's oldest schools, which means the area's also home to the country's oldest spooks—not that you could tell by looking at them. Most of them look as young as they did the day they first entered these schoolyards.

If you've got a hall pass to the Spirit World, let's take a look around.

Maine

Oak Grove Academy lies in the woods of Vassalboro. Legend has it that several students were murdered there and hung from meat hooks. The killer was never found. Spectral voices whisper the children's names, their ghosts are seen on the main school building's roof, and lights flicker throughout the academy.

Over in Brunswick, the old high school is haunted by a schoolgirl, but no one knows who she is or why she's returned. The custodians have named her Mimi. She moves objects and slams doors, and her apparition is occasionally seen walking the halls of Brunswick High.

Massachusetts

Sessions House at Smith College in Northampton was once a farmhouse and served as a station on the Underground Railroad. It's been haunted since before being incorporated into the college. The ghosts are thought to be those of slaves who died when one of the secret tunnels into the basement collapsed. The first floor of Martha Wilson House, also on campus, is haunted by an unknown presence. Its footsteps can be heard pacing the floor. Also, windows are discovered to have been opened by themselves, and occasionally, all the doors on the floor slam shut simultaneously without human assistance.

The fourth floor of Shelton Hall of Boston University is usually reserved for writing majors. The famous playwright Eugene O'Neill is said to have died in what is now Room 401 in Shelton Hall. Since his death in 1953, he has haunted the entire floor of the residence facility. O'Neill's tragic life influenced much of his own work. By haunting the dorm, is he giving his successors something to write about?

New York

Schenectady is the home of Union College. There's a beautiful garden behind the central campus that belies its horrific history. Each year, on the first full moon following the summer solstice, the ghost of "Alice" strolls along the creek that runs through the garden. According to legend, she was burned at the stake for witchcraft on the site hundreds of years ago.

Ghostly Pursuits
The legend of Alice being burned at the stake for witchcraft in Schenectady is improbable. Few people were burned for witchcraft in the United States; most were hanged. Now and then, one was pressed to death by having large stones placed on the chest to force a confession. The last notable hangings and pressings occurred as part of the witchcraft hysteria and trials at Salem Village in the Massachusetts Bay Colony in 1692. Of course, that's not to say there couldn't have been a local burning here and there.

Pennsylvania

Pennsylvania is one of the most haunted of the original 13 American colonies. With the writing of the Declaration of Independence in Philadelphia, you could say that the City of Brotherly Love is the site of the birth of the nation. Ghosts can be found all over the greater city area, not just from the Revolutionary War days, but from all eras of its historic past. Here are a few school- and library-related haunted sites in Pennsylvania:

- **Civil War Library and Museum.** Phantom soldiers have been seen playing cards on the second floor of the Philadelphia museum. The site has been featured on TV's *Unsolved Mysteries*.

- **Grundy Memorial Library.** The ghost of a man said to have been a king of Spain has been spotted in a phantom rowboat on the Delaware River behind this library in Bristol. He holds a lantern and calls out the name of a lost little girl. Reports date back to before the library was built when there was a private residence on the property.

- **Bucks County Community College.** A female ghost who's thought to be Stella Tyler, a former school administrator, haunts Tyler Hall at this Doylestown college.

- **Tate House.** In the 1770s, a Hessian solider was buried in the cellar of the Tate House in Newtown. The Revolutionary mercenary haunts the former residence, now part of The George School.

How about some contemporary phantom Pennsylvanians? The ghost of a female student haunts Butz Hall at Cedar Crest College in Allentown. She is said to have committed suicide in her dorm. Just down the road in Bethlehem, an unidentified elderly man haunts the library of Lehigh University. A few miles in the opposite direction, Central Catholic High School in Reading is haunted by a man who hanged himself in the attic, back when the building was a private residence. Students report seeing combination locks on lockers spinning by themselves, and the distinct sound of chains rattling sometimes echoes down the halls.

First-Person Phantoms

As I signed out several books on ghosts from the library, the librarian noticed the titles and raised an eyebrow. "I had a ghost," she offered dryly. When the woman first moved to Hollywood, she rented a small apartment. Almost immediately, ghostlike phenomena started happening. She'd be sitting at a table, and her cigarette would float up from the ashtray, float straight across in front of her eyes, then drop: a definite fire hazard! Her cats were always the first to know when spirit activity was coming. They'd arch their backs, bare their teeth, hiss, and spit. Soon, she found out that a man had died in her apartment some years prior to her moving in. Perhaps his ghost was still a tenant—and a nonsmoker! She was never exactly afraid of the ghost or the phenomena, but after six months, it became too frustrating and unnerving. She moved.

Out at the other end of the state, Carnegie Library in Pittsburgh was supposedly built over an ancient cemetery, and people think that ghosts of the graveyard visit the library building at night after closing hours. It's said that Room 201 of Bruce Hall, a dorm on the campus of the University of Pittsburgh in Pittsburgh, is haunted. On the Johnstown campus of the University of Pittsburgh, several nighttime spirits haunt Laurel Hall as well as the Living and Learning Center. They include a woman, a boy, and an elderly man who hollers and wakes students from their sleep.

All of Gettysburg seems to be haunted, what with the catastrophic events that took place there during the Civil War (see Chapter 17 for more on Gettysburg's haunted battlefields). But the haunting of Stevens Hall at Gettysburg College only dates back about a hundred years. "The Blue Boy," as the spectre is called, ran away from an abusive home and sought shelter among the young college women in the dorms. One frigid, snowy night, the boy hid outside on a window ledge when the headmistress did her room checks. The woman seemed to take an eternity. When she left, the girls ran to the window to let the boy back in, but he had disappeared. Terrified that he had fallen and injured himself (or worse), they rushed outside. The boy wasn't there. He was never found. But residents of the dorm now report seeing a young boy, blue as if frozen to death, in and around the dorm.

The main campus of Pennsylvania State University is located at University Park in the exact geographic center of the state. Schwab Auditorium, the site of many of the university's special events, is supposedly haunted by a handful of ghosts. One is thought to be George W. Atherton, an early president of the university, who is buried beside the hall. Another may be Charles Schwab, for whom the building is dedicated. Perhaps he hangs around his namesake auditorium hoping to be recognized.

The ghost of Old Coaly, a mule that was used during construction of the university in the 1850s, has often been seen and heard haunting Watts Hall. Also, a third-floor room of the dormitory Runkle Hall was the site of unexplained poltergeist activity in 1994.

> **Ghostly Pursuits**
>
> Could Old Coaly really have returned from the dead to haunt Penn State? Most people believe that a ghost is a soul in spirit or apparitional form. Does that mean that animals—and many have been sighted as ghosts—have souls? Paranormal experts, religious theorists, and many pet owners still debate the issue.

The grave of George W. Atherton, located outside Schwab Auditorium on the grounds of Pennsylvania State University.

(Photo by author)

Vermont

At least two ghosts still reside on the grounds of the University of Vermont in Burlington. A former medical student named Henry who committed suicide there in the 1920s haunts Converse Hall. The ghost of Margaret "Daisy" Smith haunts Bittersweet House on campus. She lived in the building from the 1930s to the 1950s, back when it was a private home; today, it houses the school's Environmental department. She usually appears wearing an ankle-length skirt and a blouse with a high collar.

In the 1960s, five students from Winooski High School in Winooski were killed in a car crash while returning from a trip to Canada. A memorial service was held for them in the school gym; ever since, custodians have reported apparitional activity there.

The Lower Depths: Dixie and Southwest

There's an old song about how nice it is to live and die in Dixie. Well, apparently a lot of belles and beaus in the South and the Southwest have decided there's a third verse to that song—something about coming back to haunt those of us still here.

But they're good kids: They've decided to stay in school! They weren't going to let a little thing like being dead get in the way of a better education.

Alabama

Some ghosts are Alabamy bound! It's said that a student who died in McCandless Hall at Athens State College in Hunstville is still seen from time to time in the halls of his old dorm. Two ghosts haunt Huntingdon College in Montgomery: A Red Lady visits the older dorms of the college; she's named for the color of clothing she wore in life and still wears in death. A lonely student who was unable to make any friends at the college, she hanged herself in despair. Apparently, she's returned, still hoping to make the friends she never acquired while alive. You can't see the other spectre. He's called the Ghost on the Green because he shot himself on the central campus public area, the green, and now walks there at night. Percipients have felt him grab at their clothing, muss their hair, or blow in their eyes.

Also in Alabama, students have seen unexplained ghosts and heard spectral footsteps at Decatur High School in Decatur.

Arkansas

A little further west in Arkansas, Old Charlie Fowler Christian School in Mountain View has unexplained footsteps descending the staircase at night. Water drips from the ceiling, even during droughts, and spectral voices chatter away in the cafeteria. Rumor has it that the school was built on an ancient Native American burial ground. Paranormal theorists say that, if that's true, it might explain some of the spirit activity.

The ghost of a female student haunts Henderson State University in Arkadelphia. She goes from dorm to dorm, looking for the boyfriend who deserted her. According to most versions of the tale, she died of a broken heart.

Florida

Flagler College is located in St. Augustine in northern Florida. Although there are several ghost legends of sightings on campus, most of the activity occurs in Ponce de Leon Hall, which is a girls' dorm. Supposedly, the fourth floor is haunted by the ghost of the mistress of Henry Flagler, who hanged herself in a fourth-floor room back in the times when the building was a hotel.

The old women's dormitory of the Ringling School of Art and Design in Sarasota in southern Florida also used to be a hotel. The building is haunted by a ghost named Mary, who committed suicide in the 1920s on the stairwell between the second and third floors. (That section of stairs is now used only as a fire escape.) Mary's apparition has been seen in the halls, but usually just out of the corner of one's eye. Students who live in what was once Mary's room sometimes come in to find their paintbrushes slowly spinning in their cups of rinse water!

Boo!

There's an old saying, "Life is not a dress rehearsal." Apparently, a lot of ghosts don't agree. They come back to do things they never got around to when they were alive. Trouble is, most of them don't succeed when they're dead, either. They just spend eternity trying. There's a lesson to be learned: Do it now! This is probably your only real chance to make your dreams come true.

To the west in Tallahassee, a female student who was killed while sunbathing on the roof revisits Cawthon Hall on the campus of Florida State University. She was struck by lightning during a sudden freak storm. According to a 1971 story in the university newspaper, *The Florida Flambeau*, students have reported poltergeistlike activity in the dorm for years. Residents who occupy what was once the girl's room are especially haunted: Objects such as books or photos move by themselves, there are unusual sounds in the room at night, and often the ghost's "presence" can be felt.

North Carolina

Here's a grisly fact: Corpses are regularly sold or donated to medical schools for use in the classroom. But perhaps one girl wasn't too happy about hers being sold to Founders College in Charlotte, North Carolina. In the 1930s, her green-eyed, slender ghost regularly haunted Chambers Hall on the small campus that used to be located in the center of the city.

South Caldwell High School in Lenoir has not one but two ghosts, although neither appears as an apparition. The first is a female student who died while rehearsing a school play. She's now a theater ghost and plays tricks just before opening night of any play, such as moving props backstage and creating havoc with the lights and sets. The other ghost is that of a man who fell down the elevator shaft while working on it one night. The elevator now seems to have a mind of its own. It often goes up and down by itself, sometimes four or five times, around the hour of his deadly accident.

Texas

Everything is bigger in Texas, so is it any wonder that its high schools, colleges, and universities have more than their share of spirits? Texas's institutes of higher education are especially active:

♦ At the University of Texas Medical Branch at Galveston (UTMB), people claim to have seen phantom faces on everything from window glass to cinnamon buns over the years. There's also a long-standing legend of an unidentified face appearing on the side of a building on the UTMB campus.

♦ The University of Texas at Brownsville used to be Fort Brown. Phantom soldiers have been seen at night, marching their drills.

♦ At Institute of Texas Culture in San Antonio, which is budgeted under the University of Texas at San Antonio (UTSA), unexplained pipe smoke is smelled in exhibition rooms, books rearrange themselves in the library, and phantom footsteps can be heard coming from the audio/visual room.

♦ The Agriculture building at Texas A&M University in College Station has a haunted elevator. Local legend attributes it to the victim of a murder that was supposedly committed in the elevator.

♦ The Housing Office and adjacent buildings of Angelo State University in San Angelo are haunted by a murder victim, a young female student who was killed in the 1970s by an ROTC cadet. Apparently, the suitor went murderously insane when she rejected him.

Two more Texas terrors: The old library building in downtown Houston is haunted by a ghost that plays the violin late at night. According to some legends, the spirit was a maintenance man in the 1920s and 1930s. Sealy High School in Sealy has an elevator that operates by itself. Doors on the second floor also open and close all by their lonesome, although the activity might be connected to the unexplained footsteps heard there.

Virginia

Even the youngest children can return to their happy haunts. At least two elementary schools are haunted in Virginia. At the first, William Bass Elementary School in Lynchburg, spectral voices are heard, and doors open and shut on their own during some of school's special events. The spirits of two African American boys who were killed in the 1960s still attend Matthew Whaley Elementary School in Williamsburg.

Several ghosts haunt the College of William and Mary, which is also located in Williamsburg. In 1980, a female student committed suicide in a classroom in Tucker Hall. Ever since, students have reported seeing her ghost in the hallways there. Two Native American boys who were forced to attend the school in the seventeenth century are still "sensed" as phantoms in Brafferton Building; sometimes one is seen on the campus grounds. Also, ghosts of a French soldier and the college's first president, the Reverend James Blair, have been spotted in the President's House.

The spectre of a Revolutionary War soldier who died of gunshot wounds on the third floor of what is now Phi Beta Kappa Hall at William and Mary returns to haunt the building. Also, a spectre identified as Lucinda, a former student, haunts the stage, a room below it, and the balcony of the theater in the hall. (Lucinda was to have performed in an upcoming college production of Thornton Wilder's *Our Town* when she was killed in an automobile accident.) Is she a "living" example of the phrase, "The show must go on?"

The Nation's Breadbasket

As the nation moved westward, so did its belief in ghosts. Perhaps the telling of ghost stories is just another one of those good old, traditional family values for which the country's Midwest is justly proud. With 3,000 miles between its coasts, the United States has plenty of space to be haunted, and hundreds of ghosts attend classrooms and take up residence in dormitories every day.

 Boo!

Suicide is never the answer. It doesn't really solve problems; often, it just carries them over into the next world. Look at how many suicides have returned as ghosts, and they still can't seem to put an end to their troubles. Work on meeting your challenges now—in this life—so you can rest in peace in the next.

Illinois

Here's a gruesome one. There's a clearing outside Gurnee that's referred to locally as The Gate. A small schoolhouse used to stand on the property, but it's long since been torn down, and the road to the site is closed. All that still stands is a large black cast-iron gate.

According to an apocryphal legend—that's a fancy way of saying no one knows for sure when or *if* it actually occurred—a lunatic burst into the school and killed all the students. He decapitated several of the children and stuck their heads onto the pointed spikes on the top of the gate. It's said that even if you don't know the gate's history, looking at it produces an overwhelming sense of grief in the onlooker. Every so often, phantom heads appear on the gate's spikes, and the screams and cries of the phantom children can be heard in the wind.

> **Boo!**
>
> The road to The Gate outside Gurnee, Illinois, was obviously closed for a reason. Never go on private property unless you have permission from the owner and/or current resident.

It's said that the English building on the Champaign-Urbana campus of the University of Illinois used to be a girls' dormitory. One of the students who supposedly committed suicide there still haunts the structure.

Spectral activity takes place at the library in Williams Hall at Illinois State University in Normal. Books fall from the shelves one by one without the help of human hands, and people have seen the flicker of a moving white object out of the corner of the eye. The apparition is thought to be that of the hall's first librarian, Angie Milner.

Indiana

Next door in the Hoosier State, a Gray Lady has been seen in the Willard Library in Evansville.

Several spots of the Indiana State University in Terre Haute are haunted. Spectral activity such as objects moving by themselves as well as spirit whispers and noises have been reported in Burford Hall. Also, the twelfth floor of one of the dorms, Cromwell Hall, is haunted by the spirit of a student who committed suicide by jumping out the window of Room 1221. His restless spirit now paces the hall. Residents have also heard other odd noises.

The University of Notre Dame in South Bend was built on lands once occupied by the Potawatomi Indians. Columbus Hall, one of the university's earliest buildings, is haunted by phantom Native Americans on horseback, galloping up and down the front steps. Notre Dame is world famous for its football team, and according to some, one of the university's star players, George Gipp, haunts his old dormitory, Washington Hall. The building now houses the theater of the university's drama club, and Gipp supposedly returns to visit the stage and the backstage green room (where actors and their guests can visit and relax before and after performances).

Iowa

In the late 1800s, a woman was walking down the staircase from the third floor of College Hall at Simpson College in Indianola when she stumbled and fell. She broke her neck, dying instantly. Ever since, according to school tradition, if you stand on the college seal emblazoned on the courtyard outside the hall at exactly midnight on any Friday the thirteenth, the woman's face will appear at (or on the glass of) a third-floor window.

Several buildings at the University of Northern Iowa in Cedar Falls are haunted. The spirit of a solider named Augie returns to a dormitory named Lawther Hall. He died there when the building was used as an infirmary. Student residents also have felt cold spots, heard unusual noises, and seen moving objects—all standard ghost and poltergeist activity. The Strayer-Wood Theatre, also on campus, is haunted by a ghost that theater students have nicknamed Zelda.

> **Ghostly Pursuits**
>
> Zelda's case history at the University of Northern Iowa is quite unusual in ghost lore, because she moved locations. She originally haunted an older theater on campus, but she moved along with the theater department to their new building. Zelda has not been seen as a ghost; rather, she's responsible for producing spectral piano music, strange noises, and operating some of the theater's equipment.

Over in Ames, at Iowa State University, an unexplainable low moaning sound often can be heard in Memorial Union. The building is dedicated to the memory of graduates of ISU who died at war, and the noise is said to be the haunting voice of the only female graduate of Iowa State to die in World War II.

Kansas

Kansas State University is located in Manhattan (Kansas, not New York City). The ghost of Duncan, a pledge who died from hazing by the Theta Xi fraternity, haunts its building, which now houses Phi Gamma Delta. (Two other fraternity houses, Delta Sigma Phi and Kappa Sigma, have also been reported as having ghosts.)

Jesse Baird haunts the third floor of the Baird Music Hall at Morehead State University in Morehead. Some people claim to have seen his apparition; others have heard sounds and detected certain scents distinctive to Baird.

A depressed student committed suicide by jumping from the sixth floor of the Fine Arts building at Murray State University in Murray. Several faculty members have seen his apparition roaming up and down the aisles of Lovett Auditorium, which is located in the building. People have also reported soft piano music coming from the third-floor practice room when no one was there.

A former head of maintenance who died at Paola High School in Paola seems to have liked his job—he's still there. A girl who died by falling down the stairs during a fire drill haunts Jackson Independent School in Jackson. And the girls' restroom of the third floor of Madison Middle School in Richmond is also haunted. A cheerleader was found there, beaten to death, in the 1950s, and it's believed her ghost is causing the weird sounds coming from the empty room in the morning and late at night when the school is closed.

Michigan

The Ladies' Library in Ypsilanti was once the residence of the Starkweather family. Maryanne Starkweather bequeathed the building to the city upon her death on the condition it be used as a library. About 15 years ago, however, the building was changed into office space. Ever since, people working after hours have heard footsteps on vacant floors overhead. Is it Maryanne, unhappy about the fact that the building's no longer a library?

Minnesota

Some students at the Minneapolis College of Art and Design claim to have been awakened in the middle of the night, unable to move and hearing the sound of screaming inside their skulls. They blame the phenomenon on the unsettled spirit of a female student who was allegedly raped and killed in one of the basement apartments years earlier.

The third and fourth floors of Heffron Hall, a dormitory at St. Mary's University in Winona, are said to be haunted by a phantom priest, Father Laurence Michael Lesches. On August 25, 1915, Father Lesches shot and killed Bishop Patrick Heffron (after whom the dorm was later named). Father Lesches was committed to the State Hospital for the Dangerously Insane in St. Peter, Minnesota, where he died in 1943.

The College of Visual Arts in St. Paul was originally a private residence. There's a spook in what is now the photography darkroom: Objects move on their own once the lights are out, and the timer resets itself. Other ghost activity occurs throughout the building. Night custodians have reported the lights turning on and off by themselves, and they sometimes hear the disembodied sounds of children, as well as other strange noises. Rumor has it that a former owner of the house was cheating on his wife with the maid. They often used the darkroom for their assignations. When the man refused to leave his wife for the maid, the servant hanged herself in despair on the banister of the main stairwell. Some have claimed to see the ghost of the man himself, dressed in flannel.

Missouri

Cottey College in the city of Nevada has two resident ghosts. One, named Vera, is the spirit of a former student who accidentally caught her nightgown on fire while making candy in her room—killing her and burning down her dormitory, Rosemary Hall. Now she haunts the whole college, playing pranks on some girls but being kind to others. The second ghost at Cottey dates back to Civil War days. He's male, possibly African American, and reportedly is dressed in black.

At Stephens College in Columbia, a young lady who hanged herself in the bell tower of the dorm haunts Senior Hall. She killed herself after her boyfriend, a Confederate soldier she had hidden in her dorm, was discovered and shot.

Nebraska

Former music teachers haunt two colleges in Nebraska. The music professor who haunts Hastings College in Hastings often appears as a ghost light in that college's Music building. He's also been seen in human form, walking the halls. Lights that turn on and off by themselves have been attributed to him.

Another ghost haunts the music building at Nebraska Wesleyan University in Lincoln, where he taught the organ. His ghost is most often seen sitting near the instrument. Often, organ music can be heard wafting from the empty music hall. The professor's ghost has also been seen and heard in his former apartment.

A teacher who was killed at York High School in York has returned as a ghost. She's been reported walking into her regular room, turning on the lights, and sitting at her desk. Then, for some unexplained reason, she scatters all the papers sitting on the desk in front of her.

Ohio

The Hinckley Library in Hinckley was once a private residence owned by Vernon Stouffer, who founded Stouffer Foods. During the building's conversion into a library in 1973, workers reported seeing two ghosts standing on the staircase: a young woman in a nineteenth-century–era blue dress and a man wearing a hat. Another ghost was also seen on the basement stairway. Staffers feel unusual, unexplainable presences on the upper floors of the former mansion, and small, self-levitating objects (such as paper clips) have been reported. Although no one's been able to positively identify the spirits, none of them resembles Stouffer. They're thought to be the ghosts of a Dr. Nelson Wilcox and his sister Rebecca, who lived in a cabin located on the grounds around the time of the Civil War.

Columbus State Community College in Columbus was apparently built on top of an old Catholic cemetery. The original residents must not be too happy: Several of them haunt the college.

A female ghost has been heard walking the third floor of the Lucas County Public Library in Toledo long after closing time. Those who have heard the noise decided that it was a woman because it sounded like high heels on linoleum.

Oakwood High School in a southern suburb of Dayton has had a reputation for being haunted for years. The fast-moving figure of a male spectre, as well as footsteps, are said to be those of the ghost of a student who hanged himself in one of the hallways in the 1960s or 1970s. The second apparition, of which little is known, is that of a pretty young girl who is almost always seen in the same hallway as the one haunted by the boy, although the two spirits never appear together. Several people have also reported seeing the girl sitting on one of the benches along the hall.

Tennessee

At a women's residence hall at East Tennessee State University Campus in Johnson City, students regularly hear noises overhead that sound like someone dropping marbles, one at a time, onto the floor. The sound is supposedly caused by the ghost of the so-called "Marble Boy," who died in the hall's elevator. If you yell at the boy, he drops all of the marbles at one time.

Go West, Young Man

"Recent" is a relative term when you're talking about eternity. But most of the ghosts of the West are newer than their East Coast counterparts. Here, then, are a few of the fresher faces on the phantom scene.

California

The San Francisco Arts Institute is thought to have been built over a cemetery after the great earthquake of 1906. Ever since, the building has been haunted by unhappy spectres that believe the grounds have been desecrated.

Down the road in Sunnyvale, Homestead High School has a ghost that roams the second-floor hallway. It's only seen at night, but other times, students and faculty have "felt" its presence. In one teacher's case, it was literal: The invisible phantom tapped the teacher on the shoulder. The spectre also locks and opens doors when no one's around.

According to Modesto High School legend, some years ago a male student fell to his death from the balcony of the auditorium onto the floor below. Ever since, his ghost has been reported walking back and forth along the balcony railing. Also, there have been rapping noises heard in the main hall outside the home economic rooms.

During some basketball games at Bakersfield High School, the gymnasium is haunted by a student couple, about 16 to 18 years old. They appear on the top row of a particular area on the "home side" of the bleachers. The girl is wearing her prom dress, and her boyfriend is wearing his football jacket with BHS on the back. They sit watching the match or kiss throughout the game. Even those who don't see the apparitions have the sensation that they're being watched by them. As is common with apparitional sightings, the immediate area around the phantom pair drops in temperature when they appear.

Down in southern California, William Cook Anaheim High School Auditorium is home to various spectral activities. No apparitions have been reported, but disembodied voices are sometimes heard in the house, and irregular, wandering footsteps can be heard on the roof.

Nevada

The ghost of Miss Suzette, a former teacher, still strolls the school grounds at Fourth Ward School in Virginia City. That's some recess supervisor! In Reno, there's a ghostly legend at Wooster High School involving the suicide of a football player. Back in the early 1970s, the Wooster Colts lost a big game to their rivals, the McQueen Lancers. Later that night, one of the defeated players went onto the field and shot himself. Now, whenever the two teams meet, players say they sometimes fumble over an invisible something—or someone—out on the field.

Also in Nevada, four different buildings on the campus of the College of Saint Rose in Albany are reputedly haunted, each by its own resident ghost. The spirits are believed to be those of:

- ◆ A gardener

- ◆ A priest

- ◆ A seven-year-old girl who was killed in a fire

- ◆ A musician who committed suicide in Chicago (no one knows how his ghost wound up in Nevada)

It's a mystery why these ghosts have chosen to haunt these particular buildings.

North Dakota

At the University of North Dakota in Grand Forks, numerous sightings have been reported of the ghost of a girl in the tunnel connecting Wilkerson Dining Hall with the five campus dormitories. As recently as 1988, three students saw her in the West Hall tunnel. The spectre is always described as being about 5'5", with short dark hair, and wearing a nightgown. Her legs often seem to be missing. The ghost is thought to be that of a young female student who froze to death about 60 feet from West Hall around 2 A.M. in December 1962, before the tunnels were built. It's believed that she was trying to go to the dining room, but slipped on the ice, fell, was knocked unconscious, and died of exposure.

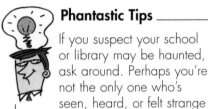

Phantastic Tips

If you suspect your school or library may be haunted, ask around. Perhaps you're not the only one who's seen, heard, or felt strange things. Check out the history of the place and find out if any deaths or other tragedies occurred on the property. If one has, that's where you should set up your ghost hunt.

South Dakota

Sparky, as the ghost has been named, haunts the stage area and auditorium's storage room in Stevens High School in Rapid City. He has supposedly made chairs burst into flames (hence his nickname) and caused nails to fall out of cement ceilings. The school is said to be located on the site of a house fire in which an entire family died. Its cause: Sparky made chairs in that home burst into flames, too.

Wyoming

In Byron, Rocky Mountain High School (which actually houses elementary through senior classes) has been haunted since 1952. Students, teachers, and superintendents have all felt presences. Much of the activity occurs in or near the weightlifting and wrestling room, which was the former library. Phenomena includes …

- Electrical appliances working, even though they're not plugged in.

- Floating, moving mist or fog.

- Foul odors.

- Icy cold spots.

- Lights turning on and off by themselves.

- The sensation of an invisible body passing by.

- The sound of doors opening and shutting on their own.

- Spectral footsteps.

So far, no one's been able to explain the phenomena or attribute it to any individual or event in the past.

What do you want to be when you grow up—that is, if you're not trapped forever in high school as a teenage prom ghost? Well, each year there are a lot of graduates who decide they want to move to California to become stars. Do *you* have what it takes?

In the next chapter, we'll go on a nighttime tour of Tinseltown. So get out your autograph book. Who knows how many filmdom phantoms we'll meet on our tour of Haunted Hollywood!

The Least You Need to Know

- Ghosts return to places where their mortal counterparts enjoyed life and/or met tragic ends. School students are no exception.

- Ghosts can be found in schools in every state of the Union.

- Be careful checking out books: There are haunted libraries in every region of the United States.

- The spirit world is an equal-opportunity employer: Ghosts of every age and rank (students, faculty, and other staff) haunt schools and libraries.

Chapter 21

Haunted Hollywood

In This Chapter

♦ Famous phantoms of filmdom

♦ Tales from haunted celebrities

♦ Haunted homes of the stars

♦ Spectral visions at movieland venues

Nothing lives forever. Even the stars in the heavens finally fade and die. But how about the stars from *movies and television?* Do you think some of them could live forever? I mean, other than in syndication and on DVD. Maybe—if they come back as a ghost!

But the quest for eternal recognition can't explain away all of the ghosts of the rich and famous. There are the famous theaters, clubs, and other night spots haunted by—dare I say it?—*non*celebrity spirits. And how about the ghosts that don't want to be in the spotlight but are content to simply shadow the stars?

They're all here in haunted Hollyweird!

A Star Is Born (Again)

Many stars of the silent and early sound eras of filmmaking were fascinated with Spiritualism and the occult. Charlie Chaplin once quipped that ectoplasm seemed to hover over Hollywood "like smog." Rudolph Valentino, Jean Harlow, and Mae West, among other stars, frequently attended séances. In fact, West sometimes *conducted* séances, acting as the medium. On occasion, she even produced spirit voices.

All the world watches Hollywood, so when one of its stars returns as a ghost, all the world notices. Let's take a look at some of the more well-known celebrity "comebacks."

Jean Harlow

In 1932, film siren and "blonde bombshell" (about whom that phrase was coined) Jean Harlow (1911–1937) was married to director Paul Bern in the living room of her home at 1353 Club View Drive in Los Angeles. They moved into Bern's Bavarian-chalet style mansion at 9820 Easton Drive in Benedict Canyon in Beverly Hills. Just two months later, Bern committed suicide there, in Harlow's bedroom.

Devastated by her husband's death, Harlow tried unsuccessfully to kill herself the next day in the master bedroom on the second floor of the house. Soon after, she moved back to Beverly Hills. Just five years later, while filming *Saratoga* (1937), the 26-year-old star died suddenly at her home of uremic poisoning. She is buried in the Great Mausoleum of Forest Lawn Cemetery in a private niche purchased by her fiancé, actor William Powell.

According to some of the later owners of the Benedict Canyon house, Harlow occasionally returns to haunt her upstairs bedroom. There have even been a few reports of her apparition at her old home on Club View Drive.

Ghostly Pursuits

Hairstylist Jay Sebring purchased Paul Bern's home in 1966. Sebring was dating actress Sharon Tate at the time, and he asked her to house-sit for him one night. Tate awoke to see Bern's ghost running around the bedroom and noisily crashing into furniture. She fled downstairs and was horrified to see an apparition of Sebring tied to the post of the staircase with his throat slashed. Eventually, the visions and sounds ended, and Tate, exhausted, fell asleep. The next day, Tate told Sebring what she had experienced, but it was soon all but forgotten. Within two years, Sebring, Tate, and three others were murdered by the followers of Charles Manson in a house just down the canyon.

Ozzie Nelson

Ozzie Nelson (1907–1975), whose beginnings were in radio, went on to star with his wife Harriet and their two sons Rick and David in the long-running television show, *The Adventures of Ozzie and Harriet* (1952–1966). In 1973, Ozzie and Harriet—without their sons—returned to television for one season in *Ozzie's Girls*.

For 25 years, the real-life Nelson family lived at 1822 Camino Palermo in Hollywood. Harriet continued to live there after Ozzie's death for another five years.

New owners moved in, and almost immediately they experienced paranormal activity throughout the house, such as lights and faucets that turned on and off by themselves and doors that opened and shut when no one was near. The owners believed that the ghost of Ozzie Nelson was pulling the pranks, even though his apparition was never seen.

Ramon Novarro

Silent-screen star Ramon Novarro (1899–1968) was a Latin-lover type—a rival, yet a close friend of Rudolph Valentino. Novarro is best remembered for portraying the title role in the 1926 film *Ben-Hur*; he was also the male lead in Greta Garbo's *Mata Hari* (1932). A lifelong bachelor, Novarro was brutally murdered on Halloween 1968 during a struggle with two young men he had met on Hollywood Boulevard and brought back to his home at 3110 Laurel Canyon. Novarro's naked body was found, beaten to death, in the master bedroom. Visitors to the estate often claim to feel an uneasy presence; many believe that Ramon Novarro, who died so violently, haunts the house.

John Wayne

The Associated Press wire service reported in the 1980s that the Santa Monica, California, lawyer who had purchased the *Wild Goose*, a yacht once belonging to John Wayne (1907–1979), regularly heard—and sometimes saw—the Duke's ghost walking the deck onboard late at night. He also heard invisible beer mugs clinking together in the ship's bar.

On one evening, the boat was on a chartered cruise when the engines were accidentally cut off, and the yacht started to drift. Oddly, the boat moved against the current and the wind, finally stopping right in front of John Wayne's old harborside home. Was there a phantom pilot onboard?

Clifton Webb

Clifton Webb (1891–1966) was one of Hollywood's most popular character actors. He was nominated for three Academy Awards, for his work in *Laura* (1944), *The Razor's Edge* (1946), and *Sitting Pretty* (1948). In his later films, he played pompous, stuffed-shirt types (including his signature character, Mr. Belvedere) in a string of comedies.

Webb lived with his mother, Maybelle, at his 1005 North Rexford mansion in Beverly Hills. After his mother's death there in 1960, Webb kept her clothes and other belongings locked in her room. Is that why, according to some sources, the actor saw the ghost of his mother in the house?

Webb later reported seeing another ghost in the estate, that of his friend Grace Moore, a Metropolitan opera star and film actress who had once leased the house.

Webb was buried in a crypt in the Sanctuary of Peace at Hollywood Memorial Cemetery (now renamed "Hollywood Forever"). His ghost is said to walk the halls of the mausoleum where he is interred.

In 1967, a year after Webb's death, the house was bought by producer Douglas Cramer and his wife, columnist Joyce Haber. They've both reported seeing two shadowy phantoms in the house that they believed to be Clifton Webb and Miss Moore. And whatever ghosts may have been in his home are now gone; a new house has since been built on the property.

One of the mausoleum hallways that actor Clifton Webb is said to haunt. White lilies mark his crypt in this photo.

(Photo by author)

> ### Ghostly Pursuits
>
> Hollywood doesn't only bury its actors. Many of the stars buried their beloved animal companions. Los Angeles Pet Cemetery is one of the most popular among the Hollywood elite. Hopalong Cassidy's horse, Mary Pickford's dog, and Petey, the Little Rascal's dog, all have their final resting places there. Rudolph Valentino may be buried in Hollywood Forever, not far from Clifton Webb, but Valentino's Great Dane, Kabar, is interred at Los Angeles Pet Cemetery. The dog died in 1929, but has apparently returned as a ghost. Several people who have passed the canine's grave have heard panting or been licked by a phantom tongue—presumably that of Kabar.

Spirit Stalkers: Warning from Beyond

It's not always the celebrity who returns to do the haunting. Sometimes, the stars become the haunted. It's one thing to be hounded by fans—but quite another to be stalked by a ghost!

Telly Savalas

Who loves ya, baby? Telly Savalas, star of TV's long-running *Kojak*, often told the story of how he was assisted by a phantom driver—and the ghost's car! Savalas was driving across a remote stretch of Long Island around 3:00 A.M. when he noticed that his car was running low on gas. He stopped at an all-night diner to ask directions to the nearest gas station.

Savalas came out of the roadside café and noticed a man standing by a black Cadillac. The guy asked him if he needed a lift, and Savalas allowed himself to be driven to get a can of gas. As Savalas went to pay, however, he realized he didn't have his wallet on him. The driver loaned the money to Savalas, who made the man write down his name and address so he could repay him.

The man drove Savalas back to his car. Savalas filled his tank, and when he looked up, the mysterious driver and his car were gone. Savalas wanted to thank him properly, so the next morning he looked up the man's name and address in the phone book. He called, but a woman answered the phone. She told him that the man he was asking for was her husband and had been dead for five years.

So the woman didn't think he was simply playing a cruel joke, Savalas visited the widow and showed her the paper. It was her husband's handwriting. She asked what the man who claimed to be her husband was wearing. It was the suit he had been buried in.

Elke Sommer

Elke Sommer, the sexy blonde film star from Germany, truly believes that a ghost saved her life, and she frequently has told the story on radio and television talk shows. Shortly after marrying writer Joe Hyams in 1964, the couple moved into a new home in Beverly Hills. The first night, they heard poltergeistlike banging and thumping downstairs in the dining room. At first they suspected burglars, but none were found. The next night, and the next, they heard the same noises, and always from the area of the dining room.

One fateful night there was a loud pounding on their bedroom door. Joe opened the door, but no one was there. Then he noticed thick smoke rising from downstairs. He fought his way down to the dining room, found it on fire, and managed to put out the flames.

Elke Sommer says that she consulted several mediums, and they all agreed that a mischievous poltergeist had set fire to the dining room, but when the fire got out of hand, the poltergeist woke them up to warn them of the danger.

Now that's some smoke detector!

Ghostly Pursuits

You might have noticed that many of the tales in these pages involve people and events from long ago. In several cases, paranormal researchers have said that ghost activity has tapered off or even stopped completely. Might the original stories have been exaggerated? Perhaps people are less superstitious or just more skeptical these days. Or maybe people today are just more hesitant about coming forward. Are advances in science and critical observation responsible for debunking more cases? It could be there are just fewer people trying to pull off hoaxes. Or perhaps, for reasons we could only guess at, fewer spirits are returning from the Other Side. What do you think?

Haunted Hollywood Landmarks

Ever since Hollywood became the movie capital of the world, it's been famous for its glittering stars and fabulous nightclubs, as well as for its notorious scandals, suicides, and murders. In such a festive atmosphere, why would any spirits want to leave? Wouldn't you want to stay to enjoy the party?

Ghosts and paranormal activity have been sighted at more than a few Hollywood landmarks. Let's take a drive down the streets of Tinseltown to see if we can turn up a macabre sight or two of our own.

Mann's Chinese Theatre

One of the most familiar sights in Hollywood, Mann's Chinese Theatre (originally Grauman's Chinese Theatre) was built by Sid Grauman in 1927 and opened with the premiere of Cecil B. DeMille's silent film epic *The King of Kings*. The movie palace, located at 6925 Hollywood Boulevard, is famous for the handprints and footprints of movie stars enshrined in cement in the forecourt.

It's been said that the ghost of actor Victor Killian has haunted the courtyard since 1982. Supposedly, he walks back and forth along the sidewalk looking for his murderer. According to police reports, Killian befriended a man at a nearby bar and invited him back to his apartment. The man allegedly beat Killian to death. Killian's body was discovered the next morning. His killer was never found.

Boo!

There's a lesson to be learned from the deaths of Ramon Novarro and Victor Killian, both of whom were brutally murdered: Don't invite strangers back to your place. They may help you on your way to becoming a ghost!

The Houdini Mansion

The property often referred to as the "Harry Houdini estate" is a four-acre tract of land in Laurel Canyon (at the corner of Laurel Canyon Boulevard and Willow Glen Road).

R. J. Walker, a Los Angeles department store magnate, built a 40-room mansion on the tract between 1911 and 1924. The mansion and adjoining structures on the property burned in the 1950s.

Houdini's name never appeared on a deed, so there's always been some question as to his actual connection with the property; however, Houdini and Walker both owned stock in a land venture that developed the area. When Houdini came west in 1919 to act in two films, *The Grim Game* and *Terror Island*, he most likely stayed in the guesthouse on the property, which burned with the mansion.

Before the estate's recent renovation, nearby residents had reported seeing and hearing unusual events such as ghost lights and unexplained sounds among the ruins on the uninhabited site. During the 1960s, it was reportedly a hang-out for occultists. Some think that Houdini himself haunts the grounds.

The renovated stairway and hillside leading up to the ruins of Houdini's haunted estate.

(Photo by author)

The Comedy Store

The Comedy Store, a nightclub featuring established and up-and-coming comedians, is located in West Hollywood. The building started as Ciro's in 1939, and it remained open until 1957. In its heyday, Ciro's was one of the largest and glitziest nightspots on the Sunset Strip.

After Ciro's closed its doors, the club operated as a rock 'n' roll venue through much of the 1960s. Then in the 1970s, Mitzi Shore reopened the club as The Comedy Store.

Comedians and night watchmen have regularly reported that the club is haunted. Chairs move without help, and sometimes the lights and sound seem to have minds of their own. For some unknown reason, this frequently happened when the (now deceased) comic Sam Kinison was onstage. Although most spirit activity there occurs at night, more than one person has reported seeing apparitions during the day, including the ghost of a man in a brown leather jacket and other men dressed in the styles of the 1940s. The back room dressing room area and the basement storage area under the stage seem to be especially haunted.

On January 11, 1999, Shore had paranormal investigators visit her Hollywood Hills home in which several comedians—including Richard Pryor, Robin Williams, and Mitzi's son Pauly Shore—had roomed while performing at The Comedy Store. Several

> **Ghostly Pursuits**
>
> Dr. Barry E. Taff and members of a parapsychology team from UCLA investigated The Comedy Store in 1982, but their data was inconclusive. Taff, who holds a doctorate in psychophysiology and frequently appears on radio and television as a paranormal expert, was a research associate with UCLA's former Parapsychology Laboratory from 1969 through 1978.

comedians had reported paranormal activity there, including seeing shadows moving through the house as well as doors opening and closing by themselves—"standard poltergeist activity in a haunting situation," according to investigators.

Dr. Larry Montz, a parapsychologist, led the investigation; Daena Smoller, a psychic medium, also attended. High-tech tools used to pinpoint ghosts included a *magnetometer* and a temperature gauge. Often, in paranormal investigations, a two-, five-, or even ten-degree temperature change is recorded. (Indeed, a five-degree drop in temperature was registered at the Shore residence.)

During the investigation of Shore's home, the ghost hunters sensed a man who had been shot dead and dragged down a set of stairs. They "saw" an "invisible" stain at the foot of the stairs. Eventually, they claimed that they felt three figures—two male, one female— all killed in the 1920s. The female, named Flo or Florence, supposedly died from a botched abortion.

Researchers are now looking for historical pictures, evidence, or other information to corroborate what they felt.

Phantom Phrases

A **magnetometer** measures the presence of a magnetic field as well as its strength, direction, and fluctuation. Normally, a magnetometer is used in geophysical and astronomical surveys, but some paranormal investigators believe that spirits have a detectable, measurable magnetic or energy aura.

Hollywood Roosevelt Hotel

The Hollywood Roosevelt Hotel, located diagonally opposite Mann's Chinese Theatre on Hollywood Boulevard, has long been a mecca for ghost hunters.

The luxury hotel in central Hollywood opened its doors in 1927. Over the years, most of Hollywood's elite have walked through its doors, either staying as guests or attending one of the many functions held under its roof. In fact, the first Academy Awards banquet was held in the hotel's Blossom Room in 1929.

In 1984, the hotel underwent a multimillion-dollar renovation, restoring it to its former glory. Since that time, there have been dozens of reported sightings of apparitions. No doubt hundreds more have gone unreported.

The next year, prior to the hotel's grand reopening, a cold spot credited to spirits was felt in the Blossom Room. The spot, 30 inches in diameter, measured about 10 degrees cooler than the rest of the room.

Remember the stories of haunted mirrors in Chapter 4? Well, the Roosevelt Hotel has its own haunted mirrors. In 1985, a staff member was looking into a mirror in the hotel manager's office when she noticed the reflection of a blonde woman standing behind her. It was Marilyn Monroe! The employee turned to look, but there was no one there. Yet when she faced the mirror again, Marilyn's reflection was still plainly visible.

The mirror had once hung in Suite 1200, which was often occupied by Monroe. The mirror has since been moved and is said to be the one now hanging beside the elevators on the hotel's lower level. Many people have reported seeing the ghost of Marilyn Monroe reflected in its glass.

Monroe isn't the only celebrity ghost spotted at the Roosevelt. Montgomery Clift lived in Room 928 for three months in 1952 while he was filming *From Here to Eternity*. Maids have reported feeling cold drafts in the hallway outside his room. Others have reported seeing strange shadows. And in 1992, a guest staying overnight in Room 928 reported feeling a spectral hand on her shoulder.

The haunted mirror, located in the lower level of the Hollywood Roosevelt Hotel. The ghost of Marilyn Monroe is said to appear reflected in its glass.

(Photo by author)

Ghostly Pursuits

That Marilyn gets around! Not only does she haunt a mirror in the Hollywood Roosevelt Hotel, but her ghost has also been seen hovering near her crypt at the Westwood Memorial Cemetery in Westwood, California. Actor Richard Conte, known for his Italian cop and gangster roles in the 1940s and 1950s, is also buried at Westwood Memorial Cemetery. Oddly, the years "1910–1975–?" are marked on his gravestone. Why the question mark? Did he intend to come back? Perhaps be reincarnated? Or return as a ghost?

First-Person Phantoms

While researching the Roosevelt Hotel, I talked with some guests who had come to town to take part in a Walk of Fame ceremony. (That's when a celebrity gets his or her own star set into the sidewalk in Hollywood.) One visitor reported seeing a phantom woman at the foot of her bed, calmly brushing her hair. Another saw the ghost of a man reflected in the room's mirror.

Several people have reported seeing the ghost of an unidentified man in a white suit. Other phantom phenomena at the hotel include empty rooms being bolted from the inside and phone calls being made from locked, unoccupied rooms. Other times, phones are knocked off their receivers inside vacant suites. The spirits had a field day when a television crew came to shoot a report on the sightings in 1989. Equipment failed without explanation, hotel lights went out, and smoke detectors set themselves off.

Pacific Theater (Formerly Warner Theater)

In 1927, Warner Brothers was filming a revolutionary movie: *The Jazz Singer*. It would be the first feature-length "talkie." For its West Coast premiere, the four Warner brothers—Harry, Albert, Sam, and Jack—began work on a new flagship movie theater on Hollywood Boulevard. Sam Warner personally supervised the installation of the sound equipment. Unfortunately, the theater was not completed in time for the movie's opening, and it's said that Sam cursed the building. On October 5, 1927, the day before the film's premiere in New York, Sam Warner died in Los Angeles of a cerebral hemorrhage.

The Warner Theater finally opened six months later, and a plaque commemorating Sam Warner was placed in the lobby. Over the years, there have been sporadic sightings of Sam Warner in the theater's lobby, in the auditorium of the theater, and in the offices upstairs. Two men on a cleaning crew saw Warner's ghost walk across the lobby and enter an elevator. Others have heard noises—scratching and chairs being moved—in vacant offices overhead.

For its last several years of operation, the theater was part of the Pacific Theater chain. It's currently closed awaiting renovation.

The Avalon Hollywood (formerly The Palace)

The Palace opened in 1927 as the Hollywood Playhouse, intended to be a home for legitimate theater. Since that time, it's also housed radio programs, television shows, and, most recently, a rock 'n' roll nightclub. In 2003 the club changed its name again, to The Avalon Hollywood, or simply Avalon. With such a long and varied history, it would actually be unusual—by Hollywood standards, anyway—if the building *weren't* haunted. But don't worry: It is!

Spectral phenomena inside have included:

- A piano, locked in a room, playing jazz music on its own

- Cold drafts

- The scent of perfume

- Phantom taps on the shoulder

An unidentifiable aura hovers over the dance floor in this October 2001 photo taken at a party at the Hollywood Palace.

(Photo courtesy of Jeremy Vargus)

One security guard reported seeing the spectre of a tuxedoed man with no face. The ghost was standing but appeared to have no feet: It was seemingly standing on the level of the former floor that was slightly lower than the current stage. The guard's dog also sensed the phantom and chased it.

Phantom voices have often been reported coming from the theater's balcony. At least two apparitions (an elderly couple) have been sighted there.

Ghosts have also been blamed over the years for electronic troubles that have plagued bands playing at the theater. Also, printouts from the theater's adding machines and cash registers often contained odd, nonsensical combinations or groups of numbers. Are they coded messages from the Other Side?

Pantages Theatre

Alexander Pantages built the Art Deco Pantages Theatre as the West Coast jewel box of his namesake vaudeville chain. Howard Hughes leased space in the theater about the time of his purchase of RKO Pictures in 1949. He and his two sons had their offices on the second floor. In 1967, Pacific Theaters bought the Pantages and, in association with the Nederlander Corporation, restored the theater.

Since that time, there have been reports of an invisible presence and cold drafts in Howard Hughes's old office. The scent of cigarettes and the clacking sounds of brass drawer knobs sometimes waft through the air. The large apparition of a man, thought to be Hughes, has been seen at least twice in the hallway outside his former office. Following a 1990 vandalism of the balcony area, there were repeated spectral thumpings and bangings there. Did someone disturb a ghost?

Beginning in 1932, the disembodied voice of a woman has been heard singing in the theater auditorium, sometimes during the day but usually at night when the theater is closed. Legend says it belongs to a woman who died in the mezzanine during a show. Once, her voice was even picked up by a microphone during a performance!

And so our tour of the stars' homes and the famous sites of filmdom's capital comes to a close. But there are plenty more places to visit. Before we finish off our section on hauntings, let's do a catch-all chapter of other venues and facilities that have attracted ghosts.

The Least You Need to Know

- The ghosts of several stars of film and television have been reported throughout the Hollywood area.
- Many stars have had paranormal experiences; some even say they owe their lives to warnings from ghosts.
- Stars return from Beyond to visit places they loved and frequented during life— be it their homes, theaters, nightclubs, or hotels.
- Many of Hollywood's top tourist attractions, including the Hollywood Roosevelt Hotel, Mann's Chinese Theatre, and several other theaters, are said to be haunted.

Chapter 22

Eat, Drink, and Be Merry

In This Chapter

- ◆ Hungering (and thirsting) to find a phantom
- ◆ Haunted hotels: Just passing through? Staying overnight? Or staying *every* night?
- ◆ Phantoms that play in the park
- ◆ Imprisoned for eternity

Remember that old saying, "Eat, drink, and be merry, for tomorrow we may die?" Well, apparently even if—or I should say, *when*—we die, we don't have to stop having fun. Let's start our merrymaking by visiting a few restaurants, bars, and amusement parks. Then we'll rest in peace in a haunted hotel or two. (How do you find these places? You'll find most of them listed in Appendix C.)

But be careful. If you party too hearty, you might get busted. You don't want to wind up in an inn of incarceration. Locked up in prison is no way to spend eternity!

Hungry for a Haunting

Be careful who sits down next to you when you're eating in a restaurant. For example, several cowboy ghosts, some of whom have been captured in photographs, haunt Big Nose Kate's in Tombstone, Arizona. A spectral woman in white appears at a dark, corner table in El Fandango Restaurant in San Diego, California. Some restaurants which are converted from private homes are haunted by their former owners. These include:

♦ Pirate Captain Flint at Pirate's House Restaurant in Savannah, Georgia

♦ Elizabeth Ford at the Country Tavern in Nashua, New Hampshire

♦ An anonymous wife who committed suicide at the Santa Clara House (now Landmark 78 Restaurant) outside Ventura, California

---

First-Person Phantoms

Frank Monaco had heard that the private businessmen's club in Niagara Falls, New York, where he tended bar was haunted. Several members had reported seeing the ghost of a man running in the basement, then disappearing after dashing behind the huge oil burner.

One night around closing, the club manager and a friend came downstairs from the office to ask Frank why he had the bar television turned up so loud. And who were those people singing on the show? Puzzled, Frank explained that the TV wasn't on.

Another evening, Frank heard his name being called out in the hallway, even though he knew no one else was in the club because he had just locked up. Frank dashed out into the corridor, but it was empty. He searched the club and came up empty-handed.

The building in Niagara Falls, New York, dates to the late 1800s. It's believed that the ghost is most likely one of the original caretakers, who was found dead on the third floor of the club. It wasn't until after his death that the strange things started happening …

Good-Time Ghost

Looking for a good time before you head up into the Yukon gold fields? The spirits at the Red Onion Saloon in Skagway, Alaska, might be able to wet your whistle. Built near the outskirts of town in 1897 as a "house of pleasure," the saloon was moved to its present location on the main street in 1914. A female ghost has been seen at the window of the former madam's room on the second floor, and heavy perfume has been smelled in the area. Customers in the saloon sometimes hear footsteps overhead walking the hallway of the empty upper story.

They're Not Amused

Amusement parks should be among the happiest places on Earth. They are—unless tragedy strikes. The spirits of those who die at theme parks are often trapped there, having "fun" forever. But beware: If *you* run across one of those ghosts, you might find that scary ride more chilling than thrilling.

Seven ghosts or more are thought to haunt Disneyland in Anaheim, California. The "It's a Small World" attraction, populated by singing dolls dressed to represent children from all over the earth, debuted at the 1964 World's Fair in New York. It's said three cast members loved it so much that their spirits have returned to haunt it. Lights inside the attraction turn on and off by themselves, and, after hours, the dolls sometimes move when there's no electricity working them.

Two or more different apparitions have been seen on Tom Sawyer's Island after it was closed for the night. Cast members search the island but invariably come up empty-handed. It's thought that the ghosts may belong to the three boys (at least) who are said to have drowned in the "Rivers of America" surrounding the island, even though the water is no more than five feet deep.

The most infamous ghost story about Disneyland—and one of the saddest— is that of Dolly's ghost, which haunts the Matterhorn ride. According to legend, Dolly was riding in the front of one of the toboggan-style cars and turned to check her two children who were riding in the back. She unfastened her seat belt and stood up just as the car entered a sharp slope on the tracks. She was thrown out of the car, up over the heads of her children, and onto the track behind them. The next toboggan then struck and killed her. Some people swear they feel her presence at the hollow (now known as "Dolly's Dip") where she died.

CAUTION

Boo! _____

Accidents happen, especially when you take unnecessary risks, when you're not paying attention, or when you're in the dark. Whether you're at an amusement park (where you think nothing could possibly go wrong) or you're out in the middle of nowhere—say, on a ghost hunt—be careful at all times. The ghost you prevent could be your own!

Finally, there are the ghosts of Gracey Mansion, which is known simply as the Haunted Mansion. According to the legend created to go with the attraction, there are "999 Happy Haunts" residing there.

The exterior of the Southern antebellum-style mansion was built in New Orleans Square in 1963, but completing the interior took another six years. The Haunted Mansion finally opened its doors to the public on August 16, 1969. But Walt Disney, who died in 1966, never got to see his haunted house. Unless, of course, he became the thousandth spirit to move in.

In the next chapter, we'll take a look at some of the magical effects used to simulate ghostly phenomena in the Haunted Mansion. But is it possible that the Haunted Mansion really *is* haunted? There are several legends that say it is. Two cast members swear that, as they watched in their security monitors, a woman boarded one of the cars, rode through the attraction, but never got off at the end. By the time the car returned to the loading area, she had disappeared. Is she still inside the mansion?

> **Ghostly Pursuits**
>
> Disneyland Park at Disneyland Resorts Paris has its own version of the Haunted Mansion, a Gothic mansion called Phantom Manor. Although no ghosts have been seen there, employees and guests have reported hearing spectral screams and seeing objects in the building move on their own. Also, unexplained glowing balls and streaks of light have shown up in photographs taken of its exterior, as well as inside the attraction.

In another story, a cast member working near the exit caught a glimpse of a man in a tuxedo. Because he was in costume, she assumed that he was another employee, but when she turned to talk to him, nobody was there. He later reappeared but walked past without speaking or acknowledging her. Again, she turned, but he had already vanished. Later that night, the mysterious man did try to talk to her, but no sound came from his moving lips. He then walked behind her, and she felt him put his hand on her shoulder. She spun to face him, but he was gone.

The tale is told of a woman who wanted to spread the ashes of her recently deceased son in the Haunted Mansion because it was the boy's favorite attraction at Disneyland. She asked permission, but, of course, the park couldn't allow it. Nevertheless, the mother snuck in the ashes and scattered them anyway. From that time on, several guests and cast members have seen a phantom boy, sitting and crying, near the exit of the Haunted Mansion.

Finally, here's a story that's not a myth or folklore. It's absolutely true! Gordon Williams, one of the original sound designers of the Haunted Mansion, was putting finishing touches on his work when he heard soft, nonstop music coming from behind one of the walls. He knew that no speakers were positioned there, and the music wasn't bleeding over from another part of the mansion.

Williams thought that perhaps a radio had accidentally been sealed up. He waited hours for an announcer to break in, but the music never stopped. With no time to tear down the wall to find the source of the haunting refrains, he placed a large speaker there instead. The attraction's theme music completely covered over the quieter, ghostly sounds. For all anyone knows, the unexplained phantom music may still be playing behind that wall to this day.

Haunted Hotels

How does a hotel become haunted? To paraphrase a popular pest-control commercial, the guests check in, but they don't check out. Some hotels are rather tight-lipped about their ghostly residents. Others delight in the notoriety and are more than happy to share their haunted histories. Maybe one of these hotels would make the perfect getaway for you.

Ante-Up, Apparition

Room 17 at the St. James Hotel in Cimarron, New Mexico, is haunted by the ghost of a man who was killed there after winning the hotel in a poker game. The scent of perfume pervades "Mary's Room" at the St. James, and the ghost of "The Imp," a short man with a pockmarked complexion, has been seen there, too. (The St. James Hotel has been featured on television's *Unsolved Mysteries*.)

First-Person Phantoms

Kate Ward, a receptionist at the Magic Castle, tells of seeing a ghost at historic Clunie House in San Francisco, which operated from 1981 to 2003 as an exclusive bed-and-breakfast, the Victorian Inn on the Park. The beautiful Queen Anne-style home was built in 1897 for California politician, Thomas Jefferson Clunie. During one visit to the hotel, Kate stayed up late reading as her husband slept beside her. She heard a faint female voice whispering, as if the sound were coming from the next room. She paid it little attention until she, later, got up and entered the bathroom. Standing at the mirror, Kate could plainly see the reflection of a translucent female figure standing behind her. Kate turned, and, of course, there was no one there. It suddenly became obvious to Kate that the murmuring must have come from the bathroom. It had been the spectral voice of the ghost. The identity of the ghost remains unknown.

Ghostly Guests at the Menger Hotel

The Menger Hotel was built in 1859 in downtown San Antonio, just steps away from the Alamo (see Chapter 17). It's one of the oldest hotels west of the Mississippi, and it proudly claims to be home to at least 32 different ghosts.

Here are the stories of just four of the spectral guests:

- ◆ A standoffish female ghost is sometimes seen knitting in the old lobby of the hotel. She wears small, wire-rimmed glasses, a blue dress and a tasseled beret. If anyone disturbs her, she simply vanishes.

- ◆ The spirit of a man dressed in a buckskin jacket and gray pants sometimes appears by the bed of a guest. The ghost seems to be talking to some unseen person in the room, demanding, "Are ya gonna stay, or are ya gonna go?" After asking three times, the figure—well—goes.

- ◆ Captain Richard King, a wealthy cattleman, had his own apartment at the hotel. Several guests and staff members have seen his ghost enter his former quarters (now called the King Suite) by walking through a wall where the door used to be.

- ◆ When Sallie White, a maid at the Menger, was murdered by her husband, the hotel paid for her funeral expenses. Maybe she's trying to repay the Menger for their kindness: She's still seen walking the hotel hallways, carrying towels, with a scarf on her head and wearing a long gray skirt.

If you're in San Antonio to visit the Alamo, don't forget that famous cry: "Remember the Menger!"

The Wraith of "The Whistler"

The small Black Hawk Hotel in Davenport, Iowa, was built around the beginning of the twentieth century and became a popular stopping-off point for travelers between Chicago and St. Louis. The ghost of a woman dressed in red has been seen outside the hotel. Guests have complained about having the covers pulled off their beds in the middle of the night by unseen hands. One girl checked out in a panic, claiming that the ghost had grabbed the sheet off her and clucked, "Now here's a pretty one!"

First-Person Phantoms

Fitzgerald, a friend and fellow magician, was staying at the Black Hawk Hotel while in Davenport on business. He woke up suddenly around 4 A.M. and noticed that the room was unusually cold. In the darkness to his left, he heard noise that sounded like radio static. Underneath it, he could make out mumbling voices.

Fitzgerald checked the corridors and looked out the window. There was no one around. But as soon as he returned to bed, the staticlike sound started up again. Suddenly, there were two sharp whistles, as if someone were calling a dog. Then, Fitzgerald felt someone or something pressing down on his feet through the blankets.

Well, that did it! Fitzgerald jumped up, turned on the light, dressed, and hurried down to the lobby.

When one of the women working on the same project came downstairs later, she told Fitzgerald that she'd heard a disembodied voice at the foot of her bed. She called the hotel's security guard, who told her that he'd just been in the basement and heard the voice down there, too!

Fitzgerald asked the staff about the hauntings, but all of them were mum. That afternoon, he found a teenager working the front desk who confirmed that the hotel was haunted. He knew all about the ghost that had disturbed Fitzgerald. They called him "the Whistler." He was a scientist who'd lived at the hotel during World War II and worked across the street. He used a walkie-talkie to communicate between his room and the shop. The hotel employee mimicked the walkie-talkie noise and duplicated the whistling that had startled Fitzgerald the night before.

An Ethereal Enigma

The Hotel del Coronado, known locally as "the Del," is a landmark seaside resort near San Diego. The 115-year-old hotel is haunted by the black-garbed ghost of Kate Morgan, who shot herself—although some say she was murdered—on November 28, 1892, on a hotel staircase that leads down to the beach.

Kate's ghost has been seen for years at the hotel. Usually it glides silently down a hallway or stands by a window. She sometimes, but not always, appears dressed in black.

Guests who have stayed in the room Kate occupied in the days preceding her death—now Room 3327—have experienced several ghostly phenomena:

◆ Doorknobs rattling

◆ Bathroom lights turning on and off by themselves, or flickering

◆ Bedcovers being yanked off in the middle of the night

Is her ghost real? Maybe it's worth taking a holiday to the Hotel del Coronado to find out. Tell them "Kate sent me!"

First-Person Phantoms

When she was around 8 years old, Roxana Brusso was sharing a bed with her grandmother in the old Marina Hotel on the Las Vegas Strip. Her grandmother was asleep, but Roxana was wide awake. The ghost of a man wearing a golf cap with a snap-brim was standing at the foot of the bed! It didn't move or speak, but gave the girl a smirk. Not wanting to wake her grandmother, Roxana simply pulled the covers over her head and tried to go back to sleep. Years later, when the hotel was being torn down to make room for the MGM Grand, Roxana heard a newsman casually mention that the Marina had the reputation of being haunted.

Way Up (at the Golden) North

Skagway, Alaska, was one of the main starting-off points for the trek into the Yukon during the days of the Gold Rush. The Golden North Hotel was built there in the 1890s to accommodate the hordes of pioneers heading north to strike it rich.

"Mary" came to Skagway at the tender age of 18 to meet her fiancé who was already in the Klondike gold camps. She settled into Room 24 at the Golden North Hotel, but while waiting for his return Mary fell ill and died of tuberculosis. The hotel manager found her dead in her bed, dressed in her lace wedding gown. That was in 1898.

Ten years later, after the Gold Rush boom had ended, the two owners tore down the hotel. But they purchased another building, moved it to the main street of town, opened it as the new Golden North Hotel.

Today, the building houses a gift shop, and the guest rooms upstairs are rarely used. But many who *have* stayed at the Golden North Hotel overnight have been haunted by the apparition of a young woman in a long white gown that has appeared outside Room 24 on the third floor; her footsteps have also been heard shuffling down the carpeted hallway. A guest in Room 13 felt an invisible presence sit on the bed next to her, then leave the room. A pulsating light form has been seen in Rooms 24 and 14, and at least two people became very ill, without any physical explanation, while staying in Room 9.

Did Mary move into the second Golden North Hotel to wait for her beau?

The Honolulu Hilton Haunting

Even a "name" hotel can become haunted. One of the six towers of Hilton Hawaiian Village on Oahu in Honolulu, Hawaii, is haunted by a female spectre in a red dress. In 1959, a bellhop following the ghost to a room saw it vaporize before his eyes. It's said that she's the apparition of a guest who died or was murdered in the hotel. Locals have claimed that it's an incarnation of Madame Pele, the Huna native's mythic volcano goddess.

The Pirate and His Bride

Bluebeard's Castle Hotel sits on a hilltop overlooking the bay in Charlotte Amalie, St. Thomas, in the U.S. Virgin Islands. In its central court is a five-story former watchtower that was built in 1679 to augment the town's shoreline defenses at Fort Christian.

According to legend, the notorious pirate Bluebeard actually built the tower (or converted it) to be a home for his lover, Mercedita Cordovan. (In some versions of the tale, he married her as well.) But she was unfaithful to him, so he killed her and sailed off—as pirates are wont to do. He never came back to the island. Or did he? The ghosts of both Bluebeard and Cordovan are said to still be in St. Thomas, haunting the tower.

The tower of Bluebeard's Castle Hotel in St. Thomas may be haunted by the spirits of the pirate Bluebeard and his bride.

(Photo by author)

Singapore Spirits

The celebrated Raffles Hotel in the small Southeast Asian island nation of Singapore opened in 1887. Part of an expansive colonial bungalow known as Beach House, the hotel itself was named after Sir Stamford Raffles, the country's founder. Among the hotel's many claims to fame is its creation of the famous cocktail, the "Singapore Sling."

For more than 50 years, the hallways and rooms in the back part of the hotel have been haunted by the voice of a little girl singing nursery rhymes. She's thought to have been a student at an English boarding school that once stood on the property.

Jailhouse Rock

Jails hold some of the most vicious and brutal types that humanity has to offer. Prison walls have enclosed so much violence, pain, misery, and, of course, death, that it somehow seems only natural that residents of the spirit world are holed up here.

Here are five ghost-infested sites found around the world.

Alcatraz

Located on an island in San Francisco Bay, Alcatraz was an Army fort and prison until it was converted into a federal penitentiary in 1934. Society's most hardened criminals were sent there, and it was considered inescapable. Among its many residents were Robert "The Birdman" Stroud, "Machine Gun" Kelly, and Al Capone.

Guards and tour guides have reported hearing the sounds of cells being opened and shut, footsteps, whistling, screams, and voices echoing down the halls. Banjo music has been heard coming from the shower room: Capone was allowed to play his banjo there. Many visitors have reported cold spots throughout the facility, especially around the solitary confinement "holes" in Cell Block D. Often guests report the feeling that they're being watched by invisible presences.

> **Ghostly Pursuits**
>
> Ironic, isn't it? You'd think that after spending your life in prison, death would set you free. But for some of the unlucky ones, that's not the case. Their spirits remain bound forever, for whatever reason, to the jailhouse sites where they were confined. Are these the true ties that bind?

The Tower of London

The Tower of London, which once served as a prison and execution site, is one of the most haunted places in England. The ghosts are thought to be the spirits of the many people—of both sexes and all ages—who lost their lives there. Spirits have been known to walk the grounds, pass through doors and windows, or stare dolefully out of tower windows. Most remain unidentified—especially the ones that are headless.

There are many notable phantoms that haunt the Tower, however. Perhaps the first famous ghost to be recognized at the Tower—in fact, in all of England—was that of Thomas Becket, Archbishop of Canterbury. He was first seen in 1241, which was a full 71 years after he was murdered in Canterbury Cathedral. It's thought that his spirit returned to the Tower grounds because he was once Constable there.

Also among the Tower's ghosts is Anne Boleyn, the second wife of Henry VIII. She was beheaded at the Tower in 1536. Her headless spirit has been spotted walking in front of the Tower chapel, in the hall below the room in which she was imprisoned the night before her execution.

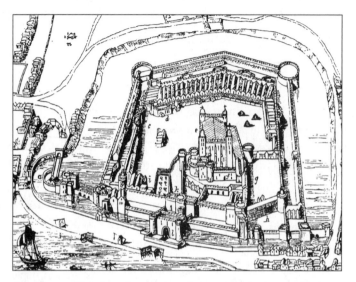

The Tower of London, the prison and execution site known for its multitude of famous ghosts, as it appeared in 1597.

The Tower of London, infamous for its imprisonments, executions, and hauntings, as seen today.

(Photo by author)

Another one of Henry VIII's unlucky wives was Catherine Howard. Some say her screaming ghost is seen, still running the length of the corridor outside her prison apartment. (Yes, she *also* haunts a hallway of Hampton Court.) Sentries have also reported seeing the ghost of King Henry VIII himself.

Lady Jane Grey was executed in the Tower of London after reigning for only nine days as queen of England. Her ghost has often appeared in the Tower, usually around the anniversary of her beheading on February 12, 1554. She was a frequent visitor throughout the 1950s.

> **Ghostly Pursuits**
>
> It's not all that unusual that Catherine Howard haunts both Hampton Court and the Tower of London. Many ghosts, especially celebrity ghosts, it seems, have been known to haunt a number of places.

Margaret, the Countess of Salisbury, had a grisly end at the Tower in 1541. The executioner missed his mark on the first three tries. He finally connected on the fourth swing, but his ax only succeeded in cutting her head halfway off. The fifth chop was the *coup de grâce*. The horrific screams of the Countess are sometimes still heard on the nights of the anniversary of her death.

Other famous phantoms at the Tower of London include:

- ◆ Sir Walter Raleigh, who was executed in 1618 by the order of King James I.

- ◆ King Edward V and Prince Richard, brothers who were executed while still children by their usurping uncle, King Richard III.

- ◆ The Duke of Northumberland, who appeared so often that sentries dubbed the usual path he took between Martin Tower and Constable Tower as "Northumberland's Walk."

The Bridge of Sighs (the Ponte dei Sospiri)

Designed and built in Venice, Italy, in 1600 by Antonio Contino, the Ponte dei Sospiri crosses over a narrow canal called the Rio di Palazzo. The decorated enclosed bridge has the seemingly romantic nickname "The Bridge of Sighs." But the phrase actually has a dark origin.

The enclosed bridge connects the Doge's Palace to the stronghold's dungeons. After their trials in the palace, prisoners passed through this elevated corridor into incarceration. For many, a brief glimpse out of one of the four small, latticed windows over the canal—accompanied by their mournful sighs—was their last look at the outside world.

The Bridge of Sighs in Venice, Italy.

(Photo by author)

Residents and visitors to Venice have long been hearing muffled sounds, cries, and—yes—sighs, coming from the bridge's windows during its unoccupied hours. Perhaps the ethereal voices of former prisoners are still being heard as they yearn for escape and freedom.

Melbourne Gaol

The old Melbourne Gaol (or jail) is one of Melbourne, Australia's most popular tourist attractions, not in the least because it's said to be haunted by the ghost of the infamous nineteenth-century outlaw Ned Kelly, who was executed there. Kelly became a *cause célèbre* in his own lifetime by escaping prison and eluding capture for many years by hiding in the bush of the Outback. He was finally caught, hanged in

1888, and buried near the gallows. Kelly's coffin was accidentally broken open during construction in 1929, and macabre trophy hunters made off with much of his corpse. The remaining bones were re-interred at Pentridge Prison. Yet Kelly's spirit seems to have remained behind!

The Melbourne Gaol, haunted by the ghost of the notorious Ned Kelly, among others.

(Photo by author)

Port Arthur Prison and the Isle of the Dead

Many of Australia's original colonists were forced settlers, "transported" as prisoners of the British crown, with little or no chance of ever returning to their homeland. Many were held at Port Arthur Prison, which was built in 1852 on the island of Tasmania, off mainland Australia's southeast coast.

Even though the site has long been abandoned, the ghosts of its many former inmates, the prison staff, and their families still make their presence known. Ethereal bells ring near the old church grounds; unearthly screams are attributed to a 14-year-old boy who hanged himself rather than spend his life in prison. Iron gates open and close on their own, and a phantom elderly lady is sometimes seen in a rocking chair inside a former guard's house. Perhaps most unsettling are dark forces felt in some of the old cells. One, Cell 4, was so upsetting that it was finally closed off to tourists.

The Isle of the Dead, located just off the coast at Port Arthur, is uninhabited, unless you take into account the more than 2,000 people—prisoners, guards, and officials alike—who are buried there. The island's now a popular attraction during the day, but it empties every night. It's said that those who get left behind can often meet the local residents firsthand.

By now you might think we've looked at just about every kind of place a ghost could hide. But, no, there are still plenty more. Can you think of another setting that could be haunted? If so, jot it down for a future ghost hunt. You might be the first person to spot a phantom in that location.

Well, that just about wraps up our Spirit Survey. Now turn out the light, say your prayers, and try to get a good night's sleep. Then it'll be time to turn to our last section and see how ghosts and spirit phenomena have been reflected in our popular culture.

The Least You Need to Know

- Ghosts can be very accommodating—haunting hotels, restaurants, and saloons.
- Sites connected with joy that suddenly turns deadly, such as amusement parks, are ghost magnets.
- Prisons sometimes hold onto their tenants even after their leases of life are terminated.
- Ghosts can—and do—appear anywhere, in any type of venue.

Part 5

Apparitions and the Arts

Many people think ghosts are real. But for many others, they're all just an illusion. In ancient times, wizards and sorcerers could be condemned to death for conjuring up the spirits of the dead. But not so today. For more than a century, modern stage magicians have been devising increasingly clever ways to produce ghosts—or, to be fair, incredible simulations—during their performances. Then there are the magicians, like Houdini, who debunked the frauds that claim supernatural powers by exposing their secret methods.

Ghost stories make up a significant part of our artistic culture, with hundreds of examples in literature, theater, and film. In this final part, I've profiled just a few of the most popular in each genre. Have I mentioned yours?

Chapter 23

The Magic Connection

In This Chapter

♦ Ancient magic and the spirits

♦ Magicians produce ghostly phenomena and pseudo-séances on stage

♦ Houdini exposes fraudulent mediums

♦ The popularity of the spook show

Can you keep a secret? Not all ghosts are real! But that hasn't stopped people throughout history from using trickery to create the illusion that they were able to summon up ghosts and spirits. Ancient temple priests, necromancers like the Witch of Endor (see Chapter 2), and tribal shamans used their "tricks of the trade" to prove their control over the spirit world.

So it's only natural that stage magicians wanted to create the same illusions. Let's see how some of them pulled it off! Along the way, we'll visit some spooky stage shows and a couple of amusement venues where magic's being used to produce a hauntingly good time for the guests.

Remember, a good magician never tells how the tricks are done, so keep all these secrets under your top hat!

Open Sesame: Spirit Doors

Imagine that you're standing in front of an Egyptian or classical Greek temple. Slowly, the massive temple doors begin to open by themselves, as if pushed by the invisible hands of powerful gods or spirits. Awesome! Obviously you'd be impressed by the power of the priest inside.

But in an illustrated manuscript, Hero of Alexandria explained a secret technique to produce this phenomenon. A fire built on the altar warmed the air in an animal skin bag hidden below. The bag inflated, pulling a rope over a pulley, which in turn rotated concealed columns that were connected to the doors.

Spirit doors. Lighting the altar fires produced the magical effect through pneumonics.

(From a manuscript by Hero of Alexandria)

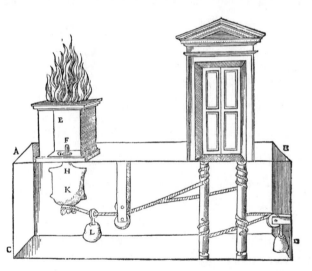

Throughout the Dark and Middle Ages, wizards and sorcerers, steeped in the occult teachings of the Kabbalah, sought to contact and control angelic and demonic forces. As we've seen, these magicians also used necromancy to try to invoke or manifest spirits of the dead.

By the late eighteenth or early nineteenth century, however, the performance of magic was accepted as a legitimate form of stage entertainment. No longer were magicians branded as devils—at least, not usually.

Smoke ...

It was an age of scientific discovery, and magicians were using many new principles to create their illusions. One of the most popular effects was the production of ghosts on the stage. In 1784, Belgian stage performer Robertson (Etienne-Gaspard Robert) debuted his "Fantasmagorie" in which images were projected onto smoke. Ten years later, he presented the ghost illusion during a six-year run in a Paris theater.

Then, in 1803, magician Paul de Philipsthal created his own version of the trick, which he called "Phantasmagoria." Standing in the middle of a stage within the "safety" of a magic circle, de Philipsthal would wave his wand to produce spectres of the "Dead or Absent." Audiences swore that they were seeing an actual materialization of a real, honest-to-goodness ghost. De Philipsthal advertised that he was performing the entertainment "to expose the Practices of artful Imposters … and to open the Eyes of those who still foster an absurd belief in Ghosts or Disembodied Spirits."

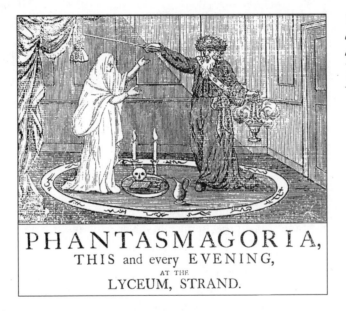

With a wave of the wand, de Philipsthal conjures up a phantom at the Lyceum Theatre on the Strand, in London, England.

… and Mirrors: Pepper's Ghost

Other magicians followed Robinson's and de Philipsthal's lead. In the 1860s, Dr. John Henry Pepper created an elaborate stage trick using a mirror to create the illusion that the performers on stage were interacting with ghosts, spirits, skeletons, and the like. Magicians now know the special effect and the principle itself as Pepper's Ghost.

It worked like this: The actors were really standing behind a wall of glass that was placed at an angle to the audience. Actors costumed as ghosts or other spirit entities were stationed in the orchestra pit in front of the stage but below the audience's line of vision. With the use of special and precise lighting, the reflection of the actors in the pit would appear on the glass. From the audience's point of view, the translucent "ghosts" seemed to be real, standing next to the actors on the stage.

An 1874 engraving detailing the method and angles of reflection required to achieve the Pepper's Ghost illusion.

(From Fulgence Marion's L'Optique, *published by Librairie Hachette, 1874)*

The creative French conjuror, Jean Eugene Robert-Houdin (1805–1871), often called the "Father of Modern Magic," used the Pepper's Ghost principle in a Paris stage production named *La Czarine* at the Ambigu Theatre in 1868.

With the assistance of a Mr. Walker, Pepper adapted his ghost illusion in the 1870s. Using gradual light changes, he could make the ghostly reflection fade away at the same time as another appeared. From the audience's point of view, one object would visibly transform into the other. A living person could be seen turning into a ghost— or a ghost could come to life!

Pepper called the new illusion "Metempsychosis." Years later, it would be adapted by American stage illusionist Harry Kellar (1849–1922) under the title "the Blue Room" for use in a playlet as part of his full-evening touring show.

Today, many magicians use the term *spirit theater* to refer to individual tricks, routines, acts, shows, or events in which ghosts or other paranormal phenomena are apparently produced. Magician Eugene Burger and his work personify spirit theater. Burger is considered by fellow magicians to be the authority on the subject, and his 1986 book *Spirit Theater* is considered a modern classic magician's text.

The Master Mediums and the Sorcerer's Apprentice

The magic world is actually a small community. Many of the professional performers know and have often worked with each other.

Harry Kellar was America's leading magician at the turn of the twentieth century. Born Harry Keller, he spent four years early in his career as the stage manager for the Davenport brothers. In 1873, he teamed with William Fay, another Davenport associate, to tour Cuba, Mexico, and South America. Three years later, he was back in the United States, having changed the spelling of his name to Kellar to avoid being confused with one of his peers. Kellar's full evening show included several spiritualism routines, including such standard séance fare as slate writing, table-tilting, and a self-levitation. He placed a mannequin hand on a table, and it rocked and tapped answers to questions. A highlight of his act was a version of the Davenport brothers spirit cabinet. He devised a new method to quickly escape from ropes tied behind his back; the so-called "Kellar Rope Tie" is still used by magicians today.

Magicians Supply the Phantom Paraphernalia

Let me be clear: Séances were *not* magic shows. They were supposedly legitimate attempts to contact the spirits of the deceased. Although almost all mediums were suspected of trickery from time to time, there were many, many who were never caught in the act.

Often, any "magic" that occurred took place in the sitters' minds. The setting, lighting, and atmosphere instilled a muted sense of dread, fear, and expectation. The slightest movement, special effect, or sound was magnified out of proportion by the participants' imaginations, *especially* as they sat in silence in the dark. (Maybe you've discovered this for yourself if, after reading Chapter 9, you "haunted" your own house for friends.)

To remain popular, however, mediums had to produce results—and spectacular ones at that! As a result, many of them resorted to trickery. Magic supply shops were more than willing to provide the tools necessary for fraudulent mediums to fool their clients.

Magicians also purchase the supplies and paraphernalia to duplicate séance phenomena. Among the most popular pieces of apparatus are:

- Spirit slates, similar to those used by Henry Slade (see Chapter 8).

- A rapping hand (a mannequin hand like the one used by Kellar, which rocks and taps by itself when set on the table).

◆ Mechanical talking skulls.

◆ Spirit cabinets.

◆ Floating and tipping tables.

In medieval times, it was often thought that wizards trafficked with the devil. Today, many magicians still incorporate this "dark side" into their acts, their wardrobe, or their advertising. Posters from the first half of the twentieth century (and even a modern poster by performer Ricky Jay) show miniature devils whispering into the magicians' ears. Illusionist Howard Thurston (1869–1936), for instance, took advantage of the public's fascination with spiritualism by asking the question "Do the Spirits Come Back?" on several of his posters. The spectral séance activity illustrated on his posters implicitly answered "Yes."

Left: Abbott's Spirit Séance, a complete spirit act as offered in the catalog of Abbott's Magic Company of Colon, Michigan. Right: Abbott's Floating Table, a magical version of the Spiritualists' tipping table.

(Used by permission of Abbott's Magic Company, Colon, Michigan)

An advertising poster of illusionist Howard Thurston, asking "Do the Spirits Come Back?"

Houdini Among the Spirits

The most famous magician of the twentieth century was Harry Houdini (1874–1926). He was best known as an escape artist, but, in the last years of his career, a sizeable portion of his full-evening show was given over to recreating and exposing spirit séances.

How much of a believer in Spiritualism was Harry Houdini? Was he a complete skeptic? Or, as many suggest, was he actually seeking a real medium so that he could once again communicate with his late, beloved mother? The truth will probably never be known.

What *is* certain is that Houdini was a master showman, and he knew that Spiritualism was a craze. He realized that he would draw huge audiences by debunking famous mediums as part of his show.

Houdini began a crusade, exposing the methods of mediums, challenging them to produce true phenomena under test conditions, and writing articles, pamphlets, and even a book (*A Magician Among the Spirits*) about his experiences. In the book, Houdini tells how, in 1910 in upstate New York, he met up with Ira Davenport, the surviving member of the Davenport brothers (see Chapter 7). Ira supposedly confessed that the brothers were, indeed, simply escape artists and then taught Houdini many of their secrets.

Harry Houdini, escape artist.

(Photo from the Mark S. Willoughby collection)

Houdini, Meet Sherlock Holmes

Houdini was a friend of Sir Arthur Conan Doyle, but Doyle's blind belief in Spiritualism sometimes caused tension between them. Doyle, for example, believed that Houdini escaped from a locked trunk by changing into spirit form, passing through cracks in the box, and rematerializing on the other side. Nothing the magician said could convince him otherwise. In fact, Doyle frequently asked Houdini to admit his paranormal abilities for the sake of the Spiritualism movement.

 Boo! _____

> Sherlock Holmes explained how he solved his cases: To paraphrase, eliminate the impossible, and all that's left is the possible. It's hard to believe that Sir Arthur Conan Doyle penned those words. As an avid Spiritualist, he frequently chose to ignore rational explanations. *You should heed Sherlock's advice, however.* Don't automatically assume that any spirit phenomenon you witness is proof that ghosts exist. Eliminate all other explanations first.

At one séance that Houdini and Doyle attended together, the medium (whom some say was Doyle's wife) received a message for the showman supposedly written by his deceased mother. But the writing was in English, a language his Hungarian mother had never learned. Doyle's comment that Houdini's mother must have learned English on the Other Side infuriated the master magician.

The Scientific Investigation of Margery

In 1924, the prestigious *Scientific American* magazine formed a committee to investigate mediums. It was really the inspiration of J. Malcolm Bird, the magazine's associate editor. Two prizes of $2,500 each were offered, one for a demonstration of true mediumship, the other for an actual psychic or spirit photograph. The five judges were American psychic researcher Walter Franklin Prince; Hereward Carrington, an English-born writer about the paranormal who had a fascination with magic; magician Harry Houdini; Daniel F. Comstock (who developed Technicolor for movies); and Bird.

The committee's major investigation was of Mina Stinson Crandon (1884–1941), a Boston medium who worked under the name of "Margery." Houdini left the committee after a year, claiming that the rest of the group ignored Margery's obvious trickery. The rest of the committee continued séances with Margery on-and-off for a half year. All but Carrington eventually agreed with Houdini that she was a charlatan. The contest was ended, and no award was ever given out.

Houdini demonstrates how a spirit cabinet is no impediment to a trained trickster in this 1924 booklet exposing the medium Margery.

(Back cover illustration from the author's collection)

Houdini Performs an Encore

Houdini died of peritonitis on Halloween 1926. It was rumored that he and his wife Bess had worked out a coded message so that, should the survivor ever receive the words in a séance, there would be proof of contact with the Afterlife.

For ten years after Houdini's death, however, Bess tried to contact her husband. She held a séance every Halloween on the roof of the Knickerbocker Hotel, which had just opened its doors in Hollywood in 1925. Finally, Bess called an end to the annual ritual, saying that it was her opinion that even if Houdini *had* survived death, he wasn't coming back.

In the years that followed, a number of mediums claimed to have contacted Houdini. Near the end of her life, Bess agreed that one of them, American medium Arthur Augustus Ford (1897–1971), had actually received the coded message. But she soon retracted her endorsement, saying that she had been too ill to understand what she was agreeing to. Magical historians suggest that Ford could have read, overheard, or otherwise learned the secret word. There's still controversy surrounding the medium's stunning announcement.

Did Houdini ever return? To this day, magicians worldwide hold sénaces on Halloween in an attempt to contact his spirit. Perhaps it's only a matter of time. Believe.

The New Skeptics

Although several magicians carried on Houdini's tradition of debunking paranormal claims, the gauntlet was really picked up by performer and author Milbourne Christopher (1914–1984). In his books *ESP Seers and Psychics* (1970), *Mediums Mystics and the Occult* (1975), and *Search for the Soul* (1979), he examined the role that magic, outright fraud, and superstition play in fooling a gullible public that wants to believe in the paranormal. In more recent years, the role of professional skeptic has been assumed by James Randi (b. 1928). A recipient of the MacArthur Foundation "genius" grant, the Amazing Randi is perhaps best known for his attempts to debunk the Israeli psychic Uri Gellar.

Right Before Your Very Eyes

The *spook show*, also known as a ghost show or more colloquially as a spookeroo, was a magic show especially designed to target audiences with a fascination for horror and ghosts. The heyday of the spook show was the postwar 1940s and the 1950s, although they did continue into the 1970s. The show usually began around midnight and featured horror-themed magical tricks, such as sawing a person in half or chopping through a neck with a guillotine (without hurting the volunteer, of course). Sometimes, they would re-create a spirit séance onstage. Often, there were short sketches: In the two most famous, the Frankenstein monster was brought to life, and Dracula visibly turned into a bat and flew out over the auditorium. Spook shows also included the showing of one or two horror movies.

The climax of the spook show was always the dark segment, or blackout, in which ghosts, spirits, and other creatures of the night supposedly traveled out into the audience. Spectators were told what they would experience, such as the touch of the cold, clammy hands of a mummy. Worms, maggots, spiders, or snakes might crawl up their legs. Then, in the dark, assistants dressed in black crept up and down the aisles and brushed people with strands of thread or their ice-cold fingertips. To create a real panic, the men in black would throw strands of cooked wet spaghetti or macaroni into the crowd. Likewise, glowing ghosts, luminous skeletons, and the like (all painted models on strings, of course) would be dangled over the heads of the audience.

Many magicians have performed spook shows as a segment of their acts. Some performers specialized in the genre. William Neff (1905–1967), presenting his *Madhouse of Mystery* show, George Marquis, and Jack Baker (working as Dr. Silkini) were among the best-known performers in the field. Though a latecomer to the field, Philip Morris enjoyed success touring his "spooker" from 1950 to the mid-1970s, often appearing in his character of Dr. Evil.

Conjuring Under Canvas

In addition to magic shows that performed in theaters, there were several shows that toured under canvas throughout the early and middle parts of the twentieth century. Perhaps the best known in the United States was the full-evening illusion show performed by Harry Willard (1896–1970), known as Willard the Wizard.

One of the features of his show was the re-creation of a spirit séance, including, as one of his posters promised, a medium named Nellie Davenport producing "startling feats of Spirit and Power in full gas light." In the spirit séance segment, Davenport would have volunteers from the audience tie her wrists and neck with strips of cloth, then nail the ends to the bench on which she sat. She was then enclosed with a curtained-draped framework, which acted as her spirit cabinet.

Immediately, according to one advertising broadside, "knocks are heard … tables and chairs float in mid-air … [spirit] hands and faces are plain[ly] seen and musical instruments are played and passed to the audience. Flowers are materialized and etherealized spirit forms are seen on the stage." Spectators were promised "Spirit Concerts Upon a Dozen Instruments, All Playing at One Time without a Living Soul Touching Them."

Advertising piece for the Willard the Wizard show. The wizard promised to produce genuine spirit phenomena during his performance.

(Courtesy of Frances Willard and Glenn Falkenstein)

Willard's daughter, Frances, who began her career as an assistant to her father, still convincingly performs the remarkable spirit cabinet act today. Acting as the medium, she performs a spirit cabinet routine with her husband, mentalist Glenn Falkenstein. Frances Willard is generally recognized as the best psychic entertainer performing the spirit cabinet today.

Spirit activity surrounds the bound medium, Frances Willard, as Glenn Falkenstein opens the spirit cabinet.

(Photo by Cory Flynn; courtesy of Frances Willard and Glenn Falkenstein)

Welcome to the Haunted Mansion

In our last chapter, we talked about all the real ghosts in Disneyland's Haunted Mansion attraction. But the ghosts that most visitors see during their visit are created by special effects.

It's amazing how many ghost legends are represented within the mansion's haunted halls. As you ride through the attraction, doorknockers rap by themselves, doors bulge, and a candelabrum floats in the middle of an endless corridor. In the attic, screaming ghosts mischievously pop out of suitcases and trunks, and you're confronted by a phantom bride with a throbbing red heart shining through her wedding dress. There's a complete sénce room, with glowing tambourines and spirit horns levitating overhead; its table holds a giant crystal ball, inside of which is the disembodied, talking head of your medium, Madam Leota.

But the best is yet to come! As you ride past the ballroom, ghosts fly into the room from a hearse carriage parked by the door. A phantom musician plays a huge pipe organ at the other end of the room. Two portraits come to life and fight a duel with pistols, and, of course,

> **Ghostly Pursuits**
>
> On November 26, 2003, Walt Disney Pictures released *The Haunted Mansion,* a movie loosely based on the Disneyland attraction of the same name. You can read more about it in Chapter 24.

there are the spectral dancers. Then, as you pass through a graveyard, hundreds of ghosts fly overhead. Sculpted heads on tombstones come to life and sing. As you leave, you're joined by a hitchhiking ghost, and a tiny wisp of a Lady in White bids you farewell.

> ### Ghostly Pursuits
>
> The Ballroom of the Haunted Mansion is the largest Pepper's Ghost ever built. With slight variations in design, the Haunted Mansion, complete with its ballroom and other special ghost effects, can be found at all five Disney theme parks: Disneyland, Walt Disney World, Tokyo Disneyland, Disneyland Park at Disneyland Resort Paris, and the new Hong Kong Disneyland.

Magic Castle

The Magic Castle, located in Hollywood, California, was created by Milt Larsen and his brother William W. Larsen Jr. as a private club for magicians and their friends. Unique in the world, the Magic Castle can be visited only by its members or by invitation from a member.

The Magic Castle opened in 1963, housed in a Victorian mansion built by the Rollin B. Lane family in 1908. In addition to dining and bar areas, there are three showrooms featuring magical entertainment each evening.

The Houdini Séance Room at the Magic Castle must be specially reserved. After dinner, a medium joins the sitters to summon the spirits. As the lights are darkened, a tambourine shakes and flies through the air, the table floats, and the chandelier lowers and sways. Even a ghost puts in a brief appearance.

The Magic Castle in Hollywood, California.

(Photo by author, with permission by the Magic Castle)

First-Person Phantoms

The Magic Castle doesn't need to create ghost legends. It actually has *real* ghosts! Manager and host Michael Gingras has heard rapid footsteps following him on the main staircase after he has closed the club for the night.

One night, Castle receptionist Cindy Freeling, one of her friends, and Gingras were in the club after locking up when they heard voices murmuring in the lobby. When Cindy peered into the lobby, the noises stopped; no one was there. In a few minutes, the sounds started up again, closer to the entrance of the room. Cindy's dog, Booker, snapped to attention, perked up his ears, and stared into the darkness. Was there an apparition in the house? The spectral noises moved up the stairs and into the dining room, where they faded away.

Milt Larsen reports that several guests have told him that they've seen the ghost of a former bartender, Loren, in the Haunted Cellar where he used to serve drinks. The phantom presence, including an accompanying icy chill, has also been felt by Mark Nelson, a former host at the Castle.

Even the club's main theater is haunted! Stage manager Bryan Lee heard a man and woman talking behind a rear curtain, even though the area had been locked up for the evening. When he investigated, the sounds stopped. The stage was empty. Two minutes later, the voices started up again. Once more, the mumbling stopped when Bryan checked behind the curtain.

Then there was the time Bryan was sitting outside the showroom with Peter Pit, a Castle performer and its long-time entertainment director who is now deceased. They mentioned the founder Bill Larsen, who had recently died, and at that moment the grandfather clock near them unexpectedly started to chime, even though it was nowhere near the hour. A coincidence, or was someone eavesdropping from the Spirit World?

A haunted phone booth is located near the main showroom on the upper floor. When a guest sits in this old-fashioned hotel lobby-style phone booth and closes the door, a skeleton appears in a mirror next to the caller.

Perhaps the most enchanted room at the Magic Castle, and one of the most popular, is the music parlor, or, as it is better known, Invisible Irma's room. A baby grand piano fills one corner of the room. Irma, a ghost that can't be seen, sits at the keyboard. All a visitor has to do is request a song—*any* song—and Invisible Irma immediately plays it! Invisible Irma also has a wicked sense of humor and often answers questions put to her by playing songs with appropriate lyrics or song titles. She's sometimes accompanied by her phantom pet bird (which now "lives" in a gilded cage next to the piano).

Irma the Invisible Ghost. Though normally invisible, Invisible Irma is captured here on a (promotional) spirit photograph.

(Photo by Young & Robin, courtesy of Pamela Young Photography, with permission by the Magic Castle)

So that's just a sampling of how magicians have created ghost illusions over the centuries. In our final chapter, let's see how ghosts, poltergeists, and other paranormal entities and activities have been portrayed in popular culture, in books, on the stage, and on the screen.

The Least You Need to Know

- ◆ Priests, shamans, and oracles used magic in ancient times to convince worshippers of their power over deities and spirits.

- ◆ Many magicians have created and performed ghost-themed illusions. Some depend on special lighting, smoke, or mirrors to produce the spirits.

- ◆ Some magicians, like Houdini, made a career out of debunking, or at least demystifying, those who claimed to be able to communicate with ghosts.

- ◆ Disneyland's Haunted Mansion just might *be* haunted!

- ◆ The Magic Castle, a private club for magicians and their friends located in Hollywood, California, is haunted by friendly ghosts—or is it just an illusion?

Chapter 24

Cultural Visions

In This Chapter

- ◆ Ghosts as reflected in popular culture
- ◆ Ghosts on the written page
- ◆ Spirits on the stage
- ◆ Phantoms of the silver screen

Quick! Think of a movie about ghosts. Were you able to come up with one—or maybe a hundred and one? That's because art, in whatever form, reflects the culture in which it's created. And ghost stories have been a part of every civilization's folklore as far back as anyone can discover.

It would be impossible to put together a complete list of all of the ghost characters and tales that have appeared in literature, theater and films since Pliny the Younger described that haunted house in the first century. But let's pause long enough to look at a few notable examples in the written and visual arts.

Ghost Writing

As we've seen, people have written and collected tales about spirits and hauntings for thousands of years. But the "ghost story" as literature dates only to about the nineteenth century.

"The Legend of Sleepy Hollow," an early nineteenth-century American short story written by Washington Irving (1783–1859), tells the tale of a headless horseman—a phantom rider that haunts a New England roadway. His famous story, which first appeared in *The Sketch Book* (serialized in the United States 1819–1820), was adapted from an old German fable.

Phantastic Tips

If you like ghost stories, there's no need to spend a fortune to read them. You'll find dozens of books filled with such tales for readers of all ages at your local public library.

There have been five major feature film releases based on this classic Washington Irving story using its original title. Perhaps the most unusual adaptation is Disney's animated *Adventures of Ichabod and Mr. Toad* (1949); the most recent version was named simply *Sleepy Hollow* (1999).

God Bless Us Everyone

Charles Dickens (1812–1870) was perhaps the greatest writer of fiction in nineteenth-century England. In 1843, he published *A Christmas Carol* (subtitled *A Ghost Story of Christmas*), a story of redemption in which ghostly spirits try to goad Scrooge into altering his miserly ways. Scrooge first receives a Christmas Eve visit from the ghost of his old business partner Jacob Marley, who's bound in chains and dragging his money chest behind him.

Ghostly Pursuits

Partly as a result of the success of *A Christmas Carol,* the "Christmas ghost story" emerged as a literary genre. By 1860, the ghost story was a regular feature in the *Christmas Annual,* a special holiday issue put out by many British and American magazines. Some people compiled ghost stories or made up their own specifically for telling at the family get-togethers during the December holidays.

Scrooge dismisses the spectre as a "piece of undigested potato." But in the course of one evening, three more spirits visit Scrooge: The Ghost of Christmas Past, the Ghost of Christmas Present, and the Ghost of Christmas Yet to Come. This last ghost reveals to Scrooge what will happen if he doesn't mend his ways. By the end of the novella, Scrooge is a changed man!

A Christmas Carol was an instant and incredible success. In the 150 years since its publication, there have been innumerable renderings in books, on stage, and on film. Perhaps the most memorable version, though, is the 1951 adaptation starring Alastair Sim as Scrooge.

Scrooge confronts Marley's ghost in this illustration from an early edition of A Christmas Carol.

Phantastic Tips

At first, Scrooge thought he was having hallucinations because of an upset stomach. It's important to take your own physical condition and state of mind into account at the time of a ghost sighting. Were you wide awake? Were you bored? Were you sober? Your results are much more reliable if you know they were collected when you were totally alert with a clear mind and rested body.

Do You Have a Screw Loose?

New York novelist Henry James (1843–1916) published his classic ghost book *The Turn of the Screw* in 1898 after having serialized it in *Colliers* magazine. In the tale, a young governess named Miss (who acts as the story's narrator) comes to believe that the two children in her charge, Miles and Flora, are being threatened by the ghosts of an ex-valet, Peter Quint, and her own predecessor, Miss Jessel. During the governess's final confrontation with the spectres, Flora is hurried away to safety, but little Miles is not so lucky. The governess attempts an exorcism of Quint, which results in the boy's death. Because no one but Miss ever sees or feels the presence of the apparitions, it's left to the reader to decide whether the ghosts were real or the hysterical fantasy of an impressionable young woman.

A movie version of *The Turn of the Screw*, retitled *The Innocents*, was released in 1961, with Deborah Kerr portraying the governess. There have also been notable television adaptations in 1959 (starring Ingrid Bergman), 1989, and 2000.

A Wilde Ghost

In London, Oscar Wilde (1854–1900), the Irish author, playwright, and wit, penned the short story "The Canterville Ghost," which was first published in 1887 as a serial in the magazine *Court and Society Review*. It was republished four years later in his book *Lord Arthur Savile's Crime and Other Stories*. In the tale, an American family buys an old British mansion that's been haunted by a ghost for 300 years. Not only are the Americans not afraid of the phantom, they actually set out to make the spectre so miserable that it decides to leave! The short story served as the basis for films in 1944 (starring Charles Laughton as the ghost), a 1986 remake, a 1966 TV musical adaptation by Jerry Bock and Sheldon Harnick, and TV movies in the 1980s (with John Gielgud) and in the 1990s (with Patrick Stewart).

It's Good to Be the King

Stephen King (b. 1947) is undeniably the most commercially successful author writing in the horror genre today. His novel, *Carrie*, put him on the map in 1974. Since then, he has published more than 30 novels with over 100 million copies in print.

King has said, "I retain my childish love of the uneasy dead." Is it any wonder, then, that ghosts and hauntings have found their way into many of his works?

Let's look at some perfect examples:

- *The Shining* (1977). When a family becomes the caretakers of a haunted hotel, its spectral residents try to entice Danny, the young boy in the family, to join them in their world. When their efforts fail, the spirits (especially the ghost of the hotel's former custodian) drive his father insane so he attempts to kill his son.

- *Bag of Bones* (1998). Mike Noonan, a best-selling author, suffers writer's block after the death of his wife. He retreats to his lakeside cottage, which turns out to be haunted.

◆ *Rose Red* (2002). In this original television screenplay, a college professor and several of her students investigate a vacant, haunted manor named Rose Red. The original owner of the mansion thought she would never die so long as she continued to build onto it. (King acknowledges that the legend of the Winchester House—see Chapter 13—formed the basis for his story. But he hypothesized, "Suppose that at some point the house took over ... and started building itself?")

The Diary of Ellen Rimbauer: My Life at Rose Red, purported to be the lost journal of the hotel's first owner, was published in conjunction with the premiere of the TV mini-series. The book was "edited" by Stephen King under the penname Joyce Reardon.

◆ *Kingdom Hospital* (2004). King's first foray into series television, was based on the 1994 Danish miniseries *The Kingdom*, directed by Lars von Trier, about a hospital haunted by the spirits buried in the marshland on which the facility was built.

And, Now, Something for the Kiddies

Ghost stories aren't just for adults. More than 50 books by R. L. Stine have appeared in the children's book series *GOOSEBUMPS*, about a dozen of which are stories about ghosts. The first *GOOSEBUMPS* book, *Welcome to Dead House* (1995), established the fun, tongue-in-cheek but slightly scary tone for the series. *GOOSEBUMPS* remains one of the best-selling book series for children ever: More than 200 million books, translated into 16 languages, have been sold worldwide.

Unless you've been living in a cave for the past few years, you know there's a worldwide phenomenon going on in children's literature that goes by the name "Harry Potter." The books, written by British author J. K. Rowling, follow Harry Potter through his years of training at Hogwarts School of Witchcraft and Wizardry.

That ghosts exist in Harry's supernatural world of wonders is a given. In fact, 20 or more ghosts populate Hogwarts. Among the spectral beings introduced by name in the Harry Potter series so far are ...

◆ Moaning Myrtle, who primarily haunts a girls' bathroom on the second floor.

◆ Prof. Binns, a history teacher at Hogwarts (and its sole ghost academic).

◆ Peeves, a poltergeist, who loves to cause mischief whenever possible.

In addition, each of the four student "houses" at Hogwarts has its own resident ghost:

◆ Nearly Headless Nick (the Gryffindor house ghost)

◆ The Bloody Baron (Slytherin)

- The Fat Friar (Hufflepuff)
- The Grey Lady (Ravenclaw)

More than 100 spectral guests attend Nearly Headless Nick's deathday bash in *The Chamber of Secrets*, the second book in the series, including a band of Headless Huntsmen, the Wailing Widow from Kent, a group of ghost nuns, a tattered man in chains, a knight with an arrow stuck in his forehead, and an unnamed fat phantom.

The Play's the Thing

As far as anyone can tell, spirits and hauntings have always been a part of the theater. Ghosts appeared as characters as early as the plays written by Roman philosopher, statesman, and dramatist Seneca (4? B.C.E.–65 C.E.). Typically, his ghosts acted as a chorus, offering the prologue and commenting on the central events in the story. Occasionally a spectre entered into the action of the play; if so, it was usually to seek revenge on one of the living.

CAUTION

Boo! _____

Don't be frightened away by the iambic pentameter and weird words you'll find in Shakespeare. His plays really *are* worth reading and seeing. They must be, or they wouldn't still be around 400 years after they were written. If you want tips on how to tackle the Bard of Avon, you might take a peek at *The Complete Idiot's Guide to Shakespeare* (Alpha Books, 1999).

A new form of apparition, the whining ghost that begs favors from the living, appeared in medieval drama. The moaning-and-complaining ghost was a popular character up to the end of the sixteenth century.

By the time of Elizabethan England, the theater was depicting ghosts more sympathetically, although the appearance of a spectre was frequently of little importance to the main plot. In *Doctor Faustus* (1588, possibly 1590), for example, playwright Christopher Marlowe (1564–1593) has Mephistopheles conjure up several spirits of the dead, including that of Helen of Troy. (Her beauty prompts Faustus to declare the immortal question, "Was this the face that launched a thousand ships?") But neither her ghost, nor the others, ever interact with Faustus.

To Be or Not to Be …

Perhaps the first ghosts that audiences could take seriously appeared in the plays of Shakespeare. They were fully developed human characters; they just happened to be dead. In addition to the ghosts that appear onstage, characters often mention the spirit world.

People living in Elizabethan London believed in ghosts—even though the Church of England was telling them that they didn't exist. Even when ghosts didn't appear in Shakespeare's plays, his characters often discussed them. Ghosts feature prominently in at least four Shakespeare plays. Why not experience them for yourself by picking up the scripts or attending a performance?

♦ *Hamlet.* Hamlet's father comes back from purgatory to ask his son, the prince, to "revenge his foul and most unnatural murder."

♦ *Richard III.* The ghosts of those murdered by Richard III return to vex the cruel and vile king.

♦ *Julius Caesar.* Caesar's ghost makes two nighttime visits to Marcus Brutus, who was one of Caesar's assassins. (As was popular in ghost folklore of Elizabethan times, a candle begins to flicker when the spirit arrives.)

♦ *Macbeth.* Apparitions accompany the Three Witches and Hecate, their queen. Also, the ghost of Banquo, who was murdered on Macbeth's order, materializes at the king's celebratory banquet.

Knock, Knock: I'm Coming In

The nature of ghosts and spirit possession is often explored in Jewish folklore. In the tales, a *dybbuk* is said to be a restless soul that enters the body of a living person. The dybbuk's spirit overwhelms the mortal soul, but it can be driven out by exorcism. *The Dybbuk* (1914) by Russian-born Solomon Anski is the most notable play based on the legend.

That's the Spirit

Noel Coward's *Blithe Spirit* was written and produced (both in London and New York) in 1941. The play centers on Charles Condomine and his wife Ruth, both members of the smart society in Kent, England. They decide to hold a private séance in their home, as was then fashionable. The sitting, led by the larger-than-life medium Madame Arcati, conjures up the ghost of Charles's first wife, Elvira, who then decides not to leave.

The play is full of comic references to séances, mediums, mesmerism, ghost sightings, and paranormal activity. Even the Society for Psychical Research doesn't escape a bit of friendly razzing. *High Spirits*, a musical version of the play *Blithe Spirit*, was produced in both London and in New York in 1964.

Dressed to Haunt

In January 1989, Stephen Mallatratt's stage adaptation of Susan Hill's ghost story novel, *The Woman in Black*, opened in London's West End, where it's been running ever since. It also had a brief run off-Broadway in New York.

In the play, a young London barrister is sent to an outlying province to settle the affairs of a recently deceased elderly woman. He's unaware that his client's deserted mansion and the bogs that surround it are haunted. A chalk-faced ghost, dressed in a black dress and black hooded cape—hence, the play's title—appears suddenly and unexpectedly throughout the suspenseful drama.

A Touch of the Irish

The Weir, the acclaimed drama by Conor McPherson, opened on London's West End in 1998 and premiered on Broadway the following year.

In the play, a quiet woman who's just moved to a remote village in Ireland is brought to meet the regulars at the local pub. In a transfixing evening, three men share their personal encounters with ghosts and the paranormal. Finally, she tells her own compelling and heart-breaking tale involving a telephone call from the dead: It had come from her young daughter who had recently drowned.

Musical Comedy Masters

Ghosts also appear in musical theater. Sometimes the apparition is a character throughout, as we've just seen in *Blithe Spirit*; more often the phantoms are used as a theatrical device to give the characters one last chance to interact with those they left behind. Not incidentally, coming back from the dead often gives the actor portraying the ghost one last chance to belt out a big sentimental show-stopping ballad. Need some examples? Here are just four more classics from the mid-to-late twentieth century musical theater:

◆ *Les Misérables* (1985, London; 1987, New York). Early in the show, the young mother Fantine dies after ensuring that her illegitimate daughter will be cared for after her death. But the character isn't allowed to rest in peace; she returns as a vision in Act Two to reprise her big song.

◆ *Carousel* (1945). *Carousel*, with music by Richard Rodgers and lyrics by Oscar Hammerstein II, was based on the play *Liliom* by Ferenc Molnár. Billy Bigelow, a carousel worker, has been killed in a botched robbery attempt, and returns from the next world to make things right with the daughter he never knew. By the show's end, the girl and her mother realize that the stranger who appeared in their lives was Billy's spirit.

- *Follies* (1971). This seminal musical by Stephen Sondheim (music/lyrics), James Goldman (book) and Harold Prince (director/producer) tells the story of a reunion party for former Follies girls. Theater ghosts of showgirls from past productions glide though the proceedings, mingling with their aged counterparts.

- *The Lion King* (1997). Based on the animated Disney blockbuster (with music by Elton John and lyrics by Tim Rice), *The Lion King* was brought to Broadway with the imaginative staging and designs of Julie Taymor. As in the film, the young lion Simba is comforted and counseled by the ghost of his father Mufasa, whose spirit appears in the form of a constellation in the night sky.

Filmdom's Phantoms

There have been dozens of spooktacular feature films produced with ghosts as central characters. For you obsessives who are *really* into ghost films, I've included a selective list of feature films involving ghosts and hauntings from the last 75 years of filmmaking. Many are available for rental or purchase on video or DVD.

Everyone has favorite films. So here are thumbnail sketches of *my* 13 favorite ghost flicks. They really tickled me, and I think they deserve to haunt us for years to come:

- *Topper* (1937). Cosmo Topper, an uptight banker, is haunted by the ghosts of the Kirbys, who were two of his society friends. Needless to say, the spirits are invisible except to him. There were two sequels, *Topper Takes a Trip* (1939) and *Topper Returns* (1941). The films served as the basis for the *Topper* television series (1953–1956).

- *The Ghost and Mrs. Muir* (1946). The ghost of a sea captain haunts a widow living in an oceanside house. Before long, they fall in love. This film served as the basis for a television series (1968–1970) of the same name.

> **Phantastic Tips**
>
> A ghost film may be the perfect movie for a date. You might be surprised how close your date wants to grab and hold onto you—or vice versa—when something scary comes onto the screen!

- *13 Ghosts* (a.k.a. *Thirteen Ghosts*) (1960). A down-on-his-luck scholar inherits a house, but it's—surprise!—haunted. During the initial release of this William Castle thriller, audience members were given special glasses called "ghost viewers" so that they could see the spirits on the screen. The marketing gimmick was called Illusion-O. A remake of the film (without the special glasses) was released Halloween weekend 1999.

- *The Haunting* (1963). A doctor doing ghost research, a paranormal skeptic, a clairvoyant, and a psychic decide to spend a weekend together to investigate a 90-year old haunted house in Boston. The movie was based on Shirley Jackson's 1959 book, *Haunting of Hill House*. (A special effects–laden remake was released in July 1999.)

- *The Shining* (1980). Based on the best-selling 1977 Stephen King novel mentioned earlier in this chapter, the movie is most often remembered for Jack Nicholson's no-holds-barred performance as a father who's driven mad. Not only does the actor chew the scenery, he literally axes his way through it.

- *Poltergeist* (1982). A young girl watching TV inadvertently opens a door to the spirit world. Havoc ensues as avenging spirits and ghouls invade the house and try to capture the family's children. (The dead are unhappy because the house was built over the cemetery in which they're buried.) Zelda Rubinstein, who provided the foreword to this book, portrayed the medium Tangina Barrons in *Poltergeist* and its two sequels.

- *Ghostbusters* (1984). Four out-of-work parapsychologists set up shop as ghostbusters to help rid New York City of its monstrous apparitions. There was a sequel, *Ghostbusters II* (1989).

- *Beetlejuice* (1988). The eccentric ghosts haunting a barn in New England try everything in the book—and then some—to scare off the new owners who move in.

- *Ghost* (1990). A stockbroker returns from the Other Side to track down his murderers. Whoopi Goldberg won an Oscar for her portrayal of the reluctant medium who helps him cross over.

- *The Sixth Sense* (1999). A young boy makes an unsettling claim: "I see dead people … all the time." His last hope to banish the (presumably) mental demons is a child psychologist, who is "haunted" by the memory of a similar case he treated years before.

- *The Others* (2001). A mother must keep her house dark because her son and daughter are dangerously sensitive to sunlight. Before long, she begins to believe that the old, shadowy mansion is haunted.

- *The Ring* (2002). A young journalist investigates a strange videotape that, somehow, causes anyone who views it to die within a week. The search leads to a mysterious girl with evil powers whose spirit is able to reach from beyond the grave. The film is based on Kôji Suzuki's 1991 novel *Ringu* and a 1998 Japanese film by the same name.

- *The Haunted Mansion* (2003). A New Orleans family is stranded overnight in an antebellum mansion, which turns out to be haunted by its former owner, Master Gracey. There are also ghostly servants, a spectral orb of light, the disembodied phantom head of psychic Madame Leota inside a crystal ball, a cemetery full of spirits, and more.

A Century of Phantom Films

A Christmas Carol (1908, 1951)

The Legend of Sleepy Hollow (1915, 1938)

Hamlet (1921) Most notable remakes: 1948, 1964, 1969, 1990, 1996, and 2000

The Ghost Goes West (1936)

Topper (1937) Sequels: *Topper Takes a Trip* (1939) and *Topper Returns* (1941)

The Ghost Breakers (1940)

Here Comes Mr. Jordan (1941) Remade as *Heaven Can Wait* (1978)

Hold That Ghost (1941)

The Ghost of Frankenstein (1942)

The Canterville Ghost (1944; 1986, remake)

Ghost Catchers (1944)

The Uninvited (1944)

Blithe Spirit (1945)

The Ghost and Mrs. Muir (1946)

The Time of Their Lives (1946)

The Ghosts of Berkeley Square (1947)

Adventures of Ichabod and Mr. Toad (1949)

Carousel (1956)

House on Haunted Hill (1958)

13 Ghosts (1960, aka *Thirteen Ghosts*) Remade in 2001 as *Thir13en Ghosts* (also spelled *13 Ghosts* and *Thirteen Ghosts*)

The Innocents (1961)

The Ghost (1963)

The Haunting (1963; 1999, remake)

The Ghost and Mr. Chicken (1966)

Ghost in the Invisible Bikini (1966)

Ghosts Italian Style (1969)

Scrooge (1970)

The Exorcist (1973) Sequels: *The Exorcist II: The Heretic* (1977), *The Exorcist III* (1990), and *Exorcist, The Beginning* (2004)

The Legend of Hell House (1973)

The Other (1973)

The Evil (1978)

The Amityville Horror (1979) Sequels: *Amityville II: The Possession* (1982), and *Amityville 3-D* (1983)

The Changling (1979)

Oh Heavenly Dog (1980)

The Shining (1980)

Somewhere in Time (1980)

Ghost Story (1981)

Poltergeist (1982) Sequels: *Poltergeist II: The Other Side* (1986), *Poltergeist III* (1988)

Soul Survivor (1982)

One Dark Night (1983)

The Entity (1983)

The Keep (1983)

All of Me (1984)

Ghostbusters (1984) Sequel: *Ghostbusters II* (1989)

Maxie (1985)

The Fog (1985)

The Heavenly Kid (1985)

The Legend of Hell House (1985)

The Oracle (1985)

The Supernaturals (1985)

The Wraith (1986)

Beetlejuice (1988)

High Spirits (1988)

Scrooged (1988)

Always (1989)

Field of Dreams (1989)

The Other (1989)

Flatliners (1990)

Ghost (1990)

Ghost Dad (1990)

Dead Again (1991)

Defending Your Life (1991)

Switch (1991)

Candyman (1992) Sequel: *Candyman II* (1995)

The Muppet Christmas Carol (1992)

The House of Spirits (1993)

The Crow (1994)

Casper (1995)

To Gillian on Her 27th Birthday (1996)

The Sixth Man (1997)

The Sixth Sense (1999)

Sleepy Hollow (1999)

What Lies Beneath (2000)

Harry Potter and the Sorcerer's Stone (2001, U.S.); *Harry Potter and the Philosopher's Stone* (UK and international English title)

Moment in Time (2001)

The Others (2001)

Soul Survivors (2001)

Ghost Ship (2002)

GhostWatcher (2002)

Harry Potter and the Chamber of Secrets (2002)

Mother Ghost (2002)

The Ring (2002)

Terror at Tate Manor (2002)

Gothika (2003)

Mind Forest (2003)

The Haunted Mansion (2003)

Harry Potter and the Prisoner of Azkaban (2004)

The Last Sign (2004)

Spectres (2004)

Harry Potter and the Goblet of Fire (2005)

Well, I hope you've enjoyed our travels through the world of ghosts, apparitions, spirits, and the paranormal. The next time you hear a strange noise in the dark, or you think you catch a glimpse of something eerie fly by, you'll be ready!

Ghost hunters, arise! You know what to look for and how to search for it. And if you're already out there, reading this as you sit all alone in some haunted house or ancient graveyard, don't be scared. Remember, it's always darkest before the dawn.

The Least You Need to Know

◆ The treatment of ghosts in popular culture has always reflected the beliefs of the civilizations that produced them.

◆ Ghost literature came to the forefront in the nineteenth century. Today children's literature in also populated with spirits, such as those found in J. K. Rowling's Harry Potter books.

◆ Ghosts and apparitions have always been important characters in the theater, from Greek tragedies and the works of Shakespeare to the light comedy of Noel Coward and the Broadway musical stage.

◆ Movies are able to produce terrifying images of ghost phenomena. More than a hundred films have featured apparitional characters.

Continuing the Ghost Hunt

Most paranormal researchers recommend that if you wish to undertake a serious investigation, you should contact an organization or individual that can do so professionally and scientifically. This is especially true if you're having problems with a haunting—either by a ghost or poltergeist. You'll need help.

Three Classic Ghost-Hunter Organizations

If you think your case is serious enough to interest one of the long-standing leading paranormal research organizations, such as the Society for Psychical Research or one of its associates, by all means contact one of them. If the society feels it's not the appropriate agency to investigate your haunting, it may recommend other options.

Here are three respected organizations of note:

Society for Psychical Research (SPR)
49 Marloes Road, London W8 6LA England
Phone/Fax: 020-7937-8984
Website: www.spr.ac.uk
The SPR was founded in London in 1882 to investigate the claims of Spiritualistic mediums. It became the most important early organization dedicated to the study of ghosts and other paranormal activity.

American Society for Psychical Research (ASPR)
Patrice Keane, Executive Director
5 West 73rd Street, New York, NY 10023
Phone: 212-799-5050
Fax: 212-496-2497
Website: www.aspr.com
Although founded with the assistance of the SPR, the American Society for Psychical Research remains an independent group dedicated to investigating paranormal phenomenon.

Committee for the Scientific Investigation of Claims of the Paranormal (CSICOP)
P.O. Box 703, Amherst, NY 14226-0703
Website: www.csicop.com
CSISCOP's investigations are not limited to ghost phenomena. Indeed, their inquiries cover the full range of paranormal activities. They also publish *Skeptical Inquirer* magazine. If you have access to the Internet, I'd recommend contacting them there and visiting their many links.

Ghosts on the Internet

Several notable individuals and organizations have web pages on the Internet describing their services. Whenever possible, I've listed the group's founder, director, or chief investigator. The following is a brief list of who and what's out there.

Please note that their mention on this list is not necessarily a recommendation or endorsement of their expertise or success rate. As with any consultant, you'll have to interview a ghost hunter to make sure the two of you are in sync. Nevertheless, all of these individuals and groups are seriously interested in ghost phenomena and deal with paranormal activity. A good way to start out finding your spectre-seeking soul mate is by visiting some of these websites.

Borley Ghost Society
Vincent O'Neil, President
E-mail: mail@borleyrectory.com
Website: www.borleyrectory.com
Vincent O'Neil formed the Borley Ghost Society on October 31, 1998 to examine existing records and ongoing research related to the reported haunting of the rectory and church of Borley, Essex, England. Associate members have access to a monthly newsletter.

D. Trull, *Enigma* Magazine
E-mail: dtrull@parascope.com
Website: www.parascope.com/articles/0397/ghostin.htm

Ghost Research Society
Dale Kaczmarek, President
P.O. Box 205, Oak Lawn, IL 60454-0205
Phone: 708-425-5163
Fax: 708-425-3969
Website: www.ghostresearch.or
Dale Kaczmarek also leads "Excursion into the Unknown" ghost tours in the greater Chicago area.

International Ghost Hunters Society
Dave Oester and Sharon Gill, co-founders
E-mail: MagicDimensions@aol.com
Website: www.ghostweb.com

International Society for Paranormal Research
Los Angeles, California
Websites: www.hauntings.com; www.ISPR.net

New England Society for Psychic Research
Ed and Lorraine Warren, Directors
P.O. Box 41, Monroe, CT 06468
E-mail: info@warrens.net (general information) and help@warrents.net (for investigations and supernatural questions)
Website: www.warrens.net
Although based in New England, the Warrens or members of their staff conduct research throughout the United States.

Paranormal Research Society of New England
John Zaffis, Ghost Investigator
Phone: 203-375-6083
E-mail: info@prsne.com
Website: www.prsne.com

Philadelphia Ghost Hunters Alliance
Lewis and Sharon Gerew
E-mail: Rayd8em@aol.com
Website: http://members.aol.com/Rayd8em/index.html
PGHA has a western Pennsylvania affiliate in Gettysburg, led by Andrew and Tonya Keyser, at www.Gettysburgghostreach.com.

Richard Senate
Website: www.ghost-stalker.com
Author and ghost hunter Richard Senate leads ghost tours and publishes the *Ghost Watch Newsletter*. His site provides an ever-changing array of ghost photos, generally submitted by amateur ghost hunters. He can be contacted through his website or through Phantom Bookshop, 2989 Foothill Road, Ventura, CA 93003; phone 805-641-3844.

Shadowlands
Dave Juliano, Shadow Lord
E-mail: djuliano@theshadowlands.net
Website: http://theshadowlands.net
In addition to his work as a ghost hunter, Dave Juliano has maintained this superb ghost site since 1995. It includes multiple links to other sites of interest. Various search engines regularly rate this as one of the most popular ghost sites on the web.

The Atlantic Paranormal Society (TAPS)
Grant Wilson, co-founder
E-mail: grant@the-atlantic-paranormal-society.com
Website: www.the-atlantic-paranormal-society.com
TAPS is a nonprofit paranormal investigation group based in Rhode Island. It's networked with a number of other credible paranormal investigative groups in 36 states and 12 countries. The goal of the society is to maintain a high level of professionalism among all the affiliated organizatons.

Ghost Tours

Some towns offer ghost tours, taking amateur ghost hunters on a sightseeing expedition of area haunted houses and sites. It's worth checking with local tourist offices and the Yellow Pages when you're in a city you think might be haunted. Here are just a few ghost tours that are currently available in the United States, Great Britain, and elsewhere.

Charleston, South Carolina

"Ghosts of Charleston" walking tour
18 Broad Street, Suite 709, Charleston, SC 29401
Phone: 1-800-854-1670
Website: www.tourcharleston.com
E-mail: info@tourcharleston.com

Chicago, Illinois

Chicago Supernatural Ghost Tours
Richard T. Crowe
P.O. Box 557544, Chicago, IL 60655-7544
Phone: 708-499-0300
Richard Crowe has been conducting various ghostly itineraries for 25 years.

Fredericksburg, Virginia

"Phantom of Fredericksburg" Ghost Tour
The Living History Company of Fredericksburg
904 Princess Anne Street, Suite C7, Fredericksburg, VA 22401
Phone: 540-899-1776
Toll-free: 1-888-214-6384
Website: www.historyexperiences.com

Gettysburg, Pennsylvania

Ghost Tours of Gettysburg
Phone: 717-337-0445
Website: www.ghostsofgettysburg.com
Seasonal tours.

Harpers Ferry, West Virginia

Ghost Tours of Harpers Ferry
Conducted by Shirley Dougherty
Phone: 304-725-8019
Website: www.harpersferrywv.net
Tours depart at 8 P.M. from Lori's Cafe on Potomac Street on Saturdays in April and May, then Fridays and Saturdays from Memorial Day through the first weekend in November. Reservations are required in October and November.

Hollywood, California

Haunted Hollywood® Tour
Operated in conjunction with Starline Tours, this motorized tour of Hollywood's ghost sites is led by your ghost guide Brian Sapir. (Ask him about his own ghost experience!)

Phone: 818-415-8269

Website: www.hauntedhollywoodtours.com

Haunted House Walking Tour

Parapsychological investigator Michael J. Kouri offers day and evening ghost tours of Pasadena, Orange County, and elsewhere in southern California, all within easy driving distance of Hollywood.

Phone: 626-791-1129 or 714-731-6829

Website: www.icghosts.com

Queen Mary

Docked in Long Beach, at 1126 Queens Highway, 30 miles from Hollywood, the RMS Queen Mary offers a "Ghosts and Legends" tour several times daily. It visits many of the purported haunted spots throughout the ship.

Phone: 562-435-3511

Websites: www.queenmary.com; www.ghostsandlegends.com

In addition, paranormal researcher Peter James offers occasional evening ghost tour/dinner packages on the *Queen Mary.*

Phone: 562-499-1657

Honolulu, Hawaii

Chicken Skin Ghost Tours

2634 S. King Street

Suite 3, Honolulu, HI 96826

Phone: 808-943-0371

Websites: www.chicken-skin.com; www.chicken-skin-ghost-tours-hawaii. hawaiifanatic.com

Key West, Florida

Ghost Tours of Key West

The original walking tour of Key West's haunted, historic district.

Phone: 305-294-9255

Website: www.hauntedtours.com

The 90-minute tour covers just under a mile and departs nightly from the Crowne Plaza, 430 Duval Street.

Ghost & Legends of Key West

Phone: 305-294-1713

Website: www.keywestghosts.com

The Old Town tour is on foot. It lasts about 90 minutes and departs twice nightly at 7 and 9 P.M. from Porter Mansion on the corner of Duval and Caroline.

New Orleans, Louisiana

Gray Line
E-mail: tours@graylineneworleans.com
Website: www.graylineneworleans.com
Two-hour walking tour departs from the Gray Line booth at Jackson Brewery at 7 P.M. nightly.

Haunted History Ghost Tour
Phone: 504-861-2727
Website: www.hauntedhistorytours.com
Two-hour walking tour of the French Quarter or the Garden District available. Tours depart from Rev. Zombie's Voodoo Shop, 723 St. Peter Street at 2 P.M., 6 P.M., and 8 P.M. daily. Tours also depart from The Corner Restaurant, 500 Peter Street at 8 P.M. nightly.

New Orleans Ghost Tour
Phone: 504-524-0708
Website: www.neworleansghosttour.com
Two-hour walking tours depart from Flanagan's Pub, 625 Philip Street (between Royal and Chatres streets) at 7 P.M., 8 P.M., and 9 P.M. nightly.

Ghost and Vampire Walking Tour
New Orleans Spirit Tours
Phone: 866-314-1224 or 504-314-0806
Fax: 504-314-0807
Website: www.neworleanstours.net
Tour departs from Royal Blend Coffee and Tea House, 621 Royal Street, at 8:15 P.M. nightly.

Newport, Rhode Island

Ghost Tours of Newport
A Graveyard Walking Tour is also offered.
Phone: 401-841-8600 or 866-33GHOST (toll-free)
Website: www.NewportWalks.com

New York City, New York

Ghost Tours
Street Smarts N.Y. Walking Tours
Phone: 212-969-8262
Five different tours are available: Ghostly Greenwich Village; Pubs and Poltergeists—A Haunted Tavern Tour; East Village Ghosts; Ghosts On Broadway; and Soho Ghosts. Tours are weekends only, at 2 P.M. and 6 P.M. on Saturday and 2 P.M. on Sunday.

Philadelphia, Pennsylvania

Ghost Tours
Phone: 215-413-1997
E-mail: Philadelphia@ghosttour.com
Website: http://ghosttour.com/Philadelphia.htm
One-and-a-quarter-hour walking tour begins from Independence Hall at 7:30 P.M., April through November, however days of the week vary. Reservations highly recommended. Tickets can also be purchased at Willie & Duffy's Philly Grill, located at 6th and Chestnut Streets.

This same operator also offers a ghost tour to nearby Lancaster County:
Ghost Tours of Lancaster
Phone: 717-687-6687
E-mail: Lancaster@ghosttour.com
Website: http://ghosttour.com/lancaster.htm
The hour-and-ten-minute Lancaster County Ghost Tour departs from Mrs. Penn's Shoppe at the light in Strasburg (at the intersection of Routes 896 and 741). Tickets are purchased inside the shop. Days and times vary, with up to four tours beginning at 7:30 P.M., from June through the first weekend in November. Group and private tours beginning in the city of Lancaster are available any day or time from April through November. Call 610-587-8308 for details.

Salem, Massachusetts

Haunted Footsteps Ghost Tour
175 Essex Street, 2nd Floor, Salem, MA 01970
Phone: 978-745-0666
E-mail: salemhfgt@onegecko.com
Website: www.hauntedfootstepsghosttour.com
Ninety-minute walking tour.

New England Ghost Tours
P.O. Box 812128, Wellesley, MA 02482
Phone/fax: 781-235-7149
E-mail: nehaunts@aol.com
Website: www.members.aol.com/nehaunts
New England Ghost Tours operates a three-and-a-half-hour bus tour of Salem and
Marblehead and a 75-minute "Boston Spirits Walking Tour," beginning at 7:30 P.M.
on selected evenings, led by ghost hunter and storyteller Jim McCabe.

Vampire & Ghost Hunt Tour
Spellbound Tours™
Conducted by Mollie Stewart
Phone: 978-745-0138
Website: www.spellboundtours.com/vampire.htm
Tours depart from the Visitor Center in the Salem Armory Building at the corner of
New Liberty and Brown Streets at 8 P.M. nightly, mid-April through November.

Better known for its place in the history of witchcraft than for its ghosts and appari-
tions, Old Salem nevertheless boasts several haunted sites, including the Old Jail, the
Corwin home, the Ropes Mansion, the Athaeneum Library, and the residence of
Susan Ingersoll. Ingersoll's home inspired her cousin, Nathaniel Hawthorne, to write
the gothic horror novel *The House of the Seven Gables.* Salem holds an annual 10-day
Haunted Happenings with more than 50 events. For information, contact the Visitor
Center at Old Town Hall, 32 Derby Square, Salem, MA 01970; phone 508-744-0004.

San Antonio, Texas

The Hauntings History of San Antonio Ghost Hunt
Conducted by Martin Leal
Phone: 210-436-5417
E-mail: jleal@stic.net

San Francisco, California

San Francisco Ghost Hunt
Daily walking tour guided by Jim Fassbinder
Phone: 415-922-5590

Savannah, Georgia

Savannah Walks, Inc., Low Country Ghost Tour
Phone: 1-888-SAV-WALK
Website: www.savannahwalks.com

Canada

Ghost Tours of Québec
Evening walking tours offered in French, English, and Spanish, daily, May 1–October 31.
Phone: 418-692-9770
Websites: www.ghosttoursofquebec.com; www.fantomesdequebec.com

The British Isles

London Walks
P.O. Box 1708, London NW6 4LW England
Phone: 020-7624-3978 or 020-7794-1764
Recorded information: 020-7624-9255 or 020-7624-WALK
Fax: 020-625-1932
E-mail: london@walks.com
Websites: www.walks.com; http://london.walks.com
London Walks conducts at least four different nighttime walking ghost tours of London: "Ghosts of the West End" (Monday, Thursday); "Ghosts of the Old City" (Tuesday, Saturday); "Ghosts, Gaslight, and Guinness" (Wednesday); and "Haunted London" (Friday, Sunday). All four ghost walks are offered on Halloween!

London Ghost Walk
Phone: 020-8530-8443
Website: www.london-ghost-walk.co.uk
E-mail: enquiries@london-ghost-walk.co.uk
Nighttime tours, daily except Wednesday. Author and ghost researcher Richard Jones leads this two-hour walking tour.

Creativity Travel
Yvonne Leach
39 Kingsdown Park, Tanekrton, Whitstable Kent CT5 2DE England
Website: www.CreativityTravel.com
Specialty tours, including tours of ghost sites throughout Dover, Pluckley, and elsewhere in County Kent.

Pluckley
For information on self-guided ghost tours of Pluckley, England, visit www.pluckley.net/history/ghosts01.htm.

Spooky Brighton Ghost Walks
E-mail: info@brightonwalks.com
Website: www.brightonwalks.com/ghostwalk
The 90-minute walking tour conducted by Glenda Clarke departs from the Visitor Information Center opposite Town Hall, The Lanes, Brighton, England, at 8:00 P.M. on the first Saturday of every month.

The Dublin Ghost Bus Tour
Dublin Bus
59 Upper O'Connell Street, Dublin 1 Ireland
Phone: 01-873-4222
Fax: 01-703-3031
Website: www.dublinbus.ie/your_journey/ghost_bus_tour.asp
Departures at 8:00 P.M., Tuesday through Friday, and 7 and 9:30 P.M. on Saturday and Sunday

The Ghosts and Ghouls Tour
Mercat Tours
Phone: 0131-557-6464
E-mail: info@mercattours.com
Website: www.mercattours.com
Mercat Tours offers a variety of ghost-themed walking, including "Ghosts and Ghouls," "The Haunted Underground Experience," "Ghost Hunter Trail," and "GhostBust Tours." All tours depart from central Edinburgh, Scotland. Times vary seasonally.

Mercat Tours also offers a "Horror Walking Tour" of Glasgow, Scotland. For more information, contact Mercat Glasgow, phone: 0141-586-5378; fax: 0141-586-5378; e-mail: info@mercat-glasgow.co.uk; website: mercat-glasgow.co.uk.

The Real Mary King's Close
2 Warriston's Close High Street, Edinburgh EH1 1PG Scotland
Phone: 08702-430160
Website: www.realmarykingsclose.com
Tours depart every 20 minutes beginning at 10 A.M. Last tour departs at 9:00 P.M. from April through October and at 4:00 P.M. from November through March. Closed Christmas Day.

South Africa

The Mystery Ghost Bus Tour
E-mail: tour@mysteryghostbus.co.za
Reservations: 011-27-83-915-8000 (Computicket)
Operated by Mark Rose-Christie. Tours available in Johannesburg, Pretoria, Cape Town, and at the annual Grahamstown Festival.

Boo-Boo-Boo, Books!

There are literally hundreds of books out there on ghosts, apparitions, paranormal activity, and psychic societies. There are directories of where to find ghosts and compendiums full of ghost stories—some fictional, and many purporting to be true case histories. Some of these books are available in major bookstores, but most of them can be found in specialty bookstores or on the shelves of your local library. Most nonfiction books about ghosts can be found at 133.1 under the good old Dewey Decimal system. A few of them are currently out of print, but all are well worth seeking out.

Of General Interest

Atwater, P. M. H. *The Complete Idiot's Guide to Near-Death Experiences* (Alpha Books, 2000).

If you've ever wondered what it's like to be turned back from that "light at the end of the tunnel"—and some possible explanations of what causes this more-common-than-you-might-suspect phenomenon (which some claim is proof of survival of the spirit after death), this book is for you! Filled with dozens of first person accounts.

Bayless, Raymond. *The Enigma of the Poltergeist* (Parker Publishing Co., 1967).

A scholarly but subjective examination of the nature of poltergeists and how they differ from ghosts, apparitions, and other spirits. Many famous poltergeist cases are detailed, especially pre-twentieth century phenomena.

———. *Apparitions and Survival of Death* (Citadel Press, 1973).

A discussion of what might possibly survive the body after death. Distinctions are made among the soul, apparitions, and spirits.

Burger, Eugene. *Spirit Theater* (Richard Kaufman and Alan Greenberg, 1986).

Written by a magician and spirit-theater performer, this is a lively discussion chronicling the roots of spiritualism and the movement's most famous mediums. This book includes interviews with modern psychic entertainers as well as the methods for several convincing spirit-themed magical illusions.

Cavendish, Richard, ed. *Man, Myth & Magic: An Illustrated Encyclopedia of the Supernatural* (Marshall Cavendish Corporation, 1970).

In 24 volumes. A comprehensive encyclopedia of articles about supernatural, ghost, psychic, and paranormal phenomena.

Cohen, Daniel. *The Encyclopedia of Ghosts* (Dodd, Mead & Co., 1984).

An easy and entertaining introduction to familiarize readers with some of the most famous ghost stories. In chapter rather than A-to-Z format.

Finucane, R. C. *Ghosts: Appearances of the Dead & Cultural Transformation* (Prometheus Books, 1996).

An excellent and thoughtful examination of how the belief in and perception of ghosts have changed throughout the ages.

Guiley, Rosemary Ellen. *The Encyclopedia of Ghosts and Spirits* (Facts on File, 1992).

A thorough and entertaining compendium of mostly American and British ghostly lore and legend, plus biographies of luminaries in the fields of Spiritualism and paranormal research.

Hauck, Dennis William. *Haunted Places: the National Directory* (Penguin Books, 1996).

This is an indispensable U.S. travel guide for hobbyist ghost hunters. More than 2,000 haunted places are listed state-by-state, along with brief descriptions of the sites and their legends. It also includes a bibliography of more than 200 books on ghosts, spirits, and other paranormal phenomena.

———. *The International Directory of Haunted Places* (Penguin Books, 2000).

Although not as comprehensive as his earlier directory of U.S. hauntings, this companion volume lists more than 700 haunted places, divided by the areas of the world, then by the countries, in which they occur.

Jacobson, Laurie, and Marc Wanamaker. *Hollywood Haunted: A Ghostly Tour of Filmland* (Angel City Press, 1994).

Although covering much of the same territory as Hans Holzer's earlier *Haunted Hollywood* (The Bobbs-Merrill Co., 1974), this updated overview surveys the best-known haunted spots, phantom encounters, and celebrity ghosts of Tinseltown.

Tyrrell, G. N. M. *Apparitions* (Collier Books, 1963).

This classic book is the result of Tyrrell's survey of ghost and paranormal investigation up to the mid-twentieth century. It also expounds his theories on the nature of apparitions. The text was adapted from a speech Tyrrell made in 1942 as the Myers Memorial Lecture before the Society of Psychical Research. First published posthumously in 1953.

Underwood, Peter. *Gazetteer of British, Scottish and Irish Ghosts* (Bell Publishing Company, 1985).

As the title suggests, this is a listing of hundreds of ghosts and haunted locations throughout Great Britain.

Regional Books

The following books are specific to a particular location or city. This type of work is particularly interesting if you're going into that region, because it's often filled with many more examples than more general volumes on ghost activity. Most are published by small presses and sold in local bookstores and tourist locations.

Alexander, John. *Ghosts: Washington's Most Famous Ghost Stories* (Washington Book Trading Co., 1988).

Jonas, Shirley. *Ghosts of the Klondike* (Lynn Canal Publishing, 1996).

Murray, Earl. *Ghosts of the Old West* (Contemporary Books, 1988).

Sloan, David L. *Ghosts of Key West* (Mirror Lake Press, 1998).

Wicker, Christine. *Lily Dale: The True Story of the Town That Talks to the Dead* (HarperCollins, 2003).

Wlodarski, Robert, Anne Nathan-Wlodarski, and Richard Senate. *A Guide to the Haunted Queen Mary* (Ghost Publishing, 1998).

How-To Books

These last two books are written for people who want to create their own pseudo-séance rooms and haunted houses to entertain, surprise, and fool their friends. Although aimed primarily at young readers, the books give all ages the do's and don'ts about setting up some spooky surroundings, plus easy-to-follow directions on rigging gags and constructing special props. Both books are highly recommended!

Friedhoffer, Robert. *How to Haunt a House for Halloween* (Franklin Watts, 1995).

Witkowski, Dan. *How to Haunt a House* (Random House, 1994).

Seeing Is Believing: Haunted Places You Can Visit!

There are literally thousands of sites throughout the world that are allegedly haunted. No single directory can ever hope to give a complete listing.

Many of the locations detailed here are either residences, places of business, or other institutions not open for tourism. Only the exterior of most of these buildings can be viewed. As a result, I haven't included their street addresses. I *have* included some Hollywood addresses readily available on "Maps to the Stars Homes," but *please*, ghost hunters, don't go camping out on their front yards! A polite request at a business can sometimes result in a quick look around their premises. But, out of common courtesy, don't go knocking on the doors of private homes—as tempting as it might be.

Here are some of the most popular sites mentioned in this book that *are* open to the public. Most are found in the United States, but a few selected international locations are also listed. Whenever possible, I've included addresses, directions, and a phone number for these places. Admission is charged to enter many of the museums and tourist locations. Even so, some areas in the buildings may not be open to visitors. Many, such as theaters, can only be entered only when events are taking place inside. Opening hours vary and telephone numbers may change, so please check with the venue or local tourism boards before setting out on a major journey.

The United States of America

Alaska

Golden North Hotel
Third and Broadway
Skagway, Alaska
Phone: 907-983-2294

Red Onion Saloon
Second and Broadway
Skagway, Alaska
Phone: 907-983-2222

Arizona

Big Nose Kate's (saloon)
Tombstone, AZ 85638
E-mail: whiskers@bignosekate.com
Website: www.bignosekate.com

California

Alcatraz Island
Located in San Francisco Bay, San Francisco
Website: www.nps.gov/alcatraz
Operated as part of the National Park Service. Hours of operation vary seasonally, generally from 9:30 A.M. to 4:30 P.M. (6:30 P.M. in the summer months). Closed on Christmas and New Year's Day. Boats depart from Pier 41 on Fisherman's Wharf in San Francisco. Alcatraz is a very popular tourist attraction, so advance ticket sales are *highly* recommended. For information, contact the Blue & Gold Fleet, which operates the boats to the island, at 415-705-5555, or stop at their booth on Pier 41.

Avalon
(formerly the Palace Theater)
1735 Vine
Hollywood, CA 90028
Phone: 323-467-4571

The Clifton Webb crypt
Hollywood Forever (formerly the Hollywood Memorial Cemetery)
Tomb located in the Sanctuary of Peace
6000 Santa Monica Boulevard
Hollywood, CA 90028
Phone: 323-469-1181
Mausoleum open to the public. A map to the stars' graves is available at the offices
by the cemetery's front gate.

The Clunie House
(operating as Victoria Inn)
Victoria Inn on the Park, 1981–2003)
301 Lyon Street
San Francisco, CA 94117

The Comedy Store
(formerly Ciro's nightclub)
8433 Sunset Boulevard
Los Angeles (West Hollywood), CA 90027
Phone: 323-656-6225 (show information); 323-656-6268 (offices)

Disneyland
1313 Harbor Boulevard
Anaheim, CA 92803
Phone: 714-781-4000
Operating hours vary seasonally.

El Fandango Restaurant
2734 Calhoun Street
San Diego, CA 92110
Phone: 619-298-2860

Harmony Grove
The Harmony Grove Spiritualist Association
2975 Washington Circle
Escondido, CA 92029
Phone: 760-745-9176
Fax: 760-745-3482
Website: www2.4dcomm.com/hgchurch
Not a haunted site, but Harmony Grove is one of the few remaining year-round resi-
dential Spiritualist camps. The meeting grounds are located about 4 miles outside
Escondido, about 34 miles northeast of San Diego.

Hollywood Roosevelt Hotel
7000 Hollywood Boulevard
Hollywood, CA 90028
Phone: 1-800-833-3333 or 323-466-7000

The Houdini Mansion
2398 Laurel Canyon Boulevard
(at Willow Glen Road, near the junction of Lookout Mountain Avenue)
Hollywood, CA 90028
While this is private property and no visitors are permitted, from Laurel Canyon
Boulevard you can view the few original foundations that remain.

Landmark 78 Restaurant
(formerly the Santa Clara House)
211 E. Santa Clara Street
Ventura, CA 93001
Phone: 805-643-3264

Los Angeles Pet Cemetery
5068 Old Scandia Lane
Calabasas, CA 91302-2507

Mann's Chinese Theatre
(formerly Grauman's Chinese Theatre)
6925 Hollywood Boulevard
Hollywood, CA 90028
Phone: 323-464-8111

Pantages Theatre
6233 Hollywood Boulevard
Hollywood, CA 90028
Phone: 323-468-1770

The *Queen Mary* (hotel and museum)
Berthed at Pier J in the Port of Long Beach
Mailing address: 1126 Queens Highway
Long Beach, CA 90802-6390
Tour and event information: 562-435-3511
Information and hotel reservations: 1-800-437-2934
Guided tours take guests to many of the allegedly haunted spots throughout the inte-
rior of the ship, and additional ghost tours are usually added around Halloween.

Tahquitz Canyon Trail
Tahquitz Canyon Visitor Center
500 W. Mesquite Avenue
Palm Springs, CA 92262
Phone: 760-416-7044
Website: www.indian-canyons.com

Whaley House
Old Town
2482 San Diego Avenue (at Harney Street)
San Diego, CA 92110
Phone: 619-297-7511
Historic monument open to the public as a museum. Exit I-5 at Old Town Avenue.

William S. Hart Museum
(now the Hart Mansion)
24151 San Fernando Road
Newhall, CA 91321
Phone: 661-254-4584
Newhall is a part of Santa Clarita, California, about 20 miles northwest of Los Angeles.

Winchester House
525 S. Winchester Boulevard
San Jose, CA 95128
Phone: 408-247-2000
Fax: 408-247-2090
Open daily (except Christmas) for guided tours from 9 A.M. Located on Winchester Boulevard, near the intersection of I-280 and I-880 and State Highway #17.

Florida

Cassadaga Spiritualist Camp
The Southern Cassadaga Spiritualist Camp Meeting Association
Summerland House (Camp and Association Offices)
1325 Stevens Street
P.O. Box 319
Cassadaga, FL 32706
Phone: 386-228-3171
Website: www.cassadaga.org
Not a haunted site, but Cassadaga Spiritualist Camp has about 100 resident psychics, readers, and mediums year-round. Regular office hours are Monday through

Thursday, 10:00 A.M. to noon, others by appointment. The camp also operates the
Cassadaga Bookstore and Information Center, 1112 Stevens Street, P.O. Box 319,
Cassadaga, FL 32706; 386-228-2880.

Ernest Hemingway Home and Museum
907 Whitehead Street
Key West, FL 33040
Phone: 305-294-1575

Georgia

Chickamauga-Chatanooga National Military Park
(especially Snod Grass Hill)
Chickamauga, GA
Phone: 706-866-9241
Battlegrounds open to visitors. Located 10 miles south of Chatanooga, Tennessee, on
U.S. Highway 27.

Pirate's House Restaurant
20 East Broad Street (at Bay Street)
Savannah, GA 31404
Phone: 912-233-5757

Hawaii

Hilton Hawaiian Village
2005 Kalia Road
Honolulu, HI 96815
Phone: 800-774-1500 or 808-949-4321
Fax: 808-947-7898
Website: www.hiltonhawaiianvillage.com

Illinois

Bachelor Grove Cemetery
(one-acre plot near the Rubio Woods Forest Preserve)
Midlothian, IL 60445
Located west of Midlothian, a southern suburb of Chicago, in the Rubio Woods
Forest Preserve. From Chicago, travel I-294 south to Cicero Avenue, then go west on
the Midlothian Turnpike to the Rubio Woods exit. Visitation may be restricted due to
recent vandalism.

Beverly Unitarian Church
(also called the Irish Castle)
10244 South Longwood Drive (at 103rd)
Chicago, IL 60643
Phone: 773-233-7080

Evergreen Cemetery
3401 W. 87th Street (at Kedzie Avenue)
Chicago, IL 60805

Graceland Cemetery
4001 North Clark Street (at Irving Park Road)
Chicago, IL 60613
Phone: 773-525-1105
From downtown Chicago, travel north on Lakeshore Drive, then exit at Irving Park Road.

Holy Family Church
1019 South May Street
Chicago, IL 60607
Phone: 312-492-8442

Hull House
(at UIC)
800 South Halsted Street
Chicago, IL 60607
Phone: 312-413-5353
Now operated as a museum. At the corner of Halsted and Polk streets.

Lincoln Tomb State Historic Site
1441 Monument Avenue
Springfield, IL 62702
For more information, contact the State Historical Sites Division, 313 6th Street North, Springfield, IL 62701; 217-782-2717.

Resurrection Cemetery
7600 South Archer Avenue
Justice, IL 60458
Phone: 708-458-4770
Resurrection Mary's ghost appears on stretches of Archer Avenue in Justice, south of Chicago. Take I-294, exit at 95th Street, and travel west to Roberts Road, then head north to Archer.

St. Turbius Church
56th Street and Karlow Avenue
Chicago, IL 60646

Indiana

Willard Library
21 First Avenue
Evansville, IN 47710
Phone: 812-425-4309

Iowa

Grand Opera House
135 Eighth Street
Dubuque, IA 52001
Phone: 563-588-4356

Louisiana

Beauregard-Keyes House and Garden Museum
(also known as LeCarpentier House)
1113 Charles Street
New Orleans, LA 70116
Phone: 504-523-7257
Guided tours by docents in period costumes, 10:00 A.M. to 3:00 P.M., Monday through Saturday.

Destrehan Plantation
13034 River Road
Destrehan, Louisiana 70047
Phone: 985-764-9315
Fax: 985-725-1929
E-mail: DestPlan@aol.com
Website: www. destrehanplantation.org
Eight miles from New Orleans International Airport on LA Route 48. Open for public viewing 9:00 A.M. to 4:00 P.M. daily except on major holidays.

Hermann-Grima Historical House
820 St. Louis Street
New Orleans, LA 70116
Phone: 504-525-5661
Open for tourism.

Laveau House
1020 St. Ann Street
New Orleans, LA 70116

St. Louis Cemetery
400 Basin Street
New Orleans, LA 70116
The first grave of Marie Laveau is in St. Louis Cemetery No. 1, 25 feet to the left of the entrance. The other grave of Marie Laveau is in St. Louis Cemetery No. 2.

Maine

Boothbay Opera House
Boothbay Harbor, ME 04538
Phone: 207-633-6855
Located on Maine's southwestern coast, on Highway 27, 10 miles south of U.S. Highway 1.

Maryland

Edgar Allan Poe House
203 North Amity Street
Baltimore, MD 21202
Phone: 410-396-7932
Since 1949 (exactly 100 years since Poe's death) the house has been open as a public museum. Poe is laid to rest in the nearby Burying Ground at Westminster Church located at Fayette and Greene Streets.

Fort McHenry
End of East Fort Avenue
Baltimore, MD 21230-5393
Phone: 410-962-4290 (recorded information)
Website: www.nps.gov/fomc
Open for visitors as part of the National Park Service (since 1933). Tours are also conducted.

Massachusetts

Fort Warren Historical Site
George's Island
Boston Harbor
Boston, MA
Ferries depart from Long Wharf and Rowes Wharf in Boston. Information on the site (including a pamphlet about the ghost) is available from the Metropolitan District Commission, 20 Somerset Street, Boston, MA 02108; 617-698-1802.

The Mount
Highway 20 and Plunkett Street
Lenox, MA 01240
Phone: 413-637-1899

Minnesota

Guthrie Theater
725 Vineland Place
Minneapolis, MN 55403
Phone: 612-377-2224
Public areas open to patrons.

Missouri

Joplin lights
Near Joplin, MO
The lights are best seen along a two-mile stretch of Devil's Promenade Road, outside the village of Hornet, about 11 miles southwest of Joplin. From Joplin, take I-44 west, then turn south on State Line Road just before entering Oklahoma. Travel about four miles to Devil's Promenade.

Montana

Bonanza Inn
Virginia City, MT 59755
Located in southwestern Montana.

The Custer House
Fort Abraham Lincoln
Crow Indian Reservation

Crow Agency, MT 59022

The historic fort is located on the Crow Indian Reservation, southeast of Billings in southern Montana.

Little Bighorn National Battlefield

Crow Indian Reservation

Crow Agency, MT

Phone: 406-638-2621

The battleground is on reservation lands, on I-90 15 miles from Hardin. The haunted stone house, formerly the park guard headquarters, is near the cemetery. Reno Crossing is located about five miles from the battlefield.

Nevada

Fourth Ward School

At the corner of B and C Streets

Virginia City, NV 89440

Phone: 775-847-0975

Open May 1–October 31. For information about the school museum, contact the Virginia City Chamber of Commerce, Box 464, C Street, Virginia City, NV 89440; 775-847-0311.

St. Paul's Episcopal Church

South F and Taylor streets

Virginia City, NV 89440

Phone: 775-847-9700

Not open for tourism. The ghost appears at the upstairs window.

New Hampshire

Country Tavern

452 Amherst Street

Nashua, NH 03063

Phone: 603-889-5871

New Jersey

The Spy House Museum

119 Port Monmouth Road

Port Monmouth, NJ 07758

New Mexico

St. James Hotel
Room 17 and "Mary's Room"
17th and Collinson Streets
Cimarron, NM 87714
Located near the junction of U.S. Highway 64 and Highway 21.
The hotel's mailing address is Route 1 Box 2, Cimarron, NM 87714; or call 505-376-2664.

New York

Eamonn's (restaurant)
(also known as Eamonn-Loudon House; formerly Loudon Cottage)
151 Menands Road
Loudonville, NY 12211
Phone: 518-463-7440
Open to restaurant patrons. Current building greatly enlarged from original cottage.
Loudonville, just north of Albany, is located at U.S. Highway 9 and Osborne Road.

Fort Ticonderoga
Fort Road, Box 390
Ticonderoga, NY 12883
Phone: 518-585-2821
On Lake Champlain at the Vermont border.

Lily Dale Spiritualist Center
5 Melrose Park
Lily Dale, NY 14752
Phone: 716-595-8721
Fax: 719-595-2442
Website: www.lilydale.org
Not a haunted site, but Lily Dale still thrives as a haven for Spiritualism and has daily activities from late June through Labor Day.

Storm King Pass
Stony Point, NY
Located along the Hudson River between Storm King Mountain and Stony Point.

North Carolina

Brown Mountain lights
Linville Gorge
Brown Mountains
Morganton, NC
The lights are best seen along Highway 181 between Morganton and Lenoir in western North Carolina.

Maco light
Along the tracks near the Atlantic Coast Railroad Crossing
(formerly the Wilmington-Florence-Augusta tracks)
Outside Maco, NC
For more information, contact the Southeastern North Carolina Beach Association, Wilmington, NC 28401.

North Dakota

Fort Abercrombie Historic Site
Abercrombie, ND 58001
Phone: 701-553-8513
Northeast of downtown Abercrombie, which is located in southeast North Dakota.

Ohio

Hinckley Community Library
Ridge and Center Roads
Hinckley, OH 44233
Phone: 330-278-4271
Near Akron in northeastern Ohio.

Pennsylvania

Baleroy
111 West Mermaid Lane
Philadelphia, PA 19118
In Chestnut Hill section of the city. Tours available upon special arrangement.

Gettysburg National Military Park
Business Route 15
Gettysburg, PA
Phone: 717-334-1124
Battlegrounds are open to visitors.

Margaret Grundy Memorial Library
Radcliffe Street
Bristol, PA 19007
Phone: 215-788-7891

Rhode Island

The Palantine **lights** (phantom ship)
(off Block Island)
Block Island, RI
Block Island is in the Rhode Island Sound, 12 miles off the south coast of Rhode
Island, about 11 miles from Montauk, Long Island. The lights, when seen, are most
visible from the State Beach or Settler's Rock Grove. For visitor information, contact
the Block Island Tourism Council, 23 Water Street, Block Island, RI 02807; 800-383-
2474 ext. 63; www.blockislandinfo.com.

South Carolina

Yeoman's Hall
Charleston, SC
On the site of the old Goose Creek Plantation, just south of Charleston.

Tennessee

Orpheum Theatre
203 South Main Street
Memphis, TN 38173
Phone: 901-525-7800 (box office); 901-525-7800 (offices)

Texas

The Alamo
Alamo Plaza
San Antonio, TX 78201

Phone: 210-225-1391

Open for tourism. For more information, contact the Alamo Visitor Center at 210-225-8587.

Marfa lights
Outside Marfa, TX

Marfa is located 26 miles west of Alpine, Texas, on U.S. Highway 67/90. One of the best viewing spots is about eight miles east of Marfa on Highway 90, where there's a plaque that describes the ghost lights. Other good viewing areas are on Mitchell Flat southwest of Marfa and on the plateau between Marfa and Alpine.

The Menger Hotel
204 Alamo Plaza
San Antonio, TX 78205
Phone: 800-345-9285 or 210-223-4361
Fax: 210-228-0022
Across from the historic Alamo.

Vermont

Lake Memphremagog
Newport, Vermont
The lake is along the Quebec-Vermont border at Newport, at I-91.

Virginia

Aquia Episcopal Church
2938 Jefferson Davis Highway
Stafford, VA 22554
Phone: 540-659-4007
Website: www.aquiachurch.com
Located in Stafford County, 20 miles north of Fredericksburg.

West Virginia

Harpers Ferry National Park
P.O. Box 65
Harpers Ferry, WV 25425
Phone: 304-535-6205

Wisconsin

Majestic Theater
12th and Mitchell Streets
Milwaukee, WI 53204
Phone: 414-299-0021 or 414-299-0021 (recorded information)

Wyoming

Fort Laramie National Historic Site
Laramie, WY
Phone: 307-837-2221
Located three miles west of Ft. Laramie on Highway 160.

St. Mark's Episcopal Church
19th Street and Central Avenue
Cheyenne, WY 82001
Phone: 307-634-7709

Washington, District of Columbia

For general information about touring Washington sites, contact the Washington Visitors Association, 1212 New York Avenue, Northwest, Suite 600, Washington, D.C. 20005; 202-789-7000.

Ford's Theatre
511 10th Street, Northwest
Washington, D.C. 20004
Phone: 202-426-6934
Website: www.nps.gov/foth
Maintained by the National Park Service as a museum. Open seven days a week, 9 A.M. to 5 P.M. Ford's Theatre is also a working playhouse, operated by the Theatre Society. The auditorium of the theatre is closed when there are matinee performances (Thursday and Sunday afternoons, in season).

The Octagon
1799 New York Avenue, Northwest
Washington, D.C. 20006-5291
Phone: 202-638-3105 (recorded information) or 202-638-3221 (museum)
Located at the intersection of New York Avenue, 18th Street, and E Street, The Octagon is open to the public as a museum Tuesday through Sunday, 10 A.M. to 4 P.M.

Petersen's Boarding House
516 10th Street, Northwest
Washington, D.C. 20004
Phone: 202-426-6934
Website: www.nps.gov/foth
Across the street from Ford's Theatre and part of the national historical site. The site of Abraham Lincoln's death on the second floor has been renovated with furnishings from the Civil War period and is open as a museum seven days a week, 9 A.M. to 5 P.M.

U.S. Capitol Building
Washington, D.C. 20006
Phone: 202-224-3121
For general information about touring Washington sites, contact the Washington Visitors Association, 1212 New York Avenue, Northwest, Suite 600, Washington, D.C. 20005; 202-789-7000.

The White House
(the Executive Mansion)
1600 Pennsylvania Avenue, Northwest
Washington, D.C. 20500
For tour information, contact the White House Visitor Center, 1450 Pennsylvania Avenue, Northwest, Washington, D.C. 20004; 202-208-1631, or for 24-hour recorded information, 202-456-7041.

U.S. Virgin Islands

Bluebeard's Castle Hotel
Bluebeard's Hill
Box 7480
Charlotte Amalie 00801 St. Thomas
U.S.V.I.
Phone: 1-800-524-6599 or 340-774-1600
Fax: 340-774-5134
The hotel is built around the haunted tower, which is open to the public as a museum and gift shop.

Australia

Melbourne Gaol
Melbourne, Victoria
Australia
Website: home.vicnet.net.au/~omgaol
To book tickets in advance, call Ticketmaster at 011-613-9694-0567.

Port Arthur Historic Site
Port Arthur, Tasmania 7182
Australia
Phone: 1800-659-101
Fax: 1800-659-202
E-mail: visitor.centre@portarthur.org.au
Website: www.portarthur.org.au
The Isle of the Dead, the cemetery for Port Arthur, is located just offshore from the grounds of the main prison site.

Barbados

Chase Vault
Christ Church Parish Church cemetery
Church Hill
Christ Church
Barbados, West Indies
Christ Church is located about seven miles from Bridgetown, the capital of Barbados. The parish graveyard, which lies on both sides of Christ Church Parish Church, is open to the public during daylight hours. The Chase vault is a low structure in the cemetery to the right of the front doors of the church. For more information: phone: 246-428-8007 (Church); 246-428-9147 (Rectory); 246-428-2319 (Centre).

Curaçao

Jan Kok Landhus
Weg near San Willibrordo
Curaçao
Phone: 599-964-8087
Located mid-island, about two miles outside San Willibrordo. There is a highway marker on the road at the end of the plantation's dirt driveway. Open to the public.

England

Chingle Hall
760 Whittingham Lane
Goosnargh, Preston
Lancashire PR3 2JJ
England
Located six miles north of Preston. Open to visitors and overnight guests from April to October.

Drury Lane, Theatre Royal
Catherine Street
Covent Garden
London WC2B 5JF
England
Phone: 020-7494-5000 (box office)
Public areas open to patrons. Backstage tours available daily. Call 020-7494-5091 for advance booking.

Hampton Court Palace
East Molesey
Surrey KT8 9AU
England
Phone: 0870-752-7777
Websites: www.hampton-court-palace.org.uk or www.hrp.org.uk
The splendid parks surrounding the palace are open daily, from 7 A.M. to dusk. Visiting hours of the palace and other buildings on the grounds vary seasonally, though usually from 9:30 A.M. (10:15 A.M. on Mondays) to 4:30 or 6 P.M. The palace is closed December 24-26.

The Haymarket, Theatre Royal
(located between Piccadilly Circus and Buckingham Palace)
London SW1Y 4HT
England
Phone: 020-7930-8800 (box office)
Public areas open to patrons. A theatre and backstage tour is also available to groups.

Kensington Palace
Kensington Gardens
London W8 4PX
England
Phone: 011-44-870-751-5170 (information)

Pluckley
Pluckley, Kent
England
Website: www.pluckley.net/history/ghosts01.htm

Stonehenge
Salisbury Plain
Wiltshire
England
Phone: 01980-624715
Website: www.english-heritage.org.uh/stonehenge
Approximately 80 miles southwest of London, about two miles west of Amesbury at the junction of A303 and A344/360. Open daily except December 24–26 and January 1, from 9:30 A.M. Closing time varies seasonally.

The Tower of London
Tower Hill
London EC3N 4AB
England
Phone: 0870-756-6060
Open daily March through October, Monday through Saturday 9 A.M. to 6 P.M. and Sunday 10 A.M. to 6 P.M. From November through February, the Tower is open Monday to Saturday 9 A.M. to 5 P.M. and Sunday 10 A.M. to 5 P.M. Closed on January 1 and December 24 to 26.

Windsor Castle
Windsor, Berkshire
England
Phone: 020-7766-7304
Fax: 020-7930-9625
E-mail: information@royalcollection.org.uk
Twenty miles west of London on the south bank of the Thames River. Visiting times to Windsor Castle vary seasonally, generally from 10 A.M. to late afternoon or, in the summer, into the early evening. Hours are further limited to the State Apartments and the Albert Memorial Chapel, both of which are located on the castle grounds. The State Apartments cannot be visited when the Queen is in residence. It's best to check opening hours before planning a visit. For more information, write Windsor Castle, Ticket Sales and Information Office, The Official Residences of the Queen, London SW1A 1AA, England.

Scotland

Glamis Castle
Glamis (by Forfar)
Angus DD8 1RJ
Scotland
Phone: 01307-840393
Fax: 01307-840733
E-mail: enquiries@glamis-castle.co.uk
Website: www.strathmore-estates.co.uk
Open to visitors from late March/early April through mid-to-late October, 10:00 A.M. to 6 P.M. The last tour departs at 4:30 P.M.

Inverary Castle
Inverary
Argyll PA32 8XE
Scotland
Phone: 01499-302203
Fax: 01499-302421
E-mail: enquiries@inverary-castle.com
Website: www.inverary-castle.com

Singapore

Raffles Hotel
1 Beach Road
Singapore 189673
Phone: 6337-1886
Fax: 339-7650
E-mail: raffles@raffles.com
Websites: www.raffles.com or www.raffleshotel.com

Index

I

T